Natural Places
of the Southwest

A TRAVELER'S GUIDE TO THE CULTURE, SPIRIT, AND ECOLOGY OF SCENIC DESTINATIONS

Fraser Bridges

An On-Route Communications Book

PRIMA PUBLISHING

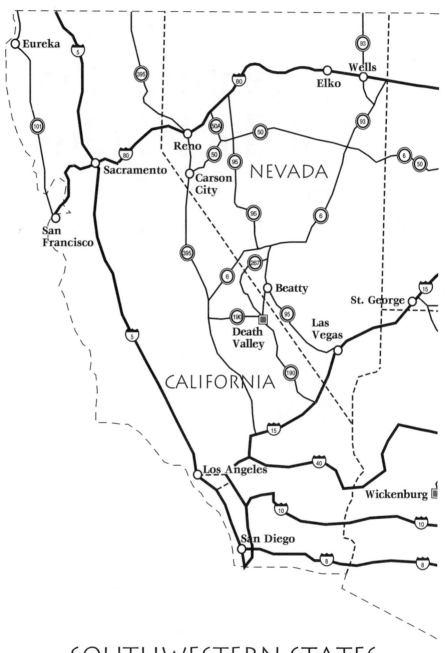

SOUTHWESTERN STATES

PRIMA PUBLISHING, NATURAL PLACES, and their respective colophons are trademarks of Prima Communications, Inc.

Map: Fraser Bridges
Illustrations: Gregory G. Gersch

Library of Congress Cataloging-in-Publication Data
Bridges, Fraser.
    Natural places of the Southwest : a traveler's guide to the culture, spirit, and ecology of scenic destinations/by Fraser Bridges

        p.   cm.— (Natural Places)

    Includes index.
    ISBN 0-7615-0158-4
    1. Natural history—Southwest, New.   2. Natural areas—Southwest, New.   I. Title   II. Series: Bridges, Fraser. Natural places.
QH104.5.S6B75   1996
508.791—dc20   95-25887
                                                                            CIP

96 97 98 99 00 DD 10 9 8 7 6 5 4 3 2 1
Printed in the United States of America

How to Order:

Single copies may be ordered from Prima Publishing, P.O. Box 1260BK, Rocklin, CA 95677; telephone (916) 632-4400. Quantity discounts are also available. On your letterhead, include information concerning the intended use of the books and the number of books you wish to purchase.

CONTENTS

INTRODUCTION

This guide to nature travel and recreation is divided into four parts for ease of reading, a system that I hope will make it easy for you to identify your own special destinations for future travels. The chapters make up the major portion of the book, introducing the features of what, for me, are the eleven most exciting nature destinations in the Southwest. Each is worthy of exploration as a vacation destination. Each has importance as a natural environment and as a place that inspires the human imagination.

In addition to background on the natural areas, you'll find an informal field guide to the regions in each chapter, with information on resident animals and plants. Included is a listing of migratory birds that frequently visit, which you may have a chance of seeing and identifying as you explore the region. Thirty prime birding areas are highlighted throughout the chapters.

Also included are places to stay in nearby towns, including bed and breakfast inns, resorts, hotels, motels, campgrounds, and guest ranches, ranging from rustic to super-deluxe.

The Wildlife Checklist at the book's end is for your records. It lists animals alongside checkoff boxes for you to keep track of your sightings.

I wrote this book because of my own interest in looking beyond the normal tourist places to gain a knowledge of natural history, and to enable readers to fully enjoy the wonders of nature in mountains, deserts, and little-known rivers. I found the human social history of the Southwest regions to be as fascinating as the ecological history. So, using the broadest dictionary meaning for natural history, I have included an overview of the human habitation of each area, which, in a few places, is a major focus.

Off the Beaten Track

In early November of 1993, while on an exploration of five nature preserves conducted by the Arizona Chapter of the Nature Conservancy, I discovered several special places. On previous sojourns in the state of Arizona, I had come within a few miles of the wildlife reserves, yet had missed them in my rush to visit traditional tourist spots.

Driving from Benson to Tombstone and Nogales, I had crossed bridges spanning the San Pedro River, not realizing that this stream—one of the very few north-flowing rivers in America—harbors the most diverse collection of wildlife in the western United States.

I had twice visited Sedona, looking for red rock, convergence zones and old mining towns, without venturing into the beautiful and lush canyon of the Verde River, one of the amazing streams that support desert life in this region below the Mogollon Rim.

And who hasn't visited the busy South Rim of the Grand Canyon, yet neglected to travel the extra 200 miles to reach the equally scenic and more naturally impressive North Rim?

This book urges you to drive and walk those extra miles, to leave the refinement and hustle of posh hotels and resorts, to venture into places which uplift the soul, and to make a connection with the other inhabitants of our natural world.

The idea that the Southwest is a desert wasteland is far from reality. The Southwest provides startling contrasts, including a great deal of hospitality. The low, hot, dry landscape is crossed by desert streams that disappear from sight under rivers of gravel only to reemerge to nurture a thriving plant and animal environment. The mountain regions—with high desert flatlands, thick forests, tumbling streams, geological magic, and many animal residents—are natural wonders of a different type.

Much of the attraction of these destinations is the powerful, life-changing nature of the southwestern wilderness. The Wilderness Protection Act of 1964 defines wilderness as an area

. . . where the earth and its community of life are untrampled by man, where man himself is a visitor who does not remain . . .

Because of their wilderness state, these special places not only provide opportunities for recreational experience, but offer solitude, the necessary ingredient for personal, spiritual renewal.

The eleven featured destinations and the many other nearby natural places in this book offer it all: haunting natural beauty, silent wilderness, and the opportunity for communion with plants, animals, and birds—all of which pre-date by eons our short human existence in the American Southwest.

One can also commune with the ghosts of occupants from prehistoric years who lived in the cliff houses of the Four Corners region, including the magnificent stone communities built by the Anasazi as distant in time as a thousand years ago. Where they came from and why they left are still mysteries to social scientists who have studied these ruins.

One can only wonder at the natural forces that have carved the glorious pinnacles in Bryce Canyon National Park and the chasm of the Grand Canyon. These places are the supreme result of eons of work by nature's powerful helpers: wind and water. The red rocks of Sedona have also been revealed by intensive erosion and the shifting of the earth over millions of years.

And while great land formations were carved from the earth, wildlife was evolving to inhabit these diverse environments. For example, one of the tiniest wild animals to be seen in the Southwest is the translucent desert pupfish, which survives in only a few scattered habitats. This plucky little fish requires a special environment, such as the short portion of the Hassayampa River that emerges from its underground course south of Wickenburg, Arizona, to provide a superb riparian habitat—not only for the pupfish but for hundreds of other creatures—in the middle of the otherwise inhospitable desert.

The Land and the Spirit

Many people find fulfillment by belonging to a branch of organized religion. I was born into, and grew up in, a minister's household. As a youth, rather than being interested in standard theology, I found myself wondering about the special qualities of nature and how the natural world related to the idea of a supreme being. In my twenties, I began to explore the nearby forests, streams, and ocean shores of Eastern Canada. A three-year stay in Newfoundland brought me the feeling of oneness with the wild beauty of this superb island wilderness bordered by dramatic fjords and quiet inlets.

Then I moved to Northern Ontario, where I paddled my canoe along the French River, drove through the endless forests north of Lake Superior, and viewed sunsets over Lake Huron and the wildlife of Hudson's Bay. All further established in my mind the dichotomy between millions of years of natural history and the evolving environment. Then, with the demands of work and other pressures of modern society, my "re-creation" was soon relegated to an occasional day-trip or a stolen long weekend.

A bureaucratic life ensued until 1986 when I began writing a series of books based on getting off busy freeways, onto scenic roads, and into the embrace of the outdoors. But, still concerned with touristy places, I barely touched the edges of the natural environment. Then I visited the Muleshoe Ranch in Arizona in November of 1993 and found the deeper meaning of my travels—a new consciousness that forever changed my life. A place like the Muleshoe has the power to put us in touch with a much greater world and spiritual dimension than we ever could imagine from our urban environments.

This book is about those natural places that bring us into a new realm of discovery—the discovery of natural life, of earth itself, of history and culture of peoples unknown, and of ourselves. My hope is that this guidebook will lead you to your own natural place, or places, where you may lose yourself—and find yourself—in the great outdoors.

Three Great Canyons

W hat is it about canyons that captures the imagination and compels adventurers to risk life and limb exploring their mysteries? Why do tourists travel to canyon rims halfway around the world, only to stand and gaze into their depths? Feeling small in stature and insignificant in the face of geographical wonder plays a large part in our human fascination with the world's enormous accomplishments. Canyons say to us that human accomplishments are picayune compared to natural architecture.

Two of our three great canyons are places where our hearts almost stand still in the face of incomparable natural majesty. The Grand Canyon is America's most visited natural phenomenon. Bryce Canyon is very different—purists would argue it's not really a canyon at all—yet it arouses the same feelings of wonder.

Our third canyon, Chaco, is not the type of deep canyon which brings feelings of wonder. Instead, it's what is in this unprepossessing canyon that causes our amazement. For here in the midst of New Mexico's high desert are the spectacular remains of a prehistoric civilization. The pueblos of Chaco Canyon were built long before Christopher Columbus "discovered" this continent. Chaco, the former cultural and trading capital of a disappeared people whose influence was felt for hundreds of miles in every direction, is a continuing mystery to historians and social scientists.

The three canyons—Grand, Bryce, and Chaco—have different features, yet all engender feelings of awe and wonder, and evoke an appreciation for the glories of nature and the fragility of our human existence.

Grand Canyon—North Rim

While the heavily visited South Rim offers stupendous views and modern lodgings, the North Rim offers truly remarkable natural experiences. First is seeing the Colorado River flowing at rim level, then descending into the deep channel it has created over millions of years. Then, farther west and south, the remote and under-traveled forests of the Kaibab Plateau and the national park's northern region present a vivid demonstration of how the forces of nature have combined to change the Arizona landscape.

Alpine meadows covered with aspen groves appear at the 8,000-foot altitude level. Snow lies deep in winter when Crane Lake is covered with a sheet of ice. Mule deer thrive in this clover-covered meadow and pine forest environment, as do wild turkeys, black bears, cougars, badgers, and the tiger salamanders that develop from larvae in Crane Lake, rarely reaching the adult stage. (How do they reproduce?)

Stunted conifer stands surround many small meadows as one passes the park entrance station. Kaibab squirrels feast on the huge cones of the ponderosa pine, stuffing themselves to a weight of two pounds in order to survive the long, cold winters.

Historians now follow the trails the Anasazi traveled from A.D. 850 and look down on the river bottom farmlands tilled by these prehistoric Native Americans who commuted from terraces close to the river and, later, from higher land on the canyon's rocky slopes.

Open only during the summer season, the North Rim trails lead quietly along the rim and into the Grand Canyon. Streams plunge down the cliffs of the canyon. The distant, southerly San Francisco Peaks—soaring to 12,000 feet—appear as tiny snow-capped fingers. The finest sunset views of the Grand Canyon are found at Cape Royal, at the end of the 23-mile Cape Royal Road.

In all of America, few short hikes surpass the trail to Bright Angel Point, which follows a sharp ridge that separates two chasms, and ends on a narrow point of rock that overlooks the two dramatic canyons. Wonder, magic, and mystery—all lie on a quarter-mile walk from the Cape Royal Road parking lot.

Chaco Canyon

This shallow canyon in northwestern New Mexico has been carved by the Chaco Wash, a sometimes dry creek. On either side of the wash, mostly close to the cliffs, are the ruins of huge multistoried pueblos. Some are still unexcavated mounds; others have been unearthed and restored.

When the moon is full, a pellucid light illuminates the great stone walls of Pueblo Bonito and Kin Kletso, two of the communities that were part of this cultural center of the Anasazi. Their population numbered in the thousands and their circle of influence extended a hundred miles in every direction.

Nine hundred years ago, following predecessors known as the Basketmakers, the Anasazi built their dry-walled communities, which included large open plazas, apartment buildings, and kivas (ceremonial rooms) of various sizes. Paths wound along the wash and up the canyon walls to fertile farm fields on the upper plateau. Straight roads led from the top of the canyon across the high plateau in all directions for 40 to 60 miles, including the Four Corners region, making Chaco Canyon the chief Anasazi trading and spiritual power center.

Between about A.D. 1140 and 1200, the Chacoan culture declined and the communities were abandoned. Today, we can only wonder why. Could it have been the drought that plagued the area during that period? Could it have been the growth of Pueblo cultures elsewhere? Such questions make a visit to Chaco Canyon even more appealing, for this enduring mystery, along with the ghosts of the Anasazi, haunts the canyon and the surrounding countryside.

Chaco Culture National Historic Park lies in the high desert, south of Aztec and Farmington and north of Gallup. It is definitely in the middle of nowhere; the nearest town of any size is 60 miles away. Accommodations in the canyon consist of a primitive campground and trailer park, a visitor center with a small museum and a water tap for filling containers. Visiting this place requires some privation, but the magic of Chaco Canyon makes it worth every inconvenience. The excavated ruins of the Anasazi culture give us insight into a vanished civilization that is now being remembered.

Bryce Canyon and the Southern Utah Parks

Bryce is the only one of the eleven natural places featured in this book that could be called over-visited. More than 2 million people come to Bryce Canyon each year to gaze on the magnificent hoodoos that rise from the floor of this bowl set into the Colorado Plateau. A prime example of the workings of nature, Bryce is only one of more than twenty geological attractions in southern Utah. Yet it is Bryce that I remember most vividly as a place of stark beauty and scenic grandeur.

Most visitors come to Bryce during June, July, and August. My own finest experiences here have come during the late spring, early fall, and in the winter months, when hats of snow crown the pink pinnacles, and few visitors mar the view or spoil the clean air and the quiet.

The intricate rock carvings here are like no others in this geologically blessed part of Utah. First, the colors of iron and manganese oxides reflect the sun in a changing kaleidoscope of reds from light pink to dark umber—from sunup to dusk. The effects of erosion over millions of years have studded the huge bowl with long finger-like pillars of every shape and size.

Trails into the canyon and along the rim—in addition to the roadway that leads along the rim to Rainbow Point—offer nature viewers and photographers unparalleled experiences. There are backcountry trails, including the "Under-the-Rim Trail," which lead to remote campsites. For those inclined to comfort, the Bryce Canyon Lodge is situated inside the park. A well-appointed motel complex is just outside the park gate, with more accommodations a few miles away.

Winter is a special time at Bryce. You'll probably find yourself alone in the stillness of the park, walking over crusted snow to the viewpoints, cross-country skiing, or hiking the few trails maintained during these months. Spring and fall are the optimum times for a visit, with nippy nighttime temperatures at the 8,000-foot altitude, and warm, sunny days that are perfect for hiking.

You'll find other notable parks within a half-day's drive, including Zion, Capitol Reef, Canyonlands, and Cedar Breaks, but none matches the sheer concentrated beauty of the huge amphitheater called Bryce Canyon.

Grand Canyon—
North Rim

The scenic majesty of the Grand Canyon of the Colorado River is somehow magnified when one visits the North Rim. Here, nature is in perfect balance. The forests of the Kaibab Plateau reach to the rocky canyon rim. Wildlife is more abundant than human life in this remote hideaway—more than 90 miles from the nearest urban area. Here a quiet solitude is to be found, unlike the claustrophobic feeling one experiences at the overly visited South Rim with its vacation motels, fine dining, Fred Harvey tower, and Native American shops, frequented by hundreds of cars and tour buses from Williams and Flagstaff who come to disgorge their human contents onto the viewpoints.

While one gets a feeling of peace here, one also senses the inexorable nature of archeological change along the North Rim. The North Rim site of Grand Canyon National Park is smaller and has a more natural dimension than the sprawling South Rim section. Because of its more remote location, there's only one lodging place inside the park and fewer people visit it—and then only during the summer and fall months. While a visit to the South Rim brings exclamations of "Wow" and other (sometimes less printable) expressions of surprise at the spectacular canyon views, a leisurely tour of the North Rim over several days incites feelings of wonder at the magnificence of nature and puts the visitor into a contemplative state—what our natural places are all about.

As the hawk flies, the south and north rims are about ten miles apart. By car, it's a drive of 210 miles—leave the South

Rim by driving east past Desert View, take Arizona Route 64 and then turn onto U.S. Highway 89 at Cameron. Drive north for 59 miles and turn west onto Alternate Route 89 at Bitter Springs (a few miles south of the town of Page). The final leg of the journey is via Arizona Route 67, the North Rim Parkway, which runs south from Jacob Lake and continues through the park, ending near the North Rim at the courtyard of the Grand Canyon Lodge.

Time Flows

The clock of geological time ticks slowly in the Grand Canyon. Over millions of years, one millimeter at a time, the Colorado River cut its way through thousands of feet of sandstone layers, which are revealed for all to see. However, the story the canyon tells began some 2 billion years ago with the building of the rock formations that the river has exposed.

One of the great mysteries about the Colorado River is why it chose to flow through high ground instead of diverting itself from the plateau. Although the theory has yet to be proven, some geologists believe that there were originally two rivers. The first emerged to the southwest as the Lower Colorado, beginning its life circumventing the Kaibab Plateau. Another smaller stream followed, in a general way, the course of the present canyon, curving across the top of the plateau, crossing Utah, and disappearing into the Nevada desert. At some later time—perhaps 4 to 5 million years ago—the lower river ran into and seized the upper river and began to cut its path through the sandstone, limestone, and shale. The colors of the rock layers— blue, pink, gray—tell the rest of the geological history of the region.

Compared to the long, slow journey in geological time, the span of human history around and in the canyon seems fleeting. However, when one sees evidence of the earliest-known habitation of the area, including the split-willow figurines found in canyon caves and thought to be more than 4,000 years old, it is evident that the Grand Canyon was home to the human species at the time civilization flowered in the Middle East— before the pyramids of Egypt were constructed.

The Basketmakers came to the canyon area about A.D. 500. Within 200 years, the Anasazi had begun farming on the South Rim and by A.D. 1050, the prehistoric tribe was well-established on the North Rim, where the annual snowfall provided water for spring and summer farming.

The Kaibab Paiutes occupied the Grand Canyon at the end of the prehistoric period and into more recent times, migrating to the plateau about A.D. 1400 and ranging across the land, hunting and gathering in the woodlands and desert areas as the seasons demanded.

The Kaibab Paiutes survived into the period when Europeans arrived in the Southwest, and captured many Native Americans, selling them into slavery in the human marketplace at Santa Fe. The remaining Paiutes continued to be mistreated for generations as American settlers arrived and the government forced them onto reservations.

One of three archeological sites in Grand Canyon National Park is located on the North Rim. The Walhalla Glades Ruin can be found across Cape Royal Road from the Glades Overlook. A small house suitable for sheltering a single family, it is thought to have been built some time after A.D. 1050.

A second site, accessible via the North Kaibab Trail, lies at the canyon floor just north of the footbridge over the Colorado River, a 14-mile hike from the North Rim. Bright Angel Pueblo was discovered by John Wesley Powell on his river expedition in 1869. Pithouses were constructed here about A.D. 1050, and the larger pueblo was constructed about 1100, housing several families who farmed beside the river and hunted for game until the time of the general exodus of the Anasazi about 1140. The third Anasazi site is the Tusayan Ruin, on the South Rim.

Another group has lived in the canyon region for thousands of years: The Havasupai have occupied the western part of the Grand Canyon—along Havasu Creek—since prehistoric times. Today, visitors may visit the Havasupai reservation and stay at the campground or tribal lodge.

Getting There

The drive between Bitter Springs and Jacob Lake is a fascinating one, as the road passes through the Cornfield Valley and then climbs to the Kaibab Plateau, passing the Vermilion Cliffs and then through House Rock Valley. Eighteen miles beyond Bitter Springs, Alternate Route 89 crosses the Colorado River over the Navajo Bridge at Marble Canyon. A short side trip of about 30 minutes will bring a whole new dimension to your enjoyment of the Grand Canyon. More about this later as we explore several excursions in the North Rim region.

From the northwest, the route to the North Rim begins just east of the town of Page, created when the Glen Canyon Dam was built to hold back the waters of the Colorado River. Driving south from Page, you encounter the Echo Cliffs a few miles south of town as the highway cuts through the cliffs and descends into the Cornfield Valley. At Bitter Springs, Alt. Route 89 leads eastward across the valley. Here are Navajo homes, some with hogans—the traditional Native American dwelling in these parts—as part of the family compound. Crossing the Colorado River on the Navajo Bridge, we enter the community of Marble Canyon and continue on Alt. Route 89, climbing to the Kaibab Plateau and turning south on State Route 67 toward the park entrance.

KAIBAB PLATEAU

For 30 miles beyond Marble Canyon, the two-lane highway leads along the base of the Vermilion Cliffs. Along the way are several small communities that have been here since pioneer days. Cliff Dwellers Lodge has two unique stone structures that housed the original trading post. Above House Rock Valley, the summit offers a wonderful view over the river to the Echo Cliffs. To the south is the dark mesa called Shinumo Altar. The Colorado River is more than 1,500 feet below the summit.

If time permits, drive from the highway to visit the House Rock Buffalo Ranch. The animals' range covers some 60,000 acres of national forest land. The first buffalo were brought here in the early 1900s by Buffalo Jones, a former buffalo hunter who drove his herd across the plains to the Kaibab Plateau. The herd is now owned by the state, which allows the buffalo to roam free with the deer and other animals.

The route to the rim turns south at the small community of Jacob Lake, then crosses the plateau. This pristine area of aspens and pines is filled with more wildlife, including deer, bears, mountain lions, and coyotes. The plateau was called Buckskin

Mountain by white settlers. Long before, Native Americans named it *kaiuw a-vwi* ("mountain lying down"). The route passes Crane Lake before reaching Demotte Park, a small community outside the national park gate, with visitor services including Kaibab Lodge and the North Rim Country Store.

INSIDE THE PARK

It's a 7-mile drive from the north entrance station to the end of the road beside the Grand Canyon Lodge. The North Rim Parkway travels beside Little Park Lake, passes a picnic area near Lindberg Hill, and meets Cape Royal Road. Beyond the junction is the trailhead to the Widforss Trail and the mule paddock. There's another picnic area closer to the North Rim Village.

As you proceed down the Parkway toward Grand Canyon Village, you'll see a series of open meadows—grassland parks in the midst of the Kaibab forest. When you reach the end of the road, it's only a short stroll to see the canyon—either from Bright Angel Point or through the hotel to the stone terraces. On a good day, when not too much smog is drifting over the canyon from the Navajo Generating Station, you can see all the way to the San Francisco Peaks far to the south.

Ten miles distant, across the Grand Canyon, you can see the Bright Angel Trail dropping down from the South Rim to the Indian Gardens on the Tonto Platform. You may also be able to see the South Kaibab Trail as it descends from the South Rim.

North Rim Trails

The North Rim park provides many opportunities for serious hikers to hike into the backcountry of the Kaibab Plateau, onto platforms that have remained after the side-canyons were created. In addition to the longer trails are several short trails, including one for people in wheelchairs, that anyone can manage.

The trails lead visitors into several ecological zones. Elevation is everything here. The North Rim is called the Boreal Zone. The vegetation here, a mixed forest environment, is reminiscent of the southern Canadian ecosystem: spruce, aspen, and fir with deep snowfall. Descending into the canyon, you will experience a transitional, high-desert zone featuring mountain mahogany, pine, and oak—similar to the Sierra Nevada Foothills or the Mule Mountains near Bisbee, Arizona. At a lower elevation lies the Upper Sonoran Zone, where yucca, agave, Mormon tea, and blackbrush grow alongside several varieties of cacti.

The inner gorge is a typical Lower Sonoran Desert environment. The river provides its own ecosystem, with cottonwoods lining the banks and willows offering a home for many insect, animal, and bird species, while raccoons, toads, tree frogs, coyote, and varieties of fish reside in and along the river.

While hiking is a rewarding way to fully experience the peace and solitude of the plateau and the various levels of the canyon, you should take precautions to make your hikes unstressful. Since there is little water along the way, plenty should be carried, particularly on trips of more than 2 hours. Two gallons of water per day is the standard for long hikes. Also, because the heat during summer months is intense and hikers become tired very easily, summer hikers are advised to double their expected hiking time. Even experienced backcountry hikers become fatigued far earlier than they would expect. Avoid hiking in the midday hours, and check your planned route with rangers before you start out on any but the shortest trails. Reservations and permits are required for backcountry camping.

Bright Angel Trail   This short trail is a *must* on your visit to the North Rim. It's only a quarter-mile long, a paved path leading along a narrow ridge between two deep gorges. The trail ends at Bright Angel Point, a narrow rock that provides an overview of Transcept Canyon (on the right) and Roaring Springs Canyon (to the left). The long canyon stretching toward the river is Bright Angel Canyon.

Roaring Springs Canyon gets its name from the noisy spring that delivers water into a stream that tumbles down the rock wall. Some of the water is pumped to the rim facilities while a second pipe carries water from the spring all the way to Indian Gardens far below, where it is pumped again to the South Rim. The elevation at Bright Angel Point is 8,145 feet.

North Kaibab Trail   Leading down the face of the canyon to the river, this trail originally led to a camp at the mouth of

Bright Angel Creek in 1905. The camp is now Phantom Ranch. The complete trail system across the canyon—from north to south rims—was completed in 1922. The trail descends for 14.2 miles, from 8,200 to 2,400 feet. For a good day-hike, walk down to Roaring Springs. This is a 4.7-mile round trip and the descent (and subsequent ascent) is 3,200 feet. You'll find the trailhead beside the paddock, north of the village. Except for very experienced backcountry hikers, those who make the trip all the way to Phantom Ranch on the canyon floor usually ride on a mule.

Transcept Trail The considerable effects of erosion may be seen in Transcept Canyon, a side-canyon which lies to the immediate west of the Village. In the winter of 1991, a huge piece of sandstone was dislodged and tumbled to the bottom of the canyon, providing a reminder of the evolution of the Grand Canyon, where the river and weather bring constant change to the landscape.

The short Transcept Trail offers good views of this and other geological effects from its trailhead north of the Village. It leads along the canyon, ending at the lodge.

Widforss Trail A gravel road leads to the west from the North Rim Parkway north of the paddock, providing access to the Widforss trailhead. This 5-mile (one-way) hike follows the rim of Transcept Canyon to Widforss Point. The first half of the walk is easy and self-guiding, with a trail guide available at the trailhead. The trail was named after Gunnar Widforss, an artist from Sweden who painted the Grand Canyon for several years and was buried at the South Rim following his death in 1914.

Point Sublime Trail You'll find the trailhead of this longer trail farther along the same side road from which you enter the Widforss Trail. Heading westward along the Kaibab Plateau, the trail passes a spring at the head of Outlet Canyon, and continues to Little Dragon Mesa. The Hindu Amphitheater lies to the south, between the trail and the river, with its eastern-named spires including Shiva, Isis, Confucius, and Mencius Temples, and the Tower of Set and Tower of Ra.

Crossing Crystal Creek, the trail veers to the southwest, running beside the Walla Valley, and ends at Point Sublime, at an elevation of 7,458 feet. This high trail provides spectacular views of the high points of land in the central canyon area, as well as frequent views of the river far below in the distance. This is a full-day round-trip, and there is also a backcountry campsite for those who wish to linger and spend adequate time absorbing the environment.

Tiyo Point Trail This side-trail leads south from the Point Sublime Trail about five miles from the trailhead near Route 67. Another Kaibab Plateau hike, this trail leads across higher land, ending at an elevation of 7,762 feet—at Tiyo Point. The geological attraction known as The Colonnade lies immediately to the south of the trail's end.

Ken Patrick Trail This 10-mile trail runs between Point Imperial—at the end of the spur road leading off Cape Royal Road—and the North Kaibab Trailhead beside the paddock north of the Village. The Walhalla Plateau is the star attraction here, as the trail winds across high country, first offering views of nearby Mount Hayden, Sullivan Peak, and Hancock Butte. Closer to the Village, the trail crosses several of the tiny tributaries of Bright Angel Creek and the head of Roaring Springs Canyon.

CAPE ROYAL ROAD: TRAILS AND VIEWPOINTS

You'll find this 23-mile road north of the Village. Our suggestion is that you plan for a full day's trip. The road leads to several viewpoints through forests of Douglas fir, Englemann spruce and blue spruce, white fir, and ponderosa pine.

Point Imperial A side road wanders beside Bright Angel Creek to this point, the highest viewpoint on either rim at an elevation of 8,803 feet. From here you can see the incredibly smooth plateau called Marble Platform 9 miles distant and 3,000 feet below Point Imperial. Both the elevation and the view are breathtaking.

Greenland Lake The Walhalla Plateau reaches out into the Grand Canyon with the road descending into a completely different ecosystem. By the time you reach the end of the road, you'll lose the pine and aspen forest. However, the forest is still evident at Greenland Lake. An interpretive exhibit here points out the eroded limestone that caused the formation of ponds and sinkholes in this area. Greenland Lake is such a sinkhole.

Vista Encantadora   Set in the mixed northern forest, this viewpoint is farther along the main Cape Royal Road, past the turnoff to Point Imperial and Greenland Lake. The view at the Indian Country pull-off spans the Marble Platform to the Echo Cliffs and beyond. The Navajo and Hopi reservations can be seen on a clear day. Those with perfect vision should be able to see the Painted Desert lying to the southeast.

Walhalla Glades Ruin   All that is left of a small Indian village, the ruin is at the end of a short trail that leads from the side of the road. It was occupied for about 100 years from A.D. 1050. There's a box at the pull-off containing guides to the trail and ruin.

Angel's Window   This is a remarkable opening in a large rock formation. It's seen from the bottom of a steep hill, where there's a pull-off for those who wish a longer view. A trailhead across the road from the pull-off leads to Cliff Spring (1-mile round-trip). The trail passes a small ruin that includes a Native American storehouse, thought to have been a granary. The top of the Angel's Window rock can also be reached from a trail that starts at the Cape Royal parking lot.

Cape Royal Overlook   At the end of the road, this is an extremely popular vista point. A short trail features interpretive signage on the various plants and animals of this forest, which is primarily a pinyon-juniper woodland. Here another path leads to Angel's Window, then proceeds on to Cape Royal. The elevation of the Cape Royal viewpoint is 7,863 feet.

The ecological changes along Cape Royal Road are striking. The colder, higher evergreen forest is home to a wide range of animal species including deer, coyote, porcupine, cougar, and red squirrel. Birds include wild turkey, several varieties of jay, flickers, and other species. Most of this wildlife is not seen at the lower elevations, even halfway down the canyon walls. As the Port Royal Road crosses the Walhalla Plateau and drops in elevation, the composition of the forests changes dramatically as the temperatures become warmer and the air drier than at the much higher reaches of the Kaibab rim.

North Rim Park Services

Grand Canyon Lodge, which overlooks the canyon, provides the only lodging in the North Rim section of the national park. There are modern motel rooms in the pine forest in addition to cabins and fairly new cottage accommodations, as well as a dining room, gift shop, and lounge inside the lodge. Other services may be arranged here, such as horseback riding and mule trips into the canyon (if they're not fully booked). The lodge is open from early May to late October, when snow shuts down the park road. For information and reservations, write TW Services, P.O. Box 400, Cedar City, UT 84720, or call (801) 586-7686.

The North Rim Campground, located north of the Village, has showers, a campers' store, and nearby gas pumps. Reservations may be made by calling MISTIX (1-800-365-2267) or writing to P.O. Box 85705, San Diego, CA 92138-5705. There are no hookups for recreational vehicles in this campground. Other campsites are located outside, at Demotte, and in the Kaibab National Forest.

Backcountry campsites on the North Rim are fully booked during the summer months. Write to the park as soon as you know your expected visit dates to request campsite reservations. These may be obtained for the following calendar year any time after October 1. A backcountry planning kit is available by calling (602) 638-7888 or by writing to the Backcountry Reservations Office, Grand Canyon National Park, P.O. Box 129, Grand Canyon, AZ 86023.

Mule trips may be arranged inside the park or by phoning Grand Canyon Scenic Rides at (602) 638-2292. The mule ride to Phantom Ranch takes a full day. Overnight accommodation is available in a dormitory or in cabins at Phantom Ranch. Although there is no road to this rustic overnight stopping place—only a hiking or mule path—it's usually booked months in advance. For reservations, call (602) 638-2401 or 638-2631, or check at the lodge in case there have been cancellations. Mule trips should also be booked well in advance of your visit to the North Rim.

The park staff has an ongoing summer interpretation program that includes guided walks and lectures. For the daily schedule, see the park newspaper or inquire at the Park Service information desk in Grand Canyon Lodge. A medical clinic is staffed by a nurse-practitioner. Please check the park newspaper for the clinic's open hours or call 638-2611.

Kaibab National Forest

The Kaibab National Forest lies north and south of the national park, providing spectacular scenery that includes views from several Grand Canyon overlooks outside the park boundary as well as recreational activity at many camping and day-use facilities. Within the national forest are several small communities, including Demotte Park (near the North Rim Park entrance) and Jacob Lake (at the junction of Highways 89A and 67). The information point for the Jacob Lake Ranger District is at the Jacob Lake intersection. At the Kaibab Plateau Visitor Center, you'll find trail guides, information on campgrounds and other forest services, and national forest maps that are invaluable for planning a stay in the area or drives through the forest. The center is open from May through November, closing when the snows fall.

LODGES AND SKI AREAS

The Forest Service has licensed several concessionaires to operate lodges and stores in this area. These include the Jacob Lake Inn, a motel with cabins, a gas and service station and dump station. The village of Demotte is closer to the North Rim, along Highway 67. Here is the Kaibab Lodge, with cabins at the 8,500 foot level and the North Rim Country Store where park visitors obtain food, hiking, and camping supplies. Forest Service campgrounds are located at Jacob Lake and Demotte, providing additional spaces for those who are not able to camp inside the park.

For those who aren't deterred by the abundant snow that falls in the area, the Forest Service has a Nordic ski center a half-mile south of Jacob Lake via Arizona Route 67 and Forest Road 461. Another winter recreation operation (Snow-Ventures) is located nearby, at the 89A/67 junction. Both have ski and snowmobile rentals, providing an opportunity to reach the Grand Canyon overlooks during winter months.

Panoramic Vistas

As Arizona Route 67 heads south toward the park gate, several forest roads lead across the plateau to overlook points:

Crazy Jug Point 32 miles southwest of Jacob Lake. Starting on the rim of the Grand Canyon Drive .3 miles south of Jacob Lake, take Hwy. 67 to Forest Road 461, and go 9 miles on FR 461 and FR 462. Then turn south on FR 422 and drive for 11.5 miles (5 miles beyond Big Springs) to FR 425. Turn west onto FR 425 and drive for 8.5 miles to Big Saddle Point. Turn south onto FR 292 and drive about 1.5 miles to an intersection. Take FR 292B for .3 miles to the viewpoint. The bumpy gravel roads are suitable for cars but not for long trailers and RVs.

Jumpup Point 35.5 miles southwest of Jacob Lake. Drive 0.25 miles south of Jacob Lake on Hwy. 67 and turn west onto Forest Road 461. Drive 9 miles on FR 461 and FR 462 to FR 422. Take FR 422 south for 2 miles to FR 423. Turn west onto FR 423 and drive 3 miles to FR 235. Drive west on FR 235 for 8 miles. Turn onto FR 423 and drive southwest to FR 201. Jumpup Point is 10.3 miles down FR 201. The one-way drive takes 90 minutes. The roads are suitable for 4-wheel-drive vehicles and pickups only.

Sowats Point Take the same rough dirt roads as to Jumpup Point except when you reach FR 422. Drive along this road for 11.5 miles (5 miles beyond Big Springs), to FR 425. Turn west (right) onto FR 425 and drive 8 miles to FR 233. Follow FR 233 for 9.5 miles to Sowats Point at the end of the road. The one-way trip takes about 1.25 hours. Not for RVs and trailers.

East Rim Viewpoint From Demotte (a mile south of the store) take Highway 67. Drive 26.5 miles south of Jacob Lake, turn east onto FR 611. Drive along FR 611 for 4.4 miles, passing the junction with FR 610, to reach the viewpoint.

Lee's Ferry

A visit to the North Rim is not complete without visiting the place where the Colorado River begins its long journey through the Grand Canyon gorge. This remarkable sight—where the north and south rims come together at water level—is located a few miles south of Page, at an historic ferry crossing. From this spot, the river meanders across the landscape for about 30 miles, then begins its descent into the canyon.

Lee's Ferry was the only crossing of the Colorado River in this entire region between 1871 and the early 1900s. The ferry boat was operated first by John Doyle Lee, a Mormon settler who moved here with his wife and family and established a farm that was irrigated by water from the Paria River.

Lee was put on trial and executed in 1877 for his part in the Mountain Meadows Massacre, when 140 California-bound pioneers were killed by Mormon settlers who resented the presence of U.S. troops in the region. Emma Lee continued to operate the ferry until she sold it to the Mormon Church in 1879. The ferry sank and was subsequently replaced by the Navajo Bridge in 1928.

The historic site of Lee's Ferry is fascinating, but there is another important reason to visit here: Lee's Ferry landing marks the beginning of the Grand Canyon and is the only spot along the canyon where one can drive to the water's edge to see the Colorado River racing into the world's most impressive gorge. Navajo sandstone, seen on the opposite side of the river as a light-colored layer, is what forms the south and north rims.

The landing is a favorite spot for anglers, who put their boats into the water here. This is also the location for the start of the one- and two-week rafting trips through the canyon. The road to the landing takes you through a scenic part of the Glen Canyon National Recreation Area. The "balanced rocks" to the west of the road are the result of boulders tumbling from the rim of the cliffs and coming to rest on softer rock, where they rest on protected pillars. There's a campground near the old Lee homestead and a trail leading across the Paria River to the original ferry crossing.

Nearby Attractions

GLEN CANYON NATIONAL RECREATION AREA (LAKE POWELL)

One of the best places in America for houseboating, Lake Powell is a place of stark contrast and stunning beauty. The lake and the recreation area surrounding it were created in

1972 with the damming of the Colorado River at Glen Canyon Dam.

The dam was not built without controversy. The Sierra Club and its founding manager, David Brower, were fresh from a bitter defeat in the environmental war of words over the damming of Yosemite's Hetch Hetchy Valley. Now at stake was the whole of the Upper Colorado project, a grandiose plan to dam significant valleys and canyons in the Green, Yampa, and Colorado rivers, including the building of the Echo Park Dam, which would damage parts of Dinosaur National Monument, which lies on the Utah-Colorado border.

From 1953 to 1955, the Sierra Club and the Wilderness Society (founded by Otto Leopold) opposed the Bureau of Reclamation plans, particularly the Echo Park Dam and its flooding of the Dinosaur Monument. In an extensive battle, with testimony before a congressional committee, both sides debated evaporation levels for the various dams. The preservationists proposed that a higher dam be built at Glen Canyon to avoid severe evaporation of stored water. As the bargaining closed, Brower and those on his side sacrificed Glen Canyon in order to retain Dinosaur National Monument. Lake Powell was thus created, and the Navajo Generating Station at Page was built to replace the planned hydroelectric station that was not built at Echo Park—again part of the bargain.

Edward Abbey, in his evocative book *Desert Solitaire,* describes a canoe trip down the Colorado River through the stupendously scenic Glen Canyon as the dam was being built, just before the flooding. While the present-day Lake Powell is a superb recreational amenity, the nation lost a magnificent desert canyon. Meanwhile, the Navajo Generating Station belches smoke from burning coal that often drifts over the Grand Canyon. Was the Echo Park/Lake Powell tradeoff a good idea, or even conscionable? Should either dam have been built? I have no idea. Only a philosopher would dare to ponder these questions at this point in time.

Enjoying Lake Powell   The prime season runs from late March to late October, the same period during which the North Rim of the Grand Canyon is open, making Lake Powell an obvious place for a side trip or a destination for a longer vacation.

The huge reservoir stretches for 186 miles from Canyonlands National Park to the Utah/Arizona border. The area is a photographer's dream with its combination of water and rock, providing unlimited opportunities for artful shooting, particularly if you have a boat to get out onto the lake, where rock islands and steeply walled inlets abound. It is also a very popular area for boating and fishing for bass, walleye (pickerel), catfish, and black crappie.

This man-made attraction is an eerie sight, particularly during dusk and moonlight hours, when the deep black of the lake contrasts with the naked sandstone cliffs that rise high above it. During sunlit hours, the lake shimmers in colors ranging from robin's egg blue to deep azure.

Boating is the major activity on the reservoir; five large marinas are located along the waterway. Bullfrog Marina is 70 miles south of Hanksville. Wahweap Marina is 7 miles north of Page. There are lodges with overnight accommodations at both marinas. Other marinas are located at Hite, Halls Crossing (across the lake from Bullfrog), and at Bullfrog (the largest marina in Utah). For information on tours and boat rentals, call 1-800-528-6154. During the busy summer weeks, rental houseboats must be reserved many months in advance.

The lake offers water trips to several remarkable places, including Rainbow Bridge National Monument. This huge rock bridge is accessible by private boat or by one of the tour launches that set out from the marinas. Indian ruins can be seen at several locations along the shoreline.

A 0.5-hour drive south of the Glen Canyon Dam, Lee's Ferry Landing is the southernmost site in the recreation area. This historic area—of great geological interest—is described earlier in this chapter.

There are seven information centers; however, the only year-round visitor center is at the Glen Canyon Dam near Page. The visitor center at the Bullfrog Marina is open most of the year. Interpretation programs are given during the summer months at campgrounds in the Bullfrog and Wahweap areas.

Getting to Lake Powell Three highways intersect Glen Canyon. At the extreme south end of the recreation area, U.S. Highway 89 leads east from Kanab to Page (Arizona) and the site of the Glen Canyon Dam. The northern route is the Bicentennial Highway (Utah Highway 95), which crosses the lake at Hite Crossing.

In the middle area, Utah Highway 276 runs to the water with the ferry John Atlantic Burr crossing the reservoir, cutting 130 miles off the route from Hall's Crossing to Bullfrog Marina.

Visitor services are available on both sides of the ferry crossing. The ferry is capable of holding cars with trailers and motor homes. It operates year-round with enhanced service during the prime season.

The crossing takes approximately 20 minutes and the ferry begins operation at 8:00 A.M. from Halls Crossing and 9:00 A.M. from Bullfrog with crossings every 2 hours through 6:00 P.M. and 7:00 P.M. from May 15 to September 30, and through 2:00 P.M. and 3:00 P.M. from October 1 to May 14. The marinas are fully equipped with stores, boat rentals, gas, restaurants, and overnight accommodations.

Glen Canyon Trails   Those who prefer to use their legs instead of a motorboat have three good trails to hike. Escalante Canyon offers several trails leading from the Highway 12 turnoff.

The Grand Gulch Trail begins at the Kane Gulch Ranger Station and leads into a deep canyon that has been the site of archeological digs. Dark Canyon is located off Highway 95. Fifty-five miles of trails lead from trailheads off several dirt roads.

Camping   Campgrounds are operated by the National Parks Service at Bullfrog, Hall's Crossing, Hite, and Wahweap. There's a charge for camping.

WUPATKI NATIONAL MONUMENT
AND SUNSET CRATER

For those traveling to or from the North Rim from the Flagstaff area, a short loop road off U.S. Highway 89 offers unusual glimpses into native history and geological disturbance. Located 10 miles north of the Flagstaff city limits, this road offers a fascinating side trip to two outstanding parks.

Wupatki Pueblo   This pueblo is one of five excavated Sinagua Indian ruins in the Wupatki National Monument (farther north on the loop road). There is a visitor center at the Wupatki Ruin where a self-guided tour will lead you through the multi-storied pueblo, and to the amphitheater and ball court.

The Wupatki Ruin was inhabited by the Sinagua, Cohonina, and Anasazi people for about 400 years, beginning in the early twelfth century A.D. The three prehistoric cultures lived here together for some of this time. They disbanded about A.D. 1225, scattering in different directions. In addition to the main ruin, other partially excavated sites include the Wukoki, Citadel, Lomaki, and Nalakihu ruins. There is no campground at Wupatki, but there is a scenic picnic area at the base of Doney Mountain, with a trail ascending 689 feet to the mountain's top.

Sunset Crater   This volcano erupted in the winter of A.D. 1064–1065 and later vented lava from its base, creating two flows. Around the base are a picnic area, a lava flow trail, and a visitor center.

Although the volcano's first blasts occurred in 1064, it continued with smaller eruptions for the next 200 years, making major changes in the landscape surrounding the vent, including the creation of a prominent lava flow to the west and north of the crater in 1180. The paved road leads through this area, past the Bonito Lava Flow to near the crater, where a trail leads to its base.

During the final blast in 1250, lava containing iron and other minerals shot out of the vent, creating the red glow at the top. There is a visitor center at the site and a picnic area next to the Bonito Lava Flow. A Forest Service campground is located across the road from the visitor center.

PIPE SPRING NATIONAL MONUMENT

Northwest of the North Rim, Highway 89 continues across the Kaibab Plateau through the town of Fredonia. Beyond Fredonia via Arizona Route 389 is the Kaibab Indian Reservation, where the Pipe Spring National Monument preserves the memory of one of the earliest Mormon settlements in Northern Arizona. A reconstruction of the original settlement and the main attraction of the town is Winsor Castle, the original frontier fort and telegraph station that features living history exhibits. Demonstrations of cheese-making, baking, woodcarving, and other pioneer skills are demonstrated daily during the summer and fall months.

FOUR-WHEEL-DRIVE ADVENTURE

Route 389 continues west, then northwest to become Utah Route 59 as it approaches the town of St. George. Southwest of St. George is the Paiute Wilderness Area, a protected natural area traversed by the Black Mountains.

Between the Kaibab Reservation (see above) and the Paiute Wilderness is a network of gravel roads that lead south toward the western section of the Grand Canyon. The Arizona State Highway Map shows these roads, all of which can be accessed from two entry points just west of the Kaibab Reservation boundary, from St. George and (farther to the southwest) from Nevada Route 170, which runs beside the Virgin River from the border town of Mesquite. Two of these dirt roads lead into Lake Mead National Recreation Area, providing additional views of the Colorado River and the Grand Canyon.

The most easterly road leads over the Uinkaret Plateau past Mt. Trumbull and Toroweep Point into Grand Canyon National Park, ending at a canyon overlook. There is a Forest Service campground at this site with a summer ranger station nearby. This road may also be accessed by taking the gravel route, which begins across the highway from the Pipe Spring National Monument in the Kaibab Reservation. For a while, the road runs beside Bull Rush Canyon. This terrain is quite different from that of the Kaibab Plateau. The arid, semi-desert land-scape is rife with draws and washes, most of which run in a southerly direction toward the Colorado River. The Hurricane Cliffs cut through the middle section, separating the Uinkaret Plateau from the lower Shivwits Plateau to the west.

LAKE MEAD AND THE VALLEY OF FIRE

After leaving the Grand Canyon, the Colorado River flows westward until it empties into Lake Mead, which is held back by the Hoover Dam, completed near Las Vegas in 1935. This is the largest but not the last diversion of water on the lower

Colorado. The Davis Dam, at Bullhead City to the south, has created Lake Mohave, another prime recreational reservoir and part of the Lake Mead recreational complex. Other dams farther south drain the Colorado to irrigate the desert for agricultural purposes.

Leaving aside any possible ranting about the value of wild and free rivers, Lake Mead is a wonderful, clear blue lake, with hundreds of miles of shoreline providing access to lonely beaches and quiet boat-in campsites. Like Lake Powell, it is a favorite houseboating venue. South of the Hoover Dam—reached by taking the highway from Las Vegas to Boulder City—rafting companies take visitors on tours of the river canyon, floating down the Colorado to Lake Mohave.

North of the dam lies the lake, which is backed up almost as far as the western end of the Grand Canyon. Hydroelectric generation fuels much of the desert economy. It keeps the Las Vegas neon flashing, and provides power for vast portions of Utah and Arizona.

Enjoying Lake Mead The nation's first national recreation area, Lake Mead—perhaps even more than Lake Powell—offers visitors the confusing but satisfying dichotomy between the vast lake (water where there would normally not be water) and the high desert of the basin and range environment. The rock surrounding the reservoir is raw, brown granite, not the sandstone and limestone of the Grand Canyon area. It lies there, seemingly desolate and lifeless. Yet wildlife is there in great quantity. Desert animals—bighorn sheep, jackrabbits, coyotes, and other creatures—emerge during the evening hours. Wildflowers bloom on the rocky hills after winter rainstorms. Shore birds, attracted by the lake, include cormorants, migratory ducks, geese, egrets, herons, and white pelicans.

Most visitors tend to stay on their houseboats. The wise tourist will explore the land portions of the recreation area as much as possible. The Parks Service has licensed six marinas—four on Lake Mead and two on Lake Mohave. Because of the huge area occupied by the lakes (274 square miles), the recreation area doesn't seem to be crowded. Boat tours are operated by the concessionaires and marinas offer boat rentals, supplies, launching ramps, water-skiing equipment, and parking. There is a 7-day parking limit. Fishing is a year-round activity, with largemouth bass, rainbow trout, striped bass, bluegill, black crappie, and channel catfish available. Once you're on the water, the possibilities seem endless. Iceberg Canyon, in Lake Mead, and Black Canyon (just south of Hoover Dam) offer thrilling exploration by boat and raft.

Overton Arm Southwest of St. George, Utah, is the northern arm of Lake Mead, providing boating, camping, and other recreational activity. To visit this underused part of the huge Lake Mead National Recreation Area, drive to St. George and take Interstate 15 southwest to Glendale and the Route 169 exit. Take Nevada Route 169 southeast past the village of Overton to Overton Beach, or continue along the lake to Echo Bay.

VALLEY OF FIRE

Situated near Overton Arm and accessible via State Highway 40, this is one of the most striking state parks in the nation. The sandstone formations were created during the Jurassic period, 150 million years ago, when great sand dunes covered the area.

   This naked landscape is a supreme piece of natural architecture. Sunsets on the red formations are nothing but spectacular. Features of the park include beehives—the rounded sandstone formations created by erosion from wind and water; petroglyphs—seen in a canyon, via a self-guided trail, and on Aratl Rock; Fire Canyon Overlook—offering a view into the deep sandstone canyons; Seven Sisters—rock formations with a nearby picnic area; and a campground suitable for tents and RVs.

SOUTHWESTERN WILDLIFE

Because the North Rim—the edge of the Kaibab Plateau—and the Grand Canyon have a vertical difference of more than a mile, a wide range of wildlife and native plants grow in the various biotic communities (a grouping of animals and plants that live together in a particular physical habitat). These communities range from the Colorado desert (beside the river on the canyon floor) to the subalpine forests of the Kaibab Plateau.

You'll see quite a difference in biotic communities when traveling between Cape Imperial, one of the highest spots on the plateau, and Cape Royal, with its lower elevation and drier climate. The water-loving wildflowers that carpet the plateau meadows (also called parks) in the early summer are not found at lower levels. However, plants and animals in one community do overlap into the next, creating fringe areas.

In each chapter, a short field guide provides descriptions of the prominent animals and plants that live in this book's eleven southwestern destinations. These descriptions cover the birds, animals, and plants you'll probably see on your visit, in addition to the resident wildlife that is rarely seen elsewhere or is unique to the particular region. For instance, the Kaibab squirrel is found only on the Kaibab Plateau and at nearby Mt. Trumbull. A few non-native species are listed, including the bison of House Rock Buffalo Ranch.

BIRDS

Golden Eagle
Aquila chrysaetos
This magnificent bird is one of the most prominent residents of the Kaibab Plateau, and is often seen from the North Rim and the forest areas.

It is perfectly suited for its range, which encompasses higher elevations including alpine tundra (none of this on the plateau), rangeland, badlands, and canyons. Shaped like a hawk, but with a much larger body (up to 41 inches long) and a wide wingspan (71 to 92 inches), the king of the canyons is overall a dark brown, with the tan or golden nape only visible at close range. Young birds in flight have a white tail with a dark terminal band.

The Golden Eagle hunts for large rodents and rabbits. You'll rarely hear it, but sometimes it lets out a high-pitched squeal, or very soft mewing sounds.

Great Horned Owl
Bubo virginianus
Sometimes called the "Cat Owl," this large bird depends on forests and cliffs for shelter, and such sites are in good supply here. Distinguishing features include ear tufts set wide apart, bright yellow eyes, and a dark, mottled brown color above with dark gray bars or stripes below. The owls here hunt for small rabbits, rodents, and birds (including other owls). Its voice is distinctive: a deep hooting sound with three *hoots* or *hoo, hoo-hoo-hoo, hoo*.

Turkey Vulture
Cathartes aura
One of the largest carnivorous birds, this raptor has a wingspan up to 72 inches and a body length of 32 inches. It is a browny black, with yellow feet. The most prominent characteristic is the red, unfeathered head. In flight, its neck is short and the wings appear as two-toned, with paler flight feathers. It flies with its wings in a shallow V, and tilts from side to side.

Having an incredible range, from southern Canada to the tip of South America, it can be seen swooping over the Grand Canyon and over the Kaibab forest. It can also be seen perched on dead trees and on the ground, feasting on road kill.

Cooper's Hawk
Accipiter cooperii
Accipiter hawks, or "bird hawks", are long-tailed raptors with rounded wings, which they use to fly between the trees of the forest. The Cooper's hawk is about the size of a crow (growing up to 20 inches) with a large head. Looking similar to the sharp-shinned hawk (another accipiter), the adult shows a dark, slate-blue back, and a rusty, barred breast. The female is larger and has a bluish-brown back.

Its habitat is primarily woodland, at the edges of forests, and along rivers and creeks.

A fast-flying bird, it can be seen flying low over the trees on the plateau. It does not fly for long periods over the canyon like other hawks, but retreats to the woods or to other hiding places between its food-searching flights.

Raven
Corvus cryptoleucus
This is the Chihauhuan raven, a desert-loving bird about the size of the American crow, but with

a heavy bill, pointed tail feathers, and a wedge-shaped tail. It is also called the white-necked raven because of a few white feathers on the neck and breast, which sometimes show when ruffled by the wind.

Its habitat is the low desert and elevations lower than the canyon rims, but not above. Unlike other ravens, it usually uses the same nest from year to year and feeds on insects, as well as carrion. You may see this raven flying in groups in the canyons.

Corvus corax
The common raven is larger than the crow and its Chihauhuan cousin, and grows to 27 inches. It has a heavy bill and the wedge-shaped tail. When it flies, it soars on flat wings. It has quite a range of sounds. The most commonly heard is the loud, hoarse croak (*kraaak*), but it is also heard uttering a hollow, knocking sound and a musical (at least for a raven) call that sounds like *kloo-kluk*.

The common raven can often be seen hopping along roadsides and in the park's parking lots. It's not afraid of anything. It lives over a wide range including high and low deserts, mountains, canyons, northern boreal forests, and is even found on the beaches of the Pacific Coast. It is considered one of the most intelligent of all birds.

Williamson's Sapsucker
Sphyrapicus thyroideus
A resident of ponderosa pine forests, Williamson's is right at home on the Kaibab Plateau and is found in some numbers here, as well as in several other sub-alpine forests of the Southwest. It is a woodpecker, living in its preferred cool climate.

The male has a black head, back, and breast, with white stripes on the face and a bright red throat. It has large white patches on its wings and rump, and its yellow belly is flanked by black and white bars. The female looks very different. It has a brown head, dark brown stripes, zebra stripes above and on the flanks, and a white rump. It has a dark bib and a smaller, darker yellow section on the belly.

One of several species of "zebra-backed" woodpeckers, the Williamson's sound is a soft *churrr* or *cheeer*. Its drumming is intermittent, with several fast thumps followed by several slower, harder thumps.

Clark's Nutcracker
Nucifraga columbiana
Like other members of the jay family, this Kaibab resident has the typical *khaaa* or *khraa* calls.

It has no crest, and looks similar to a small crow, with a light gray body and black wings with large white patches. Because of these patches, Clark's nutcracker is quite recognizable on the plateau and at high elevations in Arizona and New Mexico.

It prefers to build its nest in coniferous forests, near the tree line.

Grace's Warbler
Dendroica graciae
The wood warbler is a small bird, smaller than a sparrow, with a thin, needle-shaped bill. There are 114 identified warbler species so far, including 53 that reside in the Southwest. They are now considered to be in the same family as tanagers, blackbirds, and sparrows. Warbler food is primarily insects.

This gray-backed warbler has a bright yellow throat and two white wing bars. It resembles the yellow-throated warbler but does not have a white patch behind the ear. Since it usually lives in mountain forests, the high elevation of the Kaibab Plateau has attracted it to the canyon rim. Its song is a lengthy tune: *cheedle cheedle chee chee chee chee,* ending in a long trill.

Broad-tailed Hummingbird
Selasphorus platucercus
This hummingbird is found on the Kaibab Plateau and north from here throughout the Rocky Mountains. Arizona is its most southerly habitat. It lives in meadows, in pinyon-juniper woodlands, and in ponderosa pine forests.

Growing as long as 4.5 inches, the male has a green back and a bright rose-red throat. The female is green above with rusty sides, wings rusty at the base and black in the middle with white tips. This species is known to return to the same tree branch year after year, sometimes building a new nest on top of the old one. While a Kaibab resident during the summer, it winters in Central America.

OTHER ANIMALS

Bobcat
Felis Rufus
This member of the cat family is relatively small in size, with a body that grows to 25 or 30 inches. Its name comes from its tail, which is very short—only about 5 inches long—and black-tipped with two or three black bars. The upper legs have dark horizontal bars.

This cat's face has thin black lines (sometimes broken), fanning out onto the ruffled cheek. Males are larger than females. This cat is very secretive, not wishing to be seen by anything or anyone. Often occupying scrub chaparral areas in the

Western states, they are also seen within ponderosa pine forests, including those of the North Kaibab plateau.

Bobcats move and feed at night, hunting small mammals including rodents, rabbits and hares, as well as birds and odorless carrion.

They build their dens in rocky crevices, in hollow logs, and under fallen logs. Cubs are born in the spring.

The bobcat's trail is very narrow. Its fore and hind prints are about the same size, about 2 inches long, with four toes and no claw marks. The two sets of prints are sometimes close together or overlapping (as if it were a two-legged animal). The heel pad is lobed at the rear and concave at the front, unlike that of the dog or coyote, whose pads do not have the concave front.

The bobcat is an avid climber. It hides on tree branches, waiting for prey to pass underneath.

Kaibab Squirrel
Sciurus kaibabensis
The Kaibab squirrel is found only in the North Kaibab region, which includes the Kaibab Plateau and as far west as Mt. Trumbull, which lies beyond the boundary of the national park near the Nevada border. It is the one unique animal species in this region. Similar species are the Abert's squirrel, found south of the Grand Canyon, and the Durango squirrel of northern Mexico. The three are known as tassel-eared or tufted-eared squirrels. You will see lots of these little rodents in the forests and in park areas along the North Rim. They can be identified by their black bellies and tasseled ears. Their white, plumed tails serve them well for winter camouflage.

Why a unique species of squirrel on the Kaibab Plateau? Biologists have figured out that the Kaibab squirrel became separated from its southern counterparts a long time ago (a few million years back) during the making of the canyon. In the interim, the Kaibab developed special characteristics, including protective coloring that enables them to hide in the pine forest. At any rate, the Kaibab is similar, but quite different in its markings, to the two other tassel-eared species.

The Kaibab squirrel builds its large nest in ponderosa pine trees, and lines it with shredded bark after the nest is constructed of pine needles and twigs. It eats pine seeds and munches on the soft inner bark of pine branches. It is not averse to eating other foods, including acorns and parking lot droppings left by unthinking tourists.

Mule Deer
Odocoileus hemionus

This stocky deer changes color with the major seasons. In the summer, it is a reddish or yellowish-brown above. In winter it turns gray. There is a white throat patch and a white patch on the rump. The insides of the legs are also white, with the lower legs a creamy or tan color. The black-tailed deer is a subspecies, differing from the mule deer only because of the top of its tail, which is black or brown. The mule deer has a tail with white above, tipped with black. The buck's antlers spread to a width of 4 feet. Its total length can be as much as 6.5 feet. It has short, sturdy legs and a bounding gait, with all four feet reaching the ground together.

The history of the north Kaibab mule deer is a sorry tale. In the nineteenth century, the Havasupai used the abundant deer for skins and food. Then ranchers came and grazed large herds of cattle and sheep, which scattered the deer. The overgrazing caused most of the grass to be replaced by shrubs and broad-leafed plants. This was bad for the cattle, but good for the deer.

In 1906, Congress legislated deer protection. Deer hunting was prohibited and predators, including mountain lions, were hunted. The deer population exploded to about 100,000 by 1924. Disease and starvation then decimated the herd to about 10,000. Today, hunting and mountain lions keep the deer population controlled to a healthy level. They're seen every day on the drive to the park gate.

Bison
Bison bison

The buffalo is not a native species of the Kaibab Plateau or the Grand Canyon region, but there is a fine herd on public display near the North Rim.

While there were once great herds of bison across the American West, they did not come as far west and south as northern Arizona. The first bison were imported shortly after the establishment of the Grand Canyon Game Preserve in 1906.

The scout and buffalo hunter Charles C. "Buffalo" Jones took it upon himself to save some of the few remaining buffalo left in the West. He bought a small herd, brought them to the game preserve, and hooked them up with four partners. Jones intended to have a "cattalo" operation, interbreeding bison and cattle for meat production. The bison occupied a pasture near the site of the

Grand Canyon Lodge, next to Bright Angel Point. There were problems with the breeding experiment, and the buffalo and the few cattalo produced were sold to the state of Arizona, then moved to a more suitable, permanent home in House Rock Valley.

The descendants of these animals live at the ranch today, offering a look at a genuine buffalo herd, grazing and occasionally moving across the ranch lands. The ranch is 21 miles south of Highway 89A (41 miles from Jacob Lake), in House Rock Valley. From Highway 89A, take Forest Road 445 south for 19 miles, then FR 632 east for 2 miles to the ranch headquarters.

PLANTS

Cliffrose
Cowania mexicana
Sometimes called the Stansbury cliffrose, this small-leaf evergreen shrub (or small tree) has crooked trunks, many stubby branches, and small but plentiful white flowers.

You'll see the cliffrose in several spots around the North Rim of the Grand Canyon. One of the most prominent spots is near the beginning of the Cape Royal Trail, before reaching Angel's Window. This area is not quite as high in elevation as the Bright Angel Trail or Point Imperial. You'll also see junipers and pinyon pines near the cliffroses, a common plant community.

This hardy shrub grows in dry rock hills, on plateaus, and in high deserts. Its range is from southeastern Colorado and southern Utah to southwestern New Mexico and just inside eastern California. It is also displayed in quantity on the South Rim of the Grand Canyon. The flowers grow to a diameter of one inch, with five broad or pale yellow petals shown singly at the end of a short branch. They have a fragrant scent, and appear in the late spring and early summer.

Deer enjoy the tender shoots of the cliffrose, also called the quinine-bush. The foliage has a bitter taste.

The cliffrose is now being produced by commercial nurseries for use in landscape plantings. Its drought-resistant qualities make it a good choice for water-wise gardening.

Engelmann Spruce
Picea engelmanii
A prime tree in the forests of the North Kaibab Plateau, the Engelmann spruce grows with other conifers, particularly firs, in mixed forest settings in subalpine zones up to the tree line. It is found from central

British Columbia and Alberta south to Oregon and New Mexico. This tree is found at elevations of 8,000 to 12,000 feet in Arizona and New Mexico, and down to 2,000 feet in the northern habitats.

This is a large, straight tree, with dark blue-green needles. It has a dense, small, cone-shaped crown. It grows to heights of 100 feet, and the trunk to a diameter of up to 2.5 feet.

The needles spread out on all sides of the little twigs from short leafstalks. The bark of the tree is a grayish brown or brown with a purple tinge, and has loose scales. The twigs that bear the needles are slender and rough, with a brown color.

The cones of the Engelmann spruce are about 2 inches long, cylindrically shaped, and are a shiny brown color. The long-winged seeds come in pairs. The cone scales are long, thin, and have rough teeth at the outer edges.

At the highest elevations of the Kaibab Plateau, the principal trees in the national forest are the blue spruce, Douglas fir, white fir, aspen, and mountain ash, in addition to the Engelmann spruce. This biotic community is characterized by its cool weather and abundant snowfall. At lower elevations, ponderosa pine and Gambel oak are the pre-dominant trees.

Quaking Aspen
Populus tremuloides
Distributed across much of North America, the quaking, or trembling, aspen is the tree that fills in forest openings that have been created by fire. It is usually the first tree to grow after a fire, and in doing so, provides excellent forage for hungry deer, elk, moose, beavers, rabbits, and other animals.

You will see the aspen coexisting with ponderosa pines on the lower levels of the Kaibab Plateau, and mingling with spruces and firs at slightly higher levels.

The aspen's two descriptive names come from the leaf movements. The leaves move in a shivering fashion, at the least whisper of a breeze.

The tree's range is from coast to coast, from Alaska to Newfoundland, and from the northern Rocky Mountains south to Arizona and New Mexico. In the two southern states, the trees are found at or above the 6,500-foot level.

The bark is smooth on younger trees, with a whitish color. When mature, the large trunks bear a thick, dark gray bark.

The leaves, which grow to 3 inches, are almost round, are finely saw-toothed, and have a short point. They are shiny green above and dull green underneath.

The aspen is known for its fall foliage, with the leaves turning a brilliant yellow or yellowish-orange. The Kaibab forest in autumn is a magnificent sight.

Mormon Tea
Ephedra
The Mormon tea—there are several species—has been used for many centuries for medicinal purposes. It is browsed by native animals including deer. One prominent species is the green ephedra, so named for its bright green, jointed stems that bear upside-down, broom-like clusters of flowers in cones. This Mormon tea plant grows at elevations of up to 7,500 feet.

Another is the Torrey ephedra, growing in sandy areas from 2,000 feet to 6,800 feet—not high enough to grow on the North Rim, but on the way down to the canyon floor.

The ephedras are cousins of the pines and junipers, similar in that they produce small cones in which the female plants bear their fruit.

Rabbitbrush
Chrysothamnus (species)
The rabbitbrush is a widespread Southwest plant that also grows as far north as Canada and south into Mexico. Usually seen along roadsides and disturbed areas, this member of the sunflower family grows to 3 feet.

The sticky-flowered rabbitbrush grows at elevations up to 10,000 feet, well suited for life on the Kaibab Plateau. Golden rabbitbrush grows up to 8,000 feet and is also seen in this region. It is particularly conspicuous during the fall. Like other species, the flowers are massed in large clusters, with up to a dozen flowers in each head.

WILDFLOWERS

Aspen Bluebell
Mertensia arizonica
A member of the borage family, its cousins are often found in the herb garden. This wildflower covers large areas, mostly in spruce and fir forests, and is usually found in large clumps.

The narrow lavender-blue bell-shaped flowers hang from drooping stems. This characteristic feature makes the plant easy to identify. The smooth leaves grow in an alternate sequence, up the stem of the plant.

Silvery Lupine
Lupinus argentus
The lupine genus is found almost everywhere in North America, but the silvery lupine cannot be found in many other regions. This member of the

legume family spreads out to develop wide clumps, supported by its horizontal rootstalks. Lupines are among the first plants to grow following a fire.

The plants grow to a height of 30 inches at the time of flowering. The stalks have small leaves that radiate out like tiny fingers. There are hairs on the underside of the leaf, while the top of the leaf is shiny and green.

The flowers are either blue or blue and white. You'll see the silvery lupine in open meadows between the forests (close to the forest boundaries).

Depending on the level of snowfall and spring rains, lupine can cover large meadow areas.

Meadow Gentian
Gentianopsis detonsa
Among the finest rock-garden plants, the natural, wild gentians provide real character to a high meadow. The plant is named after King Gentius, the ruler of Illyria, an ancient country on the Adriatic Sea, who discovered medicinal uses for gentian.

A deep purple color, the flower of the meadow gentian has fringed petals that open for bright sun but close at night and in cloudy weather. It grows on the wetter meadows. Subalpine meadows can be completely filled with this gentian, offering waves of deep blue. Each stem has several pairs of opposite leaves. The petals spread from a corolla tube.

Marsh Marigold
Caltha leptosepala
A member of the buttercup family, the marsh marigold thrives in very moist places: wet meadows, the sides of ditches and other drainage areas, and in depressions that hold water.

The stamens of the flowers are a bright yellow, while the sepals (not petals) are white and surround the stamens. The flowers grow from 1 to 2 inches wide. The leaves are oval in shape with a heart-shaped base.

Like many other wildflowers, the marsh marigold was used by Native Americans as medicine, but only after they cooked the plant to get rid of the poisons within the stalks and leaves. Most animals know enough to stay away from this pretty but harmful plant.

DEMOTTE PARK, ARIZONA

Kaibab Lodge

c/o Canyoneers Inc.
P.O. Box 2997
Flagstaff, AZ 86003
(520) 526-0924 or 800-525-0924;
Lodge: (520) 638-2389

Twenty-six miles south of Jacob Lake and a few miles north of the North Rim park boundary, this historic lodge has 26 units, a restaurant, lounge, hot tub, store (across the highway), gas, riding, guided hikes, and vehicle tours ($). A cross–country ski center operates from Dec. 1. Write for advance reservations.

Demotte Campground

Southwest of Jacob Lake on Forest Road #461 via Arizona Route 67, this campground has 20 sites with restrooms and water. No hookups are available.

FLAGSTAFF, ARIZONA

Arizona Mountain Inn (B&B)

685 Lake Mary Road
(520) 774-8959

Set in the forest, with kitchens, fireplaces, TV. No smoking ($ to $$).

Best Western Woodlands Plaza

1175 Highway 66
(520) 773-8888 or 800-528-1234

Hotel has a dining room, coffee shop, pool, indoor and outdoor whirlpools, sauna, steam room, exercise room ($ to $$).

Birch Tree Inn (B&B)

824 W. Birch Avenue
(520) 774-1042

A B&B inn with pool table, no smoking ($ to $$).

Flagstaff Travelodge Suites

2755 Woodlands Village Boulevard
(520) 773-1111 or 800-255-3050

Eighty-nine units (one-room suites), free continental breakfast, pool, exercise room, sauna ($ to $$).

Big Tree Campground

(520) 526-2583

On N. Highway 89. 50 RV sites with hookups, 100 tent sites, showers, dump station. Open year-round.

Flagstaff KOA Campground

5803 N. Highway 89
(520) 526-9926

One hundred forty RV and trailer spaces with hookups, 60 tent sites, pool, store, showers, dump station, playground, laundry. Open year-round.

GRAND CANYON NATIONAL PARK— NORTH RIM

Grand Canyon Lodge
TW Services, P.O. Box 400
Cedar City, UT 84720
(801) 586-7686

The only indoor accommodations inside the north rim boundaries, this summer hotel offers modern motel rooms and cabins in the pine forest, a dining room, lounge, gift shop, park information center, tour arrangements. The lodge opens in May, when the road can be cleared of snow, and stays open until late October ($ to $$).

North Rim Campground
P.O. Box 85705
San Diego, CA 92138-5705
Reservations: call MISTIX at 800-365-2267

Located south of the Village, has showers, store, and gas pumps. No hookups. Other campgrounds are located outside the park border (see Demotte and Jacob Lake).

GRAND CANYON NATIONAL PARK, SOUTH RIM

The following listings are provided for those wishing to explore both rims of the Grand Canyon. While rooms at the North Rim are usually available on several weeks notice during the high season (summer), this is not as true at the South Rim. Here, reservations should be made several months in advance, particularly by those wishing to stay in the El Tovar Hotel.

Grand Canyon National Park Lodges
P.O. Box 699
Grand Canyon, AZ 86023
Advance reservations:
(520) 638-2401
Same-day reservations:
(520) 638-2631

Accommodations in the South Rim park include the historic El Tovar Hotel, Kachina Lodge, Thunderbird Lodge, Yavapai Lodge, Bright Angel Lodge, Maswik Lodge, and Moqui Lodge. Rates run from $ to $$$.

Phantom Ranch
(520) 638-2401
On the canyon floor beyond the north side of the river, has overnight dormitory and cabin space. Advance reservations are necessary. Call (520) 638-2401 or contact the Bright Angel Lodge Transportation desk while in the park. This desk also handles reservations for mule trips into the canyon.

Desert View and Mather Campgrounds
For reservations, call MISTIX at 800-365-2267

Both campgrounds are open during summer months. Only a portion of Mather Campground has sites that can be reserved. Desert View Campground, opposite the observation tower, has no hookups.

Trailer Village
(520) 638-2401

Located next to Mather Campground, with hookups.

HAVASUPAI INDIAN RESERVATION

Havasupai Lodges
General Delivery
Supai, AZ 86435
(520) 448-2111

In a side-canyon of the Grand Canyon, accessed by helicopter or by an 8-mile trail. Rooms with double beds and air conditioning ($ to $$).

Havasupai Campground
(520) 448-2121

In the Native American reservation, with limited accommodation and permits required.

JACOB LAKE, ARIZONA

Jacob Lake Inn
(520) 643-7232

At the junction of U.S. 89A and Arizona Route 69, north of the Grand Canyon North Rim.

Arizona Forest Service concession, with motel rooms open year-round. Summer-only accommodations include single units, larger family and group units (cabin-style), restaurant, gas, dump station ($ to $$).

Jacob Lake Campground
(520) 643-7395

Forest Service Campground with 48 units, water, restrooms, no hookups. Dump station next to Jacob Lake Inn.

KAYENTA, ARIZONA

Anasazi Inn at Tsegi Canyon
(520) 697-3793

West of the town of Kayenta, on U.S. Highway 160. Includes 56 units, restaurant ($$).

Holiday Inn, Kayenta
(520) 697-3221

In town, on Highway 160. Has 68 units, restaurant, and pool ($$).

GLEN CANYON NATIONAL RECREATION AREA, UTAH AND ARIZONA

The following places to stay are operated by ARA, the concessionaire for the national recreation area. For information and reservations at all locations, write:

ARA Leisure Services

2916 North 35th Avenue, Suite 8
Phoenix, AZ 85017
Advance reservations:
800-528-6154 or (520) 278-8888

For reservations less than 7 days in advance, call:

Wahweap Lodge & Marina
(520) 645-2433

Bullfrog Resort & Marina
800-528-6154

Lake Powell Motel
(520) 645-2477

Located 2.5 miles west of Wahweap Lodge, overlooking Wahweap Bay, on Highway 89 (west of Page, Arizona). Rooms with queen beds, TV (**$** to **$$**).

Wahweap Lodge
(520) 645-2433

The largest hotel on Lake Powell, overlooking Wahweap Bay. This fully fledged resort operation includes a large marina, standard and deluxe rooms, a dining room, lounge, gift shop, heated pool, cable TV, and entertainment during summer months (**$$** to **$$$**).

Defiance House Lodge
800-528-6154

Situated at Bullfrog Landing overlooking Bullfrog Bay, with views of the Navajo Mountain and the Henry Range. Restaurant, lounge, gift shop, TV, marina (**$** to **$$**).

Marina Housekeeping Units
Early reservations: 800-528-6154

Located at Bullfrog, Halls Crossing, and Hite Marina, these units accommodate 1 to 6 persons and are open year-round (**$$**).

RV Parks
800-528-6154

RV parks with full hookups are open year-round at Wahweap, Bullfrog, and Halls Crossing. Each park has a store, restrooms, showers, laundry, and propane.

Glen Canyon Campgrounds
(520) 645-2511

The National Parks Service operates campgrounds at Wahweap, Bullfrog, Halls Crossing, and Lee's Ferry. All have a first-come, first-served policy. Facilities include picnic tables, grills, water, and toilets. The Lee's Ferry Campground is located on a rise overlooking the Colorado River as it starts its journey into the Grand Canyon. Primitive campgrounds are located at Lone Rock (near Wahweap), Warm Creek, Bullfrog Bay, Farley, Stanton and White canyons, and at Hite Marina. Services at these sites are limited and suitable mainly for tent camping.

Backcountry camping is permitted except for within one mile of the marinas at Lee's Ferry or at Rainbow Bridge. The maximum stay along the shoreline is 30 days with inland areas limited to 14 days. Camping in the Escalante Canyon area requires a permit (520-645-2511).

PAGE, ARIZONA

Weston Inn, Best Western
207 N. Lake Powell Boulevard.
(520) 645-2451 or 800-528-1234

A large standard motel with heated pool, laundry, free continental breakfast (\$ to \$\$).

Inn at Lake Powell
716 Rim View Drive
(520) 645-5659

Motel has 103 units, pool, whirlpool, restaurant, and lounge (\$ to \$\$).

Page Holiday Inn
287 N. Lake Powell Boulevard
(520) 645-8851 or 800-232-0011
Includes 130 units, outdoor pool, restaurant, and lounge (\$ to \$\$).

Chaco Canyon

Chaco Culture National Historic Park

The most enduring human mystery in the Southwest is centered around the arrival, ascendance, decline, and disappearance of the Anasazi, the prehistoric Native American population that inhabited the desert region of the Four Corners for an all-too-brief period starting in the first century B.C. And no other place in the West is imbued with the mystery of the Anasazi like Chaco Culture National Historic Park, a shallow trench-like canyon in northwestern New Mexico through which flows a small wash and in which are located the largest and most impressive architectural remains of the Anasazi age.

About 800 years ago, the Anasazi departed from Chaco Canyon. No one knows precisely why they left, and no one understands how the Anasazi managed to develop an architectural tradition that resulted in the impressive structures now recognized as the cultural and business center of this prehistoric Native American culture.

For me and other awestruck visitors to Chaco Canyon, the first visit began as an historical search. As my stay progressed, it became a spiritual odyssey. Explorers into Anasazi culture are typically overcome with the richness of their ancient traditions and way of life; the ritual customs connected to the economic power that emanated across the desert from Chaco Canyon; and the many questions yet to be fully answered. Among the unanswered questions are these:

- Where did the Anasazi people come from?
- Where did they go?
- Why did they settle in this small, undistinguished canyon? How did Chaco become the trading and cultural center for the entire "Four Corners" region?
- How did the concept of kivas-as-ritual-centers develop?
- Why are kivas always round?
- Why are there "great kivas" and also smaller, ordinary kivas in the apartment complexes?
- What was the importance of fire in the ritual ceremonies of the Anasazi?
- Why did the Anasazi use a kiva for a few years and then fill some of them with garbage, going on to conduct religious observances in other round holes in the ground?
- Why did they farm mainly on the plateau above the canyon rather than beside the only stream in the area?
- Why did the inhabitants of Pueblo Bonito cover what could have been valuable farming land with their refuse dump?
- Why were the amazing Anasazi roads constructed in a straight line, even though it meant cutting steps into steep cliffs when it would have been much easier to curve the road around a canyon?
- What was the importance of the solstice in Anasazi life? (There are corner windows in one stone community through which the rising sun shines through two rooms at winter solstice.)
- What did the inhabitants do with human remains? (There is little evidence of burial grounds in Chaco Canyon.)
- What were the forces that led to the decline of the Anasazi culture?
- Why did they disappear as a continuing culture after only a few hundred years?

And a more immediate, personal question: Why does a full moon shining on the ruins of Chaco Canyon send shivers down your spine?

The 2,000-Year Anasazi Age

For more than 10,000 years, nomads roamed the Four Corners area, passing through the canyon. The first long-term Anasazi residents, the "Basketmakers," arrived about A.D. 700. They lived in the canyon, constructing small, one-story masonry pueblos. There is evidence that the Anasazi began building in Chaco Canyon around A.D. 900, first constructing what later became Pueblo Bonito, the largest of the structures.

At first farming was conducted on a primitive level, but as the culture developed, so did more sophisticated farming implements, utensils, and architectural skills. Chaco was one of three major Anasazi cultural regions, which included the center at Mesa Verde near Cortez Colorado, and another at Kayenta, Arizona (the Navajo National Monument).

By 1115, the Chaco culture had spread to more than seventy other pueblos, which had been established at some distance—as far as 60 miles away—and were connected to the trading and cultural center by amazingly straight roads that were as much as 30 feet wide. The largest of the Chaco buildings contained more than 800 rooms with adjoining plazas and ceremonial kivas. More than 2,000 people—perhaps as many as 5,000—lived in the canyon's stone communities.

Craftspeople of the region produced distinctive black-on-white glazed pottery and turquoise ornaments including necklaces, bracelets, and pendants. Seashells were also strung into necklaces. Chaco was an impressive trading center, first dealing with the outlying Anasazi pueblos and then trading as far as what is now Mexico.

Then, around A.D. 1100, the Anasazi began to abandon their Chaco Canyon pueblos; this was the beginning of the decline of the Anasazi across the Southwest. First the outlying communities were deserted, then by 1200 the towns in Chaco Canyon were empty. The changes in climate are often cited as the root cause of the decline. Serious drought, which the entire Southwest experienced between A.D. 1275 and 1300, may have been the reason for the evacuation, but no one is sure. There were many migrations of natives during that quarter-century, but that doesn't explain the earlier deterioration of the Chaco communities.

Other reasons given by experts include the depletion of resources such as wood and game. Wood for ceremonial fires and cooking was an important commodity, and the Anasazi were hunters who augmented their vegetable diet with meat. Also, disease may have played a part in decimating the Chaco communities. Some social scientists have theorized that religious or political strife may have brought conflict into the lives of the Anasazi. After moving to other places, the Anasazi faded into history, with the later Pueblo Indians carrying on some of the Anasazi architectural traditions.

After 1200, the Anasazi towns in the canyon sat and deteriorated for hundreds of years. For a while, Apache moved through the region but didn't stay at Chaco. Later, one of the Apachean bands, the Navajo, established settlements on the nearby mesas.

The Anasazi left an enduring legacy that began with the movement of the Basketmakers into Chaco Canyon. A few miles to the west is the present boundary of the vast Navajo Indian Reservation. One hundred miles to the west is Canyon de Chelly, another reminder of the Anasazi tradition, occupied today by Navajo who farm the river valley much as the Anasazi farmed Chaco's canyon fields and the highlands above the communities.

The sacred legacy is carried on at the Hopi, Taos, and Acoma pueblos. The pueblo religion, developed in a straight line from the Anasazi kiva rituals, is filled with mythology, intricate ceremonials, and an underlying view of nature as the all-important guiding force. At the many pueblos lying along the Rio Grande near Santa Fe, pueblo rituals are carried out on a regular basis, even though most of the pueblo inhabitants have been Christian since the days of Spanish occupation. The importance of religion and ceremony is one of the most noticed aspects of a visit to the canyon.

Getting There

Situated in the northwestern corner of New Mexico, Chaco Canyon is in a remote location, connected to the outside world by a gravel road, New Mexico Route 57. It is south of Farmington and Bloomfield and northeast of Gallup. Another route using back roads crosses the Escabada Wash; this adventure is described later in the chapter. For those with less yearning for backroad adventure, there are several easier routes.

From the north, take New Mexico Route 44 from Bloomfield (13 miles east of Farmington) and head south for 44 miles to Nageezi. Turn west and follow Route 57 to the park.

From the south, drive east from Gallup or west from Albuquerque on Interstate 40, and exit at Thoreau. Drive north on New Mexico Route 371 and turn right (east) onto New Mexico Route 57 and continue to the park (64 miles from I-40).

VISITING THE RUINS

Chaco Canyon has no farmers today. The only residents are the few Parks Service employees who maintain the historic park and provide interpretive programs. The canyon has been preserved for its unique role as the hub of prehistoric civilization in North America and as the center of an ancient culture that surpassed in complexity that of any other Native American culture in what is now the United States.

The road from the north passes through Cly Canyon, a narrow gorge leading into the historic park. After passing several Anasazi ruins, some of which are hidden from view, you'll find the one-way loop road that circles through the canyon, leading to the most important ruins.

The Visitor Center is beyond this loop road. A small museum devoted to Anasazi history is part of the Visitor Center. This is the place from which to begin your Chaco Canyon explorations.

The campground (the only place to stay in the area) is beyond the Visitor Center at the eastern end of the canyon.

The two largest and best-preserved pueblos, Pueblo Bonito and Chetro Ketl, are both located at the western end of the canyon. Visiting these two fascinating ruins will take about 90 minutes.

Pueblo Bonito   The most impressive of all the ruins is located near the west end of the canyon. Its name, "pretty village," has been known since about 1840 and is said to have been chosen by Mexican traders or soldiers.

Built in stages, the huge pueblo eventually contained more than 600 rooms and had 40 round kivas (ceremonial chambers where rituals were carried out). It is considered the classic

Anasazi group dwelling. If you are visiting with a deadline and have a single day to explore the park, this is the pueblo to see first.

The excavation of Pueblo Bonito began in 1896 by Richard Weatherill, a homesteader in the canyon, and was continued by the American Museum of Natural History under George Pepper. In the first four summers, 190 rooms were cleared of debris. After a gap, excavation work resumed in 1921 in a joint venture of the National Geographic Society and the U.S. National Museum. In the next seven seasons the work was completed—uncovering a total of 600 rooms and 33 kivas. Part of the plaza was uncovered during this period.

Pueblo Bonito was built between A.D. 1030 and 1079. The inside walls were constructed of rough stones held together with mortar. The walls were then finished on each side using drywall construction, with small, dense pieces of sandstone carefully fitted without mortar. This sandstone is of the Cliff House formation from the Cretaceous period. Ceiling beams were placed for each level and small rectangles were left open for light and air. Part of the building was five stories high.

The vast open areas inside the structure are courtyards or plazas. This was the town square for the community, where hides were scraped, pottery was made and fired, corn and other foods were prepared, and ceremonial dances were held. Two corn milling centers have been unearthed, each comprised of several rooms flanking the courtyards.

There are two Great Kivas in Pueblo Bonito, in the west and the east plazas. This has led scholars to think that the population was divided into two main groups, perhaps into the summer people and the winter people, who continue with similar ceremonies in contemporary pueblos. There are also 37 smaller kivas in the pueblo.

Chetro Ketl Chetro Ketl is a classic Anasazi pueblo with 500 rooms and 16 kivas. It is similar in design to more than twenty other structures that are located within a 20-mile radius of the Chaco Canyon. Parts of the pueblo date from about A.D. 1054 with the structure having been completed by 1100 or perhaps later.

Chetro Ketl was first uncovered in 1920 and 1921, revealing the southerly exposure of the building and the single-story room structure behind the plaza. Because the pillars and colonnades found here were unknown to the American Southwest when Chetro Ketl was built, it is thought that Mexican influences led the Anasazi to include these architectural forms. Other examples of native Mexican architecture are apparent in this and other buildings including the great kiva at Casa Rinconada, located across the valley.

There is also a great kiva here, more than 60 feet wide. The kiva was not a new thing at this age; the round pits entered from the top via ladders had been used for at least 500 years before the Anasazi arrived in Chaco Canyon. To the east of the pueblo (about 200 yards away), one of the main staircases is carved into the box canyon wall, leading to Pueblo Alto and the farm fields on the plateau. Several of the Anasazi roads converge on this mesa.

After 900 years, the long back wall of the pueblo still stands— 500 feet in length—constructed like the walls at Pueblo Bonito with a masonry core and drywall construction inside and outside of the core. The stone-laying styles of different masons are apparent as you walk outside of the wall.

Casa Rinconada   The largest of the great kivas is situated on the opposite side of the canyon. This kiva, similar in size to the great kiva at the Aztec Ruins, was not only a place for religious observance but served as a community center for the surrounding population who came here from the outlying villages. A short trail leads south to this structure from the canyon floor, passing several small villages. The path continues across the mesa where stand the remains of Tsin Kletsin, a great house, which provides a fine panoramic view of the canyon and the surrounding high points of land.

Kin Kletso   This is a smaller structure located near the west end of the canyon. It is supposed to have been built in two stages—the first from about 1125, the remainder built about 1130. Archeologists say that it probably had three stories on the north side and 100 rooms in all. Another trail leads from the park campground, encouraging evening strolls to the ruins.

Pueblo del Arroyo   Slightly east of Kin Kletso, also beside the main canyon loop road, and next to the wash, is Pueblo del Arroyo. Begun in 1075, it was completed with the construction of the plaza about 1110. This building had 280 rooms and at least 20 kivas.

Una Vida   This smaller ruin is reached by a short walk from the Visitor Center parking lot. The partially excavated structure is thought to have had as many as 150 rooms. One of the earlier structures to be built in the canyon, it was started in A.D. 930 and continued to be built and rebuilt until close to 1100. There are 5 kivas within the structure.

Pueblo Alto   Sitting on the mesa above Pueblo Bonito, Pueblo Alto is an important site at the junction of several major Anasazi roads, one of which leads northward to the pueblo now called the Salmon Ruin, near Farmington, and to the pueblo and great kiva at Aztec. Trails lead from Pueblo Alto to Casa Chiquita and Peñasco Blanco at the extreme western end of the central canyon, where the entrance road descends to the park.

Ancient Roads

An extensive Anasazi road system, which includes some roads as long as 60 miles, led out from the plateau above Chaco Canyon in several directions. While the shorter roads linking the towns of the canyon were 16 to 20 feet wide, bordered with stones and berms, the longer roads were all much wider—up to 30 feet—and remarkably straight.

A main road ran north through three small communities (each a day's walk apart) to the Salmon Ruins south of Farmington and on to the great kiva at what is now the Aztec National Monument.

Another ran due south through three smaller villages to a location near the present-day town of Crownpoint. Still another leads in a southeasterly direction, toward and almost reaching Grants. More than seventy-five communities (outliers) were connected by this network of roads that covered some 400 miles. The roads are thought to date from the eleventh and twelfth centuries. It is this road system that united the members of the Chaco culture into a single society unlike any other native culture in North America.

Trade was a major concern of the Anasazi, and there was a thriving exchange of goods among the various Chacoan communities and outside nations as far away as Mexico. Pottery was traded, as was the beadwork and turquoise jewelry made in the canyon and in the outliers. The turquoise used was not local but was imported from far-distant diggings. When the kivas of Chetro Ketl were uncovered, great quantities of jewelry were found tucked into niches in the kivas. Trading with the Toltecs is also suspected since the remains of tropical birds such as parrots were discovered in the Chaco ruins. Seashells (not an inland commodity) were also used to make Chacoan ornaments.

Long before Christopher Columbus "discovered" the Americas, these traders were crossing vast distances by foot, transporting the products of their craftspeople and engaging in commerce with other societies. It makes one wonder how future Native American societies might have developed had Europeans remained on their own side of the ocean and simply engaged in trade and benefitted from the exchange of goods and culture with the Native Americans.

Enjoying Chaco Canyon

A quick drive to the canyon, a short stay, and a fast return are counterproductive for explorers who wish to fully enjoy the remarkable attractions of the canyon. The nearest places to stay with conveniences are 60 to 80 miles away—in Bloomfield and Farmington to the north, at Crownpoint to the south, or farther south in Gallup. You will find a guide to these and other accommodations later in this chapter.

It is possible to spend the best part of a day in the canyon and come away with something—at least a feeling for the importance of these communities that once flourished and radiated their culture across the plateau. However, if you are able to camp or park yourself in an RV or trailer, I highly recommend that you stay 2 or 3 days. The park campground offers a place to stay, although there are no hookups. Water is available from a tap at the Visitor Center, and there are restrooms in the campground. Trailers longer than 30 feet cannot be accommodated.

The nearest stores for supplies are in Nageezi and at the Blanco Trading Post on New Mexico Route 44. Another store is located to the west on Route 371 near the village of Lake Valley (accessed via county roads). The best tactic is to purchase all the supplies you need in a major town before you drive to the canyon.

The museum in the Visitor Center features displays from which you can learn about the history of the Anasazi. The Visitor Center also posts schedules of ranger-led tours of the ruin sites, which I highly recommend, and has available a brochure on the four back-country trails that lead from the canyon floor to remote sites. Illustrative trail booklets, available at the larger sites, contain walking-tour information as well as historical background on the pueblos. You can also learn about the Anasazi by attending the park interpretation sessions held around a campfire during summer evening hours. The shop in the Visitor Center has a good supply of books on the Anasazi and natural history topics. Reading about the Anasazi in their own home setting is strangely rewarding.

Information Sources

Chaco Culture National Historic Park is administered by the National Park Service. You can get advance information on the park by writing to this address:

> Superintendent, Chaco Culture National Historic Park
> Star Route 4, P.O. Box 6500
> Bloomfield, NM 97413
> Or call (505) 988-6716 or 988-6727
> The park number is (505) 786-7014

The Southwest Parks and Monuments Association, which operates the sales center and bookstore in the visitor center, has an extensive list of books, maps, geological and trail guides, archeological surveys, and other materials that you may purchase before you visit the canyon. Write to the Association at the same address as the superintendent (above). The list of available materials includes many excellent reference books on Pueblo Indians and Native American culture in general, children's books, slides, and videotapes.

General information on the area surrounding the park is available from the following:

Farmington Convention and Visitors Bureau
203 W. Main Street, Suite 401
Farmington, NM 87401
(505) 326-7602

Other sources of information, particularly on the Native American communities south of Chaco Canyon, include:

Gallup Convention and Visitors Bureau
P.O. Drawer Q
Gallup, NM 87305
(800) 242-4282 (outside New Mexico)

New Mexico Office of Tourism
1100 St. Francis Drive
Santa Fe, NM 87503
(505) 827-0291 or (800) 545-2040

The **Four Corners Tourism Council**, which provides information on the four-state region, is reached at:

P.O. Box 958
Mancos, CO 81328

Nearby Attractions

BISTI BADLANDS

The ideal way to fully enjoy a visit to Chaco Canyon is to stay in the historic park for a few days to explore the sites in the canyon as well as nearby points of interest. These include the Bisti Badlands to the north, where weird-colored rock formations, petrified wood, and fossils are seen in a desolate but beautiful area on both sides of Gateway and Hunter's washes.

The Bisti Wilderness, a protected area, has no developed trails, but visitors are encouraged to walk across the badlands to experience what one would imagine a walk on the moon might be like.

The 3,946-acre preserve is pronounced "Bis-ta-hi" by the Navajo and "Biss-tie" by most others. The badlands were created during the Upper Cretaceous period some 70 million years ago, when the region was home to large reptiles and smaller primitive animals. Throughout the badlands, visitors can see the evolution of the region—a transition from coastal swamps and inland flood plains to the jumbled arid landscape of today. The main parking lot is off State Route 371, which runs south from Farmington. A large sign at the Gateway Wash announces the badlands, and a rough road leads past the old Bisti Trading Post.

You'll see coal formations in addition to shale and sandstone in unusual shapes. Camping is permitted throughout the badlands preserve, though campsites are of the primitive or non-existent variety. Water must be imported. The badlands are accessible from the east (the shortest route from Chaco Canyon) as well as from the west via New Mexico Route 371.

From Chaco Canyon, drive out to New Mexico Route 44 and turn north toward Bloomfield. Then take the road leading west at the El Huerfano Trading Post (County Road 7500). This dirt road leads beside the De-Na-Zin Wilderness and comes out at Highway 371. Turn north, and you will see the Bisti Wilderness Road after you drive a few minutes. This road leads east to the old Bisti Trading Post and to the rough parking lot that provides access to the badlands.

Cross-Country Route   Another way to reach the badlands is by the network of county back roads that crosses two washes and cuts through Navajo cattle-grazing ranches. These roads (more like trails) are suitable only for pickups and four-wheel-drive or other vehicles with high clearance. RVs and trailers are not advised to use this route.

Travel north along New Mexico Route 57 from Chaco Canyon, then turn left onto County Road 7870. Drive 7 miles west to the junction with County Road 7650. Take this road across the high desert for another 7 miles to New Mexico Highway 371. Turn north, and the Bisti Badlands road is off to the right. There is a cattle gate which must be opened and closed as you drive along the county roads. Drivers are warned to take this route only in dry weather. Fording the washes is impossible during flash flooding.

Aztec National Monument

The town of Aztec is located a few miles north of Bloomfield and Farmington on state routes 44 and 550. Its notable attraction is the Anasazi ruin called the Aztec National Monument. Here is the best-preserved and reconstructed great kiva of them all, set beside the ruin of a small Anasazi pueblo. Although there is no evidence that Aztecs were ever associated with the ruins or even the region, the town and the ruins got their name when settlers mistakenly believed that only the super-intelligent Aztecs could have created the pueblo.

The ruins are set on the Animas River, a source of irrigation and drinking water for the Anasazi. The inhabitants were basically farmers, like the people of Chaco Canyon, growing corn and other food crops. Built around A.D. 1100, the community was deserted by 1300 after the inhabitants successfully farmed here for 200 years. Historians believe drought and the overuse of natural resources including wood is the reason the pueblo was abandoned.

The multistoried pueblo contained 500 rooms, but not all the rooms were in use at the same time. As in the Chaco Canyon communities, the Anasazi builders kept adding to the pueblo, then used older rooms as trash depositories, which they eventually sealed off.

The pueblo was occupied at two separate times. The first people who built the original pueblo were from Chaco Canyon, 50 miles away. Aztec was one of the "outliers" that traded with the central communities in the canyon. The first occupation of the Aztec pueblo lasted for 90 years from about A.D. 1110. Then a second group of pueblo people occupied the town. They were not Chacoans but had ties to Mesa Verde, 40 miles to the northwest in southern Colorado. These people were here for a shorter period, from about 1225 to 1300.

There are 10 kivas apparent from an aerial view of the structure. The Hubbard Site, a smaller kiva named for an early settler, is famous because of its unusual tri-walled construction. The kiva has three concentric circular walls. The outer wall is 64 feet in diameter. The two outer compartments contained a series of rooms connected by hatchways. The central space was a kiva. Another tri-walled structure, which is in an advanced state of ruin, is located north of the main building.

The Great Kiva in the Aztec National Monument is the only such structure that has been fully restored. The great kivas were public buildings, unlike the more private family or small-group kivas found next to the living rooms. This type of kiva was for the use of the entire surrounding population, as well as the occupants of the pueblo. Forty-eight feet in diameter, it has

15 rooms at the surface and a bench circling the ceremonial chamber. Four huge pillars hold up the ceiling. The Great Kiva alone is worth the trek to Aztec.

SALMON RUINS AND ZUNI PUEBLO

After visiting Chaco Canyon, those who wish to pore more extensively over Anasazi history can take advantage of several other ruins in the immediate area.

One of the outlying villages of the Chaco culture is the Salmon Ruins, a medium-sized pueblo found 2 miles west of Bloomfield or east of Farmington on Highway 64. Heritage Park is set on the homestead of the Salmon family, who lived here around 1900. On display in the park is a Navajo hogan, tipis, wickiups, a pithouse, and unearthed artifacts from the Anasazi period. The park is open daily from 9 A.M. to 5 P.M. and is closed on major holidays.

The more recently developed Zuni Pueblo is located near the Salmon Ruins. The Zuni are renowned for their silver and turquoise jewelry.

DE-NA-ZIN WILDERNESS

Near the Bisti Badlands and Chaco Culture National Historic Park, this Bureau of Land Management (BLM) wilderness area covers nearly 24,000 acres and is reached by taking New Mexico Route 44 south from Bloomfield and then going west on County Road 15. This is high desert country, with outcroppings of rock in sculptured shapes, similar to the formations in the Bisti Badlands. Backcountry camping is permitted.

JACKSON LAKE STATE WATERFOWL AREA

This marsh and lake, located five miles northwest of Farmington along the La Plata River, covers 840 acres. An excellent birding site, the waterfowl reserve includes picnic areas and fishing access and is also open to hunters in season. To get there, take New Mexico Route 170 north from the junction with U.S. Highway 64 at the southwestern end of Farmington.

NAVAJO LAKE STATE PARK

New Mexico's largest reservoir extends north into Colorado, backing up the waters of the San Juan River. Lying just north of

New Mexico Route 64—25 miles east of Bloomfield—it offers camping, fishing, boating, swimming, birdwatching, and other activities. It is not too far away from Chaco Canyon (only an hour's drive) to serve as a point of departure for all of the destinations in this region—including a day-trip to Canyon de Chelly.

Comprised of three recreation areas, the park has a visitor center at the Pine River site on the north shore of the lake. This is the most developed area, with camping facilities and interpretive exhibits. Comforts include 40 campsites with electricity, showers, picnic areas, a marina, boat ramp, docking facilities, and a playground.

Across the lake, farther from Highway 64, is the Sims Mesa Site, accessed via Route 527. This section of the park has camping with 14 electrical hookups, a dump station, picnic area, a boat ramp, dock, marina, and a visitor center.

The San Juan River Site, near the dam, offers prime fishing access—a shrine for rainbow trout anglers with camping that includes wheelchair-access facilities. Other fish available here include kokanee, brown, largemouth and smallmouth bass, channel catfish, crappie, bluegill, and northern pike. There is also a day-use park with picnic areas at the San Juan River site. The San Juan River Easement, which lies below the dam, offers some of the best trout fishing in the state.

Staying at one of the Navajo Lake sites may be the answer for families with children who would prefer to spend more time next to and in the water than touring Chaco Canyon archeological ruins day after day.

The 6,100-foot elevation provides cool nights for good sleeping and warm, sunny days during the spring, summer, and fall months. Winter recreation is available at all three sites.

For families with boats, the reservoir can provide days of boat-camping. It has numerous bays and inlets that offer access to backcountry campsites and fine scenery.

ANGEL PEAK RECREATION AREA

Nineteen miles southeast of Bloomfield, via New Mexico Route 44, this BLM recreation area is set in prime wilderness with hiking trails and 16 campsites. The peak has an elevation of 6,588 feet. The entrance road leads east from Highway 44 for 6 miles, taking visitors to a high point with excellent views of the peak.

Trails begin at the parking lot and lead across the mountain and up to the peak.

SHIPROCK

This huge volcanic monolith rises 1,709 feet from the plateau, 30 miles west of Farmington. On a clear day, you can see the towering rock of this major landmark on the Navajo Reservation from a distance of 100 miles.

CANYON DE CHELLY NATIONAL MONUMENT

Bird-watching and other wildlife-viewing are incidental to the main attraction in this remarkable home of the Anasazi: tracing historical patterns of more than 2,000 years—from the "ancient ones" to the modern Navajo, who now inhabit and farm this fertile canyon in the northeastern corner of the state. It is one of the most beautifully serene places in the Southwest.

The floor of Canyon de Chelly (pronounced *shay*) lies 1,000 feet below its rim. Modern Navajo live here and farm the valley, using water from the Rio de Chelly, which flows west from the Chuska Mountains. The canyon and its sister gorge, Canyon del Muerto, sheltered humans long before the Anasazi arrived about A.D. 1050. First were the Basketmakers who lived here between A.D. 300 and 420. Later these early inhabitants developed a primitive form of agriculture and hunted game. After living on the plateau, the Anasazi built high cliff dwellings perched on ledges far above the river level. They decorated the rock with petroglyphs and pictographs, art forms carried on by the Navajo.

The available water, rock shelters, and flat canyon bottom fostered civilization here through the Pueblo period when, after A.D. 700, Native Americans lived in mud-masonry houses and became skilled farmers—a tradition the Navajo continue today.

Canyon de Chelly National Monument is both a park and Navajo private property. Situated near the town of Chinle, the park contains all of the impressive cliff dwellings, built high above the canyon bottoms. Administered by the National Parks Service, the monument is an essential part of anyone's tour of Anasazi and Navajo homelands. A 22-mile drive along the rim offers frequent vista points from which to view the cliff dwellings and farms that appear far below as miniatures on the canyon floor.

A 2.5-mile hike takes visitors down to the canyon, across the river to the impressive White House Ruins and back again. Parks Service rangers or authorized Navajo guides lead hikes and four-wheel-drive tours to other impressive ruins and archeological sites as well. Guided horse trips take riders through the canyons past Navajo corrals and hogans, to the remains of other prehistoric towns.

Human history is the key to Canyon de Chelly. Throughout this beautiful and haunting sandstone landscape are frequent signs of the changing civilizations—including the development by the Pueblo Culture of a highly structured religious life.

Canyon de Chelly is 65 miles south of U.S. Highway 160 and 95 miles northwest of Gallup. A 195-mile drive from Chaco Canyon (80 miles in a direct line), Canyon de Chelly is different from Chaco Canyon for this reason: Today's Navajo in the valley of the Rio de Chelly carry on the agricultural traditions of the "Ancient Ones." They irrigate their fields by waters that flow down to this deep canyon from the slopes of the Chuska Mountains, which lie to the east along the Arizona/New Mexico border.

The Basketmakers began building pithouses in this canyon and its sister gorge, Canyon del Muerto, between A.D. 300 and 420. After 550, they began to make pottery and hunted using bow and arrow.

The Anasazi pueblo people then occupied the area and their communities spread along both canyons. As the society developed, they moved into masonry houses—built above the ground—and increased their farming activity.

Anasazi religious life also developed with elaborate and structured ceremonies and rituals, much like that in Chaco Canyon. In fact, it is thought that there was communication and trade between the two major centers. They first occupied Basketmaker villages, including what are now called Antelope House, Standing Cow Ruins, Sliding Rock Ruins, and Mummy Cave. They later developed larger, more elaborate structures including White House, Battle Cove, Ledge, and the large village Tse Yaa Tsoh, which was built into a huge covered ledge on the site of Canyon del Muerto. Following the same pattern as Chaco Canyon, the Anasazi built pueblos on the plateau above the canyons. An artistic people, they not only made fine pottery but began the tradition of creating pictographs and petroglyphs, art forms the later Navajo occupants continued.

Also with amazing similarity to Chaco Canyon, by A.D. 1200 the population was in decline, and by 1300 the canyons were deserted. Some of the Anasazi migrated to the Hopi communities on the mesas of Northern Arizona. After short seasonal occupations by the Hopi during the fourteenth century, the Navajo migrated to the area from the Great Plains and began farming the canyons in the 1700s. They used the canyon as a fortress from which to defend their territory from Mexicans and white settlers. Not all the battles ended successfully for the Navajo. In 1864, Colonel Kit Carson led a cavalry unit into Canyon de Chelly and burned the Navajo crops and homes. The army succeeded in moving some eight thousand Navajo to Fort Sumner in New Mexico, an event known as The Long Walk. The Navajo have now returned, and from May to November each year, they farm and tend sheep in the two canyons.

The White House Trail has its entrance point 6 miles from park headquarters, at the White House Overlook. This 2.5-mile round-trip leads to the White House ruins, which housed a hundred Anasazi in the 1100s and 1200s. The hike involves descending 500 feet into the canyon, then wading across the river to the ruin and back with the 500-foot ascent to the overlook. The complete round-trip takes about 2 hours. This is the only walk into the canyon that park visitors may take on their own.

You can drive outside the borders of the national monument to a viewpoint that overlooks Three Turkey Ruins. To get to the viewpoint, drive from the park gate to the Spider Rock Overlook.

The Park Service conducts tours to various points of interest in the canyons and arranges tours led by Navajo guides—via bus, four-wheel-drive vehicle, or horseback. Thunderbird Tours operates the open bus that takes visitors to several attractions from Thunderbird Lodge: cliff houses, Navajo farms, and Native American rock art panels. For tour information and reservations, write or call:

Canyon de Chelly Thunderbird Tours
P.O. Box 548
Chinle, AZ 86503
(602) 674-5841 or 674-5842

Jicarilla Apache Reservation

Extending south from the Colorado border for 64 miles, the Jicarilla Reservation in New Mexico offers a look at modern Apache customs and some fine recreational opportunities.

Jicarilla, the name of the tribe, means "wicker basket," the craft for which the tribe is best known. At the Apache Museum and Arts and Crafts Center in Dulce, basketmaking and other forms of Jicarilla art, such as intricate beadwork, are on display and for sale.

This is rugged mountain country, crossed twice by the Continental Divide. Fishing and hunting areas are open to the public by permit. There is fishing at eight lakes and on the Navajo River. Hunting licenses for elk, turkey, and mule deer are available from September through December. Waterfowl hunting is permitted from October through January. For bird-watchers, the other months (February through August) can be very rewarding, as migratory and resident birds rest by the lakes and on the marshes. During winter months, the tribe operates a cross-country ski program with trails and equipment rentals.

The main access road from the south is New Mexico Route 537, which runs from New Mexico Route 44 southeast of Bloomfield and northwest of Albuquerque. Dulce, the tribal headquarters, is located on Highway 64 at the northern end of the reservation, 82 miles east of Bloomfield.

Hopi Reservation

Surrounded by the much larger Navajo reservation, the Hopi Reservation contains three mesas, and the people occupy several towns set on these high mesas of northeastern Arizona. The Hopi have lived here for centuries, and their heritage dates back many thousands of years; they have absorbed the influences of the Anasazi and other native peoples.

To reach these communities from Canyon de Chelly, drive south from Chinle on U.S. Highway 191, then drive west on Arizona Route 264 to Second Mesa. This is the site of the Hopi Cultural Center and the hub of the cluster of Hopi villages. The Cultural Center displays and sells the artwork and crafts of the Hopi, including jewelry, pottery, baskets, and kachina dolls. The Center includes a museum of Hopi history and culture.

The westernmost village in the reservation is Moenkopi, about 50 miles west of Second Mesa.

The Hopi are a people dedicated to their art and culture. While a few of the religious traditions may be observed by visitors on special occasions, many aspects of Hopi life are not open to the public. The tribe does not permit photography, sketching, or sound recording, and does not allow liquor in the reservation.

HUBBELL TRADING POST

This national historic site preserves the original Navajo trading post established here in 1878 by trader John Hubbell. Until his death in 1930, Hubbell nurtured Native American craft-making including weaving and silversmithing at this oldest, continuously operated trading post on the Navajo Reservation. These crafts are demonstrated in the visitor center.

The trading post is still an active store, open for self-guided tours as well as interpretive tours led by rangers. The Hubbell home is now a museum displaying the extensive collection of Native American crafts and Western art that John Hubbell assembled over the years.

The trading post is 58 miles northwest of Gallup, via U.S. Highway 666 and New Mexico Route 264 (which becomes Arizona Route 264 at the border). From the north, take U.S. Highway 666 from Shiprock and drive south to New Mexico Route 264 (86 miles).

ZUÑI PUEBLO

This old native pueblo is 64 miles south of Gallup off New Mexico Route 53. The Zuñi reservation is a magnet for visitors who go there not only to view the native village, but especially to see and buy the wonderful stonework of the Zuñi, including turquoise, black jet, and coral jewelry, in addition to materials formed from lapis and sugalite. Jewelry and other crafts are on view and for sale at the tribe's Zuñi Arts and Craft Center.

The Zuñi are also renowned dancers. The pueblo offers performances of its Shalako ceremony, during which native dancers wear large masks that represent many of the traditional Zuñi gods. This all-night ceremony takes place in November or early December. As on the Hopi Reservation, no photographs, sketches, or recordings are permitted. On days when ceremonies are not taking place, photographs are permitted by paying a fee to the tribe.

There is a campground nearby, at Black Rock. Visitors are permitted to fish and hunt by license, and information may be obtained from the Zuñi Tribal Fish and Wildlife Department at (602) 782-5851. Native guides are available. For general information on pueblo events, call (602) 782-4481.

NORTHERN PUEBLOS

Eight contemporary pueblos—Nambe, Picuris, Pojoaque, San Ildefonso, San Juan, Santa Clara, Tesuque, and the famous pueblo at Taos—are located mainly in the Rio Grande basin, all north of Santa Fe. They can be accessed by driving from the city on U.S. Route 84/285 and continuing northward on State Route 68.

The pueblo at Taos is featured in the Enchanted Circle and Taos chapter, starting on page 231.

While we have dealt mainly with the Anasazi tradition so far, visiting the contemporary pueblos offers insight into how the pueblo culture developed, including the continuing ritual observances evident in the Anasazi age.

Feast days and other cultural events are celebrated throughout the year at the pueblos. Unfortunately, most of these pueblos lack vitality. Nambe and Picuris pueblos are shadows of what they were centuries ago. At Nambe, on the slopes of the Sangre de Cristo Mountains, waterfalls and mountain views provide visual excitement. While there were once more than two hundred precolonial buildings in the pueblo, only twenty remain today.

Picuris Pueblo, farther north on the "High Road to Taos," was a town of three thousand people who lived in several six-story apartment houses. Few of the houses remain, and most of the inhabitants live in tract houses at the edge of the village.

Pojoaque Pueblo, 16 miles north of Santa Fe, has no village center, but the state tourist center operated by the pueblo features a large selection of northern Indian artwork including crafts from all nineteen pueblos in New Mexico. The Northern Pueblos Arts Council is located in the Poeh Center.

The residents of San Ildefonso Pueblo, some of whom came to the pueblo from Mesa Verde and Frijoles Canyon, claim a direct lineage from the Anasazi. The village has become well known for its potters and artists. The pueblo is located on New Mexico Route 502, 21 miles northeast of Santa Fe.

A small and large kiva are located within San Juan Pueblo, northwest of Espanola on U.S. Highway 70. The San Juan tribal lakes offer fishing and picnicking. There is a Native American restaurant and the O'ke Oweenge Cooperative operates a store selling turquoise and silver jewelry, pottery, embroidery, traditional clothing, and moccasins.

Santa Clara Pueblo people are descendants of the ancient Puye Cliff Dwellers. The pueblo is a center for pottery, painting, and sculpture, all of which are available from the artists in their homes. The Puye Cliff Dwellings provide the main attraction. The pueblo is located on the west bank of the Rio Grande, 1.3 miles from Espanola on New Mexico Route 30.

Tesuque, just 9 miles north of Santa Fe, features a campground, bingo hall, and two pottery shops. Pottery, sculpture, and paintings are available from the resident artists. The tribal administration office provides information on how to obtain these Indian artworks.

While it is evident that the Pueblo people of northern New Mexico have a long way to go to fully restore their culture and their communities, they have joined together to pursue these goals as a unified group. This can only lead to an eventual restoration of their cultural values and activity, which have been lost over the centuries of European occupation and influence.

CHACO WILDLIFE

Chaco Canyon could in no way be called verdant. It lies in the northern New Mexico desert, close to a major badlands region. Only Chaco Wash and several other intermittent washes make this land suitable as a living place for plants and animals.

Although more than 150 bird species have been spotted in the park, some have been identified only once or twice. Canadian geese and Sandhill cranes have been seen here, but very infrequently. The same plants that grew naturally in the canyon, before the arrival of the Anasazi, are evident today. These include a variety of edible wild plants, which the Anasazi used for dyes, medicines, and smoking. Desert vegetation is also found on the mesas above the canyon.

BIRDS

Cassin's Kingbird
Tyrannus vociferans
Its sound is often vociferous and, as a desert dweller, it prefers higher altitudes, such as the high desert of the Chaco Canyon area. This member of the flycatcher family looks like the more common Western Kingbird but is darker, with an olive-gray back, and sometimes a light tip on its tail.

Its sound is sometimes light (a low *chi queer* or *ki-dear*) and sometimes very excited (*ki-ki-ki-dear, ki-dear*).

Scaled Quail
Calipepla squamata
This small quail is suited to living in an arid landscape, such as the New Mexico desert. It survives for lengthy periods without water, although it must visit a water supply regularly. Chaco Wash is available for part of the year. The range of the scaled quail is north to Southeast Arizona, south to the Chihauhuan desert of Mexico, and Utah, New Mexico, southern Colorado, and Texas.

It has a bushy white crest on its head, and is a pale gray with a bluish tinge, with scaly markings on its breast and back feathers. Male and female look alike. You'll usually see it running, for it rarely flies. The call is nasal, usually interpreted as *pay-cos, pay-cos*—similar to the call of a guinea hen.

Rock Wren
Salpinctes obsoletus
A dweller of canyons and rocky slopes, this small wren is right

at home on the rocky ledges of Chaco Canyon. It is gray with a streaked breast, a light belly, rust-colored rump, and a light eye-stripe. It has a widespread range, from British Columbia to Central America. Look for a trail of little rock chips that leads to its nest. Why the wren places these markers is not known. Its warning call is a loud *ki-deeeee*. Its song is a series of three to five trills, a loud chant.

Canyon Towhee
Pipilo fuscus
One of two types formerly called the Brown Towhee (the other is the California Towhee), this pale, brownish-gray bird lives in low scrub and is also a resident of Arizona, Colorado, west Texas, and Mexico.

It has a rufous (reddish/brown) crown and a black spot on the breast. It is rarely spotted in the air, preferring to move quietly in the scrub plants and chaparral to look for food. Its song is varied, but sometimes you will hear a *chip-chip-chip-chip-chip* on the same note. Its call is a sharper *chink* and *tseeee*.

Say's Phoebe
Sayornis saya
Looking much like a diminutive robin, this flycatcher has a grayish brown, dusky head, neck,

and back with slightly darker wings and a pale, yellow to rust-colored belly. Its voice is a whistled *pweer, pee-ur*, or *pee-ee*.

Its range is widespread, throughout the West from Alaska to central Mexico, except west of the Sierra and Cascade ranges. It lives on the plains, in sparse, scrubby country, and often near buildings. It is often seen on western ranches, living near the barn or ranch house.

It also likes rocky ledges of canyons, which give it a sense of security. It is primarily an insect-eater, as are the other flycatchers, but will also eat other foods such as berries when insects are not available. However, lack of insects is rarely a problem in Chaco Canyon.

Violet-green Swallow
Tachycineta thalassina
This eye-catching swallow flashes its distinctive white patches, which almost meet, over the base of the tail. The tail has a purple gloss with a greenish back and greenish purple wings, plus a purple marking on the upper neck. The white of the face and breast almost encircles the eyes.

The breeding range is very widespread, from Alaska and western Canada to Mexico and Central America. Its habitat includes canyons, cliffs, holes in tree trunks, and mountain forests.

Its voice is a thin, rapid twittering sound: *chit-chit-chit wheet, wheet.*

Western Meadowlark
Sturnella neglects
Almost indistinguishable from the Eastern Meadowlark, this wonderfully musical songbird has a bright yellow breast, which is crossed by a black V-shaped "dickie." When flying, the Western Meadowlark exhibits flashes of white on each side of the tail, and has several fast wing beats, followed by gliding for a short time. Its range is from southwest Canada, throughout the western U.S. to central Mexico. It lives in grasslands, meadows, farm pastures, and prairies.

The Western Meadowlark's song is remarkable and very musical. It offers seven to ten notes, quite flute-like, double-noted and with a gurgle, unlike the Eastern Meadowlark, which sings with two loud whistles and also has a guttural, chattering sound.

OTHER ANIMALS

Badger
Taxidea taxus
Found in all the southwestern states, the badger may be seen in forest and canyon areas, but is more likely to live in the desert valleys of the lower Sonoran zone. It prefers to dig deep burrows or shallow holes in alluvial soil. While it could easily be confused for a large rodent, it is a member of the weasel family. Rodents are its main source of food, but it also preys on birds, as well as reptiles and insects.

The badger's front legs are very short, ending in thick claws up to 1.5 inches long. The hind claws are shorter. The badger weighs between 15 and 30 pounds, and has a shaggy coat of yellowish-gray body hair, with black hair on the feet and face. It has a white stripe along its cheeks and another white stripe that begins on the nose and runs between the ears, fading out on the shoulders. The male is larger than the female.

Its tracks are easy to spot. The foreprint is 2 inches wide, and longer than 2 inches when the claw marks are showing, with five toes turning in. The hind print is much smaller, about 2 inches long. Its gait is varied, with the hindfoot print behind or before the forefoot print.

The badger serves as a control over the proliferation of other species in its area by keeping populations of prairie dogs, ground squirrels, and gophers in check.

It is generally nocturnal when humans are in the area, but is often active during the daytime when it feels secure.

Desert Cottontail
Sylvilagus audubonii
The cottontail has more natural enemies in the Southwest than almost any other animal. Yet it manages to survive and even thrive in this harsh and unfriendly environment. It is prey to snakes, large birds, the coyote, badger, and almost any other hungry animal of any size. The desert cottontail is one of several subspecies of the cottontail rabbit, found in the western states.

Its back and sides are buff-colored, with darker hair on the legs and shoulders. Its ears are long for this size of animal, reaching from 2 to 3 inches. It has short hind legs (3 to 4 inches) and wide eyes. The tail is a "powder puff," about one inch long, dark gray above and white below. The overall length of the cottontail is about 15 inches.

Its style of movement gives it away. Although it can run at a fast pace, it zigzags as it runs from danger, looking for a hole or some brush in which to hide. It can climb objects and sometimes climbs the limbs of sloping trees.

These desert-dwellers usually make their nests below ground, often in a burrow that was the former home of a badger or large rodent. Its foods are grasses, cactus, and mesquite.

The desert cottontail is found in all the southwestern states, in the Upper and Lower Sonoran zones. You'll find cottontails wherever there is sufficient cover for it to hide and survive.

This rabbit is so successful at avoiding predators that its population is generally controlled through disease, rather than by its natural enemies.

White-tailed Antelope Squirrel
Ammospermophilus leucurus
Like its close cousin, Harris' antelope squirrel, the white-tailed antelope squirrel is a pale animal with buff coloring on its underparts during the summer months, and gray in winter. It has one narrow white stripe on each side. The underside of the tail is very white with a narrow black border formed of small black-tipped hairs.

This animal's habitat ranges from southwestern Idaho and southeastern Oregon into Nevada and Utah, Western Colorado (where it hibernates), the deserts of southern California, northern Arizona, and a narrow sliver of northeastern New Mexico, running south from southern Colorado. It lives in deserts and foothills, where the earth is a hard gravel. It is seen at Chaco Canyon.

When this white-tailed squirrel runs (and it runs very fast), its tail is curved over its back, exposing the white hair underneath. It can be seen foraging for food on the ground and eating cactus and yucca, since it is fond of seeds and fruit. Sometimes this squirrel lives in rock crevices, but it usually takes over burrows made by other animals.

Two other antelope squirrels inhabit portions of the Southwest. Harris' antelope squirrel is found in southern and western Arizona and the southwestern corner of New Mexico (in the Lordsburg area). The Texas antelope squirrel, which often lives under boulders, is found in south-central New Mexico, in the Big Bend area of Texas, and in Mexico.

Northern Grasshopper Mouse

Onychomys leucogaster
This mouse does not look like a grasshopper, nor does it jump like one. The grasshopper is its main food, and it eats other insects along with scorpions, smaller mice, and some (but not many) plants. It prefers to eat the flesh of warm-blooded animals but is too small to kill its prey. So it waits for another animal to do the killing, then helps itself to the remains.

The mouse is found over a wide area of western North America, from southern Manitoba and Saskatchewan to the Texas panhandle, and into Arizona and the desert parts of Utah, Nevada, and Oregon. It inhabits prairies, desert areas, and low valleys, taking over nests and burrows made by other animals.

Its relative, the southern grasshopper mouse (*O. torridus*), is found in the Lower Sonoran zone.

A medium-sized mouse, the northern grasshopper mouse has a short tail and grows to a total length of 6 inches. Its ears are small. The feet are round rather than long like the feet of most mice. This makes its tracks rather easy to spot in wet soil or mud. The hindfoot print is about .75 inches long with five splayed toes. The forefoot print is .5 inches long with four spread-out toes. The hindprints are ahead of the foreprints.

This animal is often called the "calling mouse" because of its call, a long high note. It does not squeak like other mice, and its smooth, flat note, which can be heard over a distance, is thought to be a territorial signal to other mice.

Striped Whipsnake
Masticophis taeniatus
Fast-moving, long and thin, the desert striped whipsnake hunts with its head held high. It moves swiftly, and when startled, it quickly vanishes to hide in brush or in rocky piles. It hunts in the daytime for lizards, rodents, and other small mammals.

The desert striped whipsnake is a subspecies of a group of five striped whipsnakes, two of which live in the southwestern deserts. It is blackish or dark brown, with white side stripes divided by a thin black line. Scales are smooth, with its large head scales edged in white.

Its relative, the Central Texas striped whipsnake (*M. T. girardi*) is black with lengthwise white patches on the sides. It is found only in isolated populations in north-central Texas.

All striped whipsnakes nest in May, usually in old rodent burrows. (Isn't it fascinating how many desert animals recycle abandoned burrows?) The female lays from three to twelve eggs in June and July; the young, which are 14 to 17 inches long, arrive in August.

This snake's range is widespread, extending throughout the desert West from southern Washington throughout the Great Basin and into west and central Texas. It lives in a variety of ecosystems, from brushy flatland to pinyon-juniper woodland and pine-oak woodland vegetative types to open grassland.

Its distant cousin the Sonoran whipsnake (*M. flagellum*), is found only in central and southeastern Arizona and in western Mexico.

Pallid Bat
Antrozous pallidas
While most species of bats find the Four Corners area inhospitable, at least two species live in and around Chaco Canyon.

The pallid bat, unlike most other bats, is light-colored. It is large and creamy to beige-colored above, white or off-white below. It has big ears that are separated at the base. The wings and the membrane that joins the hind legs are smooth and free of hair.

This is one bat that doesn't need a cool cave in which to hang out. It is a desert dweller, roosting in buildings, hollow trees, and in just about any shelter it can find. It comes out late at night.

A very slow flyer, it rarely flies to catch its food, feeding mostly on the ground. It grows to a length of about 5 inches.

California Myotis
Myotis californicus
Another desert bat, this one has dull brown fur, long brown ears, and a long tragus (earlobe, projecting upward).

Like the pallid bat, this myotis lives in mesquite and chaparral regions, in areas where there are rocky outcroppings. The California Myotis prefers to live in rocky canyons. Its nighttime roosts are usually in buildings. During the day it roosts under bridges, under bark, in hollow trees, and in buildings.

These bats are fascinating to watch while on the fly. They can quickly change direction and frequently do so. This makes them seem erratic in their flight.

PLANTS

Dock
Rumex hymenosepalus
The dock plant is often found in sandy desert washes of the Colorado Plateau. Considered an extension of the Great Basin biotic zone, the Four Corners area is quite unlike the remainder of New Mexico. Dock is a herbaceous perennial with a single stem. Its leaves are ruffled (like Swiss chard), large, and clustered around the base of the stalk. They flower early in the spring, producing tiny rust-colored fruits that appear from March to May. It was a medicinal plant for the Anasazi and later Native Americans, who used the root and dried leaves on infections.

Globemallow
Sphaeraicea angustifolia
Bearing a beautiful pink bloom from February to May, relatives of this plant are called apricot-mallow, desert mallow, and sore-eye poppy. The Mexicans called it mal-de-ojos. Folklore says that the hairs of the plant irritate the eyes. In southern California, this same plant is called *plantas muy malas*.

Various members of the mallow family range in height from 1 to 5 feet. Globemallow is one of the smaller varieties. The desert mallow (*S. ambigua*), which is found in the lower California and Arizona deserts, grows larger, in big clumps with many stems. Its flowers are a bright orange-red.

Of the mallows, *S. angustifolia* is the only one normally found in New Mexico and Texas.

Black Greasewood
Sarcobatus vermiculatus
Greasewood is often used synonymously with creosote bush, but the black greasewood is quite a different plant. It is a member of the Goosefoot family

and sometimes called checo or chicobush.

Its range is west to California, south to Mexico, and north to Canada, although it usually grows on alkaline ground in elevations from 2,000 feet to 8,000 feet.

This is a coarse, unkempt-looking shrub with many branches, growing from 2 to 8 feet tall. It is easily identified by its fleshy and quite narrow leaves. It has whitish-gray or tan bark.

The male flowers are spikes at the ends of the branches. The female flowers are single, round upside-down bells, which are in the leaf axis. The seeds develop here, surrounded by a green wing for propagation.

The light green leaves were eaten by Native Americans, who enjoyed their salty taste. They also used seeds as food. Animals such as pronghorn and prairie dogs also use parts of the shrub as food. Jackrabbits like greasewood a lot, using it as a major food source.

This shrub grew in Chaco Canyon and the Four Corners region long before the arrival of the Anasazi, and survived their occupation. It does not seem to have been used for construction, and perhaps its use as food (probably as a snack) saved it from being cut down for firewood or other purposes.

One-seed Juniper
Juniperus monosperma

This member of the cypress family is the most common juniper in northern Arizona and New Mexico. It is found from the Grand Canyon to Santa Fe, mixed with pinyon pine. The Spanish name for the berry of this plant is nebrina. The shrub is also called cherry-stone and redberry-juniper.

Unlike the fruit of the common juniper, which is a whitish-blue, its soft berries are a copper color, and are not usually eaten, although Native Americans occasionally ate them. The berry usually has one seed, although two seeds are sometimes found. The bark is scaled and shreds easily and the stems grow to a height of about 20 feet. There are several stems to each bush.

The Navajo have used parts of the juniper to build their homes (supports for hogans), as decoration (wristlets, necklaces), and for making a green dye (from the berries). Its dry bark was (and still is) useful for starting fires. The strong stems were used for making fenceposts.

Other members of the same family are the Utah Juniper (*J. osteosperma*) and the alligator juniper, both of which grow in New Mexico. The alligator juniper (*J. dep-*

peana) has bark quite different from other members of the species. It is checkered with almost square sections divided by thin, indented separations.

The one-seed juniper grows west to Nevada, north to Wyoming, east to Oklahoma, and south to Mexico, at elevations between 3,400 feet and 8,000 feet.

Indian Rice Grass
Oryzopsis hymenoides
Indian rice grass is often found in pinyon-juniper woodlands, and on open sandy plains and hills. It is usually found at elevations of 3,500 feet to 6,000 feet, growing in the high desert areas of the Southwest. It gets its name because it appeared to be a type of rice. The genus is comprised of oryza (rice), and opsis (appearance).

This perennial grass grows in large, dense clumps, to a height of between 12 and 28 inches. Its clustered inflorescence shows tiny grains set at the ends of tiny branches. When fully grown, in the summer, the plant is quite beautiful, with black seeds enclosed in transparent bracts. You'll see the dried grass being used in pricey flower arrangements in big-city shops. This is a valuable plant, used for fodder on Nevada and

New Mexico rangelands. The grain was ground into flour by American Indians.

New Mexico Feathergrass
Stipa neomexicana
Found in elevations of 3,500 to 6,000 feet, this plant is found from Colorado to northern Mexico. It grows to a height of 4 feet. The blades are thin and 8 to 12 inches long. The brown seed bracts have noticeable long reddish hairs (awn) at the end of the lemma (lower bract). These striking awns are about 4 inches long. Like ricegrass, this feathergrass is also used in urban ornamental plantings.

Narrowleaf Yucca
Yucca angustissima
The symbiotic relationship between yucca plants and a little moth is the key to reproduction for these members of the lily family. The pronuba or yucca moth flies through the night to pollinate the yucca flowers; in return the yucca gives the larvae of the moth its seeds for food.

The type of narrowleaf yucca found on the mesas above Chaco Canyon has dry, erect seed pods and very narrow leaves. It is identified most easily by noting the fibers protruding from the sides of the leaves. Almost stemless, it sometimes has a short stem that lies on the ground. The flower stalk is tall for the size of the plant, growing to 4.5 feet, although most of the plants do not produce stalks that high.

Its range is more widespread than most narrowleaf yuccas, growing in Arizona, Colorado, Utah, and Nevada, as well as in New Mexico. It is found in high desert areas, from 2,700 feet to 7,500 feet.

The *angustissima* is closely related to other narrowleaf yuccas, including Y. *whipplei*, which is found in the California desert, and Y. *elata*, which grows in the deserts of Arizona and Texas.

The whipple yucca is a much smaller plant than the yucca elata. It produces a stout flower stalk with a wide plume of small flowers. Sometimes called "Our Lord's Candle," the whipple catches the light of the moon and seems to glow in the dark.

Big Sagebrush
Artemesia tridentata
One of the best known shrubs of the Southwest, the big sagebrush is the state flower of Nevada, so profuse is the plant throughout that state. Growing to between 2 and 7 feet tall, the "common" or "basin" sagebrush

has a trunk that can grow to a diameter of 3 inches and, when sufficient water is available, will grow to tree size. It grows to a height of about 6 feet but has been seen to grow to 15 or 16 feet. It is found as far north as the small desert in south-central British Columbia, as well as in Oregon and as far south as Baja California.

This variety of sagebrush (not to be confused with sage– the *salvia* family) is also called black "sage," blue "sage," "wormwood," and (in Spanish) *chamiso hediondo* (stinking chamiso) and *estafiata*.

It's easy to identify. The leaves are usually three-parted (sometimes as many as nine), wedge-shaped, hairy, and silvery-green in color. The stems turn a dull gray at maturity. It has many branches and the bark is shredded. Its flowers are a yellowish to a greenish-gray.

Big sagebrush is an important food for cattle and wild animals. Eaten by many small animals and the sage grouse, it also provides a browse for pronghorn and deer. It was a source of firewood for Native Americans of the region, and makes an excellent, quick-burning campfire fuel. For me, the plant is unforgettable for the pungent smell it gives off after a rainstorm.

AZTEC, NEW MEXICO

Enchantment Lodge
1800 W. Aztec Boulevard
Aztec, NM 87410
(505) 334-6143

This is a standard but comfortable motel near the Aztec Ruins with pool, laundry, and morning coffee ($).

Cottonwood State Campground
On San Juan River, on Highway 173, 18 miles from Aztec. Paved spaces, tent sites, water, and restrooms. No hookups.

Riverside Campground
A civic facility on the Animas River. Electrical hookups, water available.

BLOOMFIELD, NEW MEXICO

Navajo Lake State Park Campgrounds
(505) 632-2278

Three units on Navajo Lake, via U.S. Highway 64 and New Mexico 511, 25 miles east of Bloomfield. RV and tent sites, hookups, showers, picnicking, fishing, swimming, boating.

Bloomfield KOA Campground
1900 East Blanco Blvd.
Bloomfield, NM 87413
(505) 632-8339

RV and tent sites, 75 full hookups, restrooms, showers, store, laundry, pool, lounge.

The Beach at Bloomfield (Campground)
1011 W. Calle del Rio
Bloomfield, NM 87413

13 full hookups, tent sites.

CHACO CANYON

Chaco Culture National Historic Park Campground
(505) 786-7014

Tent and trailer sites (under 30 feet), restrooms, no hookups. Water is available from a tap at the visitor center.

CHINLE, ARIZONA

Thunderbird Lodge
Canyon de Chelly National Monument
P.O. Box 548
Chinle, AZ 86503
(602) 674-5841 or 674-5842

Modern motel-style inn, with dining room, bus tours of canyons ($ to $$).

Canyon de Chelly National Monument Campground
P.O. Box 588
Chinle, AZ 86503
(602) 674-5436

Sites suitable for RVs, trailers and tents, with restrooms and water.

DULCE,
NEW MEXICO

Best Western Jicarilla Inn
P.O. Box 233
Dulce, NM 87528
(505) 759-3663 or 800-528-1234

In Jicarilla Apache Reservation,
U.S. Highway 64 and Hawks Dr.
Dining room, coffee shop,
lounge, rooms and suites available ($ to $$).

ESPANOLA,
NEW MEXICO

La Puebla House B&B
Route 3, Box 172-A
Espanola, NM 87532
(505) 753-3981

Four rooms, handicapped access,
breakfast and tea served ($).

**Santa Clara Canyon
Recreation Area**
Tourism Dept. Santa Clara Pueblo
P.O. Box 580
Espanola, NM 87532
(505) 753-7326

1.3 miles from U.S. 64 via New
Mexico 30. Tent and trailer sites
in a treed area with restrooms,
showers, picnicking, fishing.

FARMINGTON,
NEW MEXICO

The Inn, Best Western
700 Scott Avenue
Farmington, NM 87401
(505) 327-5221 or 800-528-1234

Large rooms, some with refrigerators, heated pool, whirlpool,
sauna, laundry, game room,
dining room, coffee shop, and
lounge ($ to $$).

Holiday Inn of Farmington
600 E. Broadway
Farmington, NM 87401
(505) 327-9811 or 800-HOLIDAY

A typical chain motor hotel
with reasonable rates, dining
room, lounge, whirlpool, sauna
and pool ($ to $$).

Anasazi Inn
903 W. Main Street
Farmington, NM 87401
(505) 325-4564

Rooms and suites, restaurant
serving Mexican food, steaks,
seafood ($ to $$).

River Grove Trailer Park
801 E. Broadway
Farmington, NM 87401
(505) 327-0974

28 full hookups.

Mom & Pop Campground
901 Illinois,
off Bloomfield Highway
(505) 327-3200

35 full hookups and tent sites,
restrooms, showers.

GALLUP,
NEW MEXICO

The Inn, Best Western
3009 W 66th Street
Gallup, NM 87301
(505) 722-2221

124 large rooms, refrigerators, restaurant, lounge, whirlpool, sauna, laundry, games room ($ to $$).

POJOAQUE, NEW MEXICO

Pojoaque Pueblo RV Park
P.O. Box 3687
Santa Fe, NM 87501
(505) 455-2965

15 miles north of Santa Fe on U.S. 84/285. RV, trailer, and tent sites; hookups and restrooms.

TESUQUE, NEW MEXICO

Tesuque Pueblo RV Campground
(505) 455-2661 or
800-TRY-RV-PARK

10 miles north of Santa Fe on U.S. 64/874/185. Full hookups, pool, showers, restrooms, laundry, and store.

SANTA FE, NEW MEXICO

The Bishop's Lodge
P.O. Box 2367,
Bishop's Lodge Road
Santa Fe, NM 87504
(505) 983-6377

Historic resort hotel in private valley setting 3 miles from downtown. Dining room, heated pool, whirlpool, sauna, tennis,

hiking, riding, skeet shooting ($$ to $$$+).

El Rey Inn
1862 Cerillos Rd., P.O. Box 130
Santa Fe, NM 87504
(505) 982-1931

56 rooms and suites in a pueblo-style inn on 3.5 acres. Breakfast, pool, laundry, whirlpool, and playground ($ to $$).

Galisteo Inn
P.O. Box 4
Galisteo, NM 87505
(505) 982-1506

A cozy B&B inn with 12 rooms and suites in the Santa Fe outskirts, with pool and horseback riding ($$).

Hotel Santa Fe
1501 Paseo de Peralta, at Cerrillos
(505) 982-1200 or 800-825-9876

Excellent pueblo revival style hotel owned by the Picuris Pueblo. 131 rooms and suites ($$ to $$$).

SECOND MESA, ARIZONA

Hopi Cultural Center Restaurant and Motel
P.O. Box 87
Second Mesa, AZ 86043
(602) 734-2401

This motel in the Hopi Reservation has 33 rooms with bath/shower and TV, restaurant with native Hopi foods and American meals ($).

Bryce Canyon

A helluva place to lose a cow.
—EBENEZER BRYCE

If the Grand Canyon could be likened to a thundering pipe organ with all stops out, Bryce Canyon should be heard as a superbly fingered classical guitar, or as the delicate strings of a chamber orchestra. While the Grand Canyon is stupendously awesome, Bryce, while less magnificent, has a finely etched subtlety that lingers in the mind long after one visits this remarkable geological wonder.

Southern Utah, with its surface layers largely constructed of soft sandstone and limestone, has been subject to erosion over many millions of years. The effects of wind and, particularly, water, can be seen across the southern half of the state, from Zion Canyon and Arches National Park to Monument Valley. It is a spreading landscape of pillars, natural bridges, spires, arches, pinnacles, and canyons. And there are breaks—eroded badlands—found on the sides of plateaus. Bryce Canyon is one such badland; it is not really a canyon, but a break sculpted from the soft, sandstone cliff of the Paunsaugunt Plateau.

And what an incredibly beautiful badland it is!

Across the Colorado Plateau, in close proximity to Bryce Canyon, is the finest aggregation of geological formations in the world. This landscape is composed of canyons carved by desert rivers, uprisen plateaus, natural arches and bridges, sandstone mazes, and colorful dunes. It is located in a line that leads from Zion Canyon near the Nevada border, to Cedar Breaks just east of Bryce, then past Bryce to the Waterpocket Fold, Kodachrome Basin, the Escalante canyons, Natural Bridges National Monument, the three otherworldly regions of the Canyonlands, the largest collection of natural arches in the world, and Monument Valley. All of this natural wonder lies within a 2-day drive across southern Utah.

Lost Cows and a New Park

While the Paiute Indians used the mysteries of Bryce Canyon to craft fanciful legends, the thousands of erosion pillars were of little use to Ebenezer Bryce, who moved with his wife Mary to the Paria River Valley, below the cliffs, in 1875. Earlier, this doughty 45-year-old Scottish immigrant had come to Pine Valley, Utah, as a Mormon pioneer. Before his trek west, Bryce had been a man of many talents: carpenter, millwright, shipyard worker, sawmill operator, and architect. Mary had not been in good health following a cholera epidemic in St. Louis, and the Bryces moved to the warmer climate of the upper Paria Valley.

Bryce operated a small farm (thus his laconic statement about lost cattle), cut and hauled timber for it, built a road across the breaks to transport logs, and provided leadership in community affairs before leaving the valley in 1880. Neighboring valley residents dubbed the strange, pink, rocky badlands near his timber road Bryce's Canyon.

After the turn of the century, the forest supervisor for the region, J. W. Humphrey, sent a request to his superiors for the sizable grant of $50 to build an automobile road to the Bryce Canyon rim. The work included building two bridges, with labor provided at no cost by local residents. Humphrey became a crusader for the canyon, wanting to attract visitors who would then spread the word about its beauty.

Reuben "Ruby" Syrett was another local mover and shaker. In 1919 Syrett opened a small, rustic lodge to house Humphrey's visitors. Early tour operators, Arthur Hanks and H. I. Bowman, brought tourists from Kanab and Marysvale. For less than $150, you could subscribe to a tour originating in Cedar City, run by the Parry brothers. The 8-day tour included Zion, Cedar Breaks, Bryce, and the Grand Canyon.

By 1923, all this touring activity had attracted the mercenary eyes of the Union Pacific Railroad. Although a train to all these attractions was an impossibility, the railroad put together a combined train and bus package, then bought and leased parcels of land in these locations, including parts of what is now Bryce Canyon National Park and Ruby Syrett's lodge. Bryce Canyon was designated a national monument in 1923, and a national park on September 15, 1928. In order to comply with federal legislation, the railroad turned over its landholdings within the park area.

How to Get There

From the west and Interstate 15, the most efficient route to take begins by exiting I-15 south of the town of Beaver on State Route 20. Drive eastward for 13 miles, then turn right onto U.S. Highway 89 and drive south to Panguitch and the junction of State Route 12.

Highway 12 is the scenic route across the plateaus, which will not only take you to Bryce Canyon, but through Red Canyon and on to several scenic areas including Kodachrome Basin State Park, the Escalante Canyons, Death Hollow Wilderness Area, and the town of Torrey. From here it leads onward to Capitol Reef and the other magnificent national parks and monuments of southwestern Utah.

From the south, take U.S. Highway 89 from Kanab, next to the Arizona border, and drive 44 miles north to the Highway 12 junction. Take Highway 12 east, through Red Canyon, to Bryce Canyon (13 miles).

From the west, take State Route 12 from the town of Torrey for 73 miles.

An Amphitheater Is Not a Canyon

Before I became hip to geological semantics, a "canyon" was any deep place that could be viewed from a high point. Using that meaning, Bryce certainly qualifies. However, a true "canyon" must be carved out of the landscape by a stream; using this meaning, Bryce has to be something else.

The magic of the series of rock amphitheaters from which Bryce Canyon has been wrought—over 16 million years—is the effect of seasonal precipitation on the soft sandstone cliffs of the southern edge of the Paunsaugunt Plateau. The Paunsaugunt is one of three high plateaus created when the Colorado Plateau was uplifted and its western edge was faulted into distinct sections, including the Markagunt Plateau (Cedar Breaks) and the Aquarius Plateau (Table Cliffs), which rises northeast of Bryce Canyon.

Drip after drip, winter after winter (with snow falling, ice forming in the sandstone cracks, then expanding, cracking the stone), the Paunsaugunt cliffs broke off and tumbled down, with some of the harder sandstone staying in place as erosion pillars, or hoodoos.

The Paria River, while not able to create a canyon, does have an effect on the cliff erosion as it flows against the plateau. Little streams, tributaries of the river, flow over the rim of the plateau and down the cliff sides, helping the erosion process by expanding many of the vertical cracks in the stone, creating gullies and hastening the deepening of the amphitheaters.

The formation, from which the pinnacles and spires are carved, is the result of layering that began more than 30 million years ago. At that time, all of southern Utah was a broad plain dotted with shallow lakes. Heavy washing of silt and other materials into the lakes deposited layers of sediment, which were stacked according to the weight of the rock, sand, clay, and silt. More lakes came and disappeared, and iron and manganese oxides colored the materials, which compressed to form the 2,000-foot-deep layer now called the Claron Formation.

The erosion continues at a relatively fast pace—about a foot every hundred years—continually carving new niches to form more and deeper gullies, while cutting back the rim and isolating new hoodoos. The varying hardness of the rock results in weird-shaped formations. At the same time, the earlier-exposed pinnacles to the south are wearing down, widening the Paria Valley. So, the geological process continues.

Life Inside the Park

In all of what seems to be sandstone desolation, life hangs on the sides of the amphitheaters. The Upper Sonoran life zone, under the rim, features the typical pinyon pine/juniper woodland species. The trees are sparsely placed, clinging to the rock. Vegetation is thicker on the canyon bottom.

As you enter the park at the visitor center, ponderosa pine dominate the transition zone. As you climb to the higher reaches of the national park, the pine gives way to the Canadian life zone, characterized by Douglas fir, spruce, and aspen, with ancient bristlecone pines at the topmost, coldest, and windiest points of land. This range of biotic communities harbors a wide range of life, including a continuous display of wildflowers throughout the growing season—from the melting of snow in the spring, until late summer and early fall.

On the upper levels, mountain marmots lie on rocks in the summer sun. Steller's jays provide the loudest of the bird sounds. Ravens and bluebirds, along with nuthatches, all inhabit the forests above the rim. On the rim and in the canyon, the Utah prairie dog digs its dens in the soil. Ground squirrels and Uinta chipmunks are also seen.

Enjoying Bryce Canyon

The national park is a long, crescent-shaped piece of land, through which a main access road runs, parallel to the canyon rim. Along its 19 miles, the road takes visitors to a series of overlooks and to several trails leading into the canyon from the viewpoints. The park visitor center, located 1.2 miles south of the entrance gate, is open every day (except Christmas day). The center includes an information desk, bookstore, and a theater featuring a slide/audio program on the geology of the park. You'll be able to get information on the timing of ranger-guided hikes and interpretative talks.

The Grand Staircase is what geologists call the descending "steps" in the Colorado Plateau as it reaches its southern edge. The Pink Cliffs at the end of the road form the top step. Other, lower steps, are named for their colors—the Pink, Gray, White,

Vermilion, and Chocolate cliffs—with the Kaibab Plateau the most southerly step in the staircase. From several viewpoints along the way, you'll be able to look out and see the steps.

The park road ends at Rainbow and Yovimpa Points, after providing access to several side roads leading to the overlooks. Several trails, starting at the various viewpoints, lead across the rim and head into the canyon. A drive from one end of the park to the other provides an excellent way to begin a visit. Scenic overload is a distinct possibility at this point, and you may wish to do the drive in two stages, with a visual rest in between.

Fairyland Point   Located north of the visitor center, this first side road runs 1 mile to a scenic overlook. From the rim, you can see Fairyland Canyon, a small gorge. Many visitors miss this fine view because of its location just inside the park. Although a small side-canyon, Fairyland is a microcosm of the larger amphitheaters, with varied displays of hoodoos and sculptured walls.

Sunrise Point   The most popular of the rim overlooks, Sunrise Point offers an expansive view of the large Bryce Amphitheater, also seen from three other viewpoints. Here, all the majesty of Bryce is on display, with hundreds of pillars and pinnacles, some wearing "pork pie" hats of harder stone. You'll see pine trees (some of them timber pine) clinging to the rocks, their roots exposed by erosion.

Sunset Point   This overlook not only provides spectacular scenes below the rim but offers long-range views of the surrounding geological formations. To the northeast is the Aquarius Plateau, rising 2,000 feet above the rest of the land-scape like a gigantic butte. The Table Cliffs are seen below the main plateau at its southern edge. From this vantage point, you'll see just about all of the Bryce Amphitheater, with Thor's Hammer to the left; the Wall Street cliffs just to the right of center; and the Silent City, a complex series of formations, to the right.

Inspiration Point   A side road leads to three overlooks, with Inspiration Point to the immediate left; Bryce Point and Paria View are reached by spur roads about a mile down the access road. Supreme examples of natural erosion at work, the formations below Inspiration Point (particularly the Silent City) show how hoodoos are created over time. The maze of shaped sandstone walls in the Silent City are in the middle stage of development, on their way to being eroded into hundreds of pinnacles. Come back several hundred years from now and the walls will have become a collection of hoodoos. This overlook is at the midpoint along the rim of Bryce Amphitheater. The grooved walls stretch to a length of 600 feet, and are about 180 to 200 feet high.

Bryce Point Looking to the north, one can see the Table Cliffs and the Aquarius Plateau above. The Silent City is seen to the left, as is most of Bryce Amphitheater. This viewpoint will allow you to catch almost the full sweep of the amphitheater, a spectacular vista at any time of day, but particularly at sunrise.

Paria View At the end of the same access road, Paria View offers views of a distinctly separate amphitheater. The floor of the valley lies some 500 feet below. The rock formations are unusual, in that the cliffs are almost perpendicular. This is the beginning of the southern edge of the plateau, where the forces of erosion work faster, and the rock is subject to fracturing off the plateau in large slabs. The distant views on a clear day reveal the White Cliffs to the east and the cliffs of Zion Canyon to the southwest.

Farview Point The route climbs several hundred feet on the drive to the end of the park, entering the northern (Canadian) life zone, with its Douglas fir, blue spruce, and trembling aspen. As its name suggests, this vista point offers a panoramic view of the Colorado Plateau components, including the Aquarius, Kaiparowits, and Kaibab plateaus, in addition to Navajo Mountain.

Natural Bridge Set at the side of the main park road, this viewpoint provides a fine view of the vertical cliffs, as well as an 85-foot stone arch, which is not a natural bridge as its name would suggest. This hole in the rock is thought to have been made not from erosion caused by running water, but by other forces. After the wall was breached, natural water runoff conspired to deepen the hole.

Agua Canyon Another roadside overlook, the Agua Canyon viewpoint, shows several series of hoodoos—some close to the rim and others far below, on massive shelves above the valley floor. Among the "named" pillars are The Rabbit and The Hunter (topped by trees).

Ponderosa Canyon   You can see the effect of warmer weather inside this canyon inhabited by the ponderosa pines, although the spruce/fir forest sits atop the plateau at this point. There are good close-up and distant views.

Yovimpa Point   Under this overlook are the Pink Cliffs, the highest step in the Grand Staircase. Here are expansive views of the cliffs, the forested valley below, and distant sightings of the plateaus.

Rainbow Point   At the end of the road, you can see more panoramic views from atop this highest part of the Paunsaugunt Plateau. From this overlook, a trail leads to a high promontory where bristlecone pines stand against the winds and survive after more than 2,000 years. The viewpoint is at an elevation of 9,105 feet, offering visitors inspiring views to the north and east, toward the Colorado and Green River canyonlands, the Aquarius Plateau, and the Waterpocket Fold (Capitol Reef).

HIKING

As marvelous as the overlook views may be, the most satisfying way to really get the Bryce experience is on foot. Even if you are allergic to hiking, the shortest walk along the rim, or down a few hundred feet below the rim, will give you visual memories that will stick with you for a long time. Venturing even the shortest distance below the rim will place you in the midst of a hoodoo forest, with towering pinnacles all around. Bryce is ready-made for the day-hiker. There are trails for everyone— from very short to lengthy, from easy (most are easy) to moderately difficult, including two interconnecting backcountry trails suitable only for experienced and hardy hikers. The following listing of trails is organized from north to south, followed by the backcountry routes.

Rim Trail   This 11-mile (17.6-km) walking trail runs from Fairyland Point at the north end of the park, to Bryce Point at the southern edge of the main Bryce Amphitheater. The trail provides views that cannot be experienced at any of the viewpoints. It can be accessed from the viewpoints along the way, including Sunrise, Sunset, and Inspiration. The average hiking time for the full length is about 4 hours. The total ascent is 559 feet. Almost all of the trail is in the easy class, more a walk through a park than a hiking challenge. The section between Sunrise and Sunset points is suitable for wheelchairs. This trail is ideal for those who wish to take a short walk by entering and leaving the trail at one of the several viewpoints.

Fairyland Trail This loop trail covers 8.3 miles (13.2 km) round-trip from the trailhead at Fairyland Point, leading down through some very scenic hoodoo country before cutting through Campbell Canyon and returning on the ascent to meet the Rim Trail near Sunrise Point. For a shorter trip, walk to the Sunrise Point overlook and parking area. To complete the circle loop, walk the final 2.5 miles on the Rim Trail. The trail passes a multitude of fanciful formations, including the Chinese Wall. Tower Bridge is reached by a side trail about a half-mile long, found about 1.5 miles from Sunrise Point. The round-trip walk between Sunrise Point and Tower Bridge is 4 miles. The 5-hour hike is classed as difficult, with an ascent of 900 feet.

Queen's Garden Trail A short, moderate hike of 1.6 miles (2.6 km) round-trip, this trail begins at Sunset Point and has the advantage of offering a self-guided interpretive tour. The difference in elevation is 320 feet. The trail ends at a viewpoint near the Queen Victoria formation, where hikers can rest on benches. A short connecting loop located near the end of the Queen's Garden Trail provides access to the Navajo and Peekaboo trails.

Navajo Loop Trail Also starting at Sunset Point, this is one of the shorter trails (1.4 miles, 2.2 km round-trip), to be hiked in less than 2 hours. With an ascent of 520 feet, it tends to be energy-sapping. The trail offers fine views of several of the more prominent named formations, including Thor's Hammer, the Pope, and Two Bridges. The walk through narrow Wall Street, with its two tall fir trees, is particularly thrilling. From the bottom, the hiker has the choice of completing the circle loop, or taking the connecting trail to Queen's Garden Trail (see above). The Peekaboo Loop is also accessed by a connecting trail. This is an option only for the hardy hiker.

Peekaboo Loop Trail   This trail, which leads under the rim, must be accessed by taking a connecting trail from Sunrise, Sunset, or Bryce points. It covers much of the southern portion of the Bryce Amphitheater. The total hiking time along the complete loop (starting at Bryce Point) is a little over 3 hours (5.2 miles, 8.3 km). The walk is longer if accessed from the other viewpoints, and it is fairly strenuous, with several steep climbs. However, the views are stupendous, including unforgettable sightings of the Silent City, the Wall of Windows, and the Cathedral. There is a picnic area with pit toilets west of the connecting trail to Bryce Point.

Hat Shop Trail   This walk, starting at Bryce Point, gives you a taste of the backcountry via Under-the-Rim Trail. It is the first part of that longer trail, providing a quick descent through balanced boulder formations. The ascent is 900 feet, making the return effort quite strenuous. The round-trip is 3.8 miles (6.1 km), about a 4-hour hike.

Bristlecone Loop Trail   Starting at the Rainbow Point overlook, the round-trip length is 1 mile (1.6 km), with a hiking time of about 1 hour. It is a flat, easy walk, and one of the easiest ways to see the ancient trees—much more accessible than several other habitats of the bristlecone pine in Utah and Nevada. The trail offers good views from the rim at the southern edge of the park.

Under-the-Rim Trail (Backcountry)   Hiking the complete 22.6-mile (36.4 km) length of this superb trail is only for the most serious and fit hikers. Running between Bryce Point and Rainbow Point, the trail has many descents and ascents. However, for those who wish to get a taste of this trail without all the ups and downs, portions can be hiked by using the access trails from the park road at Agua Canyon, Swamp Canyon, and Sheep Creek. The full trail takes between 2 and 3 days to hike. Overnight trips require free backcountry permits, which can be obtained at the park visitor center.

Riggs Springs Loop Trail   Joining the Under-the-Rim Trail, the Riggs Springs Trail leads from Yovimpa Point into the valley, then ascends to the rim at nearby Rainbow Point. The total distance is 8.8 miles (14.2 km). The hike takes between 4 and 5 hours.

PICNICKING

One could only wish that there were several additional picnic areas in the park, particularly in the serene forest areas of the southern half. However, there are five picnic areas to enjoy. Three are located near Sunrise Point—next to the campground just north of the park amphitheater, beside the nature center, and at the Sunrise Point overlook. A small roadside picnic area is located about halfway along the drive to Rainbow Point, across the highway from the Whitman Connecting Trail. The most southerly picnic spot is found at Rainbow Point.

The only picnic area off the rim is on the Peekaboo Trail, accessed from Bryce Point. Sometimes it's necessary to get away from the stupendous beauty of Bryce Canyon, to rest the overloaded brain. Having a quiet picnic is just the thing to relax the mind and prepare for more hoodoo viewing.

PARK SERVICES AND CONCESSIONS

The following services offer diverse ways to enjoy the beauty of the region.

Visitor Center This interpretive center with an audio-visual theater, bookstore, and first aid service, is located 1 mile south of the park entrance. Overnight hiking permits are obtained here, along with trail maps and general information. The visitor center is open daily from 8:00 A.M. to 4:30 P.M., with afternoon hours extended during the summer months. It is closed on Thanksgiving Day, Christmas Day, and New Year's Day.

Nature Center Open during summer months, the Sunrise Nature Center provides in-depth information about the park. Backcountry camping permits are also available. Many of the nature talks and guided hikes are conducted from this center. The Junior Ranger program, available for children twelve years of age and under, provides an activity booklet.

Shuttle Buses With 1.5 million visitors visiting Bryce each year, and most of them driving to the park, the park has launched an experimental shuttle bus system to transport visitors to the major viewpoints and to Bryce Canyon Lodge. For those who wish others to do the driving, shuttle buses are available across the highway from Ruby's Inn, just outside the park.

Horseback Riding   You can ride a horse on some park trails. To book your ride, contact Bryce-Zion Trail Rides, P.O. Box 128, Tropic, UT 84776, or call (801) 834-5219. Bryce Canyon Lodge has a counter at which you may schedule horseback rides.

TRAVEL ADVISORY

The narrow 7 miles of roadway at the southern end of the park has been inadequate to handle the large number of summer visitors. The Park Service has now widened the road, enlarged the parking areas, and has made needed improvements to several viewpoints. During the summer of 1995, the southernmost 7 miles of road were closed to cars, RVs, and foot traffic so that the work could be finished by the end of the year. At this writing, most of the work has been completed, including enlarging the Bryce Point parking area. The improvements make visiting Bryce Canyon all the more enjoyable.

It pays (in more ways than one) to visit Bryce Canyon during the spring, or from mid-September through October. And if you like snow, you'll love the Bryce views in wintertime—snow-capped hoodoos, silent snow-clad forests, and cross-country skiing—when few others visit.

Nearby Attractions

RED CANYON

Highway 12 runs through this colorful—deep red and orange— canyon, between the Highway 89 junction (to the west) and Bryce Canyon. The Forest Service has developed a recreation area including a campground centered on the canyon, across the highway from the visitor center.

Trails fan out from the area near the Red Canyon Visitor Center. The trails range in length from 0.5 miles to 8.7 miles. Horses are permitted on the three longer trails. Pink Ledges Trail, near the visitor center, is the shortest—an easy walk past some of the prettiest formations. The mile-long Buckhorn Trail, which climbs to a viewpoint high above the canyon floor, takes from 1 to 2 hours to walk. Because of the high elevation of the area, this climb is considered moderate to strenuous.

An easier, .6-mile-long trail accommodates both horses and people, leading through old-growth ponderosa pine forest to a vantage point overlooking the canyon from the north. Perhaps the easiest, and most interesting, walk can be experienced by taking the short Tunnel Trail. For hikers only, this .7-mile, moderate trail begins at the highway near a short tunnel and provides wonderful views.

The longest trail (8.7 miles) is the Cassidy Trail. For hikers and horses, the trail leads through red rock formations and beside stands of ponderosa pine. The Cassidy in the name refers to Butch, who is said to have used this trail while being pursued by the law. A spring is available for humans and horses at the head of Casto Canyon, with another at Hancock Spring. Casto Canyon Trail is open to hikers, horseback riders, and off-highway vehicles. It runs for 5.3 miles along the floor of this spectacular canyon, and takes between 4 and 8 hours to walk. This trail, which has a moderate rating, connects with the Cassidy Trail.

While the two longer trails cross wide areas of canyon and forest, the Birdseye Trail offers a short (.8-mile) walk into Red Canyon formations that vary in color from pink to scarlet. This moderate trail leads northwest from the visitor center, climbing above Highway 26.

Cedar Breaks National Monument

Located less than an hour's drive west of Bryce Canyon, Cedar Breaks is rougher, higher, and deeper than its neighbor. Lacking the delicacy of the Bryce badlands, it exhibits a raw energy that is captivating.

The rim lies on the 10,000-foot-high Markagunt Plateau. The huge amphitheater is more than 2,000 feet deep and more than 3 miles wide. The vivid colors are produced by iron and manganese oxides that are held in the eroding rock, producing purple, yellow, and red hues. Juniper trees (the supposed cedars) grow sparsely along the steep slopes, which are made up of deep ravines, pinnacles, and buttresses or walls.

From several topside viewpoints, one can gaze across the breaks and see the Cedar Valley, about 20 miles to the west. Because of the high elevations, the top of the sloping plateau is covered with subalpine fir, Englemann spruce, and aspen. In late spring and early summer, the mountain meadows are set ablaze with carpets of wildflowers.

How to Get There

Cedar Breaks provides a superb beginning to a road that continues to Bryce Canyon. From the west, take State Route 143 from Parowan. It is 21 miles to the park from Interstate 15. The route passes through the little resort town of Brian Head before cutting through the northern section of the park. Turn south on State Route 148 for the visitor center (near the southern gate), the campground, and amphitheater viewpoints.

From the south and southeast, take U.S. Highway 89 north from Kanab or Mt. Carmel Junction, turn left (west) onto State Route 14 and drive 23 miles. Turn left (north) onto State Route 148, which leads through the park to the visitor center. From the east, take State Route 143 from Panguitch and drive west to State Route 148, then turn south to the visitor center.

Enjoying Cedar Breaks

Although one can access the park during the long winter season by using cross-country skis or by riding a snowmobile, the park road (Highway 148) is open only after the piles of snow disappear, anywhere from late May to early July. The 1995 spring was so delayed that the campground opened just in time for the July 4th weekend. The park closes during November.

Alpine Pond Trail Two hiking trails on the forested plateau offer fine views of the amphitheater and quiet strolls through the verdant underbrush. The Alpine Pond Nature Trail is a 2-mile loop that leads through the forest, passing by a meadow and around the small pond. You may begin your walk at either the Chessman Ridge Overlook or from the pull-off to the north of the overlook. This is flat country and the hike is considered easy.

Wasatch Ramparts Trail The trailhead is beside the park visitor center. This 2-mile (one-way) trail leads along the rim, curving around the south edge of the amphitheater. The trail goes down a slight slope (65 feet) to Spectra Point, which offers the first of the major views and a stand of bristlecone pine. The trail continues along the rim to a viewpoint overlooking

Crescent Hollow and The Meadows, among other named valleys and rock formations. The total climb on the return hike is 398 feet.

Rattlesnake Creek Trail   The trailhead for this longer hike—to the bottom of the amphitheater—is found just outside the north gate of the park, via a short gravel road. The trail descends 3,000 feet over 4 miles, reaching Ashdown Creek. If you wish to explore Cedar Breaks, you head up the creek and into the various canyons (Chessman, Bristlecone, Slip). The trail follows the creek south through Ashdown Gorge, descending another 1,000 feet to reach a trailhead on State Route 14, east of Cedar City. The trail, which leads through the Dixie National Forest, is not maintained.

Camping   The campground has 30 sites, all available on a first-come, first-served basis. It is open from June (snow willing) until mid-September. The campground has picnic tables, grills, water, restrooms, and an outdoor amphitheater where nature interpretation programs are held. A picnic area is located near the campground. Nighttime summer temperatures at the 10,000-foot level can be chilly (in the 30s and 40s). The daytime readings are generally in the 60s and 70s. Indoor accommodations are available in nearby Brian Head, as well as in Parowan and Cedar City.

NEARBY STATE PARKS

Kodachrome Basin State Park   East of Bryce Canyon, this photogenic area of hoodoos, rock chimneys, spires, arches, and canyons so impressed the National Geographic Society that they gave the park this name. It is located 7 miles south of Cannonville, via a side road. The chimneys are the major feature of the park. These tall erosion pillars stand high off the valley floor or jut out from sandstone ledges. The chimneys and other hoodoos are eerily beautiful at sunrise and sunset. There are hiking, mountain biking, and horse trails in the park. Facilities include a store (Trail Head Station) stocked with food and campers' supplies (including Kodak film). You may arrange a guided horseback ride, or a ride through the park in a horse-drawn coach. The campground has 24 units with tables, cement slabs, and grills. Firewood is supplied and spring water is available year-round.

Another outstanding feature is Grosvenor Arch, 10 miles south of the park. This large double arch is one of the finest such formations in the state. Also down the same road is Cottonwood Canyon and the Paria River area, offering more recreation opportunities including four-wheel-drive adventure, hiking, and biking.

Escalante Petrified Forest State Park   Located 1 mile west of Escalante on Highway 12, the park features deposits of mineralized wood and is a significant source of petrified dinosaur bones. Wide Hollow Reservoir is located next to the state park, providing campgrounds, fishing, and other water sports.

Anasazi Indian Village State Park   This largely unexcavated ancient Anasazi community was a large and important settlement between A.D. 1050 and 1200. Some artifacts have been uncovered and are on display in the park museum.

Coral Pink Sand Dunes State Park   An otherworldly place, this park is a large expanse of shifting pink dunes, which can be climbed, driven on with an off-road vehicle, or merely gazed upon. There is a 21-unit campground with showers and restrooms. A paved road runs to the park, which is 11 miles south of U.S. 89 near Kanab.

FOUR BACKROAD DRIVES

These southern Utah back roads provide fascinating drives, although the gravel road beds can be bumpy and sometimes impassable.

Posey Lake Backroad   Running north from the east end of Escalante and ending at State Route 24 near Loa, this scenic road traverses the high country of the Dixie National Forest. Posey Lake, 13 miles northwest of Escalante, is a lovely alpine lake with a campground and good trout fishing. Other dirt roads provide connections to several other lakes and reservoirs with campgrounds.

Hell's Backbone Road   This road, which traverses the top of a hogsback (a narrow ridge with a sheer drop on both sides), is one of the most breathtaking and dramatic pieces of road in the Southwest. At points, the ridge top is no wider than the road. Hell's Backbone Bridge is particularly thrilling (or intimidating, if you are subject to vertigo). This road starts at the Posey Lake Scenic Byway, southeast of Posey Lake, and leads around the scarily named Box Death Hollow Wilderness, ending at State Route 12 three miles west of Boulder. The road offers opportunities to stop for camping, hiking, backcountry trekking, and off-road driving. High clearance vehicles (four-wheel-drive cars or pickups) are recommended.

Hole in the Rock Scenic Byway   A historic old trail, it was carved by Mormon settlers in 1880, as they built a passage and lowered their wagons and other supplies 1,200 feet to the floor of Glen Canyon. The byway starts 5 miles east of Escalante and runs for 57 miles to the Hole in the Rock above Glen Canyon. Views of Escalante canyon country and the Straight Cliffs are spectacular. Devil's Rock Garden, a grouping of jumbled boulders and arches, is located 18 miles south of Escalante. Hiking is available along the route. For maps, see the BLM office in Escalante.

Burr Trail Road   Leading southwest from Highway 12 at Boulder and ending at Bullfrog Marina on Lake Powell, the Burr Trail offers spectacular scenery along its 66 miles. It passes through the Waterpocket Fold of Capitol Reef National Park. The road may be impassable after rainstorms.

CAPITOL REEF NATIONAL PARK

Lying about halfway between Bryce Canyon and Canyonlands national parks, Capitol Reef National Park encloses the Waterpocket Fold, a monocline (a single fold of rock that rises from the surrounding desert), and stretches in a general north-south direction for more than 100 miles. Atop the midsection of the Waterpocket Fold is a series of domes. The most prominent of the domes resembles the dome of the Washington Capitol, thus the park's name. Access to the park is via State Route 24—which meets State Route 12 nine miles east of the park entrance—or by the rough Burr Trail Road. From the east, take State Route 24 from State Route 95 at Hanksville. The visitor center and museum provide a look into the major geological features of the park, plus present some history of the settlers who founded the community of Fruita in the early days of Mormon immigration. Remains of the village and fruit-tree orchards are seen from the highway. The one-room Fruita schoolhouse and implement shed have been restored and are on display.

Scenic Drive and Trails The park's scenic drive offers an amazing collection of geological features, including brilliantly colored cliffs, natural bridges, arches, natural water tanks (the pockets), and the domes. Taken from the visitor center, the drive leads from the Fremont River into the Grand Wash, where short foot trails lead into the narrow part of the canyon for a view of dramatic formations including Cassidy's Arch. (Yes, that's Butch again. He hid out here, too!) The drive continues past slick rock and an area where several desert plants are found, including rabbitbrush and Apache-plume, and along the reddish brown sandstone cliffs of the Moenkopi Formation. A spur road leads 2 miles into Capitol Gorge, with another fork to Pleasant Creek, a perennial stream. The white sandstone of the Navajo Formation is seen in Capitol Gorge, particularly in the white, rounded domes. Large pockets in the sandstone store rainwater. Fifteen trails lead to various geological wonders along the Waterpocket Fold. Most are short trails, from .1 miles to 2.25 miles, leading from the scenic drive route. Several longer, rugged trails lead to viewpoints. For park information, call (801) 425-3791.

Camping There is one developed campground (Fruita). Two primitive campgrounds are located on back roads (Cathedral Valley and Cedar Mesa).

Arches National Park

The world's largest display of natural arches lies within this superb piece of desert landscape, located just north of the town of Moab. Somehow, the sandstone at this place developed just the right kind of fissures and long cracks to attract eroding forces—rain, snow, frosts, and thawing—that wear down the crumbing and flaking stone. The 1,500 arches range from a height of 3 feet to 306 feet (in the case of Landscape Arch). In addition to the arches, canyons filled with hoodoos and weird balanced rock formations seen along the park roads and several trails invite hikers.

The arches are located in five major scenic areas, connected by the main park road, which leads from the visitor center at the south end of the park. Here there are several notable rock formations, including Courthouse Towers, the Organ, and the Three Gossips. The Windows section is in the southeast part of the park, accessible by a spur road. Here are the North and South Windows, Double Arch, Parade of Elephants, and several more. Farther north is the turnoff to Delicate Arch and the Wolfe Ranch. The road continues past the Fiery Furnace and Salt Valley viewpoints to the Devil's Garden arches and the park campground. An unpaved road leads 7.7 miles to the Klondike Bluffs area, which includes the huge Tower Arch.

Wolfe Ranch   The park area includes the ranch property of John Wesley Wolfe, a Civil War veteran who settled his family here in 1888. Wolfe and his son ran a cattle operation on this arid desert for more than 20 years. Others followed in Wolfe's footsteps, grazing cattle for short periods each year following winter rains. The problematical ranching history of the area is remembered at the site of the Wolfe Ranch, part of the park near Delicate Arch. A trail leads around the old irrigated garden site, the root cellar, the original corral, and a cabin that Wolfe built in 1906 for his daughter, who refused to live in the original shanty with its dirt floor and leaning sides. The original cabin has long since crumbled. Another trail leads to Native American petroglyphs.

Camping   There is one developed campground in Arches National Park, at Devil's Garden, which is open from spring through early fall. Backcountry camping permits are available. For park information, call (801) 259-8161.

Canyonlands National Park

This massive and mostly undeveloped park lies along and between the canyons of the Colorado and Green rivers, as they flow toward Lake Powell. There are three major districts in the park:

Island in the Sky   Accessed by taking U.S. Highway 191 north from Moab for 10 miles, then southwest for 22 miles along State Route 313, Island in the Sky is the high mesa between the two rivers. It's an area with fine views of the rest of the park and distant mountains, plus several short trails that lead to some arches and to the outstanding Upheaval Dome. The visitor center is open from 8 A.M. to 4:30 P.M., with extended hours from spring to fall. The only campground is classed primitive (no water, no fee). There is a picnic area and several overlooks are located along the park road. The 102-mile White Rim Road provides four-wheel-drivers with great views, and is one of the premier mountain biking roads in the country (801-259-4351).

The Needles Featuring many jumbled rock formations, numerous arches, pinnacles, and river canyon views, The Needles is located 35 miles west of U.S. 191, a 1-hour drive south from Moab or an hour's drive north from Monticello. The visitor center is open from 8:00 A.M. to 4:00 P.M. daily, with changes for winter. There is a 26-unit campground, and a store (Needles Outpost) is just outside the park gate. There are hiking and short nature trails, back roads, backcountry hiking to remote campsites, and ranger-led nature programs (801-259-6568). Along the entrance road is Newspaper Rock State Park, with one of the finest collections of Native American graffiti in the Southwest.

The Maze A much more remote area, the challenging Maze district, is on the west side of the park. Entry is via a two-wheel-drive dirt road that leads 46 miles east from State Route 24, and 24 miles south of Interstate 70 (at Green River); or via a four-wheel-drive dirt road leading north from State Route 95 near Hite Marina. Both roads lead to the Hans Flat Ranger Station, where you'll require a lot of information to find your way through what is literally a "maze" of four-wheel-drive back roads and canyon trails with primitive campsites (no water, no fee). The ranger station is open 8:00 A.M. to 4:30 P.M., spring through fall, with limited winter hours (801-259-6513).

SOUTHERN UTAH WILDLIFE

O ur tour through the southern edge of Utah takes us from over 10,000 feet at Cedar Breaks to the high desert of Moab and the Canyonlands at 4,000 feet. Because of the differences in elevation, the biotic zones vary widely, all the way from the Upper Sonoran zone around Moab and Capitol Reef—with its arid rocky soil, sage, and rabbit brush—to the Canadian life zone atop Bryce Canyon and Cedar Breaks, with thick pine groves, fir and spruce forests, dense ferny underbrush, and alpine survivors such as the whistling marmot and mule deer. The resulting range of animal, bird, and plant life is immense, making a tour of this region a naturalist's delight.

BIRDS

Flammulated Owl
Otus flammeolus
This little owl is not much larger than a sparrow or small jay. It is gray above and light below with markings of white and rusty red. The female is slightly larger than the male.

Its voice is a low hoot, single or double, and very monotonous with no variation in pitch. It repeats this call for long periods of time.

Ranging from the forests of British Columbia through the Rocky Mountains, and south to Mexico, the flammulated owl lives in the ponderosa forests of the Southwest, including Bryce Canyon.

Scrub Jay
Aphelocoma coerulescens
This jay looks larger than it really is. About the size of a robin and smaller than the more common gray jay and Steller's jay, the scrub jay grows to 13 inches, but has a long tail and bill.

Its back is a dull brown and its underparts are light gray. The white throat has a blue partial necklace. What distinguishes this jay is its blue wings, head, and tail, which flash as it glides in the sunlight. Its call is jay-like: a loud *jayy* or *jree*.

This bird's range is from southwest Washington to California and to Texas and northern Mexico. It lives in woodland and scrub chaparral. It prefers to breed in forests rather than in the unprotected scrubby desert areas, which lack the posts the jay requires to keep an eye on its nest.

White-throated Swift
Aeronautes saxatalis
This and other breeds of swift are seen flashing through the walls of Bryce Canyon. Unlike other swifts, it is white with small dark patches below, in sharp contrast to its very dark top.

Its sound is a shrill *je je je je je je je je je*, in descending scale.

Found throughout the western states, from southern British Columbia to Mexico and Honduras, it breeds on sea cliffs, as well as on canyon walls, which Bryce and Cedar Breaks have in abundance.

Red-Breasted Nuthatch
Sitta canadensis
Nuthatches are small tree-climbers, recognized by their stubby tails. Although they are like woodpeckers, with strong bills and feet, their tails are not used for balance while climbing. In fact, nuthatches come down a tree headfirst.

The red-breasted nuthatch has a reddish pink underside, as if someone had painted the bird using a rusty watercolor. It's a small bird, as nuthatches go, with a broad black line through the eye and a white line above it.

Its voice is high-pitched and nasal, making an *ank* or *enk* sound.

With a range from southeastern Alaska through the western U.S. the red-breasted nuthatch winters in the American Southwest and Mexico on an irregular basis. It likes to live in coniferous forests, such as the ponderosa pine or the fir and spruce forests of Cedar Breaks and Bryce Canyon.

Pygmy Nuthatch
Sitta pygmaea
The smallest of the nuthatches, the pygmy likes living in pine and Douglas fir forests, from British Columbia to central Mexico.

It has a grayish brown head cap with a white spot on the nape of the neck. It is whitish below. You'll see this bird flying in small flocks, rarely alone.

The pygmy nuthatch's voice is quite different from the excited song of its red-breasted cousin. The pygmy has a piping song: *kit-kit—kit*, or *pit-pi-dit-pi-dit*. It sometimes gives out a high-pitched chatter: *kee—dee*, repeated over and over again.

OTHER ANIMALS

Golden Mantled Ground Squirrel
Spermophilus lateralis

Found across the Mojave and Great Basin deserts as well as on parts of the Colorado Plateau, this little squirrel could easily be confused with a chipmunk. It's about the same size as a chipmunk, just a little larger. Its back is gray, brownish, or a buff color, and the belly is white.

Its head and shoulders are a coppery red, forming its "golden mantle." Its sides feature one white stripe bordered by black stripes. Since this hardy little squirrel lives largely in coniferous forests, you'll see it in the forests of Bryce Canyon and Cedar Breaks, at the upper elevations. It can be found from southeastern British Columbia and the Rocky Mountain regions of Alberta to the north, and west to New Mexico.

You'll rarely hear a sound out of this busy little fellow, but upon being frightened, it lets out a squeal or a growl. Its food can be insects and green plants, but its primary diet is made up of nuts and fruits.

It nests in burrows in the ground, which often stretch down 100 feet. You'll see the openings of the burrows in a sheltered area, near a log, or under a tree or large rock.

In the Bryce Canyon/Cedar Breaks area, this squirrel hibernates from mid- to late October until May or June, depending on the temperature and the amount of snow, particularly at the top of Cedar Breaks National Monument.

Yellow-bellied Marmot
Marmota flaviventris

This alpine dweller is a cousin of the hoary marmot, the familiar North American marmot, and is found in more southerly locations than its more common cousin. This one is yellowish brown with a yellow underside. Its feet are light to dark brown, and it has light spots between its eyes. The bushy-tailed creature can be seen at the higher elevations in Cedar Breaks National Monument and in a few spots in Bryce Canyon National Park. Litters are born in March and April—as soon as hibernation ends—and you'll see the fat adults, with children nearby, lazing on warm rocks during the summer and fall months.

The marmot feeds exclusively on various kinds of green plants, grasses, and wildflower plants in season. It often guards its feeding area against other animals. In late summer, the marmot puts on a thick layer of fat for winter survival.

Its range is from British Columbia and southern Alberta to eastern California and into Colorado. Although it is found in northeastern Utah, it is not generally seen in parts of southern Utah except for rarefied reaches of the Cedar Breaks/ Bryce Canyon area.

The marmot likes to live in rocky areas, and lives in a den, sometimes under rock piles or in a crevice on a hillside. It has a chirp, rather than the loud whistle sounded by the hoary marmot, and this chirp—a light whistle—is a sign of danger when it is alarmed. The marmot usually retreats to its den before making the sound.

Pika
Ochotona princeps
A fascinating little mammal, the pika looks like a fat, round mouse, but with some significant differences. It is brownish, has no visible tail, and has small rounded ears. You'll be able to find pikas in the same kind of alpine and subalpine areas as you will see the much larger marmot. This includes the higher elevation of Bryce Canyon National Park (at an elevation of 8,000 feet) and the higher rim of Cedar Breaks National Monument and the nearby treeless peak of Brian Head Mountain.

The pika lives on rocky banks, talus slides, and steep hillsides covered with boulders. Its range extends from the mountain areas of southern British Columbia to northern New Mexico.

Babies are born blind during the spring months (May and June). There is sometimes a second set produced in the late summer, depending on the length of the previous winter. Each litter is composed of two to six young.

Pikas eat green plants and aren't particular about which species they munch on. Sometimes they stay by the plant and eat. At other times, they carry the greens back to their homes where a curious ritual takes place. Pikas spread the plants to dry in the sun, like farmers stack hay to dry. After the plants dry, the pikas then store the vegetation in their dens.

Plants eaten and stored include stonecrop (sedum), thistles, fireweed, sweetgrass, and sedges.

Pronghorn Antelope
Antilocapra americana
The Pronghorn, closely related to the deer, is the fastest animal in the Western Hemisphere and

among the fastest anywhere, as it bounds 20 feet at a time and runs up to 70 miles per hour. Its cruising speed is between 30 and 45 miles per hour.

It looks like a medium-size deer with long legs. Its upper parts are a pale tan color, as are the outer parts of its legs. The rest of the animal is white, including a rump patch, cheeks, lower jaw, and white blazes across the throat.

The pronghorn buck has distinctive markings: a wide black band from its eyes down its snout to a black nose and a black patch on its neck. Its tracks are like split hearts, about 3 inches long.

The horns are black, growing to a length of 20 inches, shaped like a lyre with one broad prong jutting forward from the base (buck), with the female horns much shorter—not more than 4 inches—and usually without prongs.

The pronghorn is not a native of southern Utah but was imported to the area around Bryce Canyon by settlers. Found near the Tropic Reservoir, and sometimes wandering into Bryce Canyon National Park, it prefers to live in grassy lands or in bunch grass and sagebrush regions. It is found, naturally, from southern Saskatchewan to California, Arizona, New Mexico, and Texas. It eats grasses and other green plants, including cacti and sagebrush in the more arid areas where grass is not available.

Yellowhead Collard Lizard

Crotaphytus collaris auriceps
With a large head and a total length of up to 14 inches, this denizen of Arches and Canyonlands national parks is easily spotted by the large black and white collar across the back of its neck.

Its color is a brownish yellow (sometimes green in other subspecies of the collard lizard), with blue flashing in the sun. It sometimes has dark bands on the body, and light spots. The mature male has an orange or blue-green throat. The pregnant female has reddish-orange spots and bars on her sides. The hatchlings, which emerge from eggs laid in midsummer, are about 3.5 inches long.

Its range is from eastern Utah and most of Colorado through the central part of Texas and central Arizona. The yellowhead collard lizard lives only in the arid areas of the Southwest, including the upper Colorado and Green River basins, but not on the higher elevations of Bryce Canyon. It likes to live in hilly areas, particularly along limestone ledges. It seeks out crevices for security.

Other members of the collard lizard family are: Chihuahuan, found in southeastern Arizona, southwest New Mexico, west Texas and into Mexico; Western, seen in central Arizona and western New Mexico; and Eastern, a resident of Missouri, Arkansas, and central Texas. All are scrappy creatures that eat insects and other lizards. The collard lizard moves fast, scurrying along on its hind legs, with its body lifted.

PLANTS

Bristlecone Pine
Pinus aristata
This amazing pine tree is one of the oldest living things on earth. Trees more than 4,600 years old are found in groves in eastern California and central Nevada. The bristlecone pine found at both Bryce Canyon and Cedar Breaks are not quite as old, but are very ancient trees indeed, with some at least 2,000 to 3,000 years old. These trees, which were growing when the Egyptian pyramids were constructed, also grow in Colorado and New Mexico.

The bristlecone pine lives in the most inhospitable terrain in the American West—at the top of high, windy, rocky ledges, exposed to summer drought, as well as winter winds and cold temperatures. To survive, the tree has adapted superbly. It has very short needles crowded into small crowns. It has a low, shrubby shape, for protection from the elements. Faced with prolonged drought, it lets some of its branches die in order to keep others alive. That's why you'll see bristlecone trees that appear to be dead. Look closely; you'll find greenery somewhere on the tree's structure.

The needles are blunt and curved, five to a grouping, and crowded into dense masses. The bark of the tree is a whitish gray and smooth, turning to a rusty brown with age and developing scales. The cylindrical cones are 2.5 to 3.5 inches long, dark brown with a purple tinge. The scales are four-sided with a curved bristle at the end.

Ponderosa Pine
Pinus ponderosa
The most commonly seen pine tree in the western United States, the ponderosa pine is also the pine most often cut for commercial purposes.

Its primary habitat is in mountainous areas. It usually develops in pure stands but also is seen as a partner in a mixed coniferous forest. There are ponderosa stands in both

Cedar Breaks National Monument and Bryce Canyon National Park. Its range extends from southern British Columbia to southwestern North Dakota and California, and south as far as Texas and northern Mexico.

It grows at elevations from sea level in the northern regions to 9,000 feet in the south (including this area). It seems to grow best on mountain slopes with elevations from 4,000 to 8,000 feet.

The evergreen needles of the ponderosa pine come three to a bundle and are 5 to 10 inches long. The Arizona Ponderosa variety (found in southeastern Arizona) has five needles to a bundle. The bark is a reddish brown with scaly plates. The twigs are thick and smooth, with a gray-green color. Ponderosa cones can grow to a length of 10 inches. They're egg-shaped and a light-brown color. The cone scales have a long prickle at the end.

The ponderosa pine is quite similar to Jeffrey pine, which grows closer to the Pacific Coast, except for its lighter bark and more prickly cones. David Douglas, a Scottish botanist, identified the tree in 1826, and named it for its heavy wood, the quality that made it prime lumber.

Single-leaf Ash
Fraxinus anomala

Usually found at about the 6,500-foot level, the single-leaf ash is also found at slightly higher elevations on rim plateaus and down into the amphitheaters of Bryce Canyon and Cedar Breaks. It is seen as a small tree or as a shrub, with a rounded crown and stubby, curved branches. It grows to a height of 25 feet and has a trunk diameter of up to 6 inches.

Its habitat is on hillsides or dry canyons, and it seems to thrive in the high desert and in ponderosa pine forests. The conditions on the two plateaus are right for this tree. Its range is from western Colorado to eastern California and east as far as northwestern New Mexico. In California, it grows in elevations as high as 11,000 feet. It also grows in Grand Canyon National Park.

Its leaves are opposite, and compound, with two to three leaflets on each stem that grow to 2 inches long and 2 inches wide. The leaves are almost round, with a short tip at the end. It may have a notch at the base, and may or may not have wavy teeth. The leaves are dark green on top and paler below. Their compound nature is the key to identifying this tree.

The tree's bark is a dark brown and ridged. The twigs are brown, without hair, and have four sides. The flowers are green, without petals, and are clustered on the previous year's twigs in back of the leaves in the spring. It bears fruit in the late summer—a flat key, .75 inches long, with a rounded wing about .125 inches wide.

Greenleaf Manzanita
Arctostaphylos patula
Growing in forest openings across the Colorado Plateau, the manzanita likes well-drained, acidic soil. It is related to the pointleaf manzanita, which also grows in Utah, and to the common manzanita that inhabits mountain slopes in California.

Greenleaf manzanita is distinguished by its thick, nearly oval-shaped bright green leaves, as well as by its shiny and very twisted (almost tortured-looking) red stems. The stems grow from a swollen burl crown.

The greenleaf manzanita is more of a shrub than a tree, growing to a maximum height of 8 feet. Its flowers, about .25 inches long, are found in branched, drooping clusters. The manzanita is a member of the heather family, and the flowers give it away as such. The flowers are waxy and urn-shaped, with pinkish white blossoms with rims tinged in a slightly darker pink.

The greenleaf manzanita likes to grow in open conifer forests, and generally grows early in recently burned or logged areas. Its range includes southern Washington, south and central California, and east to Colorado and Arizona.

The name manzanita means "little apple." Its fruit is a smooth, dark brown berry, treasured by birds and bears, giving it the alternate name of Bearberry. It also provides an important browse for deer.

The greenleaf is one of about 50 species of manzanita found in the southwestern United States and in Mexico. Thirty-six of these species are native to the United States.

Alder-leaf Mountain Mahogany
Cercocarpus montanus
A member of the rose family, this alpine shrub grows from 3 to 10 feet high and has numerous stems that spread out from ground level. The mountain mahogany is no relation to the tropical mahogany tree, which is the real mahogany.

The alder-leaf species grows on dry ridges, including the ridges of Bryce Canyon. Like other plants in the pinyon-juniper zone, it lives a tenuous existence. Its leaves are broad, dark green, slightly serrated, smooth on top and somewhat hairy underneath. The thin bark has a grayish brown color. The shrub has very small pink blossoms that turn into long fruits with spiral tails.

It is another browse for the deer of the region. Native Americans used the bark to make a reddish brown dye.

Like the manzanita, the mountain mahogany is a prime tenant of southwestern chaparral country, growing particularly in the pinyon pine and juniper woodlands. Among the species are the curlleaf mountain mahogany (*ledifolius*) and birchleaf mountain mahogany (*betuloides*).

The curlleaf variety grows on the slopes of the Great Basin and is found in the Bryce area. The birchleaf is found from southwest Oregon to Baja California and Arizona. It is often found living in oak groves. Mountain mahogany are one of the first species following a fire or forest clearing, similar to manzanita.

Utah Juniper

Juniperus osteosperma
Early settlers in the area, including Ebenezer Bryce, used the Utah juniper trunks for fence posts. This tree grows in the most arid conditions one can find in the Southwest, including the sides of the great walls of Bryce Canyon. It not only has provided posts for farmers, it gives birds its cones to eat, although the seeds are not digestible. The tree is propagated largely because the hard seeds flow through the bird's digestive system, softening a little in the process and emerging to fall on the ground and germinate. What synergy!

The short tree has an upright trunk, low, spreading branches, and a rounded crown. It grows to heights of 15 to 40 feet, although at Bruce Canyon it does not reach great heights. The leaves are generally opposite, in four rows. The scale-like twigs are short, yellowish-green, and pointed. The berry-like cones grow to a diameter of 0.625 inches and are light blue, later drying to a brown color. Each cone holds one or two seeds. Juniper berries are flavorful, prized by birds and small mammals.

The Utah juniper is also found in several other states: Nevada, Wyoming, southern California, and New Mexico. It is, in fact, the most common juniper in Arizona, growing on the southern rim of the Grand Canyon and down some of the canyon walls.

In past days, junipers were called cedars, thus Cedar Breaks is named for this tree that grows in the amphitheater.

Scarlet Gilia
Gilia aggregata
Also called skyrocket, this member of the phlox family is one of the prettiest and most dramatic wildflowers found in the ponderosa pine forests of the Bryce Canyon area. These are biennial plants. During the second year, the stem is longer than during the first season, giving it its skyrocket name. The delicate flowers are in loose clusters on a stem with only a few leaves. The medium red-colored flowers are tubular and star-shaped at the ends. The plant is also seen with white, pink, and orange flowers. However, the red color attracts hummingbirds and results in greater numbers being propagated.

If you get close enough to the plant to sniff, you'll detect a decidedly skunk-like odor.

Sego Lily
Calochortus nuttallii
Receiving its name from the Shoshone word, the sego lily was sacred to the Native Americans of the region. They used the bulbs for food, harvesting them with sharpened sticks. Later, Mormon settlers also used the bulbs for food, and the flower became the state flower of Utah.

This striking plant has a flower with three large waxy petals, each bearing crescent-shaped markings of purple with bright yellow hairs on the center of the inner surface. The leaves are like grass with barely four or five leaves to a stalk. You'll find the sego lily in open glades in the fir and spruce forests at Bryce Canyon National Park.

Parry Bellflower
Campanula parryi
One of the most lovely wildflowers seen in the Cedar Breaks and Bryce Canyon area, this bellflower lives on soft, moist mountain meadows and in moist fields alongside sagebrush.

It is a perennial, with a very slender stalk. Leaves at the base of the stalk are oval in shape. The upper leaves, which grow not quite to the height of the flower, are smooth and shiny, with smooth edges. The flower, which resembles a bell, has petals that are blue to purple with purple corolla tubes bearing five lobes. These dramatic flowers are a favorite of photographers visiting the plateau country.

Dwarf Rabbitbrush

Chrysothamnus depressus
This stunted member of the sunflower family, found at Bryce Canyon, has small flower heads that bear tiny yellow flowers. The many heads at the end of the stems—each bearing five flowers—give the plant its dense look. While Navajos used the plant to obtain a yellow dye from its flower heads and a green dye from the stems, the plant is now of little use to man or beast. It is not a food for animals and tends to spread unchecked.

A more common species of rabbit brush is chrysothamnus nauseosus, the rubber rabbit brush, also seen in Bryce Canyon. It, too, has yellow flowers, but grows to a height of 7 feet—unlike the dwarf variety, which grows to a maximum height of 10 inches.

ARCHES NATIONAL PARK

Canyonlands National Park
(801) 259-4351

There are campgrounds in two of the park's three districts. The campground, located northwest of Moab in the Island in the Sky district, has primitive sites (no water, no fee) available on a first-come, first-served basis. The Needles district, southwest of Moab, has a 26-unit campground with a campers' store nearby. For information, call (801) 259-6568. The Maze has backcountry campsites accessible only with a four-wheel-drive vehicle.

Devil's Garden Campground
P.O. Box 907
Moab, UT 84532
(801) 259-8161

The only campground in the park, located at the north end, it has 50 tent and trailer sites, plus two group sites for tents, running water, and flush toilets from spring until fall, when a fee is charged. In winter there are chemical toilets, no water and no fee.

BRIAN HEAD

Brian Head Hotel
223 Hunter Ridge Road
P.O. Box 190008
Brian Head, UT 84719
(801) 677-3000 or 800-468-4898

This large hotel (170 rooms) has many amenities, including a sauna, two outdoor whirlpools, a swimming pool, TV, movies, and kitchens. Non-smoking rooms are available. It also has the Columbine Cafe for breakfast and lunch, the Summit Dining room for fine dining, and a lounge ($ to $$).

Copper Chase Condominium Hotel
150 Ridge Road, P.O. Box 190218
Brian Head, UT 84719
(801) 677-2890 or 800-468-4898

The Copper Chase is one of several facilities in town with condominium units; this one has 65 units of varying sizes, all with kitchens (fully furnished with appliances and utensils), and some with hot tubs. Also available to guests are a covered heated pool, whirlpool, and weight room ($$).

Bryce Canyon National Park
Bryce Canyon Lodge and Cabins
P.O. Box 400
Cedar City, UT 84721
(801) 586-7686

What a wonderful setting for a lodge and cabins, on the rim of the spectacular canyon, at 8,000 feet! The lodge is now a National Historic Landmark and was completely renovated in 1989. There are 4 suites available in the lodge, 106 double rooms in the motel, and 40 cabins—all with gas fireplace and private bath. Facilities also include a restaurant, bar, gift shop, and general store. Activities available here include bus tours, horseback riding, and hiking the many canyon trails. Open late April to mid-October ($$ to $$$+).

Best Western Ruby's Inn
Bryce Canyon, UT 84764
(801) 834-5341 or 800-528-1234

Ruby's is a huge complex with 216 rooms and lots of amenities. Among them are an indoor swimming pool and spa, a dining room with a seasonal buffet and deli, a gas station, and an enormous general store that alone can provide hours of entertainment; it's loaded with minerals, jewelry, and books, as well as other things such as groceries. There are other activities available as well—trail rides, helicopter flights, and chuckwagon dinner rides in the summer; snowmobiling and cross-country skiing in the winter. And best of all, it's located just minutes away from the amazing Bryce Canyon National Park ($ to $$).

Bryce Canyon Pines
Scenic Rte. 12, Box 43
Bryce, UT 84764
(801) 834-5441

Also located minutes away from the national park, this motel has 50 units, some with fireplaces, plus an indoor heated pool, restaurant, cocktail lounge, coffee shop, and laundromat ($).

BRYCE CANYON CAMPING

Bryce Canyon National Park campgrounds are located north of Sunset Point, near the park visitor center. Campsites are available for tents, trailers, and RVs at the North and South campgrounds on a first-come, first-served basis. Reservations are not taken. The length of stay is limited to 14 days per visit, with an annual total of 30 days. The sites have tables and fireplaces, with water and restrooms nearby. There are no hookups, but a coin-operated dump station is located near the North Campground (summer months only). The General Store, in the Sunrise Point area, stocks camping supplies and food. There are showers and a coin laundry at the store.

Bryce Village Resort
(801) 834-5351

Open year-round for RV and trailer camping, with 26 full-service sites plus a dump station, laundry, and showers.

Ruby's Inn Campground and Trailer Park
(801) 834-5301

200 sites (100 hookups for trailers and 100 tent sites). Open from early April until late October, it is located just south of Ruby's Inn, a large motel operation, near the national park. All services are provided including dump station, laundry, campers' store, and nearby horse rentals for Bryce Canyon and national forest trail rides.

CAPITOL REEF NATIONAL PARK

Rim Rock Ranch Motel and Restaurant
Utah Highway 24
Torrey, UT 84775
(801) 425-3843

This handy motel is located outside the west gate of the national park, 8 miles west of the visitor center, near the intersection with State Route 12. It has standard rooms with baths, and a restaurant. The complex includes a campground, see below ($ to $$).

Capitol Reef Inn and Cafe
State Route 24
Torrey, UT 84775
(801) 425-3271

Located 11 miles west of the park visitor center, this modest motel has reasonable rates and a cafe, open daily for breakfast. ($).

Capitol Reef Camping

The national park campground, at the old Fruita town site, has 70 units. Located 1 mile from the park visitor center, it has picnic tables, water, restrooms, grills, and nearby nature trails. There are two primitive campgrounds: in Cathedral Valley and on Cedar Mesa. **Rim Rock Motel** has 45 campsites for RVs and tents.

KANAB

Located just north of the Arizona border, Kanab is about halfway between the North Rim of the Grand Canyon and Bryce Canyon National Park.

Best Western Red Hills Motel
P.O. Box 758
Kanab, UT 84741
(801) 644-2675

A motel with 72 units, it has a heated pool, a whirlpool, cable

TV, and movies. A restaurant is located opposite the facility at 125 West Center Street ($ to $$).

Aikens Lodge

79 W. Center Street
Kanab, UT 84741
(801) 644-2625

A smaller motel with a more modest price tag, among its 25 units are some with two and three bedrooms and some with kitchens. There is also a heated pool ($).

KANAB AREA CAMPING

Coral Pink Sand Dunes State Park

(801) 874-2408

Open all year with 22 pull-through sites and a dump station.

Ponderosa Campground

(801) 586-2401

Smaller, with 10 sites, pit toilets, no showers or fee.

MOAB

Landmark Motel

168 Main Street
Moab, UT 84532
(801) 259-6147

This motel has 36 units (king and queen), laundry facilities, whirlpool and heated swimming pool, cable TV ($ to $$).

Castle Valley Inn

P.O. Box 2602
Moab, UT 84532
(801) 259-6012

This B&B inn has a magnificent setting at 4,500 feet, with 360-degree views of the mountains and the red formations surrounding it. There are 6 double rooms, 4 with private bath, plus 2 cottages with bath, kitchen, and hot tub. A full breakfast is included; picnic lunches and dinners are available ($ to $$).

Pack Creek Ranch

P.O. Box 1270
Moab, UT 84532
(801) 259-5505

An assortment of log cabins is available here, having one to four bedrooms, private baths and kitchens, some with living rooms and fireplaces. Both breakfast and dinner are included in the rates, as is the spectacular scenery of the La Sal Mountains. Trail rides and river rafting are among the outdoor activities available here ($$$ to $$$+).

MOAB CAMPING

There are several camping facilities in the Moab area: **Canyonlands Campark** has

130 sites including some tent sites and many with full hookups (801-259-6848).

Another large facility also open year-round is the **Slickrock Campground**, with about 180 sites (85 with hookups, 30 for tents) plus water, showers, laundry, swimming, and boating (801-259-7660).

There are also campgrounds in Arches National Park and in two sections of Canyonlands National Park.

PANGUITCH

New Western Motel
P.O. Box 73
Panguitch, UT 84759
(801) 676-8876

This motel is part of the Best Western chain and is open all year with 37 units (3 with two bedrooms). It has a coin laundry, heated pool, and winter plug-ins ($).

Marianna Inn Motel
P.O. Box 179
Panguitch, UT 84759
(801) 676-8844

Located at 669 N. Main Street, this inn is open April through October. There are 24 units, some large enough for six to eight people. There is a whirlpool and a nearby family restaurant ($).

PANGUITCH CAMPING

Panguitch Big Fish KOA is the largest in the area, with 80 sites (45 RV and 35 tent), a dump station, laundry, and pool. It's open from April 1 to October 31. (801) 676-2225.

PAROWAN

Swiss Village Inn
P.O. Box 967
Parowan, UT 84761
(801) 477-3391

Swiss decor marks this Best Western motel. It has 28 units, a restaurant, heated pool, and (in winter) an enclosed whirlpool ($).

Jedediah's Inn and Restaurant
625 W. 200 South
Parowan, UT 84761
(801) 477-3326

As the name implies, this motor inn has a restaurant attached, as well as a lounge. There are 40 sleeping units available, with cable TV, movies, and phones. The motel is open year-round ($).

Parowan Camping
(801) 477-3535

Foothills RV Park, open all year, has 79 RV sites with full hookups, as well as 40 tent sites, water, showers, toilets, laundry, and dump station.

Pit Stop Campground

(801) 477-9990

20 RV and 34 tent sites, open year-round.

TROPIC AND ESCALANTE

Bryce Pioneer Village

Highway 12, P.O. Box 119
Tropic, UT 84776
(801) 679-8546 or 800-222-0381

This complex of 29 newer motel rooms and 19 older cabins is located a few miles from Bryce Canyon. There is also a campground, a taco shop, dinners, and entertainment. A restaurant is nearby (**$** to **$$**).

Doug's Place Country Inn

141 N. Main
Tropic, UT 84776
(801) 679-8632 or 800-993-6847

With 28 recently built units, this motel has a restaurant, gas station, and a gift shop (**$** to **$$**).

Fox's Bryce Trails Bed & Breakfast

1001 W. Bryce Way, P.O. Box 87
Tropic, UT 84776
(801) 679-8700

For those who prefer quiet B&B inns, Fox's has five non-smoking rooms, all with private bath, plus a hot tub for soaking those sore joints after hiking the Bryce trails (**$$**).

Prospector Inn and Restaurant

380 W. Main, P.O. Box 296,
Escalante, UT 84726
(801) 826-4653

This motel has 51 units and even offers room service through the adjacent Cowboy Blue Restaurant. The motel provides a continental breakfast and features handicapped access (**$**).

PART 2

Mountains and Valleys

The topography of the Southwest is surprisingly varied. On my first sojourn in this part of the world, I expected nothing but flat, unending desert, but instead was astounded when I saw mountain ranges throughout the region— not only were there mountains, but they were covered by tall pines and spruces. This revelation made me feel more than slightly untutored.

The dichotomy of sky islands rising from the desert is what makes the Southwest so special. And each desert region is different from the others. The Upper and Lower Sonoran regions harbor their own wildlife and plant species, as do the Colorado and Mojave deserts. But each mountain range has its own character due to its volcanic or thrust origins, solid or fractured rock structure, and the variable effects of regional precipitation and temperature change. The Southwest (except for the southernmost tip of the Rockies) has no predominant mountain range. Instead, there are small ranges, each with a distinctive geological character, and each with its special outdoor attractions.

Three of these ranges illustrate the point. The Mule Mountains, surrounding the town of Bisbee in the southeastern corner of Arizona, would be better placed as part of the coast ranges in California. Evergreen oaks are the predominant species here, in a typical chaparral woodland.

Two hundred miles to the northwest are the Superstition Mountains, providing a backdrop for Phoenix and the Valley of the Sun. The peaks and ridges are as hard-edged as the Mule Mountains are soft and rounded. There are few trees on this reddish-brown range.

Farther to the northwest, near Flagstaff, the San Francisco Peaks comprise a range formed by volcanic eruptions over the past 2 million years. At a higher elevation and covered with green forests—pine, spruce, fir, aspen—this range offers visitors recreational opportunities all the way from summer hiking and wildflower viewing to winter skiing.

And between each set of mountains are the valleys of the Southwest. Some are expansive desert landscapes, at a wide range of elevations. Some are river valleys, some cutting (literally) through the desert as underground streams which may or may not rise to the surface for short periods. Other rivers tumble down the mountainsides, gathering water from myriad small creeks, only to disappear into the Great Basin or into the washes of the Sonoran Desert.

This contrast of conifer-clad mountains and dry desert landscape is at its most wondrous in Arizona, where life-giving rivers provide superb riparian habitats for millions of migratory and resident birds, and watering troughs for desert mammals and amphibians. In the foothills and close to rivers, springs, and other water sources, herds of javelina make their nocturnal rounds looking for food, and hungry coyote wander across salt pans and sage-covered wastes.

In this part we visit three superb regions that feature this special relationship between mountains and their adjacent valleys. In northern Arizona, the Verde River and its tributaries wander through majestic red rock uplift formations and down steep mountainsides. Here is where the Colorado Plateau meets the Sonoran Desert.

In Southeastern Arizona, the San Pedro River nurtures the largest single wildlife habitat in the American West, as it winds north from the Mexican border for 200 miles, between low and high mountain ranges, and across the desert. This least-appreciated part of the Southwest is more widely known for its Wild West towns: Tombstone, Benson, Patagonia, and Willcox. But you'll find some of the most stunning wildlife preserves and geological formations in the nation here as well.

The mountains and valleys of northern New Mexico provide a stark contrast, as we visit the Rockies—the Sangre de Cristo range—a land of clear alpine lakes, high snow-clad peaks, and evergreen valleys.

Sedona and the Verde Valley

Descending from the Juniper peaks north of Prescott, the trickling winter waters of Big Chino Wash meander to the Verde Valley, where the wash joins the Verde River to travel more than 100 miles into the Salt River near Phoenix. Creeks add to the flow. As the river increases its pace, it moves through the Verde Canyon and Valley a few miles southwest of Sedona. The northern flanks of the Juniper and Bradshaw mountains are covered with pine forests that almost—but not quite—reach the Verde riverside. The desert intervenes.

The driving trip south from Williams on Highway 89A quickly leads through the striking Oak Creek Canyon, emerging to flat land surrounded by red rock at Sedona, then continuing south for another 20 miles through the wide and ecologically diverse Verde Valley.

In recent years, Sedona has become either an object of derision or a place for spiritual fulfillment, depending upon whether you believe in convergence zones and the New Age enlightenment that comes from placing yourself in the crossroads of earthly and psychic vibrations.

The red rock geology of the Sedona region is impressive enough without sampling the effects of convergence, but the area provides an added lift to the psyche of many metaphysical crusaders. For me, the red cliffs and spires, the wooded creeklands, and the quiet vistas of Sedona are plenty to make it a natural wonder. But that doesn't invalidate the effects that many feel when they travel to the convergence zones on a Jeep tour from Sedona.

The Verde Valley is an area of recent mining history as well as prehistory, reflected in the five-story cliff dwelling known as Montezuma's Castle. Tuzigoot National Monument preserves hilltop pueblos that were occupied from A.D. 1125 and mysteriously abandoned around 1425.

From Clarkdale, the Verde Valley Scenic Railway travels up-river through the Sycamore and Verde canyons, revealing pristine cottonwood-lined ecosystems. The normally placid Verde River is a place for canoeing, fishing, and bird-watching. Here explorers abandon the beaten track and take a trip of discovery on a whole new pathway.

North San Pedro Basin

An astounding half of America's bird species can be found in the riparian areas along the San Pedro River. This productive ecosystem—nurtured by the north-flowing stream—lies along the southeastern Arizona desert from the Mexican border to east of Phoenix, where the San Pedro joins the Gila River. The northern basin is found north of Benson and Willcox, both located on Interstate 10 near Tucson. The river flanks the Winchester and Galiuro mountains for more than 60 miles, winding across the desert past the hamlets of Cascabel, Reddington, and Dudleyville. At frequent points along the river, visitors may stop to observe the abundant wildlife that rest here on the western interior's largest flyway.

From a rustic cattle ranch in the basin, one can venture onto the open range by Jeep, then drive or hike along winding canyon trails to desert overlooks and into the mountain foothills.

And at the Muleshoe Ranch Reserve (mentioned earlier), you can walk during summer months along dry creek beds through the San Pedro watershed and observe more than 160 species of birds as well as many animal species. Or you can relax in this superbly natural setting by soaking in the historic Hooper Hot Spring waters, by sitting in a converted cattle drinking tank, or simply watching the setting sun reflect on the Galiuro hills or the morning mists rise from the forest.

The Conservancy's 7,000 acres are joined by 35,000 acres of BLM lands, linked by the year-round creek that contains the largest collection of desert fishes in Arizona, including seven native species. More than two hundred species of birds can be found here, including raptors (peregrine falcons, black and zone-tailed hawks), yellow-billed cuckoos, and Bell's vireo. At the northern edge of the Galiuro Range is the Nature Conservancy's

Aravaipa Canyon Preserve, set at each end of a 10-mile gorge noted for its desert stream, high cliffs, and abundant wildlife—especially bighorn sheep.

In the basin area, modern cattle ranching is in tune with the demands of nature—reflecting a new consciousness about human coexistence with nature. It's a wonderland for bird-watchers, hikers, desert aficionados, Jeep riders, and those who simply desire to quietly commune with nature.

South San Pedro and Santa Cruz Basins

From the Mexican border to Interstate 10, the San Pedro River flows northward. In the next valley, the Santa Cruz River flows in a southerly direction. These two streams provide the most productive ecosystem for migratory birds in the desert West.

Separating the watersheds are several small mountain ranges: the Whitestones, Santa Rita, Patagonia, and Huachuca mountains. Small and large creeks wind down the sides of the ranges, feeding the rivers and contributing riparian areas that attract hundreds of migratory and resident birds varieties and provide a home for animal species.

This is also a land of history. Long before Spanish explorers arrived in the seventeenth century, this was Apache country. Apache occupied the desert and mountain habitat; the spectacular canyons provided shelter and safety from other tribes. The Spanish established their first communities along the Santa Cruz: Tubac and Tumacacori.

Later, the U.S. cavalry attacked the Apache as settlers from the east pursued their dreams of gold, silver, and copper, and built the towns of Tombstone and Bisbee. Ranchers moved into the area, and the Apache—under Cochise and Geronimo—were hunted and conquered by the army. Douglas, Patagonia, Benson, and Willcox are Old West towns that were established along the wagon roads and stage routes of the nineteenth century.

Today, the study of nature plays a large role in re-defining what is now important in southeastern Arizona, focusing on the richly diverse riparian areas of the two river basins. Several nature preserves harbor the largest collection of wildlife in the state, attracting travelers from across the continent, who find supreme joy in viewing birds, animals, and the incredible variety of plant life in these forested mountains and broad desert valleys.

The San Pedro National Riparian Conservation Area, stretching for 36 miles along the San Pedro River, is a primary destination for birders. The Nature Conservancy's Patagonia/Sonoita Creek Preserve and Ramsey Canyon Preserve are also prime natural areas that welcome visitors.

The Enchanted Circle and Taos

An extraordinary center of art and culture, the town of Taos is the stepping-off point for a remarkable circle tour of the Carson National Forest, which encircles Taos. To the north and east of Taos are the Sangre de Cristo Mountains, the most southerly range of the Rockies. These mountains with their forested valleys offer some of the most spectacular scenery and worthwhile recreational activity in the Southwest, and all are accessed by the route known as The Enchanted Circle.

We will not forget Taos as we travel through this area; it, too, is a natural wonder—influenced by more than 6,000 years of native history and cultural development. Before Columbus set sail for India and found North America instead, the Pueblo people had established the multistoried community of Taos, where they carried on the rituals and daily living passed down from the Anasazi people of the Four Corners region.

These cultural underpinnings eventually made Taos a modern arts center, as Spanish, Mexican, and American settlers came here to live and then to draw and paint this wonderful scenery. As art museums were built, more artists arrived, until Taos became the impressive cultural shrine it is today.

Northeast of Taos, the Wheeler Peak Wilderness covers the slopes and peak of New Mexico's highest mountain. On the trails leading through the wilderness area, past alpine lakes shimmering in the summer sun, you're likely to see bears, Roosevelt elk, bighorn sheep, and hundreds of bird varieties.

The Enchanted Circle route winds around Mt. Wheeler through forested valleys, past deep canyons, and through narrow mountain passes to rustic resort towns and fishing lakes and rivers. Ghost towns lie abandoned in the forests, the debris of a mining frenzy that peaked near the end of the 1800s.

This route offers the perfect vacation opportunity for those wanting to combine outdoor adventure with exploration of the arts. In Taos and around the Enchanted Circle, you'll find notable art museums, galleries, and artistic shrines such as the former home of D. H. Lawrence, the Millicent Rogers Museum of Southwestern Art, and the Taos Pueblo—still standing and in daily use after more than 800 years.

Sedona and
the Verde Valley

When T. C. Schnebly and his young wife moved to a rustic homestead in Oak Creek Canyon in 1902, the area's spectacular red rock scenery was known only to a few white farmers (the first family had arrived in 1876) and the small band of Yavapai Apache who considered the area sacred. Apache rock paintings followed much earlier rock art created by the Sinagua Indians, who lived in the area for several hundred years, dating to approximately A.D. 1150.

The Schneblys arrived in the area to find an unspoiled scene of dramatic red cliffs, towering buttes, and a deep, warm canyon that harbored amazingly lush vegetation. The combination of a temperate northern Arizona climate and a sheltered creek bed made it possible for plants and animals to thrive, and for farmers to produce a wide variety of fruits and vegetables. These settlers were not the first gardeners in Oak Creek Canyon. Apache had raised crops in the mid-canyon area now known as Indian Gardens for several hundred years.

When twenty farms hugged the banks of Oak Creek in the first decade of the 1900s, Schnebly petitioned for a community post office. He named the community after his wife, whose first name was Sedona. Some of the farms grew produce, including apples and vegetables, that were sold to the consuming market in Flagstaff, 30 miles to the north. In those early days the available roads linking the Verde Valley and Flagstaff took 4 days to navigate. Theodore Schnebly and his neighbors decided to build a shorter route that crossed the towering butte landscape northeast of the creek. This rough 12-mile track, Schnebly Hill Road, cut the trip to Flagstaff in half, and today provides an excellent scenic drive—a bit rough, but with wonderfully beautiful sights.

Over the past hundred years, the farms on the creek-side lands have been replaced by resorts and state and federal recreation areas. Only in recent years—since the 1950s—has Sedona become a major destination for travelers, but it has made up for the late start. The red rock scenery and the mystery surrounding this amazing landscape now attract hundreds of thousands of visitors each year.

The city has a full complement of accommodations, from standard motels to bed-and-breakfast inns to very fancy resorts. Sedona is probably the best place to eat in Arizona, having more fine restaurants than its population should warrant. The influence of tourism on this relatively new community has spawned several boutique shopping centers, including the superb Tlaquepaque, located next to Oak Creek at the Highway 179 junction, as well as many restaurants, bakeries, and New Age shops.

Sedona Schnebly could not have imagined the developments that have occurred in her namesake community since the mid-1950s. The red rock and a spiritual renaissance have led to its current status as the fastest-growing destination for travelers in Arizona, and one of the most treasured.

Getting There

Sedona—as the raven flies—is about 20 miles south of Flagstaff and Interstate 40, although it takes a few additional miles to get there. It is 119 miles northwest of Phoenix.

The most popular and definitely the most scenic route is via Alternate State Route 89A, which you may catch at the south edge of Flagstaff, from U.S. 180 south of Northern Arizona University, or by taking I-17 south and exiting at the airport turnoff. Alternate 89 crosses the last few southerly miles of the Kaibab Plateau, through thick ponderosa pine forest, before descending through a series of switchbacks into Oak Creek Canyon. The road parallels the creek to Sedona, passing rustic resorts and several recreation areas including Slide Rock State Park.

From Phoenix, take I-17 north to the Sedona exit (298) and drive along State Route 179 to the town. This route also offers a glimpse of the area's scenic attractions, with a display of towering buttes in the last two miles of the drive. Those who eschew interstate driving may wish to depart from Phoenix on U.S. Highways 60 and 89, passing through Wickenburg and Prescott and entering the Verde Valley from the south on Alternate State Route 89.

Sedona Geology

Several geological processes have been at work in the region over the past 1.5 billion years, and possibly much longer. The layering of rock is much the same as that comprising the walls of the Grand Canyon, 80 miles to the north. The exception in the Sedona area is the Schnebly Hill Formation, a unique, 900-foot-thick layer of red and pink sandstone, limestone, and mudstone that is exposed only here at the edge of the Mogollon Rim—the southern edge of the vast Colorado Plateau.

The layering of the plateau developed as oceans came and disappeared, followed by deserts which accumulated dunes that became thick layers of sandstone. Creeks and rivers created fresh-water floodplains. The ocean returned to create another layer of bottomland, succeeded by another desert. This process continues today. Above the Schnebly Hill Formation is a layer of white or buff-colored sandstone, and, in some places, a recently deposited cap of basalt lava. These are the most recent additions to the geological layer cake.

A second major development occurred about 65 million years ago, when a gigantic uplift began that raised the entire Colorado Plateau—including the Kaibab Plateau—to about 7,000 feet above sea level, changing the region forever.

What is most remarkable about this uplifting is that the entire Colorado Plateau—some 130,000 square miles spread over parts of four states—rose evenly, with the rock layers intact, stretching in unbroken lines across the entire plateau.

Thirty million years ago—a mere blink of an eye in geological time—there was considerable volcanic activity in the area, particularly near Flagstaff, where the San Francisco Peaks were created during the Cenozoic Era. At the head of Oak Creek Canyon, the lava flow can be seen capping the rim of the gorge. Sedona's airport is built on an old lava bed.

To the south of the plateau and the Mogollon Rim lies the Verde Valley, carved from the Supai Formation by the Verde River and its several tributaries, including Oak Creek. Because of the presence of the plateau and the lower river valley, the changes in geology and the variety in ecosystems are as wide-ranging as in any location in the American Southwest.

Plant and Animal Life

Within a few miles, the landscape changes from the ponderosa pine forest of the Mogollon Rim to a lower pygmy forest comprising pinyon pine, Utah juniper, and the rare Arizona cypress (2,500 feet below the rim). Mixed in the pygmy forest, and in the riparian habitats along the creeks, are live (evergreen) oaks. The creek nurtures the predominant cottonwood/sycamore woodland.

Because of the vast changes in ecosystems, particularly noticeable along the plateau and in Oak Creek Canyon, wildlife ranges from desert to forest species, from herds of javelina and the ring-tailed cat to the mountain lion and black bear. Birds are plentiful, including the ever-present ravens and turkey vultures that ride the valley thermals, a wide variety of other raptors including eagles, hawks, and falcons, plus water-loving birds including kingfishers and herons. South of Sedona, the Verde River wanders through the valley, providing riparian habitat in a typical cottonwood/willow environment for more than 200 species of birds, as well as fish and riverside animals. In the high desert valley, sandpipers skitter along the gravely surface, snakes hunt for rodents to devour, and lizards bask in the sun.

Those Vortices and Sedona's "New Age"

The curious arrive by the thousands, and many leave Sedona convinced that something special is happening in the land of red rock enchantment. And that special something has more to do with what's underground than with the red rock you can see above ground. Whatever the phenomenon may be—real magic or (as some believe) a craftily designed tourist lure— people are convinced that energy emanates from the Sedona landscape.

Simply put, a vortex (and there are said to be many in the area) is an energy field that comes to the earth's surface, where those who are sufficiently sensitive can feel it. Some vortices (many Sedonans say vortexes) are magnetic; some are electrical. These energy points, when identified and tapped into, are said to:

- have a calming effect.
- create bursts of energy in the person affected.
- stimulate the mind into deep thought and comprehension.
- create spiritual awareness.

Actually, Native Americans knew about energy centers, and regarded them as sacred ground. This concept is in tune with the Native American philosophy that the land and everything else is spirit. The New Age movement picked up the idea and propelled Sedona into its position as social center of today's New Age consciousness. Visiting The Worm bookstore (across the street from the town visitor center) or touring the Sedona area by Jeep will give you insight into the importance of things New Age in Sedona's business, cultural, and recreational environments.

There is probably no finer collection of books on the New Age or its music, including CDs by local Sedona New Age groups, than you can find in The Worm. Jeep tours will take you to the important vortices, some of which are located in remote locations atop huge slabs of rock.

I have been told, "If you really want to feel it, you will feel it." I'm still trying. But I have benefitted from all this through my increased focus on the spiritual nature of the outdoors (the planet, if you will) and outdoor adventure. That alone makes the vortices and the attendant New Ageism that permeates the Sedona scene worthwhile.

Red Rock Adventure

There are three ways to enjoy the Sedona area's red rock architecture: by driving your own car to tour the three major areas where eroded buttes and canyons are found, by hiking several notable trails on foot, or by taking a Jeep ride.

All the rocky wonders are located within a circular area within a five-mile radius of the city of Sedona. Some rock features can be fully appreciated from the main roads; others require driving a back road or hiking up to 2 or 3 miles. It is impossible to breeze through Sedona on a day trip and wind up savoring a sizable portion of the red rock atmospherics. An overnight stay and some advance planning is a must.

Driving Tours

Northeast Oak Creek Canyon via Alternate 89　The drive from the main Sedona crossroads (Highway 179 and Alternate 89) leads beside the creek, through a shopping and restaurant district, then past more bucolic scenes. The rock walls of the canyon show the construction of the Mogollon Rim's southern section with its Grand Canyon layers, plus the Schnebly Hill Formation and the Basalt cap. You can glimpse several major raised formations to the east, including Elephant Rock. The canyon is now a prime recreation destination along most of its length, including Slide Rock State Park, until Alternate 89 begins its switchback climb through the Coconino National Forest approaching Flagstaff.

South Oak Creek Canyon via Highway 179　You can see some of Sedona's finest red rock scenery in this sector. Drive south from the "Y" intersection along Highway 179 (the route to Phoenix). There are also excellent views of the formations to the east, featuring Submarine Rock, from Highland Drive. Continue for a short distance along Highway 179 and turn onto Chapel Road, where the prominent rock formation is the Two Nuns. A major man-made attraction is the Chapel of the Holy

Cross, a small sanctuary built with the assistance of Frank Lloyd Wright.

Marguerite Brunswig Staude, a Sedona sculptor and traveler, claimed a vision of a cross imposed on New York's Empire State Building led to her desire to build a church in cruciform shape among the red rocks of her home town. She talked about her dream to the noted architect, which led to his sharing his plans for an unbuilt cathedral, designed for the hills above Budapest before World War II intervened. The plans were scaled down to fit the Sedona landscape, and the Chapel of the Holy Cross was built on a 250-foot-high rock and opened to the public in 1956. Not only a beautiful structure in perfect tune with the twin pinnacles upon which it sits, the Chapel also offers a prime view of several major red rock formations including Bell Rock, Courthouse Butte, and Cathedral Rock. The chapel is open daily from 9 A.M. to 5 P.M.

West via Alternate 89 and Red Rock Loop Road   West Sedona, a sprawling, newer section of the city, is accessed by Alternate Highway 89 as you drive west toward Cottonwood and Prescott. After passing a long string of shopping plazas, motels, and restaurants, the road emerges from the urban area into natural terrain. Just west of Sedona's edge (beyond Foothills Drive) is the northern end of a scenic loop, named Upper Red Rock Loop Road. You may drive from this end, but I suggest you continue for another mile west on Alternate 89, then turn south at Lower Red Rock Loop Road. It is paved as far as Red Rock State Park, which straddles Oak Creek. This relatively new and fascinating little park contains a nature interpretation center, trails that lead through the upper area and down to the creek, plus picnic areas. The visitor center has information on the park ecology and wildlife.

The loop road continues, in an unpaved state, leading north from the park road. You'll catch glimpses of Cathedral Rock and other formations from the loop and the park. A spur off the main loop road, a mile northeast of the park road, leads to but does not cross the creek. This is the closest location from which to view Cathedral Rock from this far west. After another mile, the loop road reaches the highway.

Red Rock Scenery via Dry Creek Road   Although the major, continuous group of seven formations to the north of Sedona may be seen from the city center, this group of red rocks should be viewed from a closer perspective. Dry Creek Road offers an approach to the five most westerly formations. To get there, drive west from Sedona along Alternate 89, not quite as far as the Lower Red Rock Loop Road. Turn north onto Dry Creek Road and drive to Boynton Pass Road. Turn left and drive to Boynton Canyon Road. Here you can choose to turn left to obtain fine views of Cockscomb, Chimney Rock, and Capitol Butte (which does indeed bear resemblance to the U.S. Capitol).

Taking the right (northeast) turn on Boynton Canyon Road will take you to the Enchantment Resort, which is located in the canyon, as well as to great views of Sugar Loaf and Coffee Pot Rock. Farther to the northeast are Mt. Wilson and Steamboat Rock, which can be seen best from Van Deren Road or Jordan Road, both of which run off Alternate 89 just north of the "Y" intersection in town.

Schnebly Hill Scenic Drive   This is the road T. C. Schnebly and his farming neighbors carved out of red rock country in order to get their fruit and vegetables to market in Flagstaff. It runs between Highway 179, from just across Oak Creek in downtown Sedona, to Interstate 17, 15 miles south of Flagstaff at exit 320.

This 12-mile route offers some of the most spectacular rock scenes in the region, including formations such as Snoopy Rock, where the famous pooch appears to be lying on his doghouse, facing the sky. Shortly after leaving the highway (about a mile), you will see Schnebly Road winding up the grade ahead of you from an area known as Bear Wallow. Another mile along the way, you can see two striking formations—The Bench and The Thumb. At about mile four, the vegetative systems change. Manzanita, interspersed with other transitional zone plants such as century plant and yucca, takes over.

Merry-Go-Round Rock is visible at mile five, just before the newer part of the road veers off from the original road, which is now a spur. Lava flows can be seen here and at the vista point just beyond mile six. As the road climbs, it leaves the manzanita scrub woodland behind, and the pine forest begins to appear.

After the road reaches the plateau—at mile ten—you'll see a "ghost" ranch, the deteriorating remains of Foxboro, developed by the Fox family as a boys school and dude ranch in the late 1920s. The main lodge, complete with dry swimming pool and a stone garage, is easily seen from the road. The I-17 junction is 2 miles down the road.

While the modern settlement at Sedona is nondescript, this wonderful drive offers not only spectacular scenery—including the stupendous view of Oak Creek Canyon from the vista point—but also provides a glimpse into the early pioneer homestead at Foxboro, now crumbling but still evocative of those earlier days in red rock country. Foxboro was operated as a ranch school for more than three decades.

Hiking Trails

Vultee Arch/Sterling Canyon Trail   This is an easy walk of between 2 and 3 hours (round-trip), with some climbing to about 400 feet above the trailhead. To reach the trailhead, drive from the "Y" in downtown Sedona, west on Alternate 89 toward Jerome, then turn north (right) onto Dry Creek Road. Continue for almost 2 miles, then turn east (right) onto Forest Road 152, where you'll see a sign at the junction. The forest road is narrow and often rough but is suitable for a normal car driven with care. Drive for 4.3 miles to the end of the road and park on the flat, sandy area. The signed trailhead is to the east.

The canyon floor lies at 4,800 feet, with the cliffs rising almost 2,000 feet above it. The trail heads through beautiful, shaded Sterling Canyon, which drains into Dry Creek after it runs through ponderosa pine groves with abundant wildlife, especially resident songbirds that keep you company along the route.

The trail takes you under the pines, crossing the dry creek bed on several occasions, for 2 miles to the eastern end of the canyon. There a sandstone bench cries out to be climbed. From the bench you can see the magnificent 40-foot span of a natural arch named to commemorate Gerald Vultee, a well-known aircraft designer whose plane crashed near here in 1938. Both he and his wife, who was a passenger, were killed. You may spot the bronze commemorative plaque on a sandstone cliff face near the arch.

This hike through a verdant canyon points out the full effect of a perennial water supply in what otherwise would be an arid and lifeless desert gorge. The creek bed may be dry but there is water down there, sliding under the rocks and nurturing the plants, making it possible for wildlife to find an abode in unlikely territory.

Boynton Canyon Trail   In the same general area, accessed by the same Dry Creek Road, Boynton Canyon Trail offers a beautiful hike. On a flat, easy surface beside the Enchantment Resort, the trail takes you into a sandstone canyon with unusual trees on the floor and a fir forest at the upper levels.

To reach the trailhead, drive along Dry Creek Road from Alternate 89. Turn left at the first intersection onto Boynton Pass Road, then right onto Boynton Canyon Road. The total drive from the highway is 4.6 miles. At that point you'll find a parking area just before the gate to the resort and a trailhead sign.

Boynton Canyon is historically important. Sinagua Indians occupied the gorge at one time, building cliff dwellings partway up the canyon walls. The canyon is also considered (as it was by the Sinaguan residents) to be among the most powerful of the local energy vortices.

The round-trip covers about 6 miles and takes from 2 to 4 hours, depending on your pace and interests. The trail leads past the resort, offering fine views in all directions. Past the mouth of the canyon as the trail ascends beyond the 4,600-foot elevation, the alligator bark juniper—a rare and ancient tree—can be seen. It grows in few other locations and has a lifespan as long as 20 centuries.

The trail climbs to 4,720 feet, where it enters a Douglas fir forest. At this higher level you can easily see the prehistoric cliff dwellings located under overhangs in the north and east rock wall faces.

Fay Canyon Arch Trail   In the same area as the Boynton Canyon Trail, Dry Creek Road is also used to access this easy trail. Follow the same route onto Boynton Pass Road, which becomes a dirt road after the Boynton Canyon Junction. A parking area with a signed trailhead lies to the north of the road.

This trail can be walked in an hour—if you don't stop to observe the world around you—or longer. It goes for 1.5 miles, climbing to the end of the short canyon. Transition zone vegetation includes juniper, manzanita, and western soapberry. Along the way (in the first part of the hike), you'll see the ruin of a cliff dwelling and you may see a natural arch next to the ruin on the northeast side of the canyon. You can achieve a better view by walking on a side trail to the arch. A rock cairn marks the short but steep arch trail. The three trails in this immediate area off Dry Creek Road, filled with views of marvelous rock formations with varied canyon vegetation and historical significance, can easily absorb you for a full day.

Snoopy Rock Trail   The beloved beagle lying on his doghouse is preserved in sandstone just off Schnebly Hill Road. The trail close to town offers views of several other formations along its route before leading around Snoopy Rock. To reach the trailhead, take Schnebly Hill Road from the Highway 179 intersection, and drive a short distance, just past where the gravel begins. A small cairn near a dead tree marks the start of the trail. An early panorama, to the north, exhibits (from left to right) Chimney Rock, Capitol Butte, Coffeepot Rock, Brin's Mesa, Church Rock, and The Fin. Steamboat Rock is at the extreme right end of this impressive display.

The trail enters a large wash where you can see rock cairns that mark the ongoing trail that ascends from the wash. The trail crosses several additional washes and a red-colored plateau that offers a view of Cathedral Rock and the length of the Verde Valley. At this point Snoopy appears. The trail winds around Snoopy Rock, passing the canine's erect feet. The Snoopy circle route takes a left fork, then a second left fork, which leads to an area of slick rock. Up the hill are several small cairns to the left, followed by a pine tree with slabs of rock leaning against its base. A winding trail climbs to the top of the rock, offering fine views of the city and surrounding landscape.

Marg's Draw Trail   This short trail leads to the base of Munds Mountain, where several other trails follow the base of the cliffs. This trail offers a fine view of Snoopy from a lower perspective.

Drive south from the "Y" on Highway 179, turn left (east on Sombart Lane), and drive to its end. The trailhead is to the east where you'll see an opening in the fence. The trail (1 to 2 hours of hiking, round-trip) climbs up a hill and gradually rises to Marg's Draw at the base of the mountain. Varied vegetation includes pinyon/juniper and manzanita woodland, as well as a desert environment with yucca, cacti, and agave. Several side trails lead along the cliff base. This is also an important vortex area, so you may come across stone circles placed here to identify suggested energy points.

JEEP TOURS AND RENTALS

You may rent a four-wheel-drive vehicle, or hire a guide with a vehicle to take you into the depths and up to the heights of red rock country. Each tour company has its own focus and specialized tours; some will prepare a custom tour to match your interests. Four of the best are:

Pink Jeep Tours
204 N. Highway 89A/P.O. Box 1447
Sedona, AZ 86339
(520) 282-5000 or 800-8-SEDONA

This popular tour company provides a range of short and long Jeep tours 7 days a week.

Sedona Red Rock Jeep Tours
270 N. Highway 89A/P.O. Box 10305
Sedona, AZ 86339
(520) 282-6826 or 800-848-7728

This tour company specializes in trips on Sedona's only private Jeep trail, with a cowboy and ranch focus.

Earth Wisdom Tours
293 N. Highway 89A
Sedona, AZ 86336
(520) 282-4714

These tours are promoted as "more than ordinary tours . . . these are journeys." Connecting visitors with the Sedona vortices and exploring natural and historic sites are this tour firm's specialties. Local scenic and educational day time and evening tours (including hikes) range from 1.5 hours to 4 hours, and their special Hopi Mesa tour lasts 10 hours.

Sedona Photo Tours
252 N. Highway 89A/P.O. Box 1650
Sedona, AZ 86336
(520) 282-4320 or 800-9-SEDONA

This is the place to book your touring photo shoot. You'll roam the red rock outback via Jeep in the company of professional photographers.

Jeeps may be rented from the following firms:

Canyon Jeep Rentals
4548 N. Highway 89A/P.O. Box 1100
Sedona, AZ 86336
(520) 282-6061 or 800-224-2229

Desert Jeep Rentals
6626 Highway 179/40 Spur Ct.
Sedona, AZ 86351
(520) 284-1099

Sedona Jeep Rentals
Sedona Airport/P.O. Box 902
Sedona, AZ 86339
(520) 282-2227

Nearby Attractions

OAK CREEK CANYON

In its short run (only 16 miles) Oak Creek creates a lush environment that offers almost everything for those who appreciate nature. The canyon is a very busy place. Back in the early days of the twentieth century, the canyon was home to twenty farm families.

The farms have disappeared and, in their place, are shops and restaurants (at the extreme south end, in Sedona), resort operations (situated along the creek), state parks, forest campgrounds, and several marvelous hiking trails that follow along the creek, then lead up to the high ground on each side.

It is a fine bird-watching place, especially along the West Fork toward the northern end of the canyon. The summers are cool and green. Autumn brings bright leaf displays. Spring and early summer feature wildflowers and marvelous displays of ferns. Several spring waterfalls appear as the snow above melts and cascades to the canyon floor. Here are the highlights, starting from Uptown Sedona and going north:

The Gorge at Midgeley Bridge   This particularly charming scene, with castellated cliffs, lies 1 mile north of the Sedona "Y." Three trails are accessed from the roadside parking area south of the bridge. The Wilson Canyon Trail (less than a mile) is an easy walk along a wash. Wilson Mountain Trail begins behind the historical marker. It climbs 2,300 feet, a walk of 5.6 miles. Steamboat Rock Trail veers off Wilson Mountain Trail and follows an old service road.

Grasshopper Point Park   This day-use park (Forest Service) has the first of several swimming holes. The creek at Grasshopper Point has variable water levels, and it's advisable to wear shoes in the creek. It's open (summer) from 9 A.M. to 8 P.M. Allen's Bend Trail (from the north end of the parking area) leads along the creek.

Casner Canyon Trail   This path begins beside the road, 2.7 miles from the "Y." Ford the creek and climb 1,400 feet in 2 miles for fine views.

Indian Gardens   A historical marker tells the story of the early Apache farmers in the canyon. This area is particularly scenic when fall foliage is at its brightest (mid-October). A gas station and store are located across the road.

West Fork Trail   For ambitious hikers, nature lovers, bird-watchers, and rock fanciers, this is one of the most rewarding trails in the Southwest. The trailhead is located 10.3 miles from the "Y." After an easy first 3 miles, the trail crosses the stream several times. Camping is available after 6 miles, and the trail climbs past swimming pools and fine views for a total distance of 17 miles, a 1,600-foot climb to the rim.

SLIDE ROCK STATE PARK

Located 7 miles north of Sedona, the park is the site of the 1910 Pendley Homestead, one of the first canyon farms. Frank Pendley's irrigation ditch is still in use. Famous Slide Rock, located in the adjoining Coconino National Forest, is one of the most popular family attractions in the state. A picnic area is set by the old Pendley orchard. People slide down the watery rock chute and sun on the nearby sandstone ledges. The park opens at 8 A.M. and closes at 7 P.M., 6 P.M. or 5 P.M., depending on the season.

PICNIC AREAS

Two picnic parks are located along the highway. Encinoso, the first, is almost a mile north of Indian Gardens. From this area, the North Mt. Wilson Trail climbs 1,700 feet through a side-canyon, ending at the main Mt. Wilson Trail. Halfway Picnic Area is just north of Slide Rock State Park.

The Verde Valley

Spread over 1,200 square miles, the Verde Valley sits just south of Sedona, nestled between the cliffs of the Colorado Plateau (to the northeast), and a short range of mountains—called the Central Highlands—to the west, with the higher Juniper and Bradshaw ranges farther west and southwest. The major town in the valley is Cottonwood.

The town of Jerome, which clings to the side of Mingus Mountain, has been here longer than any of the more modern communities. This former copper-mining center is now an amazing little vertical town of shops, cafes, antique shops, galleries, and saloons (see page 136). A few miles northeast of Cottonwood is the historic smelter town of Clarkdale, founded in 1900 to process the copper from Jerome. Clarkdale is now the site of the Verde Canyon Scenic Railroad depot.

NATIVE AMERICAN HABITATION AND WHITE SETTLEMENT

The valley was occupied by successive groups of Native Americans—prehistoric and historic—including the Hohokam, Maricopa, Pima, Yavapai (also called Yavapai-Apache), and the Sinagua (builders of Montezuma Castle, Tuzigoot, and many cliff dwellings and pueblos). Today, there is a small Yavapai reservation near Camp Verde. The Maricopa and Pima have moved to reservations near Phoenix. Native American life was changed forever by the arrival of white fur trappers in 1826. Three years later another fur party—including Kit Carson, barely out of his teens—traveled through the valley. Farmers settled the valley, taking advantage of the water. By 1865, Fort Lincoln and Fort McDowell were built as Indian forts. In 1870, Fort Lincoln was moved downriver and named Fort Verde. It is now preserved as Camp Verde. In 1875, the Yavapai—about 1,500 men, women, and children—were force-marched to Globe, east of Phoenix. The final battle was fought on the plateau, east of the valley, in 1881.

VERDE RIVER

Flowing across what was (several times) ocean floor, the Verde River slowly cuts its way through the layers of sandstone, basalt, and mostly limestone as it meanders through this long valley before bisecting the Central Highlands and flowing into the Salt River near Phoenix. The river and its creeks harbor amazing riparian ecosystems.

The river begins in high country and flows east until it reaches the top of the Verde Valley. It then turns slowly, running southeast, and finally heads south after leaving Camp Verde. The Verde drains a watershed of more than 6,600 square miles. Its tributaries, including Sycamore, Oak, Fossil, and Beaver creeks, have created dramatic canyons. Once these streams begin to cross the valley floor, they lose their energy and flow quietly across the high plain, with a few exceptions such as Verde Falls, a short area of white water between Beasley and Childs.

The Verde is an excellent canoeing river, especially for novice and semi-skilled recreational canoeists and those who enjoy leisurely trips while viewing wildlife and riverside habitats. Except during peak winter flows, the whole river is Class 1 or Class 2, with diversion dams along the route that require portage. Bass is the primary fish in the river. The logical starting point for a trip through the Verde Valley is at Perkinsville, north of Jerome, where Forest Road 318 crosses the river. Even if you're not a canoeist, this route from Jerome is among the most scenic drives in the state, well worth taking for the scenery alone. The road continues north to Williams.

DEAD HORSE RANCH STATE PARK

This park lies along the Verde River, north of Cottonwood and south of Clarkdale, via State Highway 260. With campgrounds, fishing in the river and lagoons, picnic areas, hiking and horse trails, this is one of the most complete parks in central Arizona. The riparian habitat, one of the several prime wildlife areas on the Verde River, is a favorite of bird-watchers, who come here to see the more than one hundred bird species, and of people who enjoy the 350 native plant species that populate the park.

Because the park fronts the river, visitors have the chance to experience riparian and desert habitats. Resident birds range from black- and red-tail hawks, to great blue and green herons, belted kingfishers, sandpipers, snipes, and many others.

There are 45 campsites in the general camping area, with tables, grills, and restrooms. Park trails begin at the picnic area, near the river. The 4-acre lagoon is stocked with catfish, bass, and panfish, and trout have been stocked during winter months. A state fishing license is required.

SYCAMORE CANYON WILDERNESS

Located at the end of Sycamore Canyon Road near Tuzigoot National Monument, this extraordinarily beautiful and rugged canyon is another great riparian habitat. However, Parson's Trail, a 4-mile hike through the canyon, is relatively easy. After an early ascent of 200 feet, then a fairly level walk, it crosses the creek twice. The track is rougher for the last half of the walk. There are equestrian and backpacking trails in addition to Parson's Trail. To reach the canyon floor, find the trailhead (Trail #63) at the parking lot and hike down the slope. You'll find a bubbling spring and fine scenery. Longer trails explore the 21-mile-long canyon and the adjacent wilderness area. Information and advice is available from the Forest Service rangers in Sedona.

JEROME AND MINGUS MOUNTAIN

Mingus Mountain is one of the small mountains framing the Central Highlands of Arizona. Cleopatra Hill—part of the mountain—is the site of perhaps the most precariously located town in America. Jerome was a typical turn-of-the-century mining town—rowdy, bawdy, hard-drinking, dirty, and altogether charming. It still is.

Jerome now exists as a tourist town, attracting visitors to its unique shops, cafes, bed-and-breakfast establishments, and Jerome National Historic Park, where the hilltop home of mining magnate James S. Douglas is preserved. Many of the mansion's rooms are restored and filled with period furnishings. The tour includes a short movie that provides a capsule history of the town, displays of minerals and mining memorabilia, and (on the upper floor of the building) a scale model of Jerome mineshafts. The building is open daily from 8 A.M. to 5 P.M., with a small fee charged. There is a privately operated mining museum on Forest Road 318, a route built on copper mine tailings. Also on this road is the old United Verde Mine, which has a 3,000-foot shaft.

Over the crest of the mountain above Jerome, the Forest Service operates the Mingus Mountain Recreation Area, containing campgrounds, hiking trails, and scenic viewpoints. To get there, drive to the crest on Highway 89A. There is a campground beside the highway where Forest Road 104 leads to the left. This dirt road runs through the national forest to an overlook with another campground area. The trailhead for both the Mingus Mountain and Mingus Rim trails is found here. To hike the rim trail, follow the signs for Trail 106 for 2 miles; turn left onto Trail 105 and walk 1.3 miles to the top of Mingus Mountain. Follow the road 0.5 miles back to the campground and your car. Over the 4 miles of the walk, the elevation changes 700 feet. Mingus Mountain Trail follows Trail 106 for 2.5 miles, ending at Allen Springs Road. This walk has an elevation change of 1,000 feet.

MONTEZUMA CASTLE, MONTEZUMA WELL, AND TUZIGOOT

The three national monuments in the Verde Valley preserve the ruins of two prehistoric Indian cultures: the Hohokam and Sinagua. The Hohokam, ancestors of the Pima, were farmers who grew crops of corn, beans, cotton, and squash. They lived in small, terraced, one-room houses made of poles and mud. The remains of a small community is found at Montezuma Well, near the main site of Montezuma National Monument, close to a limestone sink that is fed by springs. The springs provided irrigation water for the farming community. The site is off I-17, northeast of Camp Verde.

The two national monuments contain Sinagua ruins. Montezuma Castle—also northeast of Verde, just off I-17—is the remains of a twenty-room communal cliff dwelling built on Beaver Creek in the twelfth century. Nearby is a crumbled mass that was once a six-story apartment building with forty-five rooms.

Tuzigoot National Monument—near Clarkdale, off State Route 279—is what is left of a Sinagua dwelling built between 1125 and 1400. It crowns a high ridge, one of several methods of ensuring security against intruders. Originally two stories high, it held as many as two hundred residents in the 1200s. The complex has few exterior entrances, but instead features ladders for gaining access to apartments—a security feature retained by the New Mexico Pueblo people, and used today at Taos Pueblo.

Montezuma Castle and Tuzigoot have visitor centers, and all three sites have walking trails around the ruins. A Yavapai Apache Visitor Activity Center, with native exhibits, is located at Montezuma Castle.

CAMP VERDE

This Verde Valley community began life as an Indian fort. The major attraction in this riverside town is Fort Verde, the preserved and restored U.S. Army cavalry fort. All buildings are originals. The Museum and the Administration Building hold displays on life in this cavalry fort and the life of settler families in the Verde Valley. Three adobe homes have been fully restored. Fort Verde Days, a celebration held in the restored fort and in Camp Verde during the second weekend of October, features barbecues, a military ball, parade, food, horse events, and an art show.

Four recreation sites near Camp Verde offer access to riparian habitats and good canoeing water, as well as picnicking.

Verde River Bridge River Access Area   On State Highway 260, 1.1 miles from downtown Camp Verde. Accessed at the east end of the bridge, it is a good spot for picnicking and fishing. The distance downstream from this point to Beasley Flats is 10 miles. Just beyond the river access area is a ranger station for the Prescott National Forest.

Beasley Flats   Take a side trip from the town of Camp Verde to reach this area. Drive along Highway 260 through Camp Verde to Salt Mine Road (Forest Road 574). Drive along Salt Mine Road and turn left on Forest Road 334. Drive to the Verde River. Fish at Beasley Flats include bass, catfish, trout, and carp. The recreation area has shady ramadas for picnicking, toilets, and boat access. If you have started a downstream canoe or boat trip in Camp Verde, this is the best place to take your craft out of the water to avoid the dangerous water to the south.

Clear Creek Campground This area offers 18 camp sites with grills, water and toilets, in a lovely setting under a line of cottonwoods beside Clear Creek. Beyond the developed campground are primitive campsites, for tenters.

Beaver Creek Campground This is located close to Montezuma Well Monument, via Beaver Creek Road. It's an open campground with 13 sites. Several hiking trails start at the nearby forest ranger station.

VERDE CANYON RAILROAD

One of the most enjoyable ways to see some prime Verde Valley wilderness is by taking a ride on the scenic railroad line that departs from the depot in Clarkdale, then runs through the Verde Canyon to Perkinsville. This line, now used only for transporting passengers, is the successor to several railway lines that were built to support mining activity in Jerome and other major claims. The first such line, the Atlantic & Pacific, was built in 1882 from Jerome to Ash Fork. Later, the Verde Valley Railroad connected the valley to the town of Drake. It is this line that is now used for the scenic train service. For reservations, call 800-293-RAIL.

The train, composed of renovated New York Metro Line coach cars (standard and first-class) with added open-air cars, leaves the depot Wednesday through Sunday at 11 A.M., returning at approximately 3 P.M. The route leads primarily through the strikingly beautiful Verde Canyon, now a protected area with much wildlife. A cottonwood/sycamore riparian habitat follows the riverside for the first stretch. Nearby is the desert. Along the way passengers can see two ancient Sinagua ruins—cliff dwellings almost hidden in ledges high on the canyon wall (at mileposts 36 and 37)—as well as the fascinating rock formations to be found across red rock country.

The open-air cars offer prime viewing spots. However, creature comforts are available with snack bars in each air-conditioned car. A valuable feature of the line is the access it offers to the superb Sycamore Canyon, a hiker's dream (at milepost 30, see page 136). Beyond the Sycamore Canyon entrance point, the train enters the Verde Canyon. The rock formations most apparent are the Supai Formation, a sandstone layer, Redwall Limestone, and the putty-colored Martin Formation. The colors of the vegetation change with the seasons.

Bald eagles and black hawks are often seen around Milepost 27. Big Springs can be seen bubbling clear water into the river at milepost 24.8. The train runs through a 600-foot tunnel, built by Swedish tunnelers at milepost 22.5. Milepost 18.5 marks the end of the line at Perkinsville, a village with fewer than ten people. The engine runs around the train and hooks up for the return trip through the canyon. Coach fare is about $35; first-class tickets cost about $53.

Three areas in the Sedona/ Verde Valley region offer superb birding opportunities. Oak Creek Canyon, particularly along the quiet West Fork Trail, provides a year-round cotton-wood/willow habitat perfect for observation. Slide Rock State Park is a good place for walking and bird identification on quiet days (never on weekends).

Red Rock State Park (south of Sedona via Highway 89A and the Red Rock Loop Road) is located in one of Arizona's most beautiful spots, with red rock views and a streamside habitat of cottonwoods, sycamores, and willows. More than 135 species have been identified in the park. Creekside trails wander through the park from the Education Center.

Dead Horse Ranch State Park (on the Verde River near Cottonwood) is another superb riparian habitat, possibly the best in the state, featuring cottonwoods and willows along the river, and a lagoon environment at one end of the park. The park is home to more than one-hundred species, including the yellow-billed cuckoo, belted kingfisher, Gambel's quail, and osprey. Drive from Main Street in Cottonwood, turn north on 5th Street, and cross the Verde River to find the park road.

Another fine observation site is Tavasci Marsh, just 1.5 miles north of the state park. This is a newer wildlife area, with marsh birds drawn by the effect of busy beavers and their dams.

BIRDS

Black Hawk
Buteogallus anthracinus
The common black hawk, which ranges from the southwestern United States to Ecuador, can be seen flying over the Verde Valley. A large bird with long legs and a wingspread of up to 4 feet, it is identified by its chunky shape and by a broad white band that crosses the middle of the tail. It breeds mainly in central and southern Arizona, as well as in New Mexico, and is also seen in western Texas and southern Utah.

You may also see a slightly smaller, slimmer raptor flying over the valley; this is the zone-tailed hawk.

Northern Harrier
Circus cyaneus
Harrier is this hawk's English name. It is also called the marsh hawk. The harrier is seen flying

over marshes and over deserts that have a good supply of sagebrush. It ranges throughout North America, but winters mainly in the western and southern states. These hawks catch small waterfowl (look for them at Tavasci Marsh or at the Dead Horse lagoon) and are renowned mousers. They fly with the wings in a slight "V" position. The male is light gray above, with white underparts and red spots, and has black wing tips and a barred tail. The female is brown with streaks below the wings. Young harriers are orange or russet below.

Green-Winged Teal
Anas crecca
This wood duck breeds and lives year-round in central Arizona, although its range extends to the northern parts of North America, and it winters in South America. This small teal is usually seen in a small flock, whether flying or floating on a marsh pond.

The male is gray with a brown head, which has a green patch that's visible in sunlight. Recognized by its compact shape, it is also distinguished by a vertical white mark near the shoulders. The female is small and speckled with green speculum. Look for this bird along the Verde River and in Tavasci Marsh. It is occasionally seen in

Oak Creek Canyon and Red Rock State Park as well.

Green Heron
Butorides striatus
Also called the green-backed heron, this dark-colored heron ranges from the northwestern United States and southeastern Canada to Argentina. Smaller than the great blue heron, it looks very much like a crow when in flight because of its bowed wingbeats.

Its short legs are yellowish-green or orange, the back has a greenish shine, and the neck is a chestnut brown. Young birds have streaks on the neck and breast. It is a vocal bird, with a series of *skuks* and a louder *skew* or *skewk* sound. It is widely found in the Sedona/Verde Valley area, along the creeks, on the Verde River, and in the marshes.

Western Tanager
Piranga ludoviciana
While there are 215 species of tanagers in the world, only four appear in the Southwest (western, summer, hepatic, and scarlet). Ranging throughout western North America, it winters from Mexico to Costa Rica. It prefers to inhabit mixed conifer forests and is commonly seen on the Mogollon Rim above Oak Creek Canyon, but is also seen in the riparian habitat

areas of the Oak Creek Canyon, at Red Rock State Park, and along the Verde River. This bird eats fruit and insects with its stout bill. The male tanager is a bright yellow with black back, wings, and tail, two white wing bars, and a red head. The female does not have the red head, is a duller yellow below and olive-colored above, and has white-and-yellow wing bars. The song of the western tanager resembles the short phrases of the robin, but they're even shorter and rougher sounding.

The summer tanager (male) is a rosy red all over, with a yellow bill. The female is an olive-color above and a deep yellow below with a slightly yellow bill. The voice is a sharp *pick-ee-tuck* or *pi-tuck*, also like a robin's song. The hepatic tanager is a darker red than the summer tanager. The female is olive above and yellow below. It has an orange-yellow throat, a gray patch on the ear, and a dark—almost black—bill. The scarlet tanager is true to its name but has very black wings and tail. The female (and male in winter) is a dull green above and yellow below.

Gambel's Quail
Callipla gambelii
This is the most widely seen of the American desert quail. Sometimes called the redhead quail, its narrow range includes southeastern California, southern and central Arizona, parts of south and central New Mexico, and the extreme southwest portion of Texas and northwestern Mexico. Both male and female have a white belly (with a black patch on the center of the male only), a chestnut brown crown, and chestnut flanks. The head plume is teardrop-shaped. It is similar to the California quail, except the chestnut color of the Gambel's quail's flanks is more pronounced and it has the black patch on an unscaled belly. Gambel's quail is often seen in the desert areas of the Verde Valley and in the arid sections of the red rock country near Sedona. It likes desert thickets and often lives near springs.

Black-Throated Gray Warbler
Dendroica nigrescens
A steady sight in Red Rock State Park and other riparian habitats in the area, this warbler has a small winter range, which includes the extreme southern part of California, Utah, Arizona, and Mexico, and along the Pacific Coast to southern British Columbia.

The male is gray, with a black throat, black patches with white stripes on the cheeks and crown, a blue to gray back with black stripes, and a yellow spot between the bill and eyes. The female and young do not have the black bib. Its song is a distinctive buzzing sound, a series of buzzes rising in pitch: *zee zee zee zee zee bzzz bzzz*. This warbler prefers a mixed woodland environment (such as the Oak Creek Canyon) or a mixed conifer forest with shrubby, open areas (Mingus Mountain). It inhabits a range of woodland types, including pinyon pine/juniper and scrub oak, as well as ponderosa pine forests.

Lucy's Warbler

Vermivora liciae

This small desert warbler is seen mainly along the Verde River and parts of Oak Creek where it flows across the desert of the Verde Valley before the creek empties into the Verde River.

Its range is across the southwestern U.S. with winters in Mexico. It has a chestnut patch on the rump, a white eye ring and a small patch of chestnut brown on its crown. Its voice is a very high-pitched *weeta weeta weeta chee chee chee.*

A good place to see this and several other warbler varieties, as well as orioles and rough-legged hawks, is the Page Springs Fish Hatchery near Cornville (via Interstate 17, McGuireville Exit 193, west for 7 miles to Casey's Corner, then north on Page Springs Road for another 4 miles). It is also seen at Dead Horse Ranch State Park. The various wood warblers are members of the *emberizidae* family, which ranges from Canada to Argentina. Out of a total of 114 warbler species, 53 are seen in the American Southwest.

OTHER ANIMALS

The following fish reside in the Verde River and the several creeks that flow into the river, including Oak and Sycamore creeks. We have chosen the smaller, distinctive fish of the region, rather than fish that are planted in the creeks and river for sport fishing. A good place to go for fishing and fish identification is Beasley Flat Recreation Site, operated by the Forest Service. It is on the Verde River, near the town of Camp Verde. To get there, drive through Camp Verde on State Route 260. Turn to Salt Mine Road (FR 574) and drive west for 8 miles to FR 529. Turn east and drive another 2 miles.

Gila Topminnow

Poeciliopsis occidentalis

This fish thrives in springs, pools, lagoons, and the edges of streams that have some vegetation in which to hide. Its range is basically the Gila River drainage from southern Arizona to southwestern New Mexico and Sonora Mexico.

This elongated minnow has a dark green (olive) back and green to tan sides with a dark stripe along the side from the upper gill cover to the tail-fin base. It grows to 2 inches.

This species was added to the endangered list in 1967. After being one of the most populous species in the Colorado River system, its numbers declined to the point where it is only found in this small area. Regional efforts are being made to protect it in springs (by removing competitive species) and rearing ponds.

Mosquitofish
Gambusia affinis
A hardy species, the Mosquitofish has been introduced to many desert ponds to control the mosquito populations.

It lives near the surface of ponds, lakes, ditches, and slow-moving streams. It is a tan-to-olive color, with pale yellow below, and the scales have small dusky spots near the edges. There is a dark bar below the eye. The female has a black spot on the belly when reproducing. The head is flat, the mouth small.

Its range covers much of the southerly states, and includes the Atlantic coast north to New Jersey.

River Otter
Lutra canadensis
A once-abundant population of otters, which is now thought to be extinct, was imported from Louisiana by the Arizona Game and Fish Department. The river otters now seen in the Verde River are descendants of these otters. The best place to see them are at the Cottonwood Basin below Beasley Flats, and downriver from Verde Ranch. These dark brown mammals have a long body (35 to 50 inches) and a dark brown color with a lighter underside. They have long, light whiskers and the throat is usually silver-gray. They live along rivers and lakes, usually in a wooded area, where they're active by day, catching fish and swimming very quickly. Often seen treading water with their heads poking above the surface, they also travel quickly over land, scuttling back and forth between the river and their dens. The nest is lined with grass, reeds, leaves, and other vegetation. It also uses old beaver lodges and hollow logs. Its range is from Alaska through the northern states to northern California and Utah, and in the East to Florida.

White-tailed Deer

Odocoileus virginianus

Sedona is just about the most northerly Arizona habitat for the white-tailed deer, which ranges from the southern part of Canada, through the United States (except much of California), and parts of Nevada, northern Arizona, New Mexico, and southern Colorado.

Primarily a nocturnal animal, this deer grazes on fresh green plants and nuts in the fall. It lives in brushy areas and woods, and can be found in the canyons of the Verde River watershed, on the rim above Cottonwood, and again in the Mingus Mountain Recreation Area. This deer is tan or reddish in its upper parts during the summer months, and grayish brown in the winter. Its belly, nose, throat, eye ring, and the inside of its ears are white. The tail is brown with white edges above, often with a white stripe down the center, and all-white below. Fawns are spotted. Male antlers spread to 3 feet. Does do not normally have antlers. It's easy to tell when white-tailed deer are present, even though they may not be in sight. Trees may have bark rubbed off by antlers. A large rubbing (up to 5 inches wide) indicates a large buck has been there. Its tracks look like narrow, split hearts about 2–3 inches long, with the pointed end forward. There may be two dots behind the main prints, made by dewclaws. A high tail, with flashes of white, is the deer's sign of danger. Although the deer usually goes to sleep at dawn, it may continue browsing for some time after sunrise.

Desert Shrew

Notiosorex crawfordi

This adaptive little mammal rarely has to have a drink, for it usually gets its water supply from the soft inner parts of the insects it eats.

The desert shrew lives in semidesert scrub, which includes a good section of the Verde Valley, and in the highland areas above Sedona that encompasses the area crossed by Schnebly Hill Road. It is often found in nests at the base of cactus, agave (century plants), or other desert plants. Gray in color with brownish touches on the top and light gray below, it has a long, gray tail. The three teeth on each side of its jaw form a single point; the desert shrew is the only North American shrew to have this arrangement.

Gopher (Bull) Snake

Pituophis melanoleucus

The nickname comes from its powerful body. The gopher snake, which grows to 100 inches, is scattered throughout the southeastern states and west of the Mississippi River to the tip of Baja California. Only two of the fifteen subspecies can be found here. It lives in dry, sandy areas ranging from pine and oak woodlands in altitudes up to 9,000 feet, to open brush, to the desert floor. It is found in the Verde Valley and on the Mogollon Rim above Sedona.

The Sonoran Gopher has a blotchy brown color, sometimes reddish, and is much darker to the rear. The Great Basin Gopher has black blotches on the forepart of its body, with side blotches and light-colored blotches on the back.

Western Diamondback
Crotalus atrox
The largest western rattlesnake, the diamondback has a heavy body with a large head. The back has a pattern of dark diamonds with light borders, or hexagonal blotches. Some diamondbacks have a mottled appearance with small dark spots.

The snake has two diagonal lines on the side of the face. The tail is circled by black and white rings.

Home for this species ranges from the low desert of southeast California, across Arizona, New Mexico, and Texas, into Arkansas, and into northern Mexico. It eats birds and desert rodents, surviving up to 25 years. Its venom is extremely toxic, and its bite, if untreated, can be fatal to adult humans. Most people are given time to depart the scene after disturbing this snake. When it raises its head and begins buzzing, this is the time to flee. It is active during evening hours, and at night during the hot summer season.

Ringtail (Cat)
Bassaricus astutus
With a fox-like face and cat-like body, the ringtail lives in canyons, boulder jumbles, and other rocky areas of the desert Southwest. It sometimes (but infrequently) lives in wooded areas, in hollow trees, making a den like a fox, padded with grasses, leaves, or moss when available. The ringtail moves by night, eating insects and small mammals. Its tail is long and bushy, with fourteen to sixteen black and white bands; its large ears and eyes have a white ring around them. Each foot has five toes.

Black-tailed Jack Rabbit
Lepus californicus
The most populous jack in the Southwest is really a hare rather than a rabbit. Common differences are that young hares are born with eyes open and fur on the body. Its range spreads from

southern California and Texas, north to southern Washington state. Its habitat is almost every-where—barren desert, prairie grassland, high-altitude mead-ows, and scrub land. It likes to hide in vegetation of two feet or more.

The body is a sandy or gray color with a salt-and-pepper wash above, and white below. The tail has a black stripe with a white border above, which ex-tends to the rump area. This jack, with its very long ears and extremely large hind feet, is a real thumper of a hare. Like most desert animals, the black-tailed jack rests during the day, in a shallow draw or in tall grass, and moves around at night. You often see large (and tiny) jacks just after the sun falls, caught in your car headlights as they cross the Verde Valley roads.

Deer Mouse
Peromyscus boylii
The most common wild mouse in America, the deer mouse inhabits semi-brush and arid brushlands, preferring to live in rocky areas. It is brownish or grayish above, with buff sides and white below. The hairy, bi-colored tail is as long as the body, and the ears are large. While this mouse usually feeds on the ground, eating insects and seeds, it can climb trees for safety.

PLANTS

Arizona Sycamore
Platanus wrightii
This relatively rare tree, one of the Planetree family, is found in abundance only beside streams and lakesides in central to south-eastern Arizona, with a few found in southwestern New Mexico.

Though common as an ac-cent tree in the pinyon/juniper woodland, it is most abundant in the Oak Creek Canyon north of Sedona, where it combines with the cottonwood to provide a superb riparian habitat for hundreds of bird species.

This sycamore has striking features—large leaves like those on a maple tree, 6 to 9 inches long and wide, divided about halfway to the base into three to five long, pointed fingers with wavy edges. It has a mottled ap-pearance, with thin bark that flakes away, exposing patches of pale green and rather white inner bark. This tall tree grows to about 80 feet, its trunk to a diameter of up to 4 feet. It sometimes divides at the ground to push up two or three large trunks, and you'll some-times find a trunk lying on the ground. The "buttonballs," round seed pods that separate and fall in the spring, swing in the breeze. The tufts attached to the seeds are much like the downy "cotton" of the cottonwood tree and have the same purpose. The Arizona Sycamore is also called the buttonwood, buttonball tree, Arizona plane-tree, ciclamor, and álamo.

Southwestern Thorn Apple
Datura wrightii
Often called the sacred datura, this plant thrives in loose sand in desert washes and on flat plains. With a range from central California to northern Mexico, it is one of the more frequently seen flowering plants in the Verde Valley.

It is easy to spot. The large, trumpet-shaped, white-colored flowers protrude from the coarse foliage. Anyone who approaches the plant will recognize the unpleasant smell, rather like that of a garbage dump. The oval-shaped leaves grow to 6 inches and have tiny hairs covering them. It has prickly fruit.

This is one of several species of datura seen in Arizona, which include jimsonweed (*datura stramonium*), the name being a corruption of Jamestown weed, which caused the poisoning of soldiers sent to Jamestown to stop Bacon's Rebellion in 1676. The use of this plant—over many hundreds of years—is fascinating. Anyone who has read books by Carlos Castaneda will get the picture. Extracts from this plant and its kin are narcotic. The datura was used prominently in religious ceremonies of Southwestern Native Americans. When prepared as a drug, the datura extract has strong hallucinogenic properties. It is thought to have been imported for medicinal use in the colonial United States. Now, it's a common roadside plant—pleasant to see with its trumpet-shaped flowers, but a deadly plant that should be left alone.

Hedgehog Cactus
Pediocactus simpsonii
Simpson's hedgehog cactus is seen in northern Arizona, as far south as the Verde Valley, and in the lower desert areas of western Nevada, western Colorado, and even into South Dakota.

A favorite of cactus collectors, the wild hedgehog has been taken from the desert so much that its population is largely decimated. Where these small cacti remain, they're found in fine sandy soil between sagebrush and in pinyon/juniper stands.

This cactus grows to about 8 inches, so it is one of the smaller cacti to grow on the desert floor. It has one, or a few, spiny, round stems that produce several white or yellow rose-type flowers at the top between May and July. The straight brownish spines, usually 0.375 inches to 0.75 inches long, are in clusters of five to eleven, spreading from the center.

These inner spines are surrounded by fifteen to twenty cream-colored spines, each about 0.25 inches long.

Desert Rosemallow
Hibiscus coulteri
Ranging from the midsection of Arizona to west Texas and northern Mexico, this desert survivor is a distant cousin to the tropical hibiscus plants, one of a genus that includes more than 300 species. A shrub-like plant that grows to 4 feet, it has undivided lower leaves and divided upper leaves. Its flowers, which appear from April through August, are cup-shaped, white to yellow, and often have a red tinge.

Century Plant and Other Agave
Agave parryi
Parry's century plant is one of the bigger species of agave, the largest of the desert succulents. This plant, with its incredibly dramatic stalk, is seen in large numbers in scenic settings along Schnebly Hill Road just outside Sedona. The leaves of this plant can grow up to 18 inches; each has a very sharp end spine, with smaller spines along the edges. Flower buds are red, but when the flowers open, they form as yellow clusters near the ends of the branches. The plant flowers only once, near the end of its life. While the plant doesn't take a century to grow to maturity, it does take many years to flower, and then the plant dies. Its most amazing feature is the flower-bearing stalk that looks like a candelabra and grows to a height of 14 feet. The stalk is often used as an indoor decor accent, or even as a southwestern-style Christmas tree. Among the many species of agave is the desert agave (*agave desertii*), which grows at low desert elevations in the Sonoran and Colorado deserts of Arizona and California. The stalks, though not as high as Parry's agave, rise to about 12 feet. Like Parry's, the desert agave buds are reddish and the flowers are yellow.

Agave americana is the largest of the Arizona agaves, with a spread of up to 12 feet. It has straight gray-green leaves. It is now widely cultivated and sold in nurseries. The stalk displays are high, but are less colorful than the smaller species.

SEDONA

Bed & Breakfast Inns

Canyon Villa B&B Inn

125 Canyon Circle Drive
Sedona, AZ 86336
(520) 284-1126 or 800-453-1166

One of the larger bed-and-breakfast places in Sedona, this charming mission-style home with swimming pool was built in 1992. All eleven rooms have a whirlpool bath, and some have fireplaces. A two-night minimum stay is required on weekends (**$$** to **$$$**).

Saddle Rock Ranch

P.O. Box 10095
Sedona, AZ 86339
(520) 282-7640

Set on an historic (1926) 3-acre estate, this B&B inn has canopied beds, antique furnishings, and fireplaces. All three rooms have private baths. Afternoon snacks are served as well as breakfast. The country setting, gardens, pool, and whirlpool make this a unique stay (**$$** to **$$$**).

Greyfire Farm Bed & Breakfast

1240 Jacks Canyon Road
Sedona, AZ 86351
(520) 284-2340 or 800-579-2340

Another pastoral getaway with great privacy, this small farm outside town, operated by Elaine and Daniel Payne, also has fine views, cozy rooms furnished with antiques, and private baths. A 3-bedroom cottage is available, and nearby hiking trails are a bonus (**$$** to **$$$**).

Cathedral Rock Lodge

61 Los Amigos Lane
Sedona, AZ 86336
(520) 282-7608

Carol Shannon owns and operates this spread-out B&B inn with scenic views. All rooms have private baths. There is a suite with kitchen and private deck, plus a cabin that is a romantic spot indeed (**$** to **$$**).

Territorial House

65 Piki Drive
Sedona, AZ 86336
(520) 204-2737 or 800-801-2737

A B&B inn with an historical focus, the Territorial House is operated by John and Linda Steele. The rooms each have a fireplace and a deck, and there is an outdoor whirlpool. Wild West movies are available for watching during evening hours. Full breakfast and afternoon snacks are served (**$$** to **$$$**).

The Lodge at Sedona

125 Kallof Place
Sedona, AZ 86336
(520) 204-1942 or 800-619-4467

This highly regarded and award-winning B&B inn is surrounded by 2.5 acres of quiet land. A perfect place for special occasions, the inn has a distinctive European ambience created by the owners, Barb and Mark Dinunzio. There are private decks off the rooms, and whirlpool tubs. A full breakfast is served daily and dinners are offered on weekends (**$$$**).

Casa Sedona

55 Hozoni Drive
Sedona, AZ 86336
(520) 282-2938 or 800-525-3756

This 15-room B&B inn is built in the adobe style and has a Southwest ambience. The rooms are large, with private baths, whirlpool tubs, and fireplaces (**$$** to **$$$**).

The Graham Bed & Breakfast Inn

150 Canyon Circle Drive
Sedona, AZ 86351
(520) 284-1425 or 800-228-1425

Highly rated by Mobil (4 stars), this Southwest-style inn has rooms and suites with fireplace, whirlpool bath, private decks, plus a swimming pool and whirlpool. A full breakfast is served. The inn is operated by Roger and Carol Redenbaugh (**$$** to **$$$**).

Resorts

Enchantment

125 Canyon Circle Drive
Sedona, AZ 86336
(520) 282-2900 or 800-826-4180

A tennis and health resort set next to Boynton Canyon at the base of dramatic red rock cliffs, this is one of two major resort operations in the Sedona Area. There are standard hotel-style rooms as well as one- and two-bedroom suites in casitas, plus 45 efficiency units. There are four heated pools, lots of tennis courts with instruction available, a putting green plus a pitch & putt golf course, croquet, and a fitness program. The excellent dining room is open from 7 A.M. until 9 P.M. Sunday brunch is served from 11:30 A.M. (**$$$**).

Poco Diablo Resort

1752 S. Highway 179
(P.O. Box 1709)
Sedona, AZ 86339
(520) 282-7333 or 800-528-4275

A golf and tennis resort, the hotel is set on 22 acres of prime landscape and features a 9-hole (par 3) golf course, lighted tennis courts, three heated pools, and three outdoor whirlpools. The resort is located beside Oak Creek, with superb views of red rock. Each room has a wet bar, coffee maker, and refrigerator. Special rooms with whirlpool and fireplace are available. There is a restaurant and lounge (**$$** to **$$$**).

Hotels, Motels and Lodges

Sky Ranch Lodge
P.O. Box 2579
Sedona, AZ 86336
(520) 282-6400

This motel and cabin complex has 94 rooms and is situated just north of Sedona on Highway 89A. The lodge sits on a mesa overlooking the town and Oak Creek Canyon. Some rooms have fireplaces. There are standard motel-style rooms and efficiencies, plus two housekeeping cottages. There is a swimming pool, whirlpool, and guest laundry. This is a good lower-priced alternative to the more expensive resorts and hotels in Sedona and the surrounding area (**$** to **$$**).

L'Auberge de Sedona
301 L'Auberge Lane
Sedona, AZ 86336
(520) 282-1661 or 800-272-6777

This deluxe operation—set along the banks of Oak Creek—has fine dining and relaxing accommodations in three different settings. Private cottages, including some with two bedrooms and two bathrooms,

are set along the creek. The European Hunting Lodge has rooms and junior suites. The Orchard unit has 41 standard hotel rooms and a gourmet restaurant featuring French cuisine and an excellent wine list. The Orchard serves up American cuisine (**$$$**)

Railroad Inn at Sedona
2545 W. Highway 89A
Sedona, AZ 86336
(520) 282-1533 or 800-858-7245

Owned by the firm that operates the Verde Canyon Railroad, this standard motor hotel offers rooms and efficiencies and a swimming pool, with special stay-and-ride combo packages, including a meal at the adjacent Bernie's Restaurant (**$** to **$$**).

Slide Rock Lodge
Box 1141
Sedona, AZ 86336
(520) 282-3531

This is one of several lodges in Oak Creek Canyon, north of Sedona. You may choose a room with fireplace. A picnic area and hiking trails are close at hand (**$** to **$$**).

The Canyon Wren
P.O. Box 1140
Sedona, AZ 86336
(520) 282-6900 or 800-437-WREN

Also located in Oak Creek Canyon, this little rustic resort has four cabins (for two people)

with kitchens and fireplaces—
a romantic getaway and a place
to recharge your batteries. Trails
leading through the Coconino
National Forest are nearby, and
there are whirlpool tubs. This is
a non-smoking place (**$** to **$$**).

Arroyo Roble Hotel
400 N. Highway 89A (Box NN)
Sedona, AZ 86336
(520) 282-4001 or 800-7-SEDONA

This Best Western operation is
centrally located near the Sedona
"Y" in Oak Creek Canyon. It
is close to the Tlaquepacque
Shopping Center and some of
the best Sedona restaurants. The
most expensive units are the
two-bedroom villas at creekside.
There's an indoor-outdoor heated
pool, whirlpools, sauna, laundry,
and exercise room. Tennis is offered for a fee, as is racquetball
and massage (**$$** to **$$$**).

New Earth Lodge
665 Sunset Drive
Sedona, AZ 86336
(520) 282-2644

The name of the place is descriptive of its ambience. With
wonderful views, this complex
of vacation cottages is designed
in the Southwest style, with
gardens and extensive natural
landscapes. Fireplaces and barbecues are available for outdoor,
self-directed dining. The cabins
are fully equipped with kitchen
facilities (**$$**).

Quail Ridge Resort
120 Canyon Circle Drive
Sedona, AZ 86351
(520) 284-9327

This resort, not quite as fancy as
the posh tennis and golf resorts,
has a good measure of privacy
for families. There are two-bed-
room chalets and efficiency
suites, complete with fully
equipped kitchens. Recreational
activities include tennis, swim-
ming, and soaking in the
whirlpool. The chalets are lo-
cated in a treed setting (**$$**).

Don Hoel's Cabins
9440 North Highway 89A
Sedona, AZ 86336-9623
(520) 282-3560 or 800-292-HOEL

This comfortable cabin resort is
a 15-minute drive north of
Sedona in Oak Creek Canyon.
Swimming, fishing, and hiking
are available, with trails leading
through the national forest.
As with other resorts in the
canyon, summer stays require
reservations (**$$**).

Bell Rock Inn
6246 Highway 179
Sedona, AZ 86336
(520) 282-4161 or 800-881-ROCK

With a Southwest adobe look,
this inn has been a popular
place to stay for some time.
Recently, 52 new suites were
added, with Southwest decor
matching the ambience of the

inn. The inn is situated a few minutes from the "Y" and downtown Sedona. There's a pool and whirlpool, plus a dining room and lounge. The staff is helpful in arranging recreational activities, including golf packages, Jeep tours, and balloon rides ($$ to $$$).

Canyon Portal Motel

280 N. Highway 89A
Sedona, AZ 86336
(520) 282-7125 or 800-542-8484

This standard motel is conveniently located just north of the "Y" in the southern Oak Creek Canyon area. It is close to shops and restaurants, and the Tlaquepaque shopping area is a minute's drive. There are 32 units, some with kitchenettes and fireplaces, and a swimming pool. The wide range of rates suits anyone's budget ($ to $$$).

Desert Quail Inn

6626 State Highway 179
Sedona, AZ 86351
(520) 284-1433 or 800-385-0927

Located in the Village of Oak Creek, the community on the southern outskirts of Sedona, this is a newer, modern, and standard motel with a swimming pool. Some rooms have fireplaces and whirlpool baths. Restaurants are nearby. The motel is 7.5 miles from the Sedona Interstate 17 ($ to $$).

Quality Inn Kings Ransom

771 State Highway 179,
P.O. Box 180
Sedona, AZ 86339
(520) 282-7151 or 800-221-2222

There are lots of trees and red rock views at this low-rise hotel located 0.5 miles south of the Sedona "Y." As with other hotels in this chain operation, the rooms are quite large and comfortable. The heated pool and spa offer resort-style relaxation. The hotel has a restaurant and coffee shop ($$ to $$$).

Oak Creek Terrace

Star Route 3, Box 1100
Sedona/Oak Creek Canyon,
AZ 86336
(520) 282-3562 or 800-224-2229

Another of the Oak Creek Canyon resorts, this operation is located 5 miles north of Sedona. It's a fine place from which to take a number of hikes. All rooms have air-conditioning, some have whirlpool tubs and fireplaces, some have kitchenettes, and the resort has cable TV. Jeep rentals can be arranged. This is one of the few places that welcome pets ($$ to $$$).

COTTONWOOD

Cottonwood Inn

993 South Main Street
Cottonwood, AZ 86323
(520) 634-5575 or 800-528-1234

This superior Best Western operation has standard rooms, some with whirlpool. There is a restaurant, lounge, and heated pool ($$).

Quality Inn
301 West Highway 89A
Cottonwood, AZ 86326
(520) 634-4207

For those who don't like adventure when they're booking a room for the night, this modern, chain motor hotel has 51 rooms and amenities, including a pool, spa, and restaurant ($ to $$).

View Motel
818 S. Main Street
Cottonwood, AZ 86326
(520) 634-4207

This low-priced motel has 34 rooms (eight with kitchens), cable TV, a pool, spa, and restaurant. It has special rates for AAA and AARP members ($).

CLARKDALE

Flying Eagle Country Bed and Breakfast
2700 Windmill Lane
Clarkdale, AZ 86324
(520) 634-0211

With rooms accommodating two people, this B&B home has reasonable rates, fine views, and a full country breakfast. It's a good place to stay if you want to explore the historic mining town before taking the Verde Canyon railroad ride to Perkinsville ($).

JEROME

Miner's Roost Inn
309 Main Street
Jerome, AZ 86331
(520) 634-5094

Set on top of the Ore House Restaurant in this historic former mining camp—situated on a mountainside—the rooms are decorated with Victorian furnishings and pioneer artifacts. The restaurant below offers large servings of "down-home" cooking ($).

Ghost City Inn
541 Main Street
Jerome, AZ 86331
(520) 634-4678

Perched on the side of Cleopatra Hill like all buildings in Jerome, this charming Victorian bed-and-breakfast home has six rooms and a whirlpool tub ($ to $$).

The Surgeon's House
101 Hill Street
Jerome, AZ 86331
800-639-1452

This historic B&B home has wonderful views of the Verde Valley from its aerie in this old mining town. Accommodations include one single room, one double room, a suite, and a guest house with kitchen ($$).

Jerome Inn

309 Main Street
Jerome, AZ 86331
(520) 634-5094

There are seven rooms in this historic old hostelry, built after the fire of 1889. At street-side, the building has a restaurant and lounge. A special gourmet package is offered, including candlelight dinner served in the room. The inn is handy to the town's shops and galleries ($).

RV Parks and Campgrounds

Sedona RV Resort

6701 W. Highway 89A
Sedona, AZ 86336
(520) 282-6640 or 800-547-8727

Located 6 miles west of the Sedona "Y" intersection, this large, paved RV park, complete with palm trees, has 196 sites with full and partial hookups, plus cabins and travel trailer rentals. There is a swimming pool, whirlpool, store, laundry, gift shop, and restaurant.

Other Camping Spots

Lo Lo Mai Springs Camping Resort

Page Springs Road,
P.O. Box 3169
Sedona, AZ 86340
(520) 634-4700

Hawkeye-Red Rock RV Park

181 Art Barn Road
Sedona, AZ 86336
(520) 282-2222

Living Springs Camp

Oak Creek Canyon,
P.O. Box 1025
Sedona, AZ 86336
(520) 282-6871

The following RV parks in the Cottonwood area have full and partial hookups:

Turquoise Triangle RV Park

2501 E. Highway 89A
Cottonwood, AZ 86326
(520) 634-5294

Rio Verde RV Park

3420 Highway 89A
Cottonwood, AZ 85326
(520) 634-5990

Mountain VU Mobile Estates

11295 Cornville Road
Cornville, AZ 86325
(520) 634-1928

Dead Horse Ranch State Park

(520) 634-5283

Located between Cottonwood and Clarkdale beside the Verde River, this superior park campground has 45 sites, suitable for tents, RVs, and trailers. It is operated on a first-come, first-served basis. Other park facilities include a dump station, picnic area, and trails that lead beside the river, under the cottonwoods and willows.

Forest Service Campgrounds

There are four campgrounds located along Oak Creek in the Coconino National Forest. **Banjo Bill Campground**, one mile north of Slick Rock State Park, has 8 small sites suitable for tents and pickup campers. **Bootlegger Campground**, another small campground to the north, has 10 sites. **Cave Spring Campground** has 11 reserved sites out of a total 78 sites. This campground is suitable for tents, RVs, and trailers to 32 feet. There's a nature trail and longer hiking trails are nearby. For reservations, call 800-283-CAMP. **Pine Flat Campground** at the northern end of the

canyon has 58 sites, and is suitable for RVs and trailers to 32 feet. While Banjo Bill, Bootlegger, and Cave Spring campgrounds are open from Memorial Day through Labor Day, Pine Flat is open from late March (after the snow leaves) until the first major snowfall. There is a primitive campground (without services) on Schnebly Hill Road, 2 miles from Highway 179.

In the Verde Valley, via Highway 260, **Clear Creek Campground** is situated on the river under cottonwood trees. There are 18 sites with grills, tables, and water. There is also a group campground, which may be reserved by calling 800-283-CAMP. Above the Verde Valley in the **Mingus Mountain Recreation Area** (Prescott National Forest), campsites are located at the crest of the mountain, south of Jerome. Follow Highway 89A to the turnoff.

North San Pedro Basin and the Galiuro Wilderness

In the United States, a river that flows north is a rarity. The San Pedro flows out of Mexico's Sonoran Desert and crosses the border into Arizona near the town of Bisbee, picks up water from the Mule Mountains, then meanders through a wide valley that lies between the Huachuca and Whitestone mountains to the west and the Dragoon Mountains to the east.

Because San Pedro's riparian areas lie on a central interior flyway, the river—with its cottonwood and willow habitat—is a haven for hundreds of species of birds. This unusual combination of desert and abundant habitat for birds and animals is only one of nature's contradictions in this southern Arizona region.

As the river flows north toward its mouth—where it empties into the Gila River near Phoenix—it changes character, but still performs its duties for wildlife. North of Interstate 10 and Benson, it slides between the foothills of the Little Dragoon, Rincon, and Winchester mountain ranges. For the remainder of its journey, the San Pedro flows beside the base of the Galiuro Mountains. It is this upper end of the river to which this section is dedicated.

The Galiuros, a pristine, rugged mountain range, adds water to the river from its many creeks, which are fed by winter and spring storms, as well as by springs located high in the mountains.

One of the finest in Arizona's collection of contrasting ecosystems—and one of the least known or visited—the North San Pedro Basin was first occupied by nomadic Native Americans in prehistoric and more recent periods. In this region, gold miners fought and killed each other for the scant riches to be found in the mountains. The Basin was also the location of hot springs, where—in the late 1800s and early 1900s—visitors came to soak their worries away after traveling for hours or days from the legendary wild-west towns of the area, including the deadly town of Tombstone. And this is the dramatic mountain landscape where settlers moved onto the high slopes of the Galiuros with their cattle, carving small ranches out of the wilderness.

The San Pedro River

For eons, the San Pedro has nurtured life. Mammoths roamed the valley of the San Pedro millions of years ago, providing food and clothing for prehistoric hunters.

It is a flood-prone river where each major storm results in channel changes that widen the flood plain, creating new wildlife habitat and agricultural land. That wildlife habitat—cottonwood and willow groves and mesquite thickets that line the banks—attracts a full half of the bird species found in the United States.

The entire length of the upper San Pedro is within Bureau of Land Management (BLM) territory, part of the vast Arizona desert region administered by the federal government. While the streamside areas lay unprotected for many years, we are seeing an increased vigilance in ensuring that the river remains a vital waterway for wildlife. Cooperative ecological programs involving the BLM and other groups such as the Nature Conservancy are now operating along several stretches. These programs see that the riparian habitats are protected and enhanced.

As the river flows north, 50 miles from the Mexican border, it crosses under Interstate 10 near the village of Pomerene, a few miles west of Benson. This flat, high desert lies at an altitude of 3,580 feet. Quickly, the valley narrows as the river encounters the Little Dragoon and Winchester mountains to the north and the Rincon Mountains to the south. Picking up speed and water from seasonal mountain streams, the San Pedro heads downhill for more than 70 miles to meet the westward-flowing Gila River.

The San Pedro River Road parallels the river for most of the upper section, beginning at Interstate 5 and leading through the little riverside villages of Cascabel, Redington, Mammoth, and Dudleyville. The San Pedro empties into the Gila River near the town of Hayden. This route takes visitors to the San Pedro ecological areas, which provide public access to the river. Although there are few organized tourist facilities along this route, the river itself makes a visit worthwhile.

Along the River

CASCABEL RANCH

Cascabel—the community—is a throwback to an earlier age, when the pioneer settlers built cabins beside the river and established orchards and small farms, drawing an existence from the riverside environment. Cascabel (Spanish for rattle, as in rattlesnake) doesn't look like a town, for it is strung along the San Pedro and the road that parallels the river for several miles.

Along the San Pedro River Road, 27 miles off the freeway (I-10), is the Redington Land and Cattle Company and its Cascabel Ranch. This is a real cattle ranch with livestock wandering over the desert hills above the village. The co-owner and ranch manager, Don Steinman, moved several years ago to Cascabel from a ranch closer to Tucson. He has become a vital part of the environmental consortium, which is working to protect the riverside habitat and the Galiuro foothills landscape. This group includes the BLM, the Nature Conservancy, and the U.S. Forest Service, as well as individuals in the area who realize that preserving and protecting nature is not only the right thing to do but can also provide a living through nature tourism.

So, while Cascabel Ranch is a working cattle operation, it is also a very different kind of guest ranch. Here families and other small groups of people experience not only ranch life but the wonders of the desert foothills, the streamside habitat of the San Pedro, and the magnificent Galiuro Mountain wilderness. The ranch offers horse and Jeep tours of the San Pedro Valley and the Galiuro desert lands, using trails that wind through small canyons to higher country, where you can see across the

San Pedro Valley to the Rincon range and beyond to the Catalina Mountains near Tucson.

Steinman, with partner Barbara Litton, provides horses, Jeeps, and guides for the higher mountain tours that the Nature Conservancy offers from Muleshoe Ranch.

A stay at the ranch—which is rustic, to say the least, but comfortable—not only provides the venue for a special vacation but also gives the visitor access to Don Steinman's endless stories—stories about the desert, stories about the history of Cascabel and the San Pedro Valley, stories about the cattle, and lots of stories about himself, all of them humorous.

The ranch uses 3,600 acres of federal land, which is surrounded by the Galiuro Wilderness, the Coronado National Forest, and more BLM land. This is wide-open space with nearly two million acres available for riding and Jeep touring.

The ranch is small enough (maximum ten people) to customize vacations for its visitors. They can herd cattle, ride fence, tend the herd and get paid for it as a 'cowpoke-for-a-day,' drive a team and wagon, make side trips to Tombstone and other wild-west towns, get rifle and six-shooter instruction, and watch birds along the riverbank. The ranch horses range from absolutely tame to spirited. Regulations and rules on how you spend your time are relaxed. You pay for your rides by the hour, and you can bring a lunch or have one provided. You don't have to do anything if you don't want to. Some guests devote their days to bird-watching beside the San Pedro.

Cascabel is unlike any other Arizona guest ranch I have visited. While small and quaint, without the big swimming pool, tennis courts, spa, fine dining, and bar, it is more like I imagined a real desert ranch would be—because it is a real desert ranch. Meals are usually eaten outside under the trees. The daily demands of the cattle provide a focus for the operation and draw visitors into the hourly jobs that have to be done. On the other hand, one can just hire a Jeep and tour forever, disappearing into the desert or mountains.

If you're traveling in your own vehicle, you can reach the ranch by driving along Interstate 10 west from Tucson and getting off at Exit 306 (Pomerene). Drive north through the village of Pomerene to milepost 24, which is 27 miles from the freeway. You may also drive from Tucson on Tanque Verde Road across Redington Pass—a 37-mile drive from the end of pavement to the ranch. If you fly in, a ranch employee will pick you up at Tucson Airport and deliver you to Cascabel.

For information and reservations, write:

Redington Land and Cattle Co.
HC 1 Box 730
Benson, AZ 85602
Or call Barbara Litton at (520) 212-5555.

BIRDS, BIRDS, AND MORE BIRDS

The term *riparian* is heard much more frequently these days as we better understand the importance of water systems to the health of wildlife. Riparian areas are found at any elevation, from the hot low desert to the tops of mountain ranges, anywhere water flows or collects. One of the finest riparian habitats in the West is located in the San Pedro River Valley.

Lying on the United States' major inland flyway, the San Pedro offers water, trees, marshes, and shrubs to millions of birds every year. Some live here year-round, nesting in the tall cottonwoods and dense willows. Others are semi-annual visitors, resting along the San Pedro during their spring and fall migrations. Still others stay beside the San Pedro during the winter while they spend their summers in Canada, Siberia, or in a more northerly state of the U.S. Then, there are summer residents who belong to the many neotropical bird species that find Arizona summers more comfortable than summers in Mexico.

The North San Pedro provides a superb habitat because of its habit of wandering. Left in its natural state without damming, the San Pedro has changed channels many times over the past few thousand years. Even today, a strong storm will flood the river past its banks, knocking down trees and carving out a new course that may be hundreds of feet from the former channel. This happened several years ago at Cascabel.

The effect of this natural disturbance is to generate a new habitat that also leaves the former streamside habitat in operation. The river (with plenty of help from nature) adds to the variety of habitat through this process—changing its course, winding across the valley, creating new banks upon which willows, cottonwoods, and shrubs will grow—thus providing more homes for birds and other animals.

The San Pedro River is considered a vital resource in the preservation of many endangered bird and animal species—simply because it is there in a natural state. During the past 100 years, Arizona has lost more than 90 percent of its lowland riparian habitats. Without the San Pedro in its present condition, the major flyway (and the species that use it) would also be endangered.

The bird numbers here are staggering. Fully half the species that inhabit North America are found in the riparian habitats of the San Pedro. Along the north San Pedro and the upper section (south of Interstate 10) lies the largest and most-used riparian bird habitat in the state.

And the birds attract human visitors. The riparian areas of the North San Pedro are almost all accessible because of the road that follows the river between Pomerene and Winkleman. Beyond the villages, it's as easy as stopping the car and walking a short way to the river. The San Pedro has gravel bars for access to the middle of the river channel. It's easy to walk along the banks or (in the dryer summer months) in and beside the river.

You'll see the permanent resident hawks flying overhead. Eagles visit the area while passing through. Water birds stop over in season. And more than one hundred species live year-round in the riverside habitat—primarily song birds, herons, woodpeckers, blackbirds, doves, owls, and more raptors. Forty percent of all the gray hawks in the United States live along the San Pedro.

In winter, the raptors really take over the region. Along with some twelve thousand sandhill cranes, which spend the winter at the nearby Willcox Playa, the wintering raptors include ferruginous hawks, rough-legged hawks, Harris' hawks, merlins, kestrels, prairie and peregrine falcons, bald and golden eagles, Cooper's and sharp-shinned hawks, harriers, and at least a dozen color variations of the red-tailed hawk.

Bird-watchers have identified more than twenty species of flycatchers along the river, plus twenty-nine varieties of shorebirds including multiple species of plovers, sandpipers, stilts, curlews, dowitchers, and phalaropes, plus sanderling, willet, and killdeer. Thirty-six varieties of wood warblers have been identified as well.

The birding community has begun to get the message that the San Pedro Valley is indeed a special place.

Galiuro Wilderness

One of the least visited mountain areas in the United States, and virtually unknown even in Arizona, the Galiuro Preserve area is a supreme example of how government and private agencies can work together to create a truly special place.

Remote, pristine, and even primeval, this rugged area of extreme beauty lies 50 miles northeast of Tucson, like an island in the desert. The Galiuro Range—some 60 miles in length—rises from the flatlands of the San Pedro Valley, its peaks running north to south, bordered by Sulphur Springs Valley on the west and the Aravaipa Valley on the northeast.

Access to most of the Galiuros is by horse or forest trail. A few roads lead to the edge of the wilderness, including the gravel road to the Muleshoe Ranch Preserve.

Spanish explorers called the range the San Calistro or San Calisto Mountains, and later named them the Sierra del Aravaipa. The highest peaks top out at about 7,000 feet, some 4,000 feet above the desert valleys.

A young mountain range, the Galiuros were created in the mid-Tertiary period through the uplifting of the earth's crust and block faulting. The upper part of the range is made up of volcanic rocks—mainly ash deposits and lava flows that lie over the much older granite and quartzite. There is not one ridge of peaks but two: parallel ridges separated by two valleys, one (Rattlesnake) sloping north and the other (Redfield) sloping south. Many creeks have cut into the slopes of these valleys, flowing to the San Pedro and Aravaipa valleys.

Three distinct ecological regions are apparent as one ascends the range. In the foothills and lower slopes are heavy thickets of manzanita, mountain mahogany, mesquite, scrub oak, and several species of cacti. Several cattle operations occupy this suitable rangeland, not only on the San Pedro slopes but also in the high mountains.

The mid-range system is home to piñon pine and several types of oak. At the higher levels, ponderosa pine is interwoven with Douglas fir, Arizona cypress, and Mexican piñon, in addition to Mexican and Chihuahua white pines. The whole of the Galiuro Mountain range has never been logged for commercial purposes.

There has been human use of the Galiuro Mountains and the river valleys for more than a thousand years. By the year 1540, when Spanish explorer Francisco Vasquez de Coronado crossed what is now southern Arizona, passing just east of the Galiuros, most of the seasonal Native American communities had been abandoned. But large, prehistoric villages occupied by farmers were scattered along both the San Pedro and Aravaipa valleys.

For the next 300 years, the Galiuros were forgotten, first by the early European explorers, then by American settlers. Father Eusebio Kino, a pioneering Jesuit priest, traveled down the San Pedro in 1697, stopping at a Sobaipuri Native American settlement called Aribabia. This small tribe sought refuge from the Apache and Jocome tribes in the sheltered valleys of the Galiuro range. Little is known about the Jocome, who are thought to have been the original inhabitants. Later, a few Spanish and Mexican army troops entered the area in search of Apache, but no existing records show an extended stay in the region by colonizers.

With the Gadsen Purchase in 1856, the Galiuros were deeded to the United States. Soon, government exploration missions traveled throughout southern Arizona with wagon and railroad routes laid out across the desert. These routes opened up the area to mining and later, to ranching. The town of Tombstone was established to the south. In 1862, the hot springs at what is now the Muleshoe Ranch became a tent hospital set up by troopers in the California column of the U.S. Army, attracting visitors who came for arthritis and rheumatism cures. The rough-and-ready spa was short-lived.

A few hardy settlers established farms in the San Pedro and Aravapai valleys, but when Apache marauders attacked and killed twenty settlers in the summer of 1876, and the Apache were eventually moved from the Chiracahua Reservation, the area was left to another kind of terrorist. As miners and cattle ranchers moved into the mountains, thugs, robbers, rustlers, and thieves—the outlaws who made Tombstone infamous—organized raiding parties with far more devastating results than any attack by Native Americans.

There was a brief mining period as well. In the mid-to-late 1800s, prospectors scoured all mountain ranges in southeastern Arizona, including the Galiuro. They discovered minerals at the western edge of the range and began mining about 1863. Twenty years later, the Copper Creek Mining District produced lead, silver, copper, and molybdenum. At least $4 million worth of these metals came out of the mountains before mining ended in 1959. Most of the operations lasted only a year or two. There were some low-grade finds along upper Rattlesnake Creek in 1902, and the tiny community of Gold Mountain sprang to life. The major buildings were a brothel and a saloon. Miners lived in rough log cabins and tent-houses. Another community called Klondyke, settled after the Yukon gold rush, was established farther to the north, along Aravaipa Creek.

On July 22, 1902—the year of the gold discoveries— President Theodore Roosevelt declared the upper part of the Galiuros a forest reserve. Six years later these rocky, thinly treed slopes became part of the Crook National Forest, protecting not the trees, but the much more precious watershed.

On the lower slopes, ranching took a firm foothold at the same time. By 1898 and through 1910, Angora goats were the principal livestock. One of the goat ranchers was Pete Spence, who had a one-room log cabin at a place called Rattlesnake Springs, now called Power's Garden. This cabin became the site of one of the biggest manhunts in Arizona history in February 1918, during World War I. U.S. Marshall Frank Haynes, Sheriff Frank McBride, and two deputy sheriffs hunted and attempted to arrest miner Jeff Power and his two sons, Tom and John (24 and 26 years of age), who had been accused of evading the draft. The Powers began shooting at the lawmen, who returned fire. After only a few minutes, four men were dead—the two deputies, the father, and Sheriff McBride. The Power boys took the officers' horses and a mule, then escaped, heading toward Redington. The fugitives crossed into Mexico with the army patrol in hot pursuit, then surrendered south of the border. The log cabin still stands at the Power's Garden site in Lower Rattlesnake Canyon.

In October 1932, the Forest Service created the Galiuro Primitive Area in the Crook National Forest. This forest was absorbed into the Coronado National Forest in 1953 and, under the 1964 Wilderness Act, the area was designated the Galiuro Wilderness. The present wilderness area was expanded in 1983 to 76,317 acres, adding the Rattlesnake Valley to the original land.

How to Get There

Basset Peak, which lies at the southeastern end of the area, can be accessed by driving along Forest Roads 651 and 660 from Fort Grant.

Other access roads include FR 159 (leading west from Bonita); FR 691 and a four-wheel-drive gravel road from Redington (both of which enter Redfield Canyon from the south); gravel roads from Mammoth, San Manuel, and Benson (all of which lead to a single entry trailhead at the midwestern edge of the wilderness); and two roads—FR 96 and FR 253—both of which lead southwest from Aravapai Road (which runs between Bonitra and Klondyke to the east of the preserve). This is a handy route from Safford via U.S. Highway 70.

Wilderness Trails

Many hiking trails traverse the wilderness area. The two longest trails follow the high ridges of land (the West and East Divide Trails) overlooking Rattlesnake and Redfield canyons. Most of the shorter trails link these two major trails.

Unlike at the neighboring Muleshoe Ranch Cooperative Management Area, no motorized vehicles are permitted in the Galiuro Wilderness. Horses are allowed and are the favored method of transportation for traveling the longer trails in the Wilderness.

The Power's Cabin and old mine site are in the approximate middle of the area. The site known as Power's Garden is 4 miles north of the cabin and 4 miles south of the northern entry point. Kennedy Peak is northeast of the cabin, Sunset Peak is southeast. Maverick Mountain is at the extreme northwestern edge of the preserve.

EAST DIVIDE TRAIL

This trail provides fine views along 22 miles of the rugged ridge. The north trailhead is at the end of FR 253. From this starting point, the trail climbs along small creeks, then to the upper portion of Oak Creek, where it follows the creek to the top of the ridge. Once you climb to the ridge, the trail leads south past Kennedy, Sunset, and Basset peaks. You can see many other ridges and peaks from the trail. A short side-trail, about 0.25 miles long, leads to the top of Kennedy peak and an unforgettable 360-degree panorama. The main East Divide Trail then drops into Douglas Canyon's mixed forest of aspen, Douglas fir, and ponderosa pine. It ends at a trailhead where Basset Peak Trail (1.4 miles) heads off to climb to the highest (7,663-foot) summit, another fine viewpoint in the Galiuro range. If you continue south along the East Divide Trail, you'll descend on a series of switchbacks into Ash Creek Canyon and the southern trailhead accessed via FR 651 and FR 660—the latter a four-wheel-drive road.

WEST DIVIDE TRAIL

Providing the longest single hike in the wilderness, West Divide Trail runs north from the Jackson Cabin (to the north of the Muleshoe Ranch Preserve) through a drainage off Redfield Canyon. The trail winds through this drainage to the main canyon and heads upstream for several miles beside some rugged and extremely scenic rock pinnacles and steep cliffs. Leaving Redfield Canyon, the trail crosses the high ridge landscape, passing the old Powers' Cabin and mine site (the location of the infamous shoot-out), then ascends to Grassy Ridge from which most of the Galiuro peaks can be seen. In addition, the Catalina Mountains stand in a dramatic formation to the west. This trail ends at Maverick Peak.

Forest Road 691, which heads 13.5 miles north from the Muleshoe Ranch, provides the only vehicle access to this trail. This rough four-wheel-drive road is used for Jeep tours from the Muleshoe. The north end of the trail is accessed via the Power's Garden Trail, which begins at the north end of the wilderness and goes 4 miles to Power's Garden. Pipestem Trail then takes over for another 5 miles to join the West Divide Trail.

A topographic map is necessary for those following this long trail and should, in fact, be used for hiking any Galiuro Wilderness trail. This map (Basset Peak, Kennedy Peak) is available from the Coronado National Forest ranger station in Safford.

Power's Garden Trail

Along this trail you follow the old roadway built by the Power family. They first established their mine, then built a house at the farmsite that is now the Power's Garden location. One can only be amazed at the tenacity of the Power family members who lived and worked in this rugged, silent country. Vehicle access to the trail is from U.S. Highway 70 to the east. Then go west on the Klondyke Road, which runs for 32 miles, to its junction with the Aravaipa Road. Turn northwest and drive 3.5 miles and turn onto FR 96, the old Power's Garden Road. This four-wheel-drive trail will take you another 11 miles to the trailhead. Access is also available from Deer Creek (FR 253) and High Creek (FR 159) by taking other trails that meet Power's Garden Trail.

From the northern trailhead on Power's Hill, the trail drops into Rattlesnake Canyon and follows the creek for the remainder of the hike. While the creek is dry most of the year, there is a healthy riparian habitat—populated with walnut, cypress, oak, and Arizona sycamores—throughout the canyon.

The Kennedy Peak topographical map covers this trail. From its beginnings at Power's Hill, the trail covers 9 miles to the junction with the East Divide Trail and another four miles to Power's Garden. It's another 5 miles to the West Divide Trail. Shorter trails include:

Tortilla Trail   From the East Divide Trail to Power's Garden, 8.5 miles.

Upper Rattlesnake Trail   Connecting the Power's Garden Trail to the East Divide Trail, 5 miles.

High Creek Trail   From the end of High Creek Road (FR 159) to the East Divide Trail, 2 miles.

Coral Canyon Trail   Connecting East Divide Trail to the Power's Garden Trail, 4 miles.

South Field Canyon Trail   Links Power's Garden Trail to the West Divide Trail, 2 miles.

Sycamore Trail   From Power's Hill to the Tortilla Trail, 5.5 miles

While there are mountain lions and black bears in this area, you are more likely to see the coatimundi, a raccoon-like creature. This desert animal is native to the Galiuros and its pesky behavior is very much like that of its better-known cousin, the raccoon. Campers may lose their victuals if food is not hoisted away from the cute but ever-hungry coati.

For information and trail maps, write:

Safford Ranger District
Coronado National Forest
P.O. Box 709
Safford, AZ 85548-0709
Or call (520) 428-4150

Muleshoe Ranch

The Muleshoe is both a mountain ranch—open to visitors—and a protected wilderness area in the Galiuro foothills. It is an example of the creative preservation efforts that government agencies and private environmental groups, in this case the Nature Conservancy, are making these days.

The Muleshoe Cooperative Management Area encompasses more than 54,000 acres, which includes rolling desert slopes, six streams, canyons, forests, hot springs, and trails for hiking and riding. The centerpiece of the area is the Muleshoe Ranch, a pioneer venture into nature tourism, owned and operated by the Nature Conservancy.

Lying at 3,900 feet at the end of 30 miles of dirt road, the ranch—with hot springs, horse paddocks, mountain views, trails, and southwestern-style casita accommodations—provides the visitor the kind of peaceful solitude no other type of "resort" can offer. I visited the Muleshoe in November 1993 and returned more recently while working on this book. On both occasions, I was caught up in the extraordinary magic of this wilderness retreat, where contemplating the glories of nature is accompanied by therapeutic exercise (if you wish to hike or ride) and blissful soaking in the hot spring tub.

The human history of the Muleshoe Ranch is as fascinating and dangerous as that of the surrounding old-west countryside. Even today, maps of the area show this site as Hooker Hot Springs, a legacy of the ranch's second owner, cattle baron Henry Clay Hooker. Hooker purchased the ranch, a small part of immense holdings he amassed in the region, following the murder of the first owner, Dr. Glendy King. Dr. King had come to Arizona because of his poor health and the dry climate found here. His son had died earlier from tuberculosis, and he had just lost his wife to disease. King had heard stories about the hot springs in the Galiuro foothills from the California troopers who had earlier set up the tent hospital.

King rode out to the property, checked to be sure no one had title to the land, then filed a homestead claim for 160 acres. Following Apache raids, and after white gunmen had come and gone, Dr. King was able to stay at the springs long enough to establish his spa resort. By 1882, two buildings had been constructed along with two rustic bathhouses.

But when another wave of outlaw violence swept over southeastern Arizona, Dr. King again had to retreat to Benson. Then a long-simmering territorial dispute with the neighboring Jones family was aggravated in August 1884. In typical Arizona fashion, Dr. King and his cowboys threatened the Jones boys who were driving a herd of horses down the canyon. Then someone ran a knife into a Jones' cowboy. When King drew his six-shooter, Jones pulled out his Winchester and shot King from a distance of 10 yards. Jones was cleared in self-defense, and King's brother put the property up for sale for an asking price of $1,050.

Buyer H. C. Hooker was more successful with the property. He made peace with the neighbors, and the Apache raids became less frequent. On September 4, 1884, Geronimo surrendered and the Indian wars were over.

Hooker built a cookhouse and a real bathhouse. He promoted the hot spring throughout the region. In 1889, 26-year-old Joseph Hooker took over management of the spa, where the waters were thought (and were promoted) to cure such diverse ailments as dyspepsia, rheumatism, and acne. Four hundred guests visited the spa during the summer season. Legend has it that the Earp brothers were among the drivers of the stages that brought visitors to the spa.

A post office and store were opened, but, by August 1883, the resort closed. First drought brought a financial crisis to the area. Then, when a flood swept part of the resort away, cattle ranching became the prime activity. By the dawn of 1900, the last visitor had soaked in the spring waters. Hooker died in 1907 at the age of 80.

The new buyer was a Philadelphian, Demming Issacson. He also bought additional property, including the Jones' ranch, and brought along two more families to help run the expanded ranch. Issacson improved the pool and expanded the house, converting the old adobe section into a bunkhouse for the ranch hands.

The vagaries of nature struck the property again and again. First more floods came, then the dust-bowl drought spread to Arizona, killing Issacson's cattle. The mortgage was foreclosed in 1927.

The next owner of the ranch, Cleveland divorcee Jessica McMurray, for a while operated the ranch for paying guests. She added a large sunroom to the dining wing and furnished the casitas with antiques and Oriental rugs. She collected Indian artifacts, later giving eighty prehistoric objects to the Amerindian Foundation in Dragoon. Many more of the museum's treasures came from archeological excursions Jessica McMurray conducted in the Winchester Mountains. Following ten years of declining health, Mrs. McMurray died in 1950. Her ashes were scattered on the hillside above the Muleshoe Ranch buildings. Following another drought, the property reverted to cattle ranching under other owners—Lyman Tinney and Jake Kittle (1950) and the Brownings (1952).

In 1975 Richard Wilson, a geoscience professor at the University of Arizona, bought the ranch. His subsequent sale of Muleshoe to the Arizona Chapter of the Nature Conservancy made possible the Conservancy's partnership with the National Forest Service and the Bureau of Land Management to form the Muleshoe Cooperative Management Area.

MULESHOE TODAY

Six year-round streams flow down the slopes of the Galiuro foothills, ending in the San Pedro River. The creeks, some of which begin as hot water bubbling to the earth's surface, provide an amazingly rich environment for birds and animal life. This is one of Arizona's finest aquatic habitats. In addition, more than 250 varieties of birds have a permanent or temporary home here, in what would be a desiccated, arid desert landscape without the creeks. That's part of the natural magic of Muleshoe.

The Muleshoe Ranch Headquarters lies at the end of 30 miles of dirt road, north of Willcox. The hour-long drive to the ranch gives the visitor time to make the mental adjustment necessary to enter this peaceful world of the Galiuro Mountains. A lane leads off the road, passing a paddock and crossing Hot Springs Creek, then winds up the hill to the U-shaped casita residence building.

The original ranch residence built by Henry Hooker, and improved by later owners, is now a comfortable court of casitas, spread around three sides of a central yard. The open side provides superb views of the Galiuro foothills with the creek below. With rooms and suites suitable for one, two, four, or six people, the complex also contains a group kitchen facility with a large adjoining lounge named "McMurray Commons."

Hot Springs

Down the hill, a few steps above the creek, is the hot spring tub, a converted cattle drinking tank into which flows the 115 degree water that originates from a spring located slightly higher on the hillside. While the Nature Conservancy holds out no promise of miraculous cures from these waters, there is something to Hooker's idea that they are therapeutic, as much for the mind as for the muscles.

At early morning and in late evening, when darkness spills over the forest, this rustic hot spring pool does offer a kind of cure found rarely in our modern world. It heats you (physically), cools you down (in a psychological sense), lifts you up (spiritually), and provides a state of quiet relaxation that continues for days after you leave the Muleshoe.

Why do only a few special places have this effect? Trails will take you close to several other springs in the preserve—some hot, some cold.

Accommodations

Muleshoe's guests stay in furnished casitas with kitchen facilities, cooking utensils, and linens supplied. From September through May and on all holiday weekends, there is a two-night minimum.

Camping facilities are available for self-contained and tent/vehicle camping, with supplied water, grills, showers, toilets, and an eating pavilion. Two cabins are available for overnight stays. The Stone Cabin, located in a private setting at ranch headquarters, has a small kitchen, a wood stove in the living room, a double bed, and a sofa bed. The Pride Ranch Cabin is a rustic backcountry cabin, with firewood and corrals provided. Water must be carried in.

TRAILS

An interpretive nature trail provides the shortest walk, three-quarters of a mile.

Bass/Hotsprings Loop The least developed of the ranch trails, this loop starts from ranch headquarters and takes you over a circular route of 3 miles.

Beth Woodin Vista Trail A trail of 5.5 miles climbs quickly from the ranch headquarters to a ridge with fine views of the surrounding foothills. You may wish to leave the main trail to walk down a hill to a small spring.

While the vehicular road ends at ranch headquarters, a track continues, climbing to higher ground north of the head-quarters. The old Pride Ranch, with its cabin, is located 6.3 miles up this trail. Along the way, the High Lonesome Trail offers 3 miles of spectacular views, providing an alternative to the main track to the Pride Ranch. You can see another spring and the Browning Ruin beside this trail. Past the Pride Ranch, the main trail continues to climb past the Jackson Cabin and into the Galiuro Wilderness, where it becomes the West Divide Trail (see page 169).

You'll find other opportunities for worthwhile hikes along dry creek beds during the summer months, offering a close-up view of the unique riparian habitats.

VISITOR PROGRAMS

Regular recreational opportunities include hiking, backpacking in the backcountry, photography, birding in season, horseback riding, and (of course) soaking. Backpackers have easy access to the magnificent Galiuro Wilderness north of ranch headquarters.

A helpful ranch staff, including horse wranglers, is available to help plan your recreational activity. The ranch offers a series of Recreational Natural History weekends that include horse-riding trips and a backcountry tour four times each year. The 4-day riding trips explore the Galiuro backcountry and offer bird viewing, hiking, and hot spring soaking. The ranch provides all horses, tack, meals, lodgings, and campfire sessions for all-inclusive rates.

Through an arrangement with the Redington Land and Cattle Co. of Cascabel, the ranch also offers Jeep tours of the Muleshoe. These remarkable jaunts on the Jackson Cabin Road trail, which range into the Galiuro high country, are available by reservation. A short trip (1.5 hours) costs from $20 to $25. A full-day trip (5 hours) will run $75 or more, and you may add extra hours to either trip by paying an hourly fee. Visitors may also arrange to have horses available for day riding trips through advance reservations.

In the spring, birding hikes are offered. In late August, the ranch has an annual fall birding hike to view the zone-tailed hawks, flycatchers, and other transients before they migrate south for the winter months. Weekly guided bird and flower hikes are held on Saturdays.

Two days might be enough in this life-changing place. More is better! A 3-day to week-long visit at the Muleshoe Ranch will restore the soul, harden muscles, bring you into close contact with birds, animals, and mountain fauna, and put you into a state of blissful relaxation.

For complete information on Muleshoe Ranch, recreational activities and overnight reservations, write:

Muleshoe Ranch Headquarters
R.R. 1, Box 1542
Willcox, AZ 85643
Or call (520) 586-7072

Nearby Attractions

ARAVAPAI CANYON PRESERVE

The central Aravapai Gorge cuts through the northern edge of the Galiuro Mountains, created by its perennial stream flanked by distinctive cliffs. Within the gorge, a superb wildlife habitat is nurtured by the creek.

The range of trees in this riparian habitat is surprisingly varied. The mixed broadleaf forest includes the standard cottonwood/willow habitat, augmented by Arizona walnut, alder, and sycamore trees.

The canyon, located about 50 miles northeast of Tucson, forms part of the most northerly section of the San Pedro River watershed. The BLM and the Nature Conservancy have set aside 35,000 acres of land as the protected area. Of special interest is the 7,000 acres assembled by the Arizona Chapter of the Nature Conservancy, which manages the preserve and offers recreational opportunities.

The canyon is noted for its fish—the best remaining collection of desert fishes in the state, with seven native species living in the creek. These include two species that the federal government lists as threatened: the spikedace and loach minnow.

Two hundred species of birds may be spotted at various times of the year, including raptors—black and zone-tailed hawks and the peregrine falcon—Bell's vireo, the yellow-billed cuckoo, and the beardless tyrannulet.

Animals roam the canyon and the surrounding hills. Bighorn sheep are the star attraction here, in addition to mountain lion, coatimundi, ringtailed cats, and brown bear. In the springtime, the creekside flowers include columbine, monkey flowers, lupine, four o'clocks, and some much rarer species (see the Field Guide section at the end of this book). The Conservancy offers several types of day hikes, as well as backpacking trips. Horseback rides are available.

The unique nature of the canyon—sheltered and protected—made it a welcome stopping place and home for many groups of people over the past few thousand years. Before the Spanish arrived in the region, the canyon was an occasional home to Hohokam, Mogollon, and Salado people—all of them farmers who grew corn and other crops close to the stream. In more recent times—from the sixteenth century—the Sobaipuri lived on the west end of the creek, in the San Pedro River Valley. They developed irrigated farms and lived in several large villages. Two hundred years later, they were replaced by the "Tse Jine" (Dark Rock People), also known as the Aravaipa Apache.

After the end of the wars with Native Americans, Mexican and European/American settlers established ranches in this same area. Copper mining in the northern part of the Galiuro range took place in the late 1800s and early 1900s. The town of Aravaipa is a ghostly reminder of those early settlement days, as is Klondyke, the old mining town at the east end of the canyon.

The Nature Conservancy properties are located at the west and east ends of the canyon, and the Conservancy and BLM share pieces of land along the south rim. Public access is allowed—without permits—at the eastern end of the canyon. There a public road passes through preserve land to the Wilderness Area parking lot. For those entering from the west, BLM wilderness permits are required. The permits are available by contacting:

Safford District Office of the BLM
711 14th Ave.
Safford, AZ 85546
(520) 428-4040

Primitive camping is permitted at the east end of the canyon, on public land beside Turkey Creek. A four-wheel-drive road leads up this side-canyon to public lands on the south rim of Aravaipa Canyon.

Also at the east end, the Nature Conservancy rents a guest house to families and small groups. This is the former Panorama Ranch, purchased in 1971 from Fred and Cliff Wood. The ranch house is now available through the preserve office at (520) 828-3443.

This old home with its treed lawn and the nearby campground provide accommodation and make it possible for visitors to get away from civilization for a day or two—to fully enjoy this superb natural setting.

It is possible to walk along the canyon floor beside the stream, and even in the usually gentle creek as it wanders around gravel bars.

CORONADO NATIONAL FOREST

Two sections of the widely scattered Coronado National Forest are within an hour's drive of Willcox, offering many sightseeing and recreational opportunities. The southern section, covering the Chiricahua and Pedregosa mountains, lies south of Interstate 10, close to the New Mexico border.

Two roads cross the forest area, taking visitors to several campgrounds and to the Chiricahua National Monument. The ghost towns of Galeyville and Hilltop are seen in the national forest along the network of gravel roads that head northwest from the village of Portal. The two sides of Hilltop, an old mining camp, are connected by a tunnel through the rock. The two ghost towns and several forest campgrounds may also be accessed by taking the gravel road south from Interstate 10 at exit 382, then turning west.

The more northerly portion of the forest spreads over the peaks and foothills of the Pinaleno Mountains a few miles north of I-10. Take U.S. Highway 666 between I-10 and the town of Safford. Arizona Route 266 leads west through the forest to the villages of Bonita and Fort Grant. There are no organized camping or other facilities along this road.

Nine miles to the north, Arizona Route 366 takes nature lovers to four camping areas, ending at Rigg's Lake, set in a sizable valley (Rigg's Flat) surrounded by the Pinalenos. Blue Jay Peak—to the northwest—has an elevation of 8,839 feet. Mount Graham, the highest peak and the tallest mountain in southeastern Arizona, tops out at 10,717 feet.

Trails lead from the campsites to mountain vistas, over high meadows and across small streams. This is one of many places where the low desert rangelands and the green mountain ecosystems of the region appear in stark contrast.

WILLCOX AND THE PLAYA

Although Willcox lies south of Interstate 10, and is covered in the next section of this book, we include it here because of its closeness to the Galiuro Wilderness. It is a logical place from which to venture into the North San Pedro Basin. Originally a railroad town, founded as a construction camp by the Southern Pacific, Willcox became the most important cattle town in the Southwest at the turn of the century. Cattle ranching and farming are still important to the area. It celebrates the cowboy legends in the Rex Allen Arizona Cowboy Museum. Allen, a cowboy singer/actor, was a longtime Willcox resident. The Willcox Cowboy Hall of Fame Museum is located in the same building as the town visitor information center.

But it is the Willcox Playa that attracts bird lovers. This lake, largely dry during summer months, takes on water from winter rainfalls and becomes an important stopping point for migrant birds. Thousands of sandhill cranes come to the Playa in January. Ninteen ninety-three saw the first Sandhill Crane Celebration, a 3-day event with guided birding tours of the Playa, Cochise Lake, the Muleshoe Ranch, and the Chiricahua National Monument. Seminars, workshops, and field trips add to the annual attractions for bird enthusiasts, and special programs are organized for children. The celebration takes place on the last weekend in January.

For information on upcoming Sandhill Crane Celebrations, write:

Willcox Chamber of Commerce
1500 North Circle Road
Willcox, AZ 85643
Or call: (520) 384-2272

SOUTHEASTERN ARIZONA WILDLIFE

B ecause the north San Pedro Valley and its neighboring mountain ranges have ecosystems that vary from the Chihuahuan and Lower Sonoran desert zones to the ponderosa pine forests of the Galiuro Range, visitors can observe a rich collection of birds and animals in the region, to say nothing of the unusual fish that are native to the mountain streams.

Our listing of wildlife is largely taken from the middle and upper zones, above the flat desert plan of the river valley. However, many of the birds are found in riparian habitats along the San Pedro, as well as along the foothill and mountain creeks.

BIRDS

Swainson's Hawk

Buteo swainsoni
This medium-sized raptor is a summer visitor to the San Pedro and Galiuro region. While it is most numerous on the Canadian prairies, it breeds from Alaska to Mexico, and winters in Argentina. It prefers plains, prairies, and meadows with few trees, as well as tundra—quite a range for this migrating bird. Growing to about 22 inches in length, it has a wingspan of about 55 inches. It is dark brown above, with a white throat and body. A reddish brown band, like a bib, lies across the throat. The top of the tail is dark gray. While the feathers are dark gray, there is a lining of white, as on the body, on the underside of the wings.

Swainson's hawk has a noticeable flying pattern. It glides in a V-angle while catching updrafts, of which there are many over the San Pedro Valley. It looks for rodents from its perches on trees and posts near the ground. It also feeds on insects. You'll see these hawks flying by the thousands, as they migrate north and south.

Prairie Falcon

Falco mexicanus
Colored and shaped much like the more common peregrine falcon, the prairie falcon has a spotted broad upper back and wings, and a lighter breast and belly that is also spotted with brown. You can recognize the falcon as it flies, by its pointed wings and narrow tail.

Its wingbeats are very fast. At close range, you will see the characteristic black bar on its face below the eye, and the triangular black patches on the wingpits. It is one of the many raptors that circle over southeastern Arizona. The range of this falcon is from southwestern Canada to the western United States and southern Mexico. It lives in grasslands, preferably in mountain regions, and also in open hill country and prairie lands. Its voice, when at its nest, is a repeated *we-chew*, and a rapidly repeated *kek*.

Yellow-billed Cuckoo

Coccyzus americanus
This is one of only four cuckoos found in the western states. There are 132 varieties worldwide. Related to the roadrunner, the cuckoo is a long-tailed, slender bird. Its feet are comprised of two toes pointing forward and two toes pointing back. It lives only in warm regions of the world.

The yellow-billed cuckoo has a brown back and white underparts. Its distinctive wings are rufous. There are large white spots at the underside tips of the feathers. The curved beak is also distinctive, with a bright yellow lower mandible. Its food includes caterpillars and other insects.

Northern Beardless Tyrannulet

Camptostoma imberbe
Also called the beardless flycatcher, this bird is a very small flycatcher, much like a kinglet or a small verdin. It has a dull grayish-green color on its head and upper back, with brownish wing and tail bars. Identifying features include a small ring around the eye, head cresting, and small bill. This bird ranges from southeastern Arizona and southwestern New Mexico to Costa Rica. It builds a globe-shaped nest with a single hole on the side in riverside habitats, low woods, mesquite bosques, and canyons that are at a low elevation. You can see the beardless tyrannulet along the San Pedro and in the foothills canyons, including canyons at Muleshoe. Its voice is a thin *peeee-yuk*, and a soft *ee ee ee ee ee*.

Bandtail Pigeon

Columba fasciata
With a distinctive narrow white collar and a light band on the end of its tail, this member of the dove family is chunky and sturdily constructed. It has yellow feet and a yellow bill with a black tip. The bandtail lives in woodlands and mountain zones, including oak canyons, foothills, and mountain forests. It is

found from southwestern British Columbia and south along the Pacific, throughout the Rockies to Argentina. Unlike many pigeons and doves, it rests on trees. Its voice is a *ooh-whooo*, much like an owl, to a repeated *whoo-oo-whoo*.

Bushtit
Psaltriparus minimus
This very plain but delightful little bird is found from southwestern British Columbia to Guatemala, including the oaks in my own back yard in the Sierra foothills. It likes the same type of chaparral and mixed woodlands that you'll find in the Galiuro foothills or at Aravapai Canyon. A member of the same family (Paridae) as the many species of chickadee, like its cousins, it gives a spirited performance at the bird feeder. The bushtit has a grayish brown back. Those found in the Rocky Mountains have gray crowns. Male bushtits in southeastern Arizona and southwestern New Mexico are more likely to have blackish cheeks. This type is known as the black-eared bushtit. Its voice is a repeated and slightly urgent *tsit tsit tsit tsit*, and a repeated *clenk*.

FISH

The fish listed here are found in the land protected by the Muleshoe Ranch Preserve. Living in the Hot Spring Creek and other nearby Galiuro foothill creeks, these fish have been decreasing in numbers since the early 1900s. The preservation of these four species was a major factor in the creation of the Muleshoe reserve.

Speckled Dace
Rhinichthys osculus
While a very widespread fish in the western U.S. and British Columbia, it has been disappearing from the Southwest. It is a prime food source for trout, and is often used for bait. It lives in creeks, rivers, and lakes, always over gravel or rock. It is also found in the waters of desert springs and the creeks that flow from the springs. The speckled dace is variable in its color, from location to location. Growing to 4 inches, it is gently rounded with a flat belly. Its back is grayish to olive green, its sides gray-green with a darker lateral stripe, and its back is covered with dark speckles. The snout is pointed.

Gila Chub
Gila bicolor
Also called the tui chub, this fish is much larger, growing to a length of 16 inches. It is a plump-fish, with a dark olive-colored

back, reddish sides, and the lower part and fins a definite reddish color. Immature gila chub have a dark stripe on each side.

The head of this fish is slightly pointed and short, and the mouth is small.

It lives in lakes, ponds, and shallow stream water, often in quiet, slow-running creeks. It is found from southern Washington through Nevada and southern California. Rarely seen in Arizona, it lives in deep pools shaded by overhanging trees in lower Redfield and Bass canyons, and in the Muleshoe preserve. Here, gila chub grow from 8 to 10 inches.

Longfin Dace
Agosia chrysogaster
The most common species of fish on the Muleshoe preserve, the longfin dace is found living in quiet pools in all the foothills streams. This speckled olive-colored fish has a blunt head; a dark stripe along the side is its most distinguishing feature.

Gila Mountain Sucker
Pantosteus clarki
Both this fish and its cousin the gila or coarse-scaled sucker (*catostomous insignis*) are easily identified by their sucker-like mouths, which are on the bottom of the head. They live in deep pools or riffles, growing up to 12 inches. Both species are found in the Hot Springs and Redfield drainage systems.

These species feed mainly on algae, although the Gila sucker is a carnivore as well. You'll find them mostly in larger pools. The Gila mountain sucker, which is the more numerous, is dark on top and light underneath. Smaller ones often have dark bands on the back. The Gila sucker is usually less banded.

OTHER ANIMALS

Blacktail Rattlesnake
Crotalus molossus
Although highly poisonous, this rattlesnake is less dangerous to humans than other species are because it has an unaggressive nature. It grows to a length of almost 50 inches, but is often shorter. Greenish, or grayish, or with a yellowish tinge, it has light crossbands on the body. The black tail offers a distinct contrast. Each scale has a single color. Its babies, which emerge 9–12 inches long, are born in the summer. Up to six are born at a time.

It is found from central and southern Arizona, east into southern New Mexico, Texas, and the Chihauhuan Desert of Mexico. Of the three subspecies of this rattlesnake, only *C. molossus* is found in the

Southwest. The blacktail rattlesnake is most common in mountain areas among rocks, including limestone formations. It lives in stony canyons that have some trees, and along rocky streambeds such as the foothill creeks of the Galiuros. It does not live above 9,000 feet.

Collard Peccary (Javelina)
Didotyles tajucu
A favorite desert "pig," the javelina is a native of southeastern Arizona, including the Tucson area, the southwestern corner of New Mexico, and central and south Texas. Definitely pig-like, this animal is small in size, growing to a length of 40 inches and weight of 50 pounds. It has a gray or blackish color on the body that gives it a salt and pepper appearance, with a yellowish tinge on the cheeks and a yellowish-gray collar that runs from shoulder to shoulder. When the animal is angry, its black mane on the back of the neck bristles. Both males and females develop tusks when they are older. The young are born in summer, usually two at a time. The young are more reddish than the parents.

The javelina has unusual cloven hooves, with four toes on the front feet and three toes on the hind feet. Each foot has two hooves. When tracking the animals, you'll see these double hooves as rounded oblong (almost oval) shapes, about 1.5 inches long.

Javelina live, and move around, in herds of anywhere from six to thirty males and females. They are often seen in the Galiuro foothills, including the Muleshoe preserve, trotting around in packs in the early morning and late afternoon. They utter a low grunt when feeding, and squeal only when frightened or hurt. The young stay close to their mothers while they feed; the others scatter quite a distance during eating sessions. When frightened, they issue an odor from musk glands located on the rump. They prefer to eat cactus, especially prickly pear, thorns and all. They also eat mesquite beans, shrubs, grasses, nuts, and berries, as well as succulent plants (for nutrition and water content). However, they do need an open water source for survival. They are found in areas where there is some form of shelter. Not fussy about their homes, javelina live in old mine tunnels and caves, and under trees in desert washes.

Coatimundi
Nasua nasua
This unusual small mammal is not a longtime native of the Southwest, but migrated into southern Arizona sometime

before the early 1900s. It has become numerous in several locations, including the Galiuro Range and the Rincon Mountains on the western side of the San Pedro Valley. It is also seen in the mountain ranges to the immediate south, next to the Upper San Pedro Basin, and in the Big Bend area of Texas.

A relative of the raccoon, the coati is a medium-sized (length of 4 feet), grayish-brown animal with a long tail that has irregular, lighter bands. It has a long, pointed snout that is white at the tip, and white markings over and under the eyes. Its ears are small. The male is twice the size of the female. With five toes on its feet, the coati leaves a track 3 inches long and 2 inches wide, with the claws showing on the foreprints only.

Coati live in mountain forests and in rocky wooded canyons. They must have water nearby. They display many of the same personality traits as the raccoon. Inquisitive and gregarious, they move in groups of two to twenty. Several females may travel together, caring for each other's young. The young wander away from the group, giving a small, plaintive *peep* call when lost. They feed on almost anything they can catch, including campers' supplies.

They eat rodents and insects, as well as berries, tubers, fruit, bird eggs, and young birds.

PLANTS

Arizona Cypress
Cupresses arizonica
This Mexican border-jumper grows naturally on gravelly slopes and rocky areas in a few isolated canyons in southeastern Arizona and in the neighboring part of New Mexico. It is found in the Galiuros, in Sabino Canyon near Tucson, and at Cochise's Stronghold and Bonita Canyon just south of Interstate 10 near Willcox. Occasionally it is found in southern California and in the Trans-Pecos area of Texas.

This relative of the Monterey cypress is a good-looking tree, conical in shape. It is also related to several Mediterranean cypress varieties that were considered sacred and used for ornamenting funerals. As an ornamental tree in the Southwest, it is often cultivated for sale as Christmas trees, urban landscape plantings, or to make fenceposts.

When there is enough moisture, this tree can grow to a height of 70 feet, although it is usually much shorter (less than 40 feet). Its trunk is from 1 to 2 feet in diameter and has reddish-brown bark, which is scaly on immature trees and develops striations (like the alligator juniper) that give it a shredded appearance. Its grayish-green leaves are similar to those of a juniper. The dark, reddish-brown cones are globe-shaped, about 1 inch in diameter with woody scales. When ripe, they open and spill their seeds onto the ground.

Arizona Walnut
Juglans major
Growing along watercourses in the Southwest and Mexico, this species of walnut is one of six found in the United States. The nuts of this tree are quite edible and are sweeter than the English (or Persian) species, although they're smaller and a bit harder to separate from the outer shell. The Arizona walnut tree grows to a height of 45 to 50 feet, with a trunk diameter of up to 4 feet, though most are about 2 feet across. Its most recognizable feature is its scaly, furrowed bark.

The leaflets are pointed and long, from 8 to 12 inches. The leaves are made up of nine to thirteen leaflets. Male and female catkins appear on the same tree, though only female catkins form fruits of nearly 1 inch in diameter. They have a smooth outer husk and a hard inner nut that looks much like the fruit of the more commonly eaten English walnut.

Mexican White Pine
Pinus flexilis–var. reflexa
This is a close relative to the limber pine, which is found more widely in the U.S. The Mexican white is distinguished from the limber pine by the sharply bent (reflexed) tips of its cone scales. Like other white pines, the Mexican has pale bluish-green needles, formed in bunches of five. The needles grow up to 4 inches in length, longer than the limber. You will find both pines growing in mixed stands in southeastern Arizona. It has several other common names: border limber pine, Arizona pine, and border pine. Mexicans call it *pino enano* (dwarfish pine). Its range extends from the mountains of southeastern Arizona to southwest New Mexico to Mexico. It is found most often in mountain canyons, which are common in the Galiuro Mountains.

Chihuahua Pine
Pinus leiophylla–var. chihuahuana
This small pine grows to a height of 50 feet, with a trunk diameter of 2 feet. You'll most often see it in a smaller size, around 35 feet. Like the Mexican white pine, this variety is not seen outside this special

area, where southeastern Arizona meets southwestern New Mexico. The slender, pale green needles grow in bunches of three, 2 to 4 inches long. Most pines keep the sheaths at the base of the needles, but the Chihuahua pine sheds its sheaths. The dark reddish-brown cones have a dullish glossy or matte finish. About 2 inches long, they stay on the trees for several years. New twigs are quite orange, but they turn a dull reddish-brown color as they mature. The bark has dark-brown, almost black scales, with grooves that are more reddish. The pine nuts follow the production of flowers. The nuts are smaller than those of the pinyon pine. Male flowers are yellow; female are green. This pine grows in the Galiuros and Chiricahua ranges.

Emory Oak
Quercus emoryi
One of six oak varieties that grow in the desert uplands of the Southwest, the Emery grows at elevations of 3,000 to 8,000 feet. It is also found in Texas and Mexico. It has a much smaller range than the common scrub oak.

This medium-sized evergreen tree has a straight trunk with very rough, black bark. It has a rounded crown and shiny, leathery, yellowish-green or dark green leaves that alternate on the twig. The underside of the leaf is paler than the upper. Each leaf has a sharp point at the tip and a few spiny teeth, which are either rounded or notched at the base. The leaves are shed in the spring as new growth occurs. The acorns are about a .75-inch oblong shape, with a deep cup that encloses almost half the shell.

Scrub Oak
Quercus turbinella
Also an evergreen, the turbinella is often found in thickets, as more of a shrub. It also forms a small tree with a rather unruly, spreading crown. The predominant species of shrub on the lower levels of Arizona's mountains, the scrub oak is found in foothills by itself, or with other oaks, junipers, and pinyon pines. Its range extends from southwestern Colorado to southern New Mexico, and west to southern California. It grows at elevations between 4,000 and 8,000 feet. Its name, turbinella, refers to the shape of the acorns, which resemble a little turban.

Arizona Alder
Alnus oblongifolia
This species is beautifully adapted for the steep creek canyons of the Galiuro foothills. You'll find it in the riparian

habitats of most creeks that feed the lower San Pedro. It is also found in southwestern New Mexico, as well as in northern Mexico. One of the largest of the native alders in the United States, the Arizona alder can grow to a height of 80 feet. It has a straight trunk with a rounded crown. From the side it has an upright oval shape. Its dark green leaves alternate in three rows, reaching a length of 2 to 4 inches. They have seven to ten parallel veins on each side. The tree's smooth, thin, dark-gray bark becomes scaled with age. The twigs are brown, slender, and pliable. Tiny flowers are followed by 2–3 inch catkins.

Pointleaf Manzanita
Arcostaphylos pungens
This manzanita grows at elevations between 3,000 and 8,000 feet in large thickets of bushes, which are 3 to 6 feet tall. Found from Texas to southern California, it grows in clumps because the slender branches often bend to the ground and immediately take root. The oval-shaped leaves are long and a bluish-green color. The leathery leaves are covered with fine hairs. Its berries, which range in color from a medium brown to a medium (Southwest) red, are somewhat flattened. Manzanita berries make a medicinal tea

that is used in Mexico as a diuretic.

WILDFLOWERS

The first of the following wildflower plants are found in the valley of the San Pedro River, and into the foothills to the east. They are also found in the lower San Pedro Basin south of Interstate 90.

Four O'clock
Allionia incarta
The trailing Allionia is found across the deserts of Arizona and Texas. The purple-to-pink blossoms appear from April until October. This flower is related to, but different from *alliona albida*, which grows only in the California desert on open sandy areas such as mesas and flat desert valleys. The trailing stems grow to a length of 30 inches, with clusters of three blossoms, several clusters to each stem. The sticky stems are held down on the ground by blowing sand, which sticks to the plant. The distinctive fruit of the four o'clock is toothed.

Monkey-flower
Mimulus bigelovii
This member of the figwort family thrives in the deserts of Arizona and California, growing to a height of about 8 inches in open, sandy areas. Though a

small plant, it produces large flowers. There are many variations of monkey-flower, including several desert species. *Mimulus glabratus* grows only in Texas. Anyone who knows penstamons and the familiar snapdragon will have no difficulty recognizing the desert monkey-flower.

Colorado Columbine
Aquilegia caerulea
Found in the higher reaches of the Galiuro Range, and at high elevations elsewhere in the Southwest (including Cedar Breaks), this columbine has very attractive large flowers made up of five (outer) white or bluish-white sepals, and inner white petals. The leaves at the base of the plant have a compound construction with rounded, divided lobes. The columbine is used as food by animals. Sheep, in particular, are fond of the plant. Grazing cattle served to largely decimate the columbine population in southern Arizona in past years. Now the plant is making a comeback.

Coulter's Lupine
Lupinus sparsiflorus
In an Arizona spring, after higher than normal rainfall, the southeastern desert blooms with a carpet of Coulter's lupine. It can be found on slopes, in the foothills, and on the desert floor. Its range extends from Baja and southern California to southern Nevada and southwestern New Mexico. Usually found in combination with globemallow and desert marigold, it is a slender, erect plant with branched stems and blue flowers (either a pale or medium lilac blue) about half an inch long. The top petal usually has a white or light yellow center. It has a compound leaf with five to nine leaflets, each growing to a length of 1.5 inches, arranged in a round "spoke" pattern.

WHERE TO STAY

ARAVAPAI CANYON PRESERVE

Nature Conservancy Guest House

This old ranch house is at the east end of the Aravapai canyon, accessible via a public road that leads to the property owned by the Nature Conservancy. The house accommodates any combination of families or small groups. To reserve accommodations, contact the preserve office at (520) 828-3443.

BENSON

Quail Hollow Inn

P.O. Box 2107
Benson, AZ 85602
(520) 586-3646

This large Best Western operation offers good accommodations—some with showers and refrigerators—at reasonable prices. The motel has a heated pool, whirlpool, and laundry. There's a restaurant nearby ($).

Desert Lodge

211 West 4th Street
Benson, AZ 85602
(520) 586-3417

A basic downtown Benson motel with TV and air-conditioned rooms and rooms with kitchenettes. Daily, weekly or monthly rates ($).

Quarter Horse RV Park and Motel

800 West 4th Street
Benson, AZ 85602
(520) 586-3371

This very basic motel has 4 rooms ($) and adjoining RV parking lot.

Chief Four Feathers KOA Kampground

(520) 586-3977

Located 1 mile north of I-10 off the Ocotillo Road exit (#304), this campground has 87 sites, many of them pull-through, most with hookups. A few sites are set aside for tenting, and cabins are available. Includes dump station, laundry, store, pool, recreation room, playground, propane.

Red Barn Campground

(520) 586-2035

Located north of I-10 on Ocotillo Road, the park offers grassy tent sites, RV spaces, a store, laundry, and propane.

CASCABEL

Cascabel Ranch

An operating cattle ranch with accommodations for ten people, the ranch offers horse and Jeep riding tours and is close to the San Pedro River, known for its birding and other attractions.

For rates and activities, contact:

Redington Land and Cattle Co.
HC 1 Box 730
Benson, AZ 85602
(520) 212-5555

CHIRICAHUA NATIONAL MONUMENT

Bonita Canyon Campground
(520) 824-3560

Located in the national monument, 36 miles southeast of Willcox via Arizona 186 and Arizona 181, this campground has tent and trailer sites (up to 21 feet), restrooms, flush toilets, and water supply. No reservations.

Coronado National Forest

There are campgrounds in several sections of the national forest within an hour's drive of Willcox. **Rigg's Flat, Hospital Flat, Shannon** and **Arcadia** campgrounds are accessed via U.S. 666 and FR 366, in the forest north of Willcox. In the Dragoon Mountains, the campground at **Cochise Stronghold** is reached via U.S. 666 and FR 584.

In the Chiricahua Mountains: **Joy Valley, Rustler Park, Pinery Canyon, John**

Hands-Cave Creek, Herb Martyr-Cave Creek, South Fork-Cave Creek, Stewart-Cave Creek and **Idlewild-Cave Creek** are all a few miles southwest of the village of Portal on the east side of the range.

MULESHOE RANCH PRESERVE

Muleshoe Ranch
Muleshoe Ranch Headquarters
R.R. 1, Box 1542
Willcox, AZ 85643
(520) 586-7072

Located north of Willcox at the end of a gravel road, Muleshoe Ranch has casita-style accommodations (with kitchens) and a common kitchen area along with the McMurray Commons lounge. Rates range from $10 (for the rustic Pride Ranch Cabin) to $100 for the large King Suite (double occupancy). Nature Conservancy members receive a discount. A 50 percent deposit is required two weeks before the reservation date. Weekly rate: 7 nights for the price of 6.

TOMBSTONE

Lookout Lodge
Highway 80, P.O. Box 787
Tombstone, AZ 85638
(520) 457-2223

Overlooking the Dragoon Mountains to the east, this Best Western motel with a heated pool is the most modern place to stay in Tombstone. A complimentary continental breakfast is served (**$** to **$$**).

Tombstone Motel
4th Street at Fremont
Tombstone, AZ 85638
(520) 457-3478

This older and smaller motel, close to the historic downtown area, has comfortable accommodations (**$**). Restaurants, saloons, and souvenir shops are a block away.

Tombstone Hills
KOA Kampground
(520) 457-3819

Just south of town on the highway, this operation is similar to many other KOA campgrounds, with tent, RV, and trailer spaces with full hookups, pool, store, and playground.

Wells Fargo RV Park
(602) 456-3850

Also located on the highway south of downtown Tombstone, this park has RV and trailer spaces with full hookups, tent sites, showers, store, laundry, and a picnic area.

WILLCOX

Best Western Plaza Inn
1100 West Rex Allen Dr.
Willcox, AZ 85643
(520) 384-3556 or 800-262-2645 (outside Arizona)

With 93 units, this is the largest of the motels in Willcox. There are rooms and suites, a pool, lounge, dining room, and free breakfast (**$** to **$$**).

Comfort Inn
724 N. Bisbee Ave.
Willcox, AZ 85643
(520) 384-4222 or 800-221-2222

This modern chain motor hotel has 73 units and a restaurant next door. Free continental breakfast is served (**$** to **$$**).

For additional places to stay, see "Where to Stay" in the South San Pedro Basin chapter starting on page 224.

South San Pedro and Santa Cruz Basins

The southeastern corner of Arizona is, at the same time, one of the most famous and one of the least recognized parts of the Southwest. This paradox becomes apparent when you visit the region.

Here, in the old towns—Tombstone, Benson, Bisbee, Patagonia—much of the continuing myth of the Wild West was set. Tombstone, particularly, is the Wild West of legend—the home of the Earp brothers and Doc Holliday, of the shoot-out at the OK Corral, and of the infamous Birdcage Theater. This is the region of rowdy mining towns, where miners scrabbled for a few years, searching for riches, and instead were mined for their dollars by gamblers, confidence men, ladies of the night, saloon keepers, and even the supposed upright merchants of the era, who charged the highest possible prices for the poorest possible merchandise.

All of this history is on display in Tombstone, where the whole town has been turned into a Wild West theme park, and in historical museums of other nearby towns. But there is more than a short, unstable period in the development of southwestern Arizona to attract visitors to the south San Pedro Valley. This basin and range region features some of the most unusual parks and monuments in the state, and the largest group of publicly accessible nature preserves—superb bird-watching areas—in the whole Southwest.

Most of the Lower San Pedro River south of Interstate 10 is a protected wildlife preserve, the San Pedro Riparian National Conservation Area. Trailheads at several access points lead to walks along the river and into the riverside marshes that contain the most extensive bird habitat in the state.

West of the San Pedro Basin, the Santa Cruz River flows south from Tucson, paralleling Interstate 19, through downtown Nogales into Mexico. Like the San Pedro, the Santa Cruz is fed by creeks that flow through the mountain valleys. After crossing the border, the Santa Cruz disappears into the sands of the inhospitable Mexican desert.

The two rivers, the creeks, and the marshes attract the largest bird population in the central and western United States. Located on the interior flyway, this unusual coincidence of desert rivers and the flyway make for the most exciting riparian bird-watching opportunities in the West. But that isn't all.

Lying just west of the New Mexico boundary, the Dragoon and Pedregosa mountains provide outstanding outdoor adventure. The Coronado National Forest covers the ranges, offering camping, hiking, mountain biking, and four-wheel-driving opportunities. The Chiricahua National Monument, located at the northern edge of the Dragoon Mountains, is a truly wondrous collection of rock formations that provides a mystifying experience at any time of day. The monument is also an excellent wildlife-viewing location.

The Whetstone and Huachuca mountains separate the two river basins, and there are more birding opportunities at the higher levels, in the Huachuca range, including Garden Canyon, Ramsey Canyon, and Bear Canyon. Hummingbird lovers will become ecstatic when they visit this region. Just to the west of the Huachucas are the Canelo Hills, with more birding.

As you travel throughout the area, within a 2-hour drive of Benson, Bisbee, or Nogales, you'll find historical monuments and memorials, one of the first U.S. Army forts to be built in the area, scenic canyons, an outstanding art colony in the old Spanish town of Tubac, and the international ambience of Nogales, Arizona, and its Mexican counterpart across the downtown border crossing.

The opportunities to engage in bird-watching are so varied throughout the region that it takes some careful planning to organize a birding vacation. To help you plan your stay in the area, we have divided the attractions into two regions: the South San Pedro Basin and the Chiricahua Mountains, and the Upper Santa Cruz Basin, including Sonoita Creek. Each region has its own charming towns in which to stay, and each town has comfortable inns, guest ranches, and motels, as well as unique bed-and-breakfast homes.

South San Pedro Basin

HISTORIC ROOTS

The central attraction of the basin is the San Pedro National Conservation Area, a wildlife preserve along the San Pedro between the Mexican border and Interstate 10. Within this area alone are more than 250 prehistoric and historic sites, and archeologists have only scratched the surface. Rivers have always had a way of attracting human habitation.

Researchers in the region, including those at the nearby Amerind Foundation, have identified the earliest human occupation by the Clovis Culture, dating back about 11,000 years from 9000 to 6000 B.C. These people are known for developing the Clovis point, a unique projectile weapon. They also used stone tools and other weapons to kill animals, including the bison and mammoths that were common to the area during this period.

Artifacts from other native cultures have identified the Archaic and Mogollon people as residents of the San Pedro Basin between 6000 B.C. and A.D. 1500.

Then came the Spanish, about A.D. 1540. Other Native American cultures occupied the region during the Spanish period, including the Sobaipuri (from A.D. 1430 to 1769) and Apache (A.D. 1600 to 1886). During the Mexican period, following Mexico's independence in 1821, the Apache lived in conflict with the settlers, particularly with the growing number of Mexican cattle ranchers. The Mexican period ended when Arizona became United States territory in 1853, through the Gadsden Purchase. Given the choice of staying or returning to Mexico, many Mexican families remained in the area, where a few of their descendants still ranch in the valley today.

Rowdy Times

The year 1850 was the dividing point between the early settlement and the modern stage, as Anglo settlers moved into the area, taking over cattle ranches and establishing new farms. The railroad mainline snaked through the northern part of the valley and miners developed claims throughout the area, causing the establishment of towns such as the present-day communities of Tombstone and Bisbee, as well as temporary towns such as Fairbank, Emery City, Charleston, and Contention City.

With all this "civilized" activity going on, the U.S. Army moved in to protect the Anglo settlers and the miners from the marauding Apache. Fort Bowie and Fort Huachuca were built as army posts. For 30 years, the army battled the Apache across the valley and into the mountain ranges, where the Apache, under chiefs Cochise and Geronimo, retreated to places such as Cochise's Stronghold in the Chiricahua Mountains, to rest and gather steam for future battles. It all ended in 1886, with the defeat of Geronimo and his followers. By 1900, most mining operations had closed and ranching predominated in the local economy.

With the development of Tombstone as a Wild West attraction, and the discovery of the charming old pioneer town of Bisbee by visitors, tourism took hold and is now the major activity in the region. The BLM acquired the riverside lands in 1986.

San Pedro Riparian National Conservation Area

Covering more than 56,000 acres on both sides of the San Pedro in Cochise County, the conservation area extends about 40 miles from the Mexican border north to the little town of St. David, a few miles south of Benson and Interstate 10. It is the most extensive protected riparian ecosystem in the basin and range area of the Southwest.

Managed by BLM staff aided by volunteers, the conservation area provides habitat to more than one hundred species of breeding birds, as well as a temporary resting place for another 250 species of migratory and wintering birds.

Birds What is most unusual about the bird population here is that the animals come from amazingly different biotic zones—from Alaska to the southern tip of South America, and from high-mountain regions to the low-desert regions of Mexico. More than 370 bird species have been identified along the river, including many species of shorebirds, twenty-eight varieties of raptors, plus herons, loons, geese and ducks, cuckoos, owls, swifts, woodpeckers, flycatchers, grosbeaks, and humming-birds.

This convergence of flyway routes makes the Upper San Pedro valley a special place indeed. The river manages to feed water to the riverside marshes throughout the year, although summertime flows are often reduced to a trickle. The river is augmented by a number of springs within the area that serve to keep the marshes wet.

Ecosystem   The uplands on both sides of the river are spread with a typical Chihuahuan desert scrub, including creosote bush, acacia, and tarbush. The areas closer to the river, the bottomland, is a mesquite bosque with large amounts of sacaton grass. The riverside is a cottonwood-willow woodland (Fremont cottonwood and Goodding willow). You'll also find other trees, including Arizona ash, hackberry, walnut, and soapberry.

One should not forget the wildlife besides the bird species that inhabits this ripe ecosystem. More than eighty species of mammals and some very special fish inhabit the conservation area. Many species that inhabit the northern San Pedro Basin can also be found here. The collard peccary, also called javelina, roams through the area in herds. These pig-like creatures are joined by many species of rodents, bobcats, a few mountain lions, white-tailed deer, mule deer, jack rabbits, and cottontails.

Long before the development of the riparian conservation area, the southern San Pedro was home to fourteen species of fish. Only two remain: the longfin dace and desert sucker. Other species now found in the river are introduced species such as the mosquitofish, common carp, and yellow bullhead.

One would think that the availability of a year-round water supply would attract amphibians, and it does. The area features a large number of lizards, including the Gila monster and desert grassland whiptail lizard. You'll probably see the Sonoran box turtle and Couch's spadefoot toad, along with many snake species, the most common of which is the western diamond-back rattlesnake. Another snake to be found (and avoided) is the seldom seen Mojave green rattlesnake. Visitors walking along the riverside trails should beware of rattlesnakes during the summer months, but will find a much less ominous companion in the resident Mexican gartersnake.

Where to Get Information   The conservation area office is located at the old townsite of Fairbank, where only a couple of buildings remain from the mining days. Largely staffed by volunteers, the headquarters provides trail maps and other valuable information for nature lovers. A useful place to look for more information is San Pedro House, operated by the Friends of the San Pedro, located to the south on Highway 90, just 7 miles east of the town of Sierra Vista. This 1930s ranch house has been recently restored and serves as a bookstore and visitor center. It is open Saturdays from 10 A.M. to 4 P.M. and on Sundays from noon to 3 P.M. It is also open on a variable schedule throughout the rest of the week, when volunteers provide information and assistance.

The conservation area is a prime area for birders, hikers, horseback riders, and photographers. Most of the trails are open to hikers and riders. Overnight camping is permitted in backcountry areas, with permits required for overnight stays. There are self-service "pay" stations at all visitor parking areas. Camping is limited to seven consecutive days in any one location, unless otherwise posted. The area is free for day visitors. For more information, call the BLM at (520) 457-2265, Monday through Friday from 7:45 A.M. to 4:15 P.M.

Trails   To put it simply, trails lead from the parking areas along the riverbanks. From north to south these are: at the Cienaga-Land Corral, at the village of St. David, at the north end of the conservation area; Fairbank (BLM headquarters), beside Highway 82, west of Tombstone; Charleston Bridge, via Charleston Road, which leads west from Tombstone and Highway 80, and east from the town of Sierra Vista; at San Pedro House, on Highway 90, east of Sierra Vista and west of Highway 80, between Tombstone and Bisbee; Hereford, accessed by taking Hereford Road north from Highway 92 west of Bisbee or east from Highway 92 south of Sierra Vista; Palominas, on Highway 92, west of Bisbee and south of Sierra

Vista. This is the most southerly section of the conservation area, touching the Mexican border.

Terrenate Presidio   You can reach this historic site by a separate trail. Drive 2 miles west of Fairbank on Highway 82, then 2 miles north on Kellar Road. The Presidio Santa Cruz de Terrenate was built in 1775 to protect Spanish farmlands in the area. It had a very brief existence, about 5 years. Continual Apache raids convinced the Spanish to desert the fort in 1780. More than eighty Presidio residents lost their lives during the raids. It is not known how many Apache were killed. The Presidio Trail leaves the parking lot on Kellar Road, continuing 1.2 miles to the ruins of the Spanish community. A stone foundation and several adobe walls are all that remain of the fort. Interpretive signs are found along the trail through the presidio area.

Boquillas Land and Cattle Company Site   The old headquarters of this sizable ranching operation is located 2 miles south of Fairbank. A bustling operation in its day, it included a railroad depot, houses, two barns, a smokehouse, and a blacksmith shop. The area is now used for private residences.

OTHER SAN PEDRO BIRDING AREAS

Cave Creek Canyon   The canyon is the location of the Southwestern Research Station of the American Museum of Natural History. The station contains a superb collection of flora and fauna. The canyon itself is a renowned birding area, featuring hiking trails that lead from the canyon floor through the Coronado National Forest. Cave Creek Canyon is near the New Mexico border. You can reach the site by taking State Highway 80 northeast from Douglas, or Highway 80 south from Interstate 10 a few miles east of the New Mexico state line. It is also possible to drive south along an unpaved road that starts at Exit 362 of I-10 (east of San Simon). This road leads south into the national forest, joining the road from the town of Portal.

Sulphur Springs Valley   The wide valley that lies between the Dragoon Mountains and the Chiricahua range is the Sulphur Springs Valley. Along the Interstate 10 corridor, Willcox is situated at the north end of the valley, the small town of Elfrida at the southern edge. Winter is the prime season for bird-watchers visiting the area, as winter rains flood portions of the huge Willcox Playa—which is a dry pan in summer. Each year, twelve thousand sandhill cranes descend upon the Playa, joining other migratory birds such as long-billed curlews, lark buntings, chestnut-collard larkspurs, and the occasional whooping crane. The town of Willcox established the annual Sandhill Crane Festival to celebrate the arrival of the enormous flock of visitors. It's held the last weekend in January.

Farther down the valley, raptors are the prime attraction. Along the Highway 666 route is the largest collection of eagles, hawks, and falcons in the state, including ferruginous, rough-legged coopers, sharp-shinned, red-tailed, and Harris' hawks, harriers, merlins, kestrels, prairie and peregrine falcons, bald and golden eagles. A good place to see waterfowl and shorebirds is at the ponds located beyond the golf course in Willcox. Shorebird migrants include pharalopes, stilts, and avocets. Sandhill cranes are the most populous species here, with peregrine falcons seen from time to time.

Motel accommodations are available in Willcox.

Sierra Vista and Ramsey Canyon Preserve The town of Sierra Vista is Arizona's fastest-growing community, located close to the Mexican border and high enough in the high desert and the Huachucha Mountains to offer pleasant temperatures. A popular retirement community, it lies in the midst of national forests. The Nature Conservancy's Ramsey Canyon Preserve has to be the finest place for viewing hummingbirds on the continent. More than 160 bird species, including up to twelve hummingbird varieties, have been identified right here, to say nothing of the other bird varieties found in the nearby lowland San Pedro riparian areas.

Sierra Vista has a full range of motel and B&B accommodations, plus thirty restaurants and other services for travelers.

While the Ramsey Canyon Preserve is best known as a birding spot, with an emphasis on hummingbirds, the preserve is also home to an amazing variety of plants, including wildflowers, mountain mosses, and fir trees—more than four hundred plant species in all. There is also a full slate of animal life, from spiny and alligator lizards to bats, butterflies, leopard frogs, coatimundi, javelina, rock squirrels, and opossums.

The main birding attraction, hummingbirds start arriving in July, with rufous hummingbirds usually the first to show up.

By mid-August, the peak hummingbird population—comprised of broad-billed, white-eared, beryline, violet-crowned, blue-throated, magnificent, plain-capped, Lucifer, Anna's, Allen's, black-chinned, and Costa's hummingbirds—is in place. Most leave before October, though a few stragglers hang on for a few weeks. Meanwhile, this is also a year-round birding destination, with raptors including golden eagles and hawks, warblers, fly-catchers, sapsuckers, and juncos arriving in season.

Two trails lead through the preserve. The Nature Trail is a short 0.7-mile loop trail along Ramsey Creek. The Hamburg Trail leads from the visitor center to a scenic overlook (one mile), and beyond into the Coronado National Forest. Guided tours are given on a seasonal basis.

The preserve has six guest cabins, which are available year-round to Conservancy members and the general public. These housekeeping cabins are heated, and each contains a fully equipped kitchen, plus a barbecue and picnic area.

A wise thing to do when you begin a visit to Ramsey Canyon is to stop at the visitor center and the well-stocked bookstore. Here you will find nature field guides and interpretive materials from around the world, as well as information on the flora and fauna of Ramsey Canyon. The capacity of the preserve is limited. Thus, it is necessary to secure a parking permit for weekend and holiday visits. Weekday parking is available on a first-come, first-served basis. RVs over 20 feet are not permitted in the parking area. The preserve is free to Conservancy members. Others are asked to donate $5 upon entering the preserve—a small sum for a superb experience.

For information and cabin reservations, call the preserve at (520) 378-2785.

Madera Canyon   Located in the Santa Rita Mountains west of Sierra Vista, this area, famed for broad-billed hummingbirds, is reached either from Interstate 19 (the freeway from Tucson to Nogales), from Green Valley by taking a side road, or by taking the unpaved Greaterville Road from State Highway 83 south of I-10.

The same hummingbird species found in Ramsey Canyon are seen here, along with other birds including elf owls. Other species such as the elegant trogon are found in the canyon. At a higher altitude, a trail starting at the upper picnic area also offers good birding, including possible sighting of the flammulated owl.

Carr Canyon East of Sierra Vista, in the Coronado National Forest, Carr Canyon offers camping with picnicking amidst many birds. This is one of very few places in the Southwest where you may camp at a prime birding site. The two campgrounds here, Reef Townsite and Ramsey Vista, offer good birding. Trails lead into the Miller Wilderness Area in the national forest. This is where the bird-watching gets really interesting. The buff-breasted flycatcher is often spotted here, in addition to other high-altitude species such as the red crossbill, red-faced warbler, yellow-eyed junco, pygmy nuthatch, and Steller's jay. Several trails, including the Comfort Springs Trail, lead from the two campgrounds. A good thing to remember is that only the lower campground has water.

To get there, drive south from Sierra Vista on State Highway 92. Turn west onto Carr Canyon Road and drive along this road for 8.5 miles. It's a narrow, curving road that's a thrill to drive—heartstopping to some—but it will get you there.

Garden Canyon On Fort Huachuca property, beautiful little Garden Canyon is usually accessible by driving into the military base off Fry Canyon Boulevard in Sierra Vista. On some days, especially during maneuvers, you will not be permitted to drive through the fort, but it's worth a try. You will have to observe all the military gate niceties such as showing your ownership papers and driver's license.

A sign along the main fort road will direct you to Garden Canyon. Along the way you may see some javelina, white-tailed deer, and pronghorn antelope. The road climbs into the Canyon beside Garden Creek. Two trails lead from the road: Scheelite Canyon Trail is a 1.1-mile ascent, with birding opportunities (Mexican spotted owl and elegant trogon). The Sawmill Canyon Trail (at the end of the road) also climbs, with frequent spottings of Montezuma quail and buff-breasted flycatcher on the lower stretch and trogons, sulphur-bellied flycatchers, pygmy owls, warblers, and other species at the higher elevations.

Coronado National Memorial This day-use area is on the southern edge of the Huachuca Mountains, with a picnic area and visitor center. Inside the visitor center is a small museum that features exhibits on the history of the area, including the Francisco de Coronado explorations. Outside is a bird-viewing area with feeders, water, and park benches from which visitors may see as many as twenty bird varieties in a single sitting. This is the lazy person's approach to bird-watching!

This is a mid-elevation area, with typical species including house finches, gray-breasted jay, acorn woodpecker, and bridled titmouse. Hummingbirds have been known to visit the feeders. Wildlife in the forest include coatimundi, javelina, and numerous Arizona gray squirrels, which visit the feeding area as well.

One should not leave the area of the memorial without taking the road to Montezuma Pass. This fine mountain drive offers excellent views and more bird-watching (Montezuma quail, of course).

Nearby South San Pedro Attractions

CHIRICAHUA NATIONAL MONUMENT

The fog rolls over the mountains—at 7,000 feet—through the eerie rock sentinels of the Chiricahua. Stone towers and buttresses climb into the sky, partially obscured as wisps of mist flow through the formations, which are still as mystifying and ennobling as when the Apache gathered inspiration here, for more than 200 years.

The awesome display of standing rocks near Willcox was created about 25 million years ago, when a volcanic eruption exploded a caldera, creating a field of rhyolite. Then, fault shifting broke the volcanic rock into standing forms and stacked blocks. Now, after eons of erosion, cracking by snow and ice, and pounding by rain, the rocks offer an unequaled display of standing and suspended rock.

This is a "sky island," mountains rising out of the low desert of southeastern Arizona. The moisture trapped by the mountains nourishes the forests and wildlife within. The miraculous placement of this range, surrounded by the Chihuahuan Desert, has created three biotic systems, the Chihuahuan and Sonoran deserts, the transition (Sierra Madre), and the Rocky Mountain zone. With all this environmental diversity, the range of wildlife is impressive. Snakes, lizards, and other desert animals share this space with more normally seen foothills species such as coatimundi, fox, and black bear. You may see the much sought-after elegant trogon, along with flycatchers and other birds. Plant life is equally diverse: mosses and ferns are found under the rock statues, firs predominate in the forest. Seventy species of mammals live in the monument, as do many amphibians such as the rare desert tortoise.

This scenic park, located in the national forest east of Benson and north of Douglas, can be accessed from either the east or west side of the Chiricahua mountain range. From the east, drive west from Benson to either U.S. Route 666 or Arizona Route 186, then drive south to Arizona Route 181.

From Douglas or New Mexico, take U.S. Highway 80 south from Interstate 10 or north from Douglas, then turn west onto the side road that leads through the village of Portal (ranger station) and the mountains.

Historic sites in the park include the Faraway Ranch in Bonito Canyon. This is the place where J. H. Stafford and his 13-year-old bride, Pauline, built a one-room cabin in 1879. They didn't stay long, but Neil and Norma Erikson arrived in 1888 to establish their farm, construct a homestead, and raise a family. All this took place in what was then a remote mountain canyon at almost the 7,000-foot level, more than a day's travel from the nearest town.

There is a campground in the monument, as well as a forest campground located past Portal, along the gravel road leading westward from Highway 80. There are interpretive trails and guided tours of monument sites. For park information, phone (520) 824-3560.

A visit to the monument isn't complete without a hike along the Echo Canyon Trail. One of the most satisfying hikes in the Southwest, the route leaves Massai Point (the location of a superb lookout at 6,870 feet) and loops through the rock formations. Covering a total of 3.5 miles, the trail begins by passing masses of towering rock clusters, then it descends gently into Echo Canyon. At any time of day, the formations in Echo Canyon are spectacular; but try a moonlit excursion when the standing rocks are illuminated, casting weird shadows on each other. The trail climbs for the final mile to return to the trailhead.

You get to Massai Point and the trailhead by driving the paved, 6-mile road from the visitor center, which is at the park entrance.

FORT BOWIE

Just outside the Coronado National Forest boundary at the northern edge of the Chiricahua Mountains, Fort Bowie is located northwest of the Chiricahua National Monument. Visitors can stroll through the ruins of the fort, which was constructed in 1862. It was a stop on the Butterfield Stage route that crossed Arizona and Nevada to the California gold fields.

In 1862, a small troop of Civil War volunteers drove several hundred Apache warriors from the mountains in order to control and protect Apache Spring, which lay in a prime location at Apache Pass, a defining notch between the Chiricahua and Dos Cabezas ranges. This event led to the series of wars with Cochise and his followers, and the 5-year battle with Geronimo. After the battle with the volunteers, a small, primitive fort was built, with a short adobe wall and tents inside.

The crumbled site is accessed via a self-guided foot trail that leads throughout the fort area. Remains of the stage stop are still here, and the adobe and stone walls have been partially restored. Visitors can see the schoolhouse, hospital, and officers' quarters. Here is the site where Geronimo surrendered, uttering, *"Don't believe any bad talk you hear about me . . . I never do wrong without a cause."* It's a unique historical landmark, redolent of the bravery of both the army bluecoats and the Native American warriors who fought valiantly for their own just cause. Geronimo's son (2 years old when he died) is buried in the old cemetery.

Below the fort (about 500 feet down) is the pass and the spring, the object of years of conflict, the cause of death, of victory and defeat.

To get there, drive south from Interstate 10 from the junction (Exit 362 just east of Bowie) or from Willcox via the paved State Highway 186. From the south and the Douglas area, drive northeast along U.S. 666, then take State Highway 181 and State Highway 186 to the unpaved road that leads to the fort and also north to Bowie and Interstate 10.

COCHISE'S STRONGHOLD

The refuge of the great chief Cochise and his Apache followers—chased into these high granite reaches of the Dragoon

Mountains—this stronghold provides a fascinating glimpse of the days when war dominated the scene in the Old West. The site, operated by the National Forest Service (520-826-3593), includes a campground, picnic area, and hiking trails. Several other prominent historic sites in Cochise County commemorate the struggles between the cavalry and the Apache, but Cochise's Stronghold provides a poignant reminder of those turbulent times.

U.S. Route 666 heads south from Interstate 10 and north from Douglas on the Mexican border. Just north of the community of Sunsites, a gravel road heads west to the stronghold. If you're driving east from Benson, another scenic route leads from Interstate 10 at the Dragoon exit. Drive east along this side road to meet Highway 666, then drive south for another 8 miles to the gravel road.

AMERIND FOUNDATION

A private research and educational organization, the Amerind Foundation is located 12 miles east of Benson via Interstate 10 (take the Dragoon exit, #318). Located in the very picturesque Texas Canyon, a rocky draw near Dragoon, it is a center for research into the native heritage of the Southwest, and has a museum that is open to the public. The museum contains artifacts of southwestern Native American life and antique Spanish furnishings, which complement the Spanish colonial-style buildings. This fine arts center also includes paintings and sculptures on early western themes by such artists as Frederic Remington, Oscar Borg, and William Leigh. For those interested in learning more about the native and colonial past of southeastern Arizona, a visit here is a must. Tours are available. For schedules, call (520) 586-3666.

FORT HUACHUCA

One of the few remaining army posts of the Indian wars period, Fort Huachuca is located just west of the town of Sierra Vista, off State Highway 92. It is both a functioning army post and a restored museum, which includes much of the original fort. The fort also provides access to the scenic Garden Canyon, a fine birding location. For information, call (520) 533-5736.

TOMBSTONE

If you're a historical purist, you will have to put those instincts on hold during a visit to Tombstone. This restored artifact of the early mining period in southern Arizona is as much theme park as real town. Yet the visitor can easily catch the flavor of the 1880s, when the Earp boys and Doc Holliday and the Clanton brothers shot it out at the O.K. Corral.

You can also drink beer in a number of saloons, including the Crystal Palace, which has been restored to its original appearance. The Bird Cage Theatre does not have musical or dramatic performances these days, but you can walk through the infamous hall where ladies of the night plied their wares in curtained boxes—at the spot memorialized by the song *Bird in a Gilded Cage*. The 1881 Bella Union Opera House continues to offer dinner along with operatic performances, and the Rose Tree Museum includes the world's largest rose bush, still growing after all these years. Boot Hill is the town's original graveyard, complete with wooden tombstones and dominated by a souvenir shop. Weekends bring staged gunfights by the Tombstone Vigilantes on Allen Street, the main drag (every 2nd, 4th, and 5th Sunday).

Five motels and three bed-and-breakfast homes provide accommodations. Besides beer and hot dogs, the standard fare in most of the saloons, you can eat in the more modern Longhorn Restaurant at the corner of Allen and 5th.

For a touch of Tombstone reality, the state-operated Arizona Territorial Museum is located in the old Tombstone Court House on Allen Street. You'll be fascinated with the displays and artifacts of rough and rowdy Tombstone.

BISBEE

This is a real living pioneer town, dating back to the same era as neighboring Tombstone. It's a copper-mining center that survives because of its fortuitous location in the cool Mule Mountains and its charming old brick Victorian buildings. Bisbee's mining days are just over, but it has become a haven for retirees. Slowly, over the past 20 years, it has also become a wonderful place for tourists, with the restoration of two fine historic hotels and the opening of a half-dozen B&B inns.

While Tombstone is mostly a museum piece, Bisbee is a living example of the early mining towns of Arizona, the rest of which grew quickly only to expire when the ore ran out.

The Mule Mountains were once occupied by the Apache, and before the 1870s, only a few white prospectors dared to enter the area. But the discovery of major copper deposits changed all that. The army drove the Apache to less valuable lands, and mining claims were staked in the mountains by 1877. By the turn of the century, Bisbee was a company town. Phelps Dodge built the Copper Queen Hotel, still a grand old hotel with an excellent dining room and a period bar that has great atmosphere.

Most of Main Street was destroyed by fire in 1908, and the town was rebuilt. The new brick construction of 1910 is still on show. Mining continued until 1975, when the town turned its attentions to tourism and retirement living.

Old miners' hostels were turned into bed-and-breakfast inns. Saloons have been converted to antique shops and art galleries. Two mines (long closed to mining) have become tourist attractions, with an underground mine tour and a view of the great open pit. The town is just north of the Mexican boundary, to the west of the border town of Douglas.

ARIZONA CACTUS AND SUCCULENT RESEARCH

Gardeners will enjoy the displays of desert plants at this nursery and research center, located 6 miles south of Bisbee at Bisbee Junction. The botanical garden contains more than 750 varieties of cacti and other plants of the high desert. The nonprofit center has an extensive library with photographs and research materials on cacti and succulents. Several greenhouses are part of the center, and classes on landscaping with desert plants are given on a frequent basis. For information, phone (520) 432-7040.

SLAUGHTER RANCH

The San Bernardino Ranch (called the Slaughter Ranch by locals) is found east of Douglas via a gravel road. This 300-acre site became the 1884 home of John Slaughter, a former Texas Ranger who became the sheriff of Cochise County. He

---

farmed the cattle ranch for 30 years. Today the ranch home is a museum, restored to its original Victorian state. Tours are given daily between 10 A.M. and 3 P.M. For information, phone (520) 364-4481.

Santa Cruz Basin

PATAGONIA–SONOITA CREEK PRESERVE

In 1966, the Nature Conservancy, with help from the Tucson Audubon Society, purchased 312 acres along Sonoita Creek in order to protect a delicate riparian environment. It was the Conservancy's first project in Arizona, leading to many other ventures. The Conservancy—over the ensuing years—has parlayed the 312 acres, through obtaining conservation easements and donations, into more than 750 acres. This outstanding example shows how nonprofit organizations such as the Nature Conservancy, along with governments, donors, and private landowners, can work together to preserve a priceless heritage.

The preserve is located at the town of Patagonia, on State Highway 82, which runs from Tombstone to Nogales. Patagonia, a pioneer Old West town (cowboys followed the miners) has matured into a charming little town that has retained much of its pioneer flavor while developing tourist facilities including several fine bed-and-breakfast homes. After arriving in Patagonia, turn west on 4th Avenue. Then turn south on Pennsylvania and cross the creek. The preserve is about 0.75 miles down the road.

Patagonia and the creek lie between the Santa Rita and Patagonia Mountains, in the Santa Cruz watershed. The perennial creek provides a variety of habitats as it wanders through the valley, joining the Santa Cruz north of Nogales. The Conservancy's preserve features a wonderful, mature cottonwood and willow woodland ecosystem. Many of the Fremont cottonwood trees are over 100 feet tall, a perfect perching and nesting place for hawks. Some are as much as 130 years old. Several varieties of willow are found here, close to the water, along with the lesser trees including Arizona black walnut, velvet ash, canyon hackberry, and mesquite. The preserve also includes marsh areas or cienegas. Over 250 species of birds are found in the preserve, and wildlife that live on and under the ground include javelina, bobcat, coyote, the desert tortoise, toads, frogs, and white-tailed deer. As in other Arizona places, rattlesnakes inhabit the area.

This is, most of all, a birder's paradise. Three trails (Creek, Railroad, and Cienega) cross through the sanctuary, along the creek, and to the marsh areas. The Railroad Trail leads along the old rail bed of the Santa Fe line, which ran the length of Sonoita Creek when it was built in 1882. A visitor center provides trail information, bird checklists, and information on current sightings. A self-guided nature trail is planned.

Guided trail tours are given each Saturday at 9 A.M., and other walks are conducted according to the seasons. For information, call the preserve office at (520) 394-2400. The prime birding period is March through September. Migrants are seen during late April and May, then again during late August and September. Winter brings a few migrants including the rufous-backed robin.

EMPIRE-CIENEGA RANCH

This prairie and marsh environment, managed by the Bureau of Land Management, is located north of the village of Sonoita via Highway 83. It is an area of open grasslands, scattered with several cienegas, as well as bird breeding and resting areas. The vermilion flycatcher is often seen here in the spring and summer. You may see pronghorn in the fields of grass as you drive down the road.

KINO SPRINGS

A private development with a golf course, Kino Springs features two ponds that harbor some unusual and rare species, along with the normally resident water birds. Among the more unusual species for this part of the country are cormorants, black-bellied whistling ducks, green kingfishers, and tropical kingbirds. Gray hawks ride the currents overhead.

The golf course area, including the ponds, is open to the public. To get there, drive south from Patagonia on Highway 82. Turn left after 7 miles. Two miles down the road is the pro shop near the club house, where you'll need to obtain permission to visit the viewing ponds.

SYCAMORE CANYON

This rugged and beautiful canyon of the Pajarito Mountains is off to the west of the other sites in the Santa Cruz watershed. Part of its attraction is a streamside woodland, nurtured by an intermittent creek. This birding experience is only for those who can endure strenuous hiking along with their sightings. As the old saying goes, "If you have the energy, the birds have the time." You may be rewarded by identifying elegant trogons, black-capped gnatcatchers, five-striped sparrows, and rose-throated becards, among others, including up to fifteen sighted species of flycatcher.

Now, here's the reason you'll need your good hiking boots. From the parking area, at Hank and Yank Spring, it takes 2 miles of hardy hiking in the stream bed to the junction with Peñasco Canyon. Now you've arrived in good birding territory.

To get there, take Interstate 19 south from Tucson or north from Nogales. Eight miles north of Nogales, take Ruby Road (State Highway 219) and drive west for 10 miles. There is a turnoff to Peña Blanca Lake. Almost 10 miles beyond the end of pavement is a sign for Sycamore Canyon. Drive another half-mile to the end of the road.

Nearby Santa Cruz Attractions

PATAGONIA

A favorite lodging place for birders, Patagonia is a little rural town wedged into the valley of Sonoita Creek, in the Patagonia Mountains. The main reason for being here—aside from the charm of this former mining community and Wild West cowboy town—is the Patagonia–Sonoita Creek Preserve, owned and operated by the Nature Conservancy (see page 210). Patagonia Lake State Park is close to town, beside Highway 82, with camping, boating, and swimming. The town is 18 miles from Nogales and the Mexican border.

The Southern Pacific Railway once came through Patagonia, and the town park and the restored railway station flank the highway on what was the railway right-of-way. The ghost towns of Harshaw, Duquesne, and Washington Camp, reminders of the mining period, are located in the nearby San Raphael Valley.

Restaurants in downtown Patagonia, and several cozy bed-and-breakfast homes, make a stay here very pleasant.

TUBAC

Established in 1752, Tubac is the oldest city in Arizona. Located northwest of Nogales on Interstate 19, Tubac is not a large town, but the art colony and the old Spanish presidio, the seat of government for the region in the mid-1700s, provide an interesting visit. A ghost town by 1853, when the Gadsden Purchase transferred Tubac to American hands, it was revived by mining for another boom period.

TUMACACORI NATIONAL MONUMENT

Just south of Tubac, the Tumacacori National Monument—an early Spanish mission—dates back to the 1800s, when Franciscan friars and Native Americans built the impressive church. It is open daily to the public. Across the road from the mission is (for me) an equally interesting local monument—in praise of the chile pepper. The Santa Cruz Chile and Spice Factory sells chile products of every kind, including bottled pastes.

BIRDS OF THE SAN PEDRO BASIN

In this chapter, we concentrate entirely on birds, for bird-watching is the major pre-occupation of most travelers to this area's nature preserves. Although hummingbirds are common in the San Pedro Basin, descriptions of hummers are found later in this section, along with other birds even more frequently seen in the Santa Cruz watershed.

Cooper's Hawk
Accipiter cooperii
Like other accipters or "bird hawks," Cooper's hawk is a long-tailed raptor that lives in woodlands and has rounded wings. Two other accipters are found in the Southwest: the northern goshawk and the sharp-shinned hawk. They fly in a similar fashion, with two or three quick beats of the wings followed by a glide. The female is larger than the male. They eat small mammals and other birds.

Cooper's hawk has short wings, and is a little smaller than a crow. The white tip on its tail is broader than on the sharp-shinned hawk. Young, immature birds are brown, streaked on the breast and white on the belly. The adult is a slate blue above, with rusty streaks below. The female is brownish blue above. Cooper's range is from southern Canada to northern Mexico. Its voice is a rapid *kek kek kek kek kek*.

Gray Hawk
Buteo nitidus
Buteos or "buzzard hawks" are large, stout raptors with wide, rounded tails and broad wings. Their diet is comprised of rabbits, rodents, reptiles, grasshoppers, and small birds. Its range is from the southwestern U.S. to Brazil. The gray hawk is small, compared to most other buteos, with a wingspread of about 3 feet and a length of 16 to 18 inches. The adults have a gray back and have gray bars underneath. It has wide bands on the tail. Immature birds have buff-colored stripes underneath.

Red-tailed Hawk
Buteo jamaicensis
You will see this hawk in every shade of red throughout the San Pedro Basin, but especially in the Sulphur Valley south of Willcox. It's a large hawk with a wide tail and broad wings, reaching a length of 25 inches.

While flying it can be identified by the rufous color on the top side of the tail (adults). From below, the tail is a pale color, but the red of the top may often be seen shining through. Immature birds have a grayish tail that sometimes has narrow bands. The top is brown and the underside is usually a deep rust (on birds west of the Rockies). Its voice is a distinctive squealing *keeer-r-r*, with the call slurring downward.

American Kestrel
Falco sparverius
This is the smallest of the American falcons, swallow-like, and about the size of a jay. It is distinguished by its reddish-brown back and tail. The male bird has blue-gray wings and a buff breast. The female is rufous across the entire back and wings, and also has a buff breast. Both have a white face with black markings that look like a double moustache, black markings behind the ears, and a black band on the end of the tail. Its range is widespread, from Alaska to Tierra del Fuego at the southern tip of South America. You'll see this bird perching on trees and telephone poles. It feeds on grasshoppers and small gophers. The voice is a rapid, loud *killy-killy-killy-killy*, unlike any other raptor.

Western Wood-Pewee
Contopus sordidulus
Many varieties of flycatchers live in the San Pedro basin, including kingbirds, phoebes, and the rose-throated becard. This bird is a small, sparrow-sized flycatcher, dusky-colored, with two narrow wing bars but no ring around the eyes. It gets its name from its call, a nasal *peeeer* or *peeyee*. It breeds from central Alaska to Central America, and winters from Panama to Peru. It lives in groves along the river in the cottonwoods, and in a variety of forest zones, including pine-oak and open conifer woodlands. It has a slightly darker neck than the eastern wood pewee. Both sexes look alike.

Gray Flycatcher
Empidonax wrightii
The empidonax family of flycatchers are all drab birds without much color, but they can be identified by their light eye rings and two pale bars on the wings. They are gray above and whitish below, with the lower bill a creamy-pink color.

An easier method of identification is by listening to its voice. The song is a two-syllable *chewip* or *cheh-we* or *chi-bit*; the call is a dry, soft *wit*. It lives in sagebrush and in pinyon-juniper woodland. The bird's range includes the Great Basin, and it ventures into north and central Arizona and this southeastern part of the state.

Burrowing Owl
Athene cunicularia
Growing to a length of 11 inches, this small owl breeds in this region and migrates throughout the Southwest into the southern Canadian prairies. It is also found on the southern tip of Florida. Pinyon-juniper woodlands (on sloping land) and deserts (where it lives in old rodent burrows in open spaces) is its habitat. It has brown feathers with black spots, light eyebrows and throat, and a dark brown collar. The tail is short, the legs long. The burrowing owl can be identified by its upright position at all times, and by its habit of bobbing up and down when surprised and excited. Normally its voice is a long, rolling *coo-coooo*, but when frightened, its note is a cackle.

Rose-throated Becard
Pachyramphus aglaiae
A large-headed and thick-billed flycatcher, the becard is dark gray above and dusky to pale below, identifiable by the rose-colored throat on the male bird. The female has a different appearance: brown above and buff below, with a dark cap and a light buff-colored nape. The becard is a subspecies of the tyrannidae or tyrant flycatcher family. Formerly known as a member of the cotinga family, it is a transient in southeastern Arizona. Its range is from the Mexican border to Costa Rica. You'll find it a summer resident of the San Pedro Valley. It also stops in the lower Rio Grande Valley in Texas. It lives in wooded canyons, on river banks (cottonwood-willow), and in sycamores.

Horned Lark
Eremophila alpestris
This bird with the beautiful voice is a brown ground-living bird, with two small black horns, black sideburns, and a black bib below the neck. It has pale yellow on its face and throat. Its colors provide good camouflage, and it may be difficult to see on the ground, where it eats seeds and insects. It does not hop, but prefers to walk or run.

Its range covers most of Canada and the U.S., except for the American southeast. It lives in open patches of ground, such as prairie lands, tundra, fields, and golf courses, where low plants grow. Its song, often in flight, is a clear, tinkling *tsee-titi* and a *buzz*.

Greater Roadrunner

Geococcyx californianus

One must be careful not to scare the roadrunner, for it speeds to its hiding place at an extremely fast pace. This is the cuckoo that runs on the ground. It's a large bird (up to 24 inches)—brown with a green glint above, streaked with black and white; buff-colored below with brown streaks on the breast. It has a heavy bill and a crest and often flicks its long, white-edged tail. Its range is from California's Central Valley throughout the Southwest and into Mexico, where it lives in desert scrub and chaparral. It seldom flies, preferring to run on its very strong feet.

Its song is a series of six to eight low cooing notes, like a dove, that drop in pitch: *cooo cooo cooo cooo-ah cooo-ah.*

Ruby-crowned Kinglet

Regulus calendula

Kinglets and gnatcatchers belong to the same family. Kinglets are tiny, busy birds, chubbier than the gnatcatcher, with small, slender bills. The ruby-crowned kinglet has a stubby tail, and is an olive-gray color with a black bar on the wings behind a white bar. The male has a scarlet crown patch that is usually invisible, but can be seen when the bird is ex-

cited. The female has a deep red crown patch. Both have a broken eye ring. Its call is a *ji-dee.* The song is comprised of three or four high notes, followed by several lower notes, ending with a chant: *tee tee tee tew tew tew, ti-didee, ti-didee, ti-didee.*

American Pipit

Anthus rubescens

Also called the water pipit, this is a slender brown bird with a slender bill. Both sexes have a brown back and wings, buffy underparts with streaks, white outer tail feathers, and black legs.

It can be identified by its movements: while walking it bobs its tail; while flying it dips up and down. While this bird winters in warmer climates, as far south as El Salvador, and in Africa and southern Asia, its summer range includes the northern parts of North America. The sound it makes is a thin *ch-eet* or *cheet.* While flying it sings *chwee chwee chwee chwee chwee.*

Whiskered Screech Owl

Otus trichopsis

Similar in size and coloration to the western screech owl, the whiskered owl is usually gray in color, with large white spots on its scapulars, and large black spots underneath. It has long bristles on its face (the whiskers) and a yellow-green bill. Its range includes southeastern Arizona, Mexico, and northern Nicaragua. It lives in mountains, preferring canyons, in pine-oak woodlands, and in sycamores. Its voice is *booboo-boo-boo*, repeated with some variations. Sometimes it gives a repeated, dove-like *choo-yoo coo-cooo*. Like all owls, it is a nocturnal creature, feeding on rodents, other birds, reptiles, and large insects. It is one of twelve owls found across the American West.

Loggerhead Shrike
Lanius ludovicianus
Often seen perching on tree-tops, this is a songbird that acts like a hawk. It feeds on insects, lizards, small birds, and mice. There are only two shrikes in North America (the northern shrike is also seen in the West). The loggerhead shrike is a large bird (grows to 10 inches) with a gray head top and back, a black mask and a white stripe underneath the mask, and a lighter gray breast. The immature shrike is brown with small bars on the breast. Ranging from southern Manitoba and Saskatchewan to the Mexican border, it winters in this region. This bird lives in semi-open country, in trees and scrub,

and requires lookout posts. The shrike's song is made up of notes and phrases repeated many times: *queedle, queedle,* or *tsurp-see, tsurp-see.* It also has a raspy call: *shack shack.*

Bell's Vireo
Vireo bellii
Vireos are small, gray or olive-colored birds, with a curved upper bill. Bell's vireo has one or two light wing bars, pale yellow sides and breast, and a whitish-yellow eye ring.

Its range is from the central and southwestern U.S., to the warmer climes of Mexico and Nicaragua, where it winters. It resides in streamside habitats, preferring willows. The strained song is voiced at short intervals: *cheedle cheedle chee cheedle cheedle chew.* When standing, it flicks its tail.

Orange-crowned Warbler
Vermivora celata
The so-called orange crown is rarely visible, so one must look carefully to identify this San Pedro Valley resident. A drab bird, compared to the yellow or Nashville warblers, it has no wing bars. This bird is yellowish-green above, and a greenish-yellow below (darker on the top), and grows to a length of about 5.5 inches. Its voice is a song, a mild trill that trails off at the end. It ranges from

Alaska and across Canada to the western U.S., and winters south to Guatemala. The orange-crowned warbler is one of many wood warblers found in the Southwest. Out of a total of 114 warblers, fifty-three have been spotted in the western U.S., including several rarely seen varieties. Warblers are usually smaller than sparrows and have thin, pointed bills. Most have shades of yellow in their coloring. Insects are their main food supply.

Nashville Warbler
Vermivora ruficapilla
Easier to identify, this wood warbler has a white eye ring and a yellow throat and breast. There is a white band between the breast and the yellow undertail. Its head is gray and it has no wing bars. Ranging from southern Canada to Honduras, it lives in mixed woods, including riparian habitats, but also lives in undergrowth, and at the edges of forests. It feeds mainly on the ground, eating insects. The song has two parts: *seebit, seebit, seebit, ti-ti-ti-ti-ti*.

Painted Redstart
Myioborus picta
Also called the painted whitestart, this member of the wood warbler family shows black on its head, back, and wings. The wings have large white patches, and there is a large red patch on the breast. It has no yellow. The American Southwest is its most northern habitat, and it ranges south to northern Nicaragua. It prefers to live in oak canyons and in pine-oak forests. Its note is a *cleee-ip*. It sings with a repeated *weeta-weeta-weeta wee*, or *weeta-weeta-weeta-chilp-chilp-chilp*.

Summer Tanager
Piranga rubra
This is one of those families in which the males are much more brightly colored than the females. Only four of the world's population of 215 tanager species are found in the western U.S., and three are found in the South San Pedro and Santa Cruz watersheds (also hepatic and western). The male summer tanager is a rosy red on top and below, with slightly darker wings and a yellowish bill. The female is an olive-green above, with darker yellow below. The immature bird has red above and on the breast, which is streaked with yellow, a yellow rump, and blackish wings. The song is much like a robin's, and its call or note is a sharp, staccato *pi-tuk* or repeated *pik-i-tuk-i-tuk*. Its range is across the central and southern U.S., and it winters in Costa Rica and Mexico. It prefers to live in oak groves, as well as in mixed woodlands.

Elegant Trogon

Trogon elegans

There are birds which cause a great stir, and raise personal passions when sighted. Of all the birds in southeastern Arizona, perhaps the elegant trogon brings the most excitement. Another trogon (*euptilotis neoxenus*) is a rare visitor to this region and is sometimes seen in the Chiricahua Mountains. The elegant trogon is also a casual visitor, but is more often seen—both in the Chiricahuas and in the canyons of the Huachuca Mountains, near Sierra Vista.

These brightly colored birds live in forests. They have a short yellow bill, a short neck, and tiny feet. The elegant trogon (also called the coppery-tailed trogon) grows to a length of about 12 inches. The male's head, chest, and top parts are a deep, shiny green. Between the chest and belly is a narrow white band. The tail has a square tip. The female is brown, with a wider light band on the chest and not as much red underneath. The female has a white spot on the cheek.

The trogon's voice is a monotonous series of low notes: *koam koam koam*, or *koa koa koa*, Its range stretches from this tiny corner of the U.S. to more southerly climes. It is also seen as a casual visitor to the Big Bend area of Texas, and to New Mexico. It lives in mountain forests, in oak and pine groves, and in sycamore canyons such as those in the Santa Cruz watershed. It is identified by noting its straight posture and its curved, parrot-like bill.

Song Sparrow

Melospiza melodia

A member of the same general family as the tanagers (*emberizidae*), the song sparrow of the Southwest deserts is smaller than song sparrows found farther north into Canada and Alaska. The upper part of this bird is a dull, light brown, with a lighter, whiter breast that is streaked with light brown. There is a brownish spot in the center of the breast where the streaks come together. Its song is a series of notes, starting with three or four sharp notes then continuing with notes that are like a buzz. Its call is a nasal *chep*. In the Southwest, the song sparrow lives in thickets, in brush, and along roadsides.

Sandhill Crane

Grus canadensis

One would not expect to see large numbers of this large gray waterbird in the Southwest, and its visits are temporary.

However, thousands of sandhill cranes descend onto the Willcox Playa and the ponds near the Willcox golf course each year. Growing to a length of 48 inches, this crane has a bald red crown with a white stripe underneath the crown. The rest of the bird is gray. A distinguishing feature is its tail feathers, which fan out (like a bustle). Their dramatic flight shows them with necks extended and strongly beating wings. Its voice is a high-pitched, rough, repeated *garoo-ah-ah-ah*. Its range extends from the arctic (including Siberia) to its winter quarters in Mexico.

HUMMINGBIRDS OF THE SANTA CRUZ WATERSHED

Rufous Hummingbird

Selasphorus rufus

The only hummingbird with a reddish-brown back, the male rufous has a bright orange-red throat. The female has an iridescent green back, light rufous on the sides and at the base of the tail. It's one of the smaller hummers, growing to about 3.5 inches.

Costa's Hummingbird

Calypye costae

Costa's stays longer in this area than most hummers. Growing to 3.5 inches, the male has distinctive markings—green back and wings, purple throat, and projecting neck feathers. The female is green above and whitish below, with a red patch on the throat. Ranging from the southwestern U.S. and northwest Mexico, it has a soaring flight.

Broad-billed Hummingbird

Cynanthus latirostris

With a very dark green top and bottom, the male looks almost black. He is identified by his bluish throat. The bill is a bright red with a black tip. The female also has a red bill, but has a light gray throat and underparts, and a white mark (line) behind the eye. The broad-billed hummingbird lives in the Southwest U.S. and in Mexico, and summers in southern Arizona and also nearby in southwestern New Mexico.

White-eared Hummingbird

Hylocharis leucotis

Similar to the male broad-billed hummingbird, this male has a larger white line behind the eye and a greener tinge to its throat. The male has the red bill with black tip. The female has small green spots on its throat, unlike the even gray color of the broad-billed hummer. This is the northern extent of its range.

It breeds as far south as Nicaragua, and lives in or near riparian areas, preferring pine-oak woodlands.

Violet-crowned Hummingbird
Amazilia violiceps
This larger bird grows up to 4.5 inches and breeds in Guadalupe Canyon, in this area, and in southwestern New Mexico as well. Identified by its pure white throat and other under-parts, it has a red bill with black tip and a violet/blue colored crown (male). The female has a greenish-blue crown. It lives in riparian habitats, in sycamore canyons, and among agave plants.

Blue-throated Hummingbird
Lampornis clemenciae
Growing to 5.5 inches, this is a very large hummer. The male and female have large white patches on each side of the tail. The male has a blue throat, while the female has all-gray underparts and white streaks on the face. The female's tail is a dark blue color, while the tail of the male is black (with those white patches). This bird's range is from the southwestern U.S. to southern Mexico, where it lives beside streams in foothill canyons.

Magnificent Hummingbird
Eugenes fulgens
Another exceptionally large hummingbird, the male has a bright green throat and a purple crown. The female is greenish on top and a much lighter greenish-gray below. The fe-male has small white patches on each side of the tail. The male's tail looks black. This is one hummer you may hear since its call is a sharp chipping sound. Its range is from the southwestern U.S. to northern Nicaragua. It breeds in the area during the summers, living in canyons, in pine-oak wood-lands, and in the mountains.

Lucifer Hummingbird
Calothorax lucifer
This devilish little bird grows to 3.5 inches and has a slightly curved bill. It is made up of several contrasting colors. The male has rusty-red sides and a bright purple throat. Sometimes it folds its tail to a sharp point. The female has a buff-colored breast, without marks. Its range includes West Texas and Mexico. The lucifer is a casual visitor to the Santa Cruz watershed.

Black-chinned Hummingbird
Archilochus alexandri
The black throat is the distin-guishing mark on the male.

Below this is a band of purple (although this is often hard to see), and below that is a white collar. The female is green above and whitish-gray below. It's hard to distinguish this female from the female Costa's. The call is a *teew*. Its range is restricted mainly to West Texas and Mexico, and it's a casual visitor to the Huachuca Mountains.

Broad-tailed Hummingbird
Selasphorus platycercus
This Rocky Mountain species is found throughout the Western U.S., and in Mexico to Guatemala. It lives strictly in mountains. Quite a large hummer (4.5 inches), the male has an iridescent green back, and a bright, deep rose-colored throat. The female is buff underneath, with reddish-brown at the base of the tail. It can be identified by the beating of its wings—a high-pitched trilling sound.

Allen's Hummingbird
Selasphorus sasin
This bird looks quite similar to the rufous hummer, which has a rusty-red back, sides, and tail. The Allen's back is green. The female in flight looks exactly like the female rufous, with a spotted throat, green back, and buff belly. This bird is a wonder to watch when it flies. It has a great swooping motion, flying in an arc and then going into a steep ascent and swooping down again with a loud sound like cloth tearing: *riiiiip*.

Beryline Hummingbird
Amazilia beryllina
This bird is an occasional visitor to southeastern Arizona and is spotted from time to time around Sierra Vista. It's easy to identify since both male and female have a deep green head and back, and a shiny green chest (although the female is duskier and has a touch of gray at the base of the belly). It lives mostly in Mexico, but sometimes breeds in the Huachucas.

BENSON

Quail Hollow Inn

P.O. Box 2107
Benson, AZ 85602
(520) 586-3646

This Best Western operation offers good accommodations at reasonable prices. The motel has a heated pool, whirlpool, laundry, and nearby restaurant. Some rooms have refrigerators ($).

Benson Camping

Chief Four Feathers KOA

(520) 586-3977

Campground has 87 sites, most with hookups, a few set aside for tenting. There are many pull-through sites, plus a dump station, laundry, store, pool, recreation room, playground, and propane. Cabins are also available. Located 1 mile north of I-10, take the Ocotillo Road exit (#304). The **Red Barn Campground** ((520) 586-2035) is also north of I-10 on Ocotillo Road. With grassy tent sites and RV spaces, the park also has a store, laundry, and propane.

Chiricahua National Monument

Dos Cabezas Route, P.O. Box 6500
Willcox, AZ 85643
(520) 824-3560

There are 26 sites in the park campground, which has drinking water, flush toilets, picnic tables, and grills. Some sites are shaded; all are allocated on a first-come, first-served basis. Backcountry camping is not allowed. The nearest motels are in Willcox, 36 miles from the park gate.

It pays to buy all necessary supplies before you set out driving to the monument. There is no gas, nor are there food or campers' stores closer than Willcox.

BISBEE

Copper Queen Hotel

Drawer CQ
Bisbee, AZ 85603
(520) 432-2216 or 800-247-5829

The old Copper Queen is a major historic landmark, built just after the turn of the century during Bisbee's greatest mining years. Around the corner is famous Brewery Gulch, and the town's Main Street is just a half-block away. The hotel is well preserved, with a fine dining room and atmospheric saloon. There are 45 rooms decorated in the Victorian style of these original hotels of the pioneer West.

The place reeks of history and makes a great base for a vacation in southeastern Arizona ($$).

Bisbee Grand Hotel
61 Main Street
Bisbee, AZ 85603
(520) 432-5900

Dating back to 1906, when it was constructed, burned to the ground, and quickly rebuilt, the hotel benefits from its 1986 restoration. There are nine rooms and two suites upstairs, all with Victorian furnishings and decor. On the ground floor, you'll find the saloon, a small theater, and the old Ladies' Parlor—now a civilized extension of the saloon. Melodramas are presented in the Bisbee Grand Theater. Continental breakfast is served to overnight guests on the veranda or in the guest rooms ($$).

Bisbee Inn
45 OK Street
Bisbee, AZ 85603
(520) 432-5131

Called the LaMore Hotel when it opened in 1917, this intimate B&B inn now has 18 rooms, which share five shower rooms and seven restrooms. All rooms have a washbasin. There is a TV room and laundry, and an evening social hour features re-freshments. Breakfast is served (all-you-can-eat!) ($). Hosts are Joy and John Timbers.

The Inn at Castle Rock
112 Tombstone Canyon Road
Bisbee, AZ 85603
(520) 432-7195

The long-standing B&B inn was closed for a while but reopened with new management in 1993. It's an oddly shaped building under the shadow of Castle Rock, which rises from across the road. The hillside behind the inn features thick plantings of trees, pampas grass, roses, and other foliage. There are twelve rooms and two suites, all with private bath. A continental breakfast is served. This inn has its own mine shaft and several porches. It's a great place to take children for an overnight stay ($).

Bisbee Camping

Bisbee is a great place to camp, with several RV parks, including the **Turquoise Valley Golf and RV Park** on Newell Road. There are full hookups, showers, and laundry, but no tent camping (602-432-3091). The **Queen Mine RV Park** has 25 spaces, including tent sites, with showers and laundry facilities. It's on Highway 80, next to the Mine Tour office, near the downtown area (520-432-5006). **Shady Dell RV Park**, at 1 Douglas Road, has 16 sites under the trees (520-432-7305).

NOGALES

Americana Motor Hotel
850 Grand Avenue
Nogales, AZ 85621
(520) 287-7211
In Arizona: 800-231-6170
Outside Arizona: 800-874-8079

This is downtown Nogales' largest motel, with 101 rooms, a heated swimming pool, and a dining room with cocktail lounge. It's close to the border for strolling to the Mexican side.

PATAGONIA

Stage Stop Inn
303 West McKeown Street
P.O. Box 777
Patagonia, AZ 85624
(520) 394-2211

This small hotel was opened in 1969, on the site of the old Hall's Mercantile Store and a soda fountain shop. The rooms are named after the old mines of the area, including Big Jim, New York, and Mowry. With a restaurant and guest laundry, the hotel has rooms and kitchenettes ($ to $$).

Patagonia Camping

Patagonia RV Park
566 Harshaw Road
Patagonia, AZ 85624
(520) 394-2491

This private camping operation has spaces with hookups.

Patagonia State Park is located on the highway southwest of town, with camping beside the reservoir.

RAMSEY CANYON

Ramsey Canyon Inn
31 Ramsey Canyon Road
Hereford, AZ 85615
(520) 378-3010

Situated in a bird-lovers paradise, this B&B inn has six rooms, all with antique furnishings and private baths. Some rooms have queen beds, some two doubles, and the one with a king bed has a deck overlooking the nearby creek. Also overlooking the creek are two 1-bedroom cottages, equipped with all appliances and kitchen necessities, including some food staples. Children are welcome here, but not in the main inn. A full gourmet breakfast is served, and owner Shirlene DeSantis is famous for her blue-ribbon pies, baked from fruit grown in the property's orchard. The inn is adjacent to the Ramsey Canyon Preserve, with the same hummingbird viewing and hiking available by using Forest Service trails that join the reserve trails (**$$**).

Ramsey Canyon Preserve
27 Ramsey Canyon Road
Hereford, AZ 85615
(520) 378-2785

The Nature Conservancy rents six housekeeping cabins in this nature preserve near Sierra Vista. The cabins are heated and each is equipped with linens, utensils, stove, and refrigerator. A barbecue grill and picnic area are available. The cabins are a legacy from the purchase of the former Mile Hi resort, which the Conservancy added to its previous holdings obtained in 1974. The cabins are available year-round. Early reservations are advised (**$$**).

RIO RICO

Rio Rico Resort
1069 Camino Caralampi
Rio Rico, AZ 85648
(520) 281-1901 or 800-288-4746

This resort, part of a country club and upscale housing development, lies a few miles north of Nogales and south of Tubac. The full range of facilities available here and the reasonable rates make it a good place to stay while exploring the Santa Cruz Basin and nearby attractions. The resort has a large swimming pool and whirlpool, tennis courts, exercise room, and offers golf packages (for the Robert Trent Jones 18-hole championship course) and horseback riding. The San Cayetano restaurant features a standard menu: steaks, prime rib, seafood, etc. There's a lounge beside the dining room.

SIERRA VISTA

Sun Canyon Inn
260 N. Garden Avenue
Sierra Vista, AZ 85635
(520) 459-0610 or 800-822-6966

This full-service hotel is located at the main gate of Fort Huachuca, in close proximity to many nearby historic attractions. Guests enjoy a complimentary breakfast buffet, a refrigerator and microwave in every room, and 24-hour access to the heated pool and Jacuzzi. Other amenities include cable TV, discounted green fees at the Pueblo del Sol Golf Course, laundry and dry-cleaning services, and membership privileges at the health and racquetball club (**$**).

Thunder Mountain Inn
1631 S. Highway 92
Sierra Vista, AZ 85635
(520) 458-7900 or 800-222-5811

Nestled at the foot of the Huachuca Mountains, this full-service hotel has 105 newly renovated rooms, each with televisions and refrigerators. Some of the amenities include room service, meeting and banquet facilities, swimming pool and Jacuzzi. There is also a coffee shop, open from 6:30 to 11:00 A.M. for breakfast, and for lunch and dinner there is Baxter's Restaurant, voted #1 in Sierra Vista by Cochise County residents. Early breakfasts and box lunches are available for birding enthusiasts, and there is a special accommodation package for birders, which includes a room with breakfast for two, evening beverages, and dinner coupons ($).

SONOITA

Crown C Ranch

P.O. Box 984
Sonoita, AZ 85637
(520) 455-5739

I had to include this unusual place to stay because it is rare that a small group of people (two or three couples) can stay together, share kitchen facilities, yet have their own privacy.

Sidney Franklin is the owner and host of this working cattle ranch. The ranch house and a guest house are rented to travelers, who usually rent the two-bedroom guest house as a unit. The same is true for the two wings of the main ranch house (one wing has four bedrooms, the other has two).

There are kitchens in the two wings and in the guest house. The ranch offers the sense of privacy a B&B cannot offer. Aside from quiet stays, the ranch has a swimming pool and tennis courts. You could bike from the ranch house, or hike through the ranchlands to the Arizona Trail, which passes through the nearby forest. Horse trail rides can be arranged through a local tour operator. The ranch is located 2.75 miles west of Sonoita on Arizona Highway 82. It dates from the mid-1930s. The prime birding sites, including Patagonia and Coronado National Memorial, are less than a hour's drive from the ranch ($$).

TUBAC

Burro Inn, Restaurants, and Suites

P.O. Box 4188
Tubac, AZ 85646
(520) 398-2281 or 800-371-2281

The Burro Inn is a fine restaurant, serving Mexican dishes as well as mesquite-broiled steaks, ribs, and chicken. It opens at 11 A.M. daily. The suites are large two-room affairs with king-size beds in the bedroom, a queen pull-out in the living room, a wet bar with microwave and refrigerator. The inn is located 1 mile west of I-19, from Exit 40 (Chavez Siding) ($ to $$).

TOMBSTONE

Lookout Lodge
Highway 80, P.O. Box 787
Tombstone, AZ 85638
(520) 457-2223

Most local accommodations are older, small motels. Overlooking the Dragoon Mountains to the east, this Best Western operation is the most modern place to stay in Tombstone. It has been recently renovated and has a heated pool. Complimentary continental breakfast is served ($ to $$).

Tombstone Motel
9th Street at Fremont
Tombstone, AZ 85638
(520) 457-3478

An older and smaller motel, close to the historic downtown area, this veteran of many years of visitors to this amazing town offers comfortable, clean accommodations. Restaurants, saloons, and souvenir shops are only a block away ($).

Buford House B&B
113 East Safford Street,
P.O. Box 98
Tombstone, AZ 85638
(520) 457-3969 or 800-263-6762

This historic 1880, two-story adobe house is now a comfortable bed-and-breakfast inn with five rooms, all furnished with antique furnishings. Some rooms have a private bath.

Brenda Reger, the owner, serves a full breakfast ($$).

Priscilla's B&B
3rd and Safford, P.O. Box 700
Tombstone, AZ 85638
(520) 457-3844

Built in 1904, this two-story country Victorian has a warm ambience. Full breakfast is served. The five rooms on two floors share two private baths ($).

Tombstone Boarding House
108 North Fourth Street
Tombstone, AZ 85638
(520) 457-3716

A bed-and-breakfast inn, seven rooms are decorated with different color themes, while the eighth unit is a historic miner's cabin. The rooms have private entrances and private baths. A full breakfast is served in the country kitchen. Rooms are furnished with antiques and collectibles. The inn is comprised of two 1880 adobe houses ($$).

Ironhorse Ranch
P.O. Box 536
Tombstone, AZ 85638
(520) 457-9361

This is a place to stay overnight, or to visit for lunch or dinner. It is a working cattle ranch with a little theme park town called Tumbleweed, which includes a hotel and saloon. It all is on the land occupied by the historic community of Bouquillas. The hotel on the ranch has large rooms and private baths. There's also a room above the Winchester Hotel in the Tumbleweed theme town. You can have a horseback ride, a chuckwagon supper, or attend the nightly dinner stage show featuring western music. Rodeos are held twice a year (**$$**).

The Enchanted Circle and Taos

North-central New Mexico is blessed with an amazingly clear, pure light. Many residents and visitors believe that this almost mystical light is responsible for Taos being what it is: a large town that still has the character of a village; perhaps America's finest artists' colony, surely brought to Taos by the light that infuses the renowned paintings and watercolors created here; a haven of Pueblo civilization and spirituality; a community where the confluence of four distinct cultures results in a felicitous architectural tradition; and a place with an amazingly varied cultural program including several notable art museums, drama and dance companies, and more than seventy galleries.

The most southerly range of the Rockies, the Sangre de Cristo Mountains lie to the north and east of Taos. The range crosses the Colorado border and stretches as far south as Santa Fe. There is an abundance of mountain recreation and sightseeing within a half-hour's drive of Taos—in any direction.

Taos and the area surrounding are not to be taken lightly, or swiftly. This is a town meant for exploring, and for experiencing the unique ambience created by the mixture of cultural influences that have brought it so much fame. The opportunities for outdoor recreation also require time to fully appreciate. This is a mountainous landscape, quite unlike any other part of the Southwest. If you're a hiker or camper, the wilderness areas of the Carson National Forest offer superb alpine recreation. If you prefer to tour in your car or RV, the two major scenic loop drives—the Enchanted Circle and Valle Vidal—will take you through the forest into wonderful valleys, across prairies, past ghost towns, and to some of the best fishing streams and lakes in New Mexico.

The Rio Grande becomes a major stream after descending from the San Juan range of the Colorado Rockies, carving a deep gorge just west of Taos. Into the Rio Grand flows the Rio Hondo, which drains the Sangre de Cristo mountains north and east of Taos. The Rio Hondo, and the alpine creeks that feed it, provides a rich series of ecosystems at many elevations.

Taos and Taos Pueblo

An hour's drive north of Santa Fe—a much more sophisticated city, or at least that's what the travel pundits say—Taos is one of a very few small cities that begin to affect, even haunt, you as soon as you arrive. Perhaps it's the clear air, snappy temperatures, pellucid light, the deeply ingrained cultural tradition flavored by the artists who live in Taos today, or the architecture—of Spain, Mexico, Victorian America, the Pueblo peoples. Whereas in Santa Fe the cultural underpinnings are there but somehow subdued and underlayed, in Taos it's all in-your-face, and all in a very small town.

In the same community is the Taos Pueblo—the regional center of community and culture since A.D. 1000—and the home of the late Kit Carson, the famed buffalo hunter and scout. Somehow, such dichotomy seems valid in this strangely affecting town.

Taos Pueblo is not only an amazing architectural marvel, but it is still a living community—now more ceremonial than residential—with roots established 500 years before Columbus' arrival in the Caribbean and 1,500 years before the first Spanish explorers reached New Mexico.

Native Americans and Spanish occupied the area, in what the Spaniards considered peaceful coexistence, until the Pueblo Uprising of 1680, when the pueblos united to drive out the colonial powers. Sixteen years later the Native Americans of Taos were defeated by Don Diego de Vargas.

The legacies of both cultures are apparent throughout Taos, with the trademark Spanish/adobe architecture, the impressive brown pueblo, and the festivals celebrating both cultures that take place at almost any time of year. The Taos Indians have also turned the pueblo into a money-making monument, charging admission to the pueblo grounds, with additional charges for picture-taking. Native American food, art work, and souvenirs are also sold in the pueblo shops that occupy some of the ground-level rooms. The old Catholic mission church is open to the public, but the pueblo buildings, except for the shops, are off-limits. Other than during a few ceremonial occasions (funerals, etc.), the pueblo is open every day.

Taos' streets are lined with small boutiques, art galleries, cafes, and crafts studios. All are within a short walk from each other in this city that has remained—in its feel—a small village. It's a renowned center for the arts, commemorated for all time by such ground-breaking western artists as Georgia O'Keeffe. Ernest Blumenschein was a founder of the Taos School of Art, part of a group of eastern artists who "saw the light" and encouraged others to come and paint the northern New Mexico landscape. Art museums and commercial galleries display the work of present-day Taos artists and other Southwest arts and crafts notables. Museums, including the Millicent Rogers Museum, the Harwood Foundation Museum, and the Ernest Blumenschein House and Museum, deal with the long multicultural traditions and the twentieth-century Taos art vogue.

Taos Plaza is a must for any visitor to the area. This is the original Spanish Plaza, bordered with many original buildings now occupied by shops, restaurants, and the Hotel La Fonda. The low-key shopping areas, on either side of the plaza, contain most of the art galleries in town, plus additional cafes, boutiques, and book stores (Moby Dickens is a fine one).

Taos has more than its due share of atmospheric hotels, inns, and bed-and-breakfast homes. It is unusual indeed to be able to stay in an urban community so in tune with its natural surroundings. You'll find wonderful period homes (mostly adobe style) transformed into unique B&B inns. The Taos Inn, the historic hotel on the town's main street, is an absolute gem. Other, larger establishments with more standard motel rooms succeed in offering fine gardens and the unique architecture of the area, a mix of Spanish and Native American styles.

For information on Taos attractions and its ongoing cultural program, contact:

Taos County Chamber of Commerce
P.O. Drawer 1
Taos, New Mexico 87571
(505) 758-3873 or 1-800-732-TAOS

OTHER THINGS TO SEE AND DO

Chama and the Cumbres and Toltec Scenic Railway   This famous narrow-gauge railroad runs between Chama, New Mexico, and Antonito, Colorado. Antonito is a 60-mile drive from Taos via U.S. 64 and U.S. 285. Chama is a longer distance (about 80 miles) from Taos, via U.S. 64. Powered by steam locomotives, the train travels through Cumbres Pass (at 10,015 feet) and the 1,100-foot-deep Toltec Gorge. Halfway trips are available from both ends of the line. A bus delivers passengers who make the entire one-way trip from either end back to their starting points.

Driving to Antonito provides an opportunity for a day-trip from Taos. A hot meal is served at lunchtime at Osier, midway along the route. The daily departure time from Antonito (for the one-way trip to Chama) is 10:30 A.M. Departure for a half-way trip to Osier and return to Antonito is 10:00 A.M. If you want to take a bus or van to Chama and return as the train climbs, the bus leaves Antonito at 9:15 A.M. For information and reservations, call the railroad at (505) 756-2151 (Chama) or (719) 376-5483 (Antonito).

San Antonio Mountain Wildlife Viewing Area   The largest free-standing mountain in the U.S. is just west of U.S. Highway 285, northwest of Taos. The lower slope of the mountain is a wintering area for one of the largest elk herds in New Mexico. The herd moves to higher ground for the summer months. Antelope are often seen close to the highway, in both winter and summer. Binoculars are a great help in spotting the browsing animals.

Bird life in this open countryside includes rough-legged hawks, mountain bluebirds, and golden eagles. Sandhill cranes follow the Rio Grande, migrating through the area each spring and fall.

The wildlife viewing area is really a parking lot, provided by private wildlife foundations, the New Mexico State Highway and Transportation Department, the BLM, and Carson National Forest. To reach the viewing area, drive north from Taos on U.S.

64. Take the turn west and drive over the Rio Grande Gorge, continuing on U.S. 64 until you reach the town of Tres Piedras. A national forest ranger station is located 1 mile west of the intersection. Turn north (right) onto U.S. 285 and drive north to the viewing area. The one-way distance from Taos is less than 55 miles. The wildlife area is about 14 miles south of Antonito, Colorado, and the depot for the scenic train ride on the Cumbres and Toltec Narrow Gauge Railroad. Combining these activities in one trip makes sense.

High Road to Taos   Between Taos and Espanola is a remarkable highway that takes the visitor back to an earlier era in New Mexico. The 58-mile route, called the High Road to Taos, is a journey through a beautiful mountain and forest region to which Spanish settlers came and established several communities including Trampas, Truchas, and Chimayo. The Sanctuario de Chimayo and the old church at Trampas are superb examples of early Spanish architecture. Both are open for viewing. Picuris Pueblo is just off this route as well. In the Espanola/Chimayo area, easily accessible pueblos include Nambe, Pojoaque, Santa Clara, Tesuque, and San Juan. For the return trip to Taos, you can take State Route 570, with a possible stopover at the Orilla Verde Recreation Area, set on the banks of the Rio Grande. For information on the recreation area, call (505) 758-8851.

Carson National Forest

A huge chunk of north-central New Mexico is made up of the forest that covers the slopes of the Sangre de Cristos. The Carson National Forest extends from the Colorado border to where it meets the Santa Fe National Forest a few miles north of the city of Santa Fe. While it doesn't include the Rio Grande Valley, the Carson areas do cover the range east of the Rio Grande, including the scenic Canjilon Lakes region. To the east, the forest lands end on a line north and south from the community of Eagle Nest, about 40 miles from Taos. Several protected wilderness areas are within the national forest, including the Wheeler Peak Wilderness, which encompasses the highest peak in New Mexico; the Latir Peak Wilderness, a wild rugged mountain area near the Colorado border; and the Columbine-Hondo Study

Area, now being considered as a potential new fully protected wilderness area. All have hiking trails through creek valleys, and to alpine lakes and mountain meadows, although the Latir Peak Wilderness has a lack of maintained trails, with one notable exception. Other highlights include the Valle Vidal unit—a former ranch property now protected by the Forest Service. As in other national forests, the Carson mixes some logging (not as much as in previous decades) with other commercial activities including mining and ranching. Taos Ski Valley, with downhill and cross-country skiing and resort accommodations and restaurants, is set beside the Rio Hondo, in the midst of the national forest.

Much of the route along the two circle loop trips leads through the Carson National Forest, beginning and ending in Taos. Both offer a diverse range of forest drives, camping, fishing, alpine and streamside hiking, and wildlife viewing. Seasonal hunting is permitted in some parts of the forest tract. The loop drives provide easy access to almost all of this recreational activity.

Enchanted Circle—Scenic Route

An 84-mile drive through the Carson National Forest, the Enchanted Circle loops around Wheeler Peak, the topmost point in the state, and the central point in the rugged Wheeler Peak Wilderness. Along the way, the route crosses the Rio Hondo, then turns west to the small resource community of Questa, then leads through the Red River Valley to the quaint, rustic resort town of Red River. Next it climbs up to Bobcat Pass, at an elevation of 9,820 feet, then descends to Eagle Nest Lake, climbs again (on U.S. 64) to Palo Flechado Pass (9,101 feet) close to Wheeler Peak, and runs through Taos Canyon along the Rio Fernando de Taos, passing several small, old villages and canyon recreation areas before it returns to Taos. In addition to these major landmarks, there are many places to visit, including museums, historic sites, wildlife viewing areas, a ghost town or two, ski areas, and trailheads.

Allow adequate time for your tour of the Enchanted Circle so you can fully enjoy the experience. While you can make the drive in a 2-hour period, this type of hurried tour will only allow a few prime mountain views. A trip lasting a full day (or perhaps longer, with an overnight stop in Red River) will reward you with an unforgettable mountain experience. Several side roads lead to natural attractions: small river valleys, a view of the northern end of the Rio Grande Gorge, and several wildlife areas where you might see elk and deer. The first part of the drive, north from Taos, is the same route you take for the longer Valle Vidal circle tour, which is covered later in this chapter.

LEAVING TAOS

Taos Plaza is the beginning and the end of the circle loop. The drive begins by taking U.S. 64 (Paseo del Pueblo Norte) north past Kit Carson State Park and the entrance roads to Taos Pueblo. To the east is Taos Mountain, thought to be a magic place. Native American legend has it that this mystical mountain has great power. If it likes you, you will return again and again. Those with whom it is displeased will find it impossible to stay. On the back side of the mountain are the downhill slopes of Taos Ski Valley.

Four miles north of the plaza is a blinking light. This marks the junction of U.S. 64 with State routes 150 and 522. Seven miles west on U.S. 64 is the Rio Grande Gorge and bridge. State Route 150 leads southeast for 15 miles to Taos Ski Valley. To continue the Enchanted Circle route, drive north on State Route 522.

One mile off the highway, on a county road, is one of the finest collections of southwestern art, including superb Hispanic and Native American art collections, at the Millicent Rogers Museum. Mrs. Rogers, who was a primary supporter of the Taos art movement, collected most of the works during the 1940s. The museum was opened in 1956. The adobe-style building is now open daily from 9 A.M. to 5 P.M.

Farther north, 7 miles north of the Highway 64 junction, we cross the Rio Hondo. A short side trip is available from this point. A gravel side road leads 3.5 miles to John Dunn Bridge, which spans the Rio Grande. The Dunn Bridge is a popular launching point for kayakers and rafters. It also provides an opportunity to see the Rio Grande as it flows toward the deepest parts of the gorge.

Enthusiasts of things literary will definitely want to drive to the Kiowa Ranch and the D. H. Lawrence Shrine. The British author, who lived his life in controversy over his saucy writings, spent several of the final years of his life here (1922 to 1925). Lawrence and his wife were presented the ranch by Mabel Dodge Luhan, a Taos society matron and a famous character in her own right. When Lawrence died in France in 1930, his ashes were brought to the ranch at San Cristobal. Frieda, his widow, built a chapel to hold the remains and continued to live at the ranch. She later married Angelo Ravagli and played host to artistic and literary notables from around the world. The ranch is now owned by the University of New Mexico. The shrine is open daily to the public.

FOREST HIGHLIGHTS

The Enchanted Circle enters the Carson National Forest just north of the Rio Hondo crossing and the road to the Lawrence Shrine. Forest Road 9 leads 4 miles to Cebolla Mesa Campground. This campground has five sites overlooking the Rio Grande Gorge. A steep hiking trail leads to the river, and a bridge crosses the gorge. The visitor center for the Rio Grande Wild River Recreation Area is on the west side of the river. The recreation site and visitor center are operated by the BLM. (For hiking in this area, see page 243).

Two miles west of the highway—via State Route 515—is the Red River Fish Hatchery. This is a 2-mile side trip to a visitor center featuring a display of the trout hatching and rearing process. There's a free, self-guided tour of a sample rearing pond and several trout raceways. Twenty-four miles north of Taos, you arrive at the town of Questa, at the intersection of State Routes 552 and 38. Nearly two hundred years old, Questa was originally a ranching village. While there are ranches in the area, most of the people who live here work at the nearby molybdenum mine. There's a store, gas station, and other visitor services, including a visitor information center, at the highway junction. The Enchanted Circle route leads east along State Route 38. You'll find the Questa Ranger Station for the Carson National Forest beside the highway at the east end of town.

The first of the national forest campgrounds located beside Highway 38 is at Goat Hill, the second—Columbine Canyon Campground—is several miles to the east. Goat Hill has three units; Columbine has 27 sites. Across the road is a large tailings pile, the accumulated debris from the huge molybdenum mine, now operated by Molycorp Inc. The stand of dead and damaged trees across the road from the mine is not the result of mine effluvia. The fir and spruce have been stricken by the western spruce budworm. The forest service has managed to halt some of the destruction in the roadside area by applying a natural agent, Baccilus thuringiensis.

Three additional campgrounds—Fawn Lakes (22 sites), Elephant Rock (22 sites), and Junebug (20 sites)—are located to the south of the highway. The small Fawn Lakes, located south of the road near Elephant Rock Campground, offer fishing opportunities.

RED RIVER

Just beyond the campgrounds, this little mountain town is situated at 8,750 feet. A popular winter ski resort with rustic-style accommodations at a reasonable cost, and several fine restaurants, it's an excellent place to stay during the summer and fall months while exploring the forest and mountain recreation areas. The lifts operate in the summer, taking visitors along with scenic rides to mountain meadows high above the town. Other available benefits of staying in the Red River area are horseback riding, off-road driving, trail hiking, and an Old West ambience, which adds to the nightlife in the several saloons and melodrama theater. You may see staged shoot-outs on Main Street.

Just beyond Red River, State Route 578 runs southeast, beside the Red River. The junction with the Jeep road that leads up Goose Creek to Goose Lake is a minute's drive from the highway. Farther down Route 578 is the Tall Pine Museum, an historic cabin housing artifacts of the pioneer days of the Red River settlement. The road continues along a stunning scenic route, crossing the river several times before coming to an end at the Bull of the Woods Mountain trailhead and Jeep road. This is one way to hike to Wheeler Peak (see page 247).

BOBCAT PASS AND EAGLE NEST

As the road climbs rapidly and approaches Bobcat Pass, you will see the entrance to the Enchanted Forest Cross-Country Ski Area, with 30 miles of groomed trails within the Carson National Forest. Then, 7.7 miles after crossing the pass, you will see the ruins of Elizabethtown off to the south of the highway.

This gold-mining town founded in 1870 was the first incorporated town in New Mexico. In those days, there were seven saloons, three dance halls, and the Mutz Hotel (the ruins can be seen from the highway). The Elizabethtown cemetery, like other pioneer graveyards, tells a lot about the short history of this rough-and-ready little town. The town of Eagle Nest was more fortunate. It still lives, located next to Eagle Nest Lake, one of northern New Mexico's most popular fishing lakes. With strong breezes blowing down from the mountains, it is also a popular windsurfing place. Wheeler Peak dominates the western sky.

U.S. Highway 64 provides the final leg of the Enchanted Circle, leading southwest to Taos. About 8.5 miles south of Eagle Nest is a simple but striking building, the D.A.V. National Memorial. It was built by Dr. Victor Westphall in memory of his son David, who died in Vietnam, and as a memorial to all Vietnam War veterans. Now operated by the Disabled American Veterans organization, the modern, curved chapel—which looks like a nun's habit—is open daily. A special service is held each Memorial Day, attracting veterans from near and far.

THROUGH TAOS CANYON

As the road leads west, Mt. Wheeler is to the right (north). There's a turnoff (State Route 434) to the resort community of Angel Fire.

Angel Fire has an 18-hole championship golf course and a fine downhill ski area. Palo Flechado Pass was a well-used Native American trail, later used by Spanish and American settlers who traveled from the east along the Cimarron River. The river was called La Flecha (the arrow) by Spanish explorers in the early 1700s. After descending, the road enters Taos Canyon and follows Rio Fernando de Taos. You'll see a group of trout pools along the river. This is the work of the Izaak Walton League, which coordinated the Taos Canyon Riparian Project, designed to protect the riverside ecosystem by keeping cattle out with fences and planting willows to cool the riparian habitat.

Forest Road 437 leads to Garcia Park. During the summer and fall months, Garcia Park is a beautiful forest area used for primitive camping, four-wheel-drive touring, and hiking. The area is used in winter for snowmobiling and cross-country skiing. A series of rough roads fan out along Rio Chiquito, Rito de la Olla to Bear Wallow Ridge, and along the Rio Grande del Rancho, a tributary of the larger Rio Grande.

La Sombra Campground (13 sites) is beside the highway in Taos Canyon, 7.4 miles east of Taos. Capulin Campground (10 sites) and Las Petacas Campground (9 sites) are farther west, toward Taos. La Vinateria picnic ground is scenically located between the two campgrounds. El Nogal picnic ground is located just inside the national forest boundary, 5 minutes from downtown Taos.

One of the lasting impressions of the Enchanted Circle is that of nature persevering: whatever humankind does to the landscape, whether through the ravages of mining, the clearing of land for building short-lived communities, bug infestations, or logging, the land returns to its original state. Sometimes it takes many generations; sometimes it takes only a few decades. Nature has already reclaimed several ghost towns within the Enchanted Circle and nature will renew other areas temporarily changed by man. In the long time span of history, nature heals the landscape; this is a good place to see the process at work, from the pine-clad Taos Canyon to the streamside habitats of the Sangre de Cristos.

Valle Vidal–Scenic Route

This loop, to the north of and longer than the Enchanted Circle, offers superb views of vast open spaces, high Rocky Mountain peaks, wildlife (including numerous birds and a magnificent herd of elk), and reminders of the early frontier days of northern New Mexico—an era dominated by mining, lumbering, and ranching.

What is now called the Valle Vidal unit of the Carson National Forest was once the huge Maxwell Land Grant—two million acres—deeded by the Mexican government in 1841 to Charles Beaubien and Guadalupe Miranda. When the Mexican-American War broke out in 1846, Miranda returned to Mexico while Beaubien, loyal to the United States, stayed in New Mexico. Beaubien's daughter Luz married Illinois fur trapper Lucien Maxwell, and the couple settled here, establishing a ranch. Maxwell began buying adjacent properties in 1864, following his father-in-law's death, and wound up owning the whole grant—a piece of land the size of Rhode Island.

Then, in 1870, Maxwell sold the land to an English syndicate. It was later sold to a Dutch firm. A local war then broke out, fueled by the owners' demand that the ranchers and other settlers who lived on the land leave. They had built homes with Maxwell's assent, and were not prepared to leave. The Colfax County war ensued, pitting the remaining settlers against the Dutch company. The company was victorious in 1887 when the U.S. Supreme Court ruled in its favor. By the turn of the century, the land was subdivided. New ranches were opened, loggers came to topple trees, and a private organization established a private retreat. Of the original land grant, 200,000 acres were used by members of the Vermejo Park Club, including the likes of such Hollywood celebrities as Douglas Fairbanks, Mary Pickford, and Cecil B. DeMille, and other well-known people such as Herbert Hoover, Andrew Mellon, and Harvey Firestone. The club closed during the Depression and the property reverted to ranching uses.

The Vermejo Park property and other lands—totaling almost one million acres—were eventually bought by Texas magnate W. J. Gourley. Wanting to expand the small existing elk herd, Gourley purchased several hundred elk from Yellowstone National Park (at $5 per head). He also bred and raised wild turkeys in order to increase the wild bird population. After Gourley died in 1970, the land was sold to the Pennzoil Company, which donated 100,000 acres to the Forest Service in 1982. With the checkered history of the area, the Valle Vidal tract is littered with historical artifacts: abandoned cabins built by the first settlers; remains of the small, early ranches including houses, corrals, and farm implements; remnants of an old railroad; and ruins that once were the foundations for a townsite. Among the other historical sites is the former Ring Ranch. Timothy Ring purchased 320 acres at $3 per acre. He built a huge home—a real mansion—in the midst of this vast tract. The ranch is located on Forest Road 1950.

The prime job for the Forest Service is wildlife preservation, although the land grant area is also used for ranching. There are two developed campgrounds along the route. Because of the elk calving season, some of the western part of the Valle Vidal unit is closed to traffic from May 1 until early-to-mid-July.

Motorized campers are restricted to the two campgrounds, although backcountry camping is permitted in the unit.

LEAVING TAOS

To get the Valle Vidal: Starting in Taos, heading north on U.S. 64, take the same route as for the Enchanted Circle, continuing north via State Route 522, past the town of Questa to Costilla and the junction with Forest Road 1950. Turn east (right), and drive toward Amalia.

Before leaving the Taos area, you may wish to sample a few sights along the way. Just north of Questa, State Route 378 leads west, through the village of Cerro, to the Rio Grande Wild River Recreation Area—8 miles west of Highway 522. The recreation area includes the Rio Grande Gorge. This area has fine scenery and striking geological features, in addition to Indian rock pictographs. The recreation sites managed by the BLM include a visitor center, campground, and picnic area. You can look into the gorge from viewpoints or hike down to the river level.

There's a fine hike available, leading into the Rio Grande Canyon. The hike is a 7-mile round-trip, starting from a trailhead at the Big Arsenic Springs campground. To get there, drive from Questa on State Route 522 for about 5.5 miles, to the road that leads to the Rio Grande Wild and Scenic River (you'll see a sign at the turnoff). Drive west on the paved road, and you'll find the campground almost 12 miles from the turnoff. You may wish to stay at this scenic campground, which lies 800 feet above the river.

From the trailhead, walk down the path, descending through a series of switchbacks, past ponderosa pine trees. There's a fork in the trail. If you take the path toward Arsenic Springs, you'll see the springs and the stream—created by the large spring—flowing under the trail. Shelters are available along the path. The loop hike takes the left-hand fork, leading toward La Junta. The trail passes Little Arsenic Springs. Stay on the downward trail (a side-trail leads back to the campground). There are more shelters along this path. At 2.7 miles, a fork ascends to the La Junta Campground. Stay on the downward trail to reach river-level, where the Red River flows into the Rio Grande.

There are several options for the return trip. If you have a spare driver who did not take the hike and stayed on the rim, you can cross the footbridge over the Red River and then ascend to the Cebolla Mesa Campground. You can also retrace part of the trail and return to the rim at La Junta Campground, or walk back, retracing the whole hike, to the Big Arsenic Spring Campground. This hike is easy and offers an unusual trip into the basalt canyon.

SIDE TRIP TO LATIR PEAK WILDERNESS

One of two protected wilderness areas in the Carson National Forest, this is a wild, rugged place without creature comforts. One maintained trail offers exceptional views, taking the hiker close to several peaks over 12,000 feet high. From Questa, drive to the wilderness area via Forest Roads 134 and 134A. FR 134A is a rough primitive road (1-mile long), suitable only for four-wheel-drive and high clearance vehicles such as pickups. You can park at the lot located at the junction of 134 and 134A, a mile south of the Cabresto Lake campground.

The trailhead for Trail 82 is found at the campground. It leads to Heart Lake and Latir Mesa, climbing into the hills and following Lake Fork. A spur trail leads 1 mile to Baldy Mountain. The main trail continues as a circle loop across Latir Mesa and then down Bull Creek Fork. Another spur trail leads southwest past Cabresto Peak and Pinabete Peak, and then through Peñasquito Canyon. A map of the Latir Wilderness (also including the Wheeler Peak Wilderness) is available from the forest ranger stations in Questa and Taos.

APPROACHING THE COLORADO BORDER

State Route 522 leads north, past the Urraca Wildlife Area, managed by the New Mexico Department of Game and Fish. The wildlife area, to the east of the highway, protects herds of elk and deer. Ute Mountain lies to the west. Our route turns east at the town of Costilla, at the junction with State Route 196. Costilla, just south of the Colorado boundary, is an historic settlement, with the old Plaza de Arriba seen on the south side of Highway 196. The route continues a few miles to the village of Amalia.

The pavement ends 4 miles beyond Amalia, at Ski Rio, a downhill and cross-country ski center. From here, the route follows Forest Road 1950. This is the only road that leads through the Valle Vidal. Another recreation opportunity is available just before you enter the forest lands. The Rio Costilla (Cooperative

Livestock) Association operates a large private tract with camping, hunting, and lake fishing for a fee; there is no fee required to fish in Costilla Creek. The Rio Costilla Association has an information and fee station across the creek, on the south side of the highway. This road provides access to the camping facilities and fishing lakes.

WILDLIFE, CAMPING, AND TRAILS

The lands of Vermejo Ranch form the western side of the Valle Vidal area. Forest Road 1900 leads north, next to Commanche Point, at the confluence of Costilla and Commanche creeks. Valle Vidal tours continue on Road 1950, toward Shuree. The trailhead for the Little Costilla Creek Trail is found 3 miles east of the junction. This horseback and foot trail leads north to Little Costilla Peak (12,584 feet), which is part of the territory closed to the public until mid-July for elk calving. To the south side of the road is Valle Vidal Vista. This is a good place to see elk, particularly in the early morning and late afternoon hours. The Clayton Corral is used by the ranchers who have grazing permits to run cattle in Valle Vidal.

Cimarron Campground, the first of three maintained campgrounds in Valle Vidal, is located 1 mile south of the route via Forest Road 1910. With 22 sites, the campground has picnic tables, grills, toilets, and water. Campsites for the disabled are available. Horse camping is also available, with several designated sites. FR 1910 continues (with FR 1914) as a loop, rejoining FR 1950 near the Ring Ranch site. This loop leads to several trailheads, including a trail to the Beatty Lakes and farther south to the Elliot Barker Wildlife Area. Another goes south from near the Rock Wall to join the trail down Middle Ponit Creek, also entering the Elliot Barker Wildlife Area. If you take the latter trail to the west, you'll pass into Greenwood Canyon and hike through the Cimarron Range. All this territory lies within the original Maxwell Grant lands.

Staying on Forest Road 1950, heading east, the Shuree Ponds are found by taking Shuree Pond Road for a half mile. There are ponds, a fishing pier, and trails, along with picnic tables and restrooms. One pond is reserved for children under 12. Fishing is permitted from July 1 through December 31. Anglers must purchase a fishing stamp (permit) at sporting goods stores before entering the Valle Vidal Unit. A campground is located at this site.

Windy Gap is located 3.3 miles east of Clayton Corral. This is a break in what is known as the Rock Wall, a long monocline that runs north and south. The black markings on the aspen trees in this area are browsing marks—wounds—made by elk that feed here in the fall. As the road goes through several switchbacks, Vista Grande, a wide spot in the road, offers great views of both the eastern and western parts of Valle Vidal. Beyond this spot is the historic Ring Ranch. The ranch house, now on the National Register of Historic Places, is reached by taking a trail to the south of FR 1950. Visitors are asked not to enter the buildings, as they have not been restored.

The forest road loops around Hart Canyon, then passes through Lookout Canyon, before it leaves the Valle Vidal Unit. It then continues through the long Cerrososo Canyon, all the way to U.S. Highway 84, east of the town of Cimarron.

CIMARRON TO TAOS

Take U.S. 84 west to Cimarron and Eagle Nest, where the tour takes the same route back to Taos as the Enchanted Circle Tour.

Cimarron is an old Wild West town founded in the 1880s as a stage stop on the Santa Fe Trail. The scene of the Colfax County War, it was a rowdy place in its early years. Twenty-six men were said to have been killed in the saloon, which became the St. James Hotel. The hotel has been restored and is a National Historical Landmark. The Old Mill Museum, converted from a grist mill to an historical museum, contains artifacts from Cimarron's turbulent past.

There's an interesting historic home on the Philmont Scout Ranch, 4 miles southwest of Cimarron on State Route 21. Each summer, Boy Scouts gather on this property, which was donated to the Boy Scouts of America by Oklahoma oil baron Waite Phillips in 1941. Villa Philmonte, the expansive Phillips ranch house, is open to the public. The nearby Kit Carson Museum includes part of a ranch home built by Carson, the famous scout of another kind. Between Cimarron and Eagle Nest Lake, the highway passes through the dramatic Cimarron River Canyon in the Colin Nesblett Wildlife Area.

The castellated rock formations of Cimarron Canyon are often the site of rock climbing. Cimarron Canyon State Park is part of the wildlife area. There are four campgrounds in the canyon (Ponderosa, Maverick, Palisades, and Tolby), with two picnic sites at midpoint in the wildlife area, and another at the extreme western edge of the area. Campers must have valid New Mexico hunting or fishing licenses. One night's free camping is provided for each license per camping party. The highway curves around the north shore of Eagle Nest Lake, passing through the town of Eagle Nest, then turns south to lead over Palo Fletchado Pass and through Taos Canyon.

TRAVEL ADVISORY

The total length of the Valle Vidal Route (Taos to Taos) is 173 miles. While it can be done in a long day-trip—about 8 hours—2 or 3 days, with camping or a stay in Cimarron, offers much more time for wildlife viewing, sightseeing, and exploring several easy trails that lead from the main route. This is a perfect trip for a picnic lunch. There are no services (gas, store, cafe) between Amalia and Cimarron, a distance of almost 70 miles. Another few words of caution: Visitors to Valle Vidal during the spring and early summer may face muddy forest roads, the result of rains; winter visitors may encounter intermittent road closures, the result of snowfall.

Nearby Attractions

WHEELER PEAK WILDERNESS

Twenty thousand acres of alpine splendor, protected for future Americans, is the legacy of a movement in the late 1950s to set aside the area around Wheeler Peak as a wilderness preserve. In 1964, 7 years after the state legislature requested the designation from Congress, the federal government acted. The preserve lies across the peaks and ridges of the Sangre de Cristo range, with elevations ranging from a low of 7,650 feet to the summit of Wheeler Peak at 13,161 feet. The Taos Indian Pueblo borders the wilderness along its south and east boundaries, and the area cannot be accessed from the pueblo without a permit. There is easy access from Taos Ski Valley, where a trail leads to Williams Lake and Wheeler Peak, and other trails (Bull of the Woods and Wheeler Peak) rise through the La Cal Basin. Forest roads from the northeastern side of the wilderness boundary— from the town of Red River—lead to other trailheads that run along the East Fork and the Middle Fork of the Red River. Another trail ascends to Lost Lake, proceeding past Horseshoe Lake to Wheeler Peak.

High mountains make their own weather, and Wheeler Peak is no exception. While snowfall is impressive, half the annual precipitation of 34–40 inches falls during the summer. July and August feature showers on an almost daily basis. The driest periods for hiking to Wheeler Peak are late June or the first half of September, when the weather is crisp and clear, and you won't find a lot of people in the preserve.

The human race is not a newcomer to these mountains. Before a startling discover was made by two Forest Service employees in 1987, it was thought that Native Americans first explored the mountains in about A.D. 1200 when they began constructing pueblos in the Rio Grande Valley. The discovery of a basalt knife at about 11,000 feet indicated that humans had hunted in the Sangre de Cristos as far back as 9,000 years ago. Later occupants of the area include the Spanish, who arrived in the 1600s and later turned the area over to Mexicans. Gold miners flocked to the local gold rush in 1885 and little mining towns survived until the early 1900s. The area was rich with beaver and other fur-bearing animals. Bill Williams, a famous trapper and adventurer, came through the area with General Fremont, who had been sent here to look for a transcontinental railroad route. Williams Lake is named for the trapper.

Major George M. Wheeler (Wheeler Peak) was a U.S. Army surveyor who mapped much of the region. His survey companion (Simpson) has a nearby peak in his name. Other nearby peaks and mountains are named for influential people of the region, including William Frazer, a prospector and investor with an unsavory reputation, who has an entire mountain named in his honor.

The mountains are the result of movement during an uplift period, about 130 million years ago. This is igneous rock, hot at first and then cooled by freezing, cracked by freezing/thawing cycles, then shaped by glaciers.

WHEELER PEAK WILDERNESS TRAILS

Wheeler Peak Trail (#90) *Access:* Drive 4 miles north of the Taos Plaza on U.S. 64 to the junction of State Route 150. Drive east on New Mexico 150 to Taos Ski Valley and the

Twining campground. Trailhead parking is located next to the campground, across from the ski area base facilities. There is an information board at the trailhead, with a map of the preserve and several trails.

The Hike: While no mountain climbing equipment is necessary, this trail provides a relatively strenuous all-day hike, or a moderate 2-day experience. The round-trip is about 15 miles, the ascent 3,771 feet. There is drinking water at the 5-mile point.

The Trail: The trail leads northeast to Bull of the Woods Pasture (2.25 miles), intersecting the trail to Gold Hill (#63). Past the junction, the trail follows an old road that ascends toward Bull of the Woods Mountain. Two old mines are located in this area. The trail rises above the tree line and leads across the La Cal Basin. There are camping areas here, suitable for an overnight stay before the climb to the peak. This is the place to stay if a rainstorm occurs. Lightning is a regular feature of the summer storms. A stream crosses the valley (about 5 miles). The trail then climbs to the summit of Mt. Walker (13,133 feet) and continues for another half-mile to Wheeler Peak.

The panoramic views from the summit are stupendous. On a clear day, you'll see the snow-capped San Juan range in Colorado, and the mountains beyond Chama. The Great Plains lie to the east. If you wish to return by another route, Trail 91 descends to Horseshoe Lake. Trail 55 (after following the ridges to Simpson Peak and Taos Cone, into Sawmill Park) drops to the East Fork of the Red River. Perhaps a non-hiker could drive your vehicle to Red River and along FR 578 to the East Fork trailhead.

Williams Lake Trail (#62)   *Access:* Take U.S. 64 and State Route 150 to Taos Ski Valley and park in the Twining Campground parking lot (same as above).

The Hike: This is a moderate-to-strenuous hike, depending on whether you wish to climb to the peak from the lake. The route from the trailhead to the alpine lake at the base of the peak is moderately easy, a 1,730-foot ascent. The round-trip to the lake is 8 miles. Drinking water is available from Lake Fork of the Rio Hondo, the stream that feeds Williams Lake. The lake elevation is 11,120 feet.

The Trail: The trail leads across the Rio Hondo Bridge, toward the Ski Valley ticket office. The trail continues southeast under the two chair lifts, following the skiers' main return trail.

The trail is not open during the ski season (for good reason). Follow the ski trail for 1.5 miles along the river, to the Phoenix Restaurant at the base of the Kachina Lift ($4). The trail continues for another .25 miles on the east side of Lake Fork Creek. Follow the old road—not the main road—and bear left. The wilderness boundary is just ahead, at 10,600 feet. After passing through the Englemann spruce forest, the trail emerges into open meadows and rocky areas. Williams Lake is a natural alpine lake with no fish (it's too cold and freezes in winter). Camping is permitted more than 300 feet from the lakeshore or from streams.

It is possible to hike (more likely scramble) to Wheeler Peak from the lake. There is no maintained trail, and the route is steep and very rocky. However, many people do it and return (carefully) down the slope. Other trails may be used to return to road level.

Trail to Lost and Horseshoe Lakes (#91)   *Access:* From the town of Red River, drive south on State Route 578 (the old Highway 150) to the junction of Middle Fork and East Fork. As the pavement ends, take the road to the right (FR 58) for 1.5 miles, where you'll find a parking area. Parking is not available beyond this point.

The Hike: The elevation here is 9,650 feet. The ascent to Lost Lake is 1,845 feet. The trail mainly follows a Jeep road to Middle Fork Lake, outside the wilderness area. A second trail leads to Lost lake, which is .5 miles inside the boundary.

The Trail: Open to both foot and horseback travelers, the hike begins at the parking lot, but follows the Jeep road for a quarter-mile. When the road forks, take the left path and cross the creek over the footbridge. The trail leads along the east side of the creek for a mile, then mainly follows the Jeep road over a series of switchbacks. Hikers and riders may meet motorcycles and four-wheel-drive vehicles along this part of the route that goes as far as the wilderness boundary. You'll find the trailhead to Lost Lake (4 miles) at the river crossing. This is where the hike becomes a natural experience—a Douglas fir forest, with some white pine. The views are frequent and impressive. After 2 miles, the trail exits the forest and continues through small meadows, a spruce/aspen zone. The wilderness boundary is crossed, and about .5 miles later, you'll reach Lost Lake, at an elevation of 11,495 feet. There is good fishing here; the lake is stocked (by helicopter) with cutthroat trout. As with other alpine sites, camping is not permitted within 300 feet of the lake or stream.

COLUMBINE–HONDO AREA

This large area, now under study as another possible wilderness area, is part of the Carson National Forest. Located north of the Wheeler Peak Wilderness and west of the town of Red River, it also includes the Rio Hondo Canyon, through which you drive on New Mexico 150 to reach Taos Ski Valley. There are several maintained forest service trails, some of which connect with the Wheeler Peak Wilderness trails.

Gold Hill Loop Hike (#90, #63 and #64)   *Access:* Start from the Taos Ski Valley parking lot, the same parking area as for the Wheeler Peak hikes, and drive from Taos via U.S. 64 and State Route 150 to the Kachina campground (northeastern edge of the valley).

The Hike: Although this loop is taken from the same trailhead as the Wheeler Peak Trail, it proceeds in a different direction—across the mountains toward Red River. This loop, made up of three numbered forest trails, crosses the Gold Hill area above the resort town. The entire loop is 7.5 miles. The ascent is 3,200 feet, rising from the trailhead at 9,500 to 12,700 feet. It is considered a moderate to strenuous hike.

The Trails: Begin by taking the Bull of the Woods Trail from the Ski Valley trailhead. The trail rises slightly to Bull of the Woods Pasture (2 miles) and a small pond. You'll reach an intersection with Gold Hill Trail (#63). Continue by taking Gold Hill Trail, which climbs in a northerly direction. Several peaks are apparent on the climb to a meadow 1 mile from the junction. The trail climbs again through forest and meadows, passing an old mine (with a decaying cabin and mine remains). Gold Hill is ahead and the trail continues, with a good view of Goose Lake below. If you have the time, it's a fine idea to take a short detour to see the lake and the peaks visible from the ridge. The Gold Hill Trail continues to meet Trail #72, which leads toward Questa and the Columbine campground, and Trail #57 to Lobo Peak.

However, to return to the Ski Valley, walk west (left) to the junction with the Long Canyon Trail, where you'll see a sign marking the trail. This trail makes the return to the Rio Hondo. As it descends, it follows along the east side of a lovely creek for 2.5 miles to the Bull of the Woods Trail. The parking lot and trailhead are at the bottom of the Bull of the Woods Trail.

Other Hondo–Columbine Trails   Several other forest service trails lead from the rivers and creeks of the area, up into the Sangre de Cristos. The Yerba Canyon Trail (#61) is found beside State Route 150, on the way to Taos Ski Valley. This trail goes almost 4 miles, along and across a creek and through a narrow canyon, which is an amazing riparian habitat. The trail crosses to the west side of the creek after a mile, crossing the canyon above a spring. The trail continues to climb, reaching a ridge to the south and west of Lobo Peak. You'll soon reach the junction with Manzanita Canyon Trail.

Our Yerba trail leads toward the peak; at this height (about 11,600 feet) there are marvelous views in several directions. From the peak you can take another trail to Gold Hill. On the other hand, Manzanita Canyon takes you back to the highway from whence you came, a 4.2-mile descent through another canyon with a creek. The path becomes a road before reaching the highway. It's another mile to the Yerba Canyon trailhead and your car.

Because of the wide range of elevations, from high desert to more than 13,000 feet, there is a great diversity in the wildlife, particularly of birds and plants. The landscape varies from sagebrush, prairie grass, and pinyon pine woodlands around Taos, to the severe alpine conditions of Wheeler Peak and the other Sangre de Cristo mountains. There are seven biotic zones, including arctic tundra. This remarkable diversity is a bonus for wildlife-watchers, who are able to observe mountain, forest, riparian, and desert species—all in one short vacation.

BIRDS

Rough-legged Hawk

Buteo lagopus

This large hawk grows to a length of 24 inches with a wingspan of 48–54 inches. Most have a buffy head, chest, and leg feathers that grow down to the talons. The belly has a wide black band, and the tail has a broad terminal band. The leading tips and trailing edge of the wing are black, and a white patch is located at the "wrist" of the underwing. There is a darker version of this hawk, but it is rarely seen. Its range is around the world, in the northern hemisphere, from southern Canada to Arizona and Texas. A winter visitor to the British Isles, it also shows up in some areas of California and New Mexico, including the areas to the north and northwest of Taos such as the San Antonio Mountain Wildlife Viewing Area and Valle Vidal. It nests in high, upland tundra, and in winter, nests on open plains and prairie, or marshes.

This hawk can often be spotted by watching its flight pattern. When looking at its prey, it hovers like a sea bird. It feeds on rodents and ptarmigan.

Osprey

Pandion haliaetus

This bird is found throughout the world, except Antarctica. There is only one species, but it is sometimes called the American Osprey. It is the only raptor that hovers over water and plunges into it feet-first to pick up its dinner. A large bird, growing to 24.5 feet with a wingspan of 4.5 to 6 feet, it is blackish above and white below. Identifying characteristics are the mostly white head that bears a broad black cheek patch, and its flying with a crook in the wing, displaying a black forward patch. The osprey lives wherever there is water: ocean coasts, lakes, and rivers. It is not found widely in the Southwest but does breed in a small number of locations, including the river valleys around Taos, which have sufficient fish to keep it interested.

Its call is a series of crisp whistles: *cheep cheep* or *kewk, kewk, kewk*. Its danger call is a loud, frantic *cheereek*.

White-tailed Ptarmigan
Lagopus leucurus
While common in Canada, like its cousins the rock and willow ptarmigans, this is the only ptarmigan normally found in the United States. It does not have a wide habitat in the Southwest. This little alpine dweller lives in the Colorado Rockies and in the Sangre de Cristo range, and is also found in a small section of the central Sierra Nevada, in the northern Washington Cascades, and in Montana. In summer it lives above timberline, and in winter at lower elevations. In summer, this bird has a mottled brown or gray back and a white belly, with large, white, outer tail patches. In winter, it is pure white, except for the eyes and the black bill.

Killdeer
Charadrius vociferus
Found from Alaska to central Mexico, the coast of Peru, and the West Indies, the killdeer is a member of the plover family. All are waders, eating small fish and other marine life, as well as insects and plant matter. It is identified by its two black breastbands, separated by a band of white. Its head and upper parts are brown with white wing markings, and its long, golden tail has black at the back. The bird gets its name from its voice: a loud *kill-deer, kill-deer,* etc. It also has a repeated *dee-dee-dee* and a low trill. In the wild, killdeer's habitat is riverbanks, shores, mudflats, and fields.

Northern Flicker
Colaptes cafer
A colorful member of the woodpecker family, the flicker that lives in the Taos region is called the red-shafted flicker. It is one of three flicker variations in the western states, including the "yellow-shafted" and "gilded." Its wings and tail are salmon red. The male has a red moustache, like its more southerly cousin, the gilded flicker, found in the deserts of southeastern California and southern Arizona. The northern flicker has a hopping motion when on

the ground, and normally feeds on ants and other insects. Flickers live in open forests and woodlands, as well as in groves and more open areas. Its voice is a loud *wick wick wick wick*, also *flick-a flicka flicka,* and a loud *kleeer.*

Mountain Bluebird
Sialia currucoides
The mountains of central New Mexico are the most southerly breeding territory for this turquoise blue bird (male) with a light blue breast and white belly. The female is more drab, a gray-brown color with traces of blue on tail, wings, and rump. Immature birds are brown above with light blue on the wings and tail and a faintly spotted belly. Its range is from Alaska, through northern British Columbia and southern Alberta, south to the mountain areas of southern California and into Mexico. In New Mexico, it lives in open forested (subalpine) areas, alpine meadows, and aspen groves. Its voice is a quiet *phew, yor,* and *terr.*

OTHER ANIMALS

Elk
Cervus elaphus
A few of the isolated elk herds to be found in New Mexico are in the Taos area—in Valle Vidal and on San Antonio Mountain and its foothills. This large deer has a stout neck and thin legs, and is tan-colored above, darker underneath. It has a yellowish-brown rump patch, as well as a tail of the same color. The male has a deep brown mane on its throat. The male's antlers have six tines on each side when the animal is mature. The female does not have antlers, and is about 25 percent smaller than the male. The peak breeding period is late October and November, when male elk join the females in the herd. The males fight over their herds of cows by butting antlers. This activity results in few injuries, and is rarely fatal. Each male has a "harem" of up to 60 cows. Gestation can be as long as 275 days, when one or two calves are born, away from the herd.

Elk inhabit high, open mountain areas in the summer, and lower slopes (including thick woodland) in winter. They are most active at dawn and dusk. They run at a very fast pace (up to 35 mph). The elk's range extends south from Vancouver Island and central Washington. There are many large herds in Colorado, Wyoming, and Montana. After the elk of northern New Mexico were almost wiped out by the 1900s, they were imported to the Valle Vidal area in the late 1940s to enhance the small herd that had survived.

Beaver
Castor canadensis
In the last half of the nineteenth century, beaver was the prime object of fur trappers, who hunted the mammal almost to extinction. Much beaver trapping was done in and around the Sangre de Cristo range, particularly in the Enchanted Circle area. This is a very widespread animal, inhabiting most of Canada and the United States, except for Florida and the desert areas of southern California and Nevada. It lives in rivers, creeks, marshes, ponds, and lakes, damming the flow of water to create enough depth in its pond to build a comfortable two-level lodge for its family. Beaver are thought to mate for life. The young are born between late May and late June, after four months of gestation. The one-pound newborns are skilled swimmers within a week. The beaver lodge—made of sticks, grasses, and mud—has a dome shape, with its entrance under water. You'll see gnawed and beaver-felled trees in the area of the lodge. Aspen and other poplars are its construction materials of choice. It also uses willow and birch, which it eats as well.

Primarily nocturnal, the beaver repairs its lodge at night. It signals alarm by slapping its broad tail on the water. Its webbed hind feet leave a fan-shaped track, sometimes as wide as 5 inches. The front feet are much smaller, less than half the length of the hind feet. The beaver has five toes, yet the tracks often show only three or four toes. Although it takes patience, it is a real joy to see a beaver family on its pond.

Red Squirrel
Tamiasciurus hudsonicus
This small, noisy squirrel is found in the Rocky Mountain states, as well as throughout much of western Canada and Alaska. In the Southwest, the red squirrel is found in the White Mountains of Arizona and in the Sangre de Cristo range. Its color is a rusty-red or a grayish-red above, the brightest color on the sides, and whitish below. The tail has a wide black band with white edges. In summer, the color is muted. In winter, it has tufts on its ears. One way to look for this forest-living squirrel is to look on the ground for the gnawed remains of pine cones, which are often seen in piles. These squirrels live in coniferous and mixed forests, and even in hardwood forests. Their range extends almost to the East Coast. They often build

nests in trees, utilizing bark and grass, but also occupy holes in the ground. They sometimes make a nest in a hollow tree or a tree crotch. The young are born, three to five at a time, in March and April. A second litter can be born in the fall. While preferring pine seeds, the red squirrel also stores and eats acorns and other seeds, in addition to bird eggs, baby birds, and even mushrooms.

TREES AND SHRUBS

Chamisa
Chrysothamnus nauseosus
This southwestern plant is also called golden rabbitbrush. Like other rabbitbrush varieties, it is a member of the sunflower family. It is an uplands plant, growing on mesas, in foothills, and across the high deserts. It is often seen along roadsides.

It is most often noticed during the fall months, as the head becomes a gold color. The tiny flowers are seen in dense masses. The flower heads are organized as groups of about a dozen tubular flowers. Each cluster of flowers has a rounded shape at the top. The shrub grows to a height of between two and five feet (sometimes higher), and has woody stems with bark that seems to be shredded. The twigs are covered with tiny hairs. The plant is used by the Hopi Indians for basket-making. The seeds and foliage are food for rabbits and other animals.

Apache Plume
Fallugia paradoxa
Sometimes called cluster bush or feather-rose, this member of the rose family is something like a cliffrose, but the fall flower clusters are much larger and more impressive. Single flowers appear in the spring, followed by the feathery clusters. The blossoms resemble small, single white roses. The slender, whitish branches have a shredded appearance. Parts of the shrub were used by Native Americans for making brooms and arrows. It is said that a tea was made to assist in hair growth.

Gambel Oak
Quercus gambelli
Found in both tree and shrub form, the gambel oak is often found in combination with ponderosa pine, on slopes and in valleys, on foothills and plateaus. The most common oak of the Rocky Mountain region, it is found in the Sangre de Cristo range, as well as in Arizona, particularly in Grand Canyon National Park. It is also called scrub oak, Utah oak, Rocky Mountain oak, white oak,

and blue oak. You will see this tree in dense thickets, occasionally beside streams.

It can reach a height of 70 feet but rarely grows that high in the Southwest, where it is more often seen as a lower tree or large shrub. This oak is a deciduous tree, with leaves from 2 to 7 inches long and from 1.5 to 3.5 inches wide with seven to eleven lobes. The leaf-tops are shiny green and smooth, while the undersides are hairy. Male and female catkins are formed on the same tree. The oval acorns are about 1 inch long, with a cup at one end that curves around half the acorn. Native Americans prized the acorn and ground the nuts into a meal, removing the extremely strong acidic taste by running water through it. Acorn meal was sometimes mixed with corn meal to make bread and pancakes. The foliage is eaten by deer.

Box Elder
Acer negundo
Also called ashleaf maple, box-elder maple, or maple-ash, this is a real maple (not an elder or a boxwood), growing to about 50 feet in height and also as a leggy shrub of 10 to 15 feet. It has white wood and elder-type leaves, and grows in areas where other maple varieties don't grow, as far south as Mexico and north into Canada. Found mainly in riparian areas, it always grows in fairly moist land. It has double-winged seeds and leaves that are un-maple-like, divided into either three or five sections (leaflets), on smooth green twigs. The bark on the trunk is a grayish brown and is cracked on older trees. In fall, the leaves turn a pale yellow.

Birchleaf Buckthorn
Rhamnus betulaefolia
Several buckthorns grow in the Southwest, including the California Buckthorn and Desert Ceanothus. This shrubby plant generally grows along stream-sides, to a height of 15 feet. It has tiny green flowers. Shiny purple or black fruit appear early in the year and ripen in the fall. There are no thorns on this plant, unlike some buck-thorns. The leaves are oval-shaped, bright green and shiny on top, pale and fuzzy under-neath, with very tiny "teeth." Bark is gray and smooth. New twigs are green to red, and hairy. The bark was soaked and made into a medicine by Native Americans. It was used as a lax-ative because of the cascarin contained in the plant, and was also brewed for this purpose by European settlers who came to the area. Wildlife eat the fruit, which is considered too bitter

for consumption by humans. Deer and other animals browse the twigs and leaves. Bees pollinate the flowers and produce a tasty honey.

Shrubby Cinquefoil
Potentilla fruticosa
The name of this small shrub comes from Latin *quinque* (five), and *folium* (leaf). The plant bears leaves with five parts (although it can have three or seven leaflets), greenish colored with silvery hairs. The underside of the leaf is lighter than the top. A cousin of several landscape potentillas and a member of the rose family, this shrub grows to 3 feet, and has golden-yellow blossoms with five petals that bloom from June through the remainder of the summer. The stalks have a brown bark with a shreddy appearance and feel. It bears brown, fuzzy fruit in the fall, which cling to the plant through winter.

Red-Osier Dogwood
Cornus stolonifera
Growing at higher elevations (it's commonly found in Canada and the northern states), this medium-sized shrub has a distinctive red bark with thin stems like a willow (*osier*), thus the name. In the Southwest, it grows at elevations from 5,000 feet to 9,000 feet. In suitable climates, the plant is used in landscape plantings, where the red stems brighten winter days. The shrub grows from 3 to 6 feet tall. The branches are so pliable that they bend to the ground and take root. The very small flowers are clustered, with four spreading white petals. The fruit (berry) has a stone with two seeds, turning red in late summer or fall.

WILDFLOWERS

Parry Primrose
Primula Parryi
This primula grows at very high elevations (at and above the tree line on Wheeler Peak). Its large leaves grow up to a foot in length. The flowers are held in clusters of three to twelve flowers. Each flower has a bell-shaped calyx (the lower, outside part) and a five-part corolla tube, which is a rosy pink. Both flowers and leaves have a strong, unpleasant odor. It is found in marshy areas and in sheltered places near large rocks or cliffs.

Parry Gentian
Gentiana parryi
Another high-elevation wildflower, this gentian is seen among grasses and low shrubs. Like the Parry primrose, it likes moist areas that retain

some water throughout the dry summer. Flowers are found in a crowded bunch at the end of the stems. The base of the plant sprouts several stems, which have pairs of leaves. The calyx is a purple-green, funnel-like tube with pointed lobes. The corolla is narrow, with five lobes, and deep blue (sometimes mottled with green).

Monkshood
Aconitum columbianum
A tall meadow plant, this buttercup has deep blue or purple flowers. The stems range from 1 to 4 feet tall. The leaves have deep incisions and teeth. The flower has only two petals, found under a hood. All of the plant is poisonous, and is used to make a sedative.

TAOS

American Artists Gallery House
132 Frontier Road
Taos, NM 87571
(505) 758-4446

In keeping with the artistic ambience that permeates Taos, this inn is a gallery in itself, hung with the works of many well-known artists of the Southwest. The owners, Ben and Myra Carp, are former educators, and their love of learning shows in many areas of their hospitality. There are five rooms, including one suite and one cottage, all with private bath. Breakfasts here are lavish (Myra has published a cookbook on them) and dessert is served in the evening (**$$**).

Brooks Street Inn
207 Brooks Street
P.O. Box 4954
Taos, NM 87571
(505) 758-1489

Built in the 1950s in the traditional adobe manner, this inn offers a location convenient to the Taos Plaza, Kit Carson State Park, and other attractions. There are seven rooms, five with private bath. Each room is named for a native tree and is eclectically furnished (**$** to **$$**).

Casa Benavides
137 Kit Carson Road
Taos, NM 87571
(505) 758-3934

This inn was the family home of its owner, Taos native Barbara McCarthy, along with her husband and son. The McCarthy home, combined with other neighboring adobe buildings, has resulted in 22 guest rooms, all with private bath and TV, some with kitchenettes. All rooms are authentically decorated in New Mexican style with kiva fireplaces and tile. Breakfast might include eggs with green chile and cheese and homemade flour tortillas (**$$** to **$$$**).

Casa de las Chimeneas
405 Cordoba Road
P.O. Box 5303
Taos, NM 87571
(505) 758-4777

Two-and-a-half blocks from the Taos Plaza, this distinguished inn has seven-foot adobe walls, a formal garden with fountains, Taos-area art on the interior walls, and tiled fireplaces. It is a fine place to stay, summer or winter. Named for the chimneys adorning the kiva fireplaces found in each room, this B&B is well known for the extra touches owner Susan Vernon provides: sheepskin mattress covers and luxury bed linens, to name two. There are two double rooms and one suite, all with private bath and TV. For this kind of accommodation in any other town, you would pay well over $200. The rates are half that (**$$ to $$$**).

Hacienda del Sol

109 Mabel Dodge Lake
P.O. Box 177
Taos, NM 87571
(505) 758-0287

This old adobe house was originally bought by art patron Mabel Dodge Luhan as a hideaway for her Taos Indian husband Tony. Georgia O'Keeffe painted her *Sunflowers* here. The home adjoins the Taos Pueblo and has a beautiful view of Taos Mountain from the outdoor hot tub! The seven rooms, four with private bath, are all furnished with authentic Southwest decor including kiva fireplaces and original art. The owners, Marcine and John Landon, serve afternoon wine and cheese as well as breakfast (**$ to $$$**).

Sagebrush Inn

P.O. Box 557
Taos, NM 87571
(505) 758-2254

Another of the places where Georgia O'Keeffe painted is this lovely pueblo-style inn built in

1929. There are 63 rooms in all, most on two stories and one on the top floor; all have private baths. There are many facilities, including two hot tubs, tennis courts, swimming pool, and a steak house, restaurant, and bar with live entertainment (**$ to $$$**).

Taos Inn

P.O. Drawer N
Taos, NM 87571
(505) 748-2233

The Taos Inn is an utterly charming hotel with a lobby sitting on the former Taos town square. Parts of the building date back to the 1600s. The old town well still adorns the room, but is now a sitting place near the hotel's wonderful watering hole, the Adobe Bar. Also located off the lobby is Doc Martin's Restaurant, serving three meals daily. There are now 40 rooms in the inn, all with private bath, TV, and phone (**$$ to $$$+**).

Kachina Lodge

P.O. Box NN
Taos, NM 87571
(505) 758-2275 or 800-522-4462

This Best Western operation is close to Taos Plaza, built in a pseudo-adobe style, in a square structure set around a central lawn, whirlpool, and swimming pool. There is a dining room and a coffee shop. The rooms feature southwestern art. Dancers from Taos Pueblo give frequent performances here, from Memorial Day through Labor Day. The Kachina Cabaret features performances by rock, jazz, folk, and country acts, including groups from the '50s and '60s (**$$**).

Taos Country Inn
Upper Ranchitos and Karabas
P.O. Box 2331
Taos, NM 87571
(505) 758-4900

Slightly out of town, at Rancho Rio Pueblo, this small inn is located across the Rio Pueblo, 2 miles from Taos Plaza via Ranchitos Road and Upper Ranchitos Road. The inn is set among cottonwoods and willows at the river's edge. The grounds are pasture lands with gardens next to the building. Parts of the building date back to the early nineteenth century. There are nine luxury suites, with private bath, sofas, and king- or queen-sized beds. A full breakfast is served in the dining room (**$$$**).

Old Taos Guesthouse
Box 6552
Taos, NM 87571
(505) 758-5448

This historic adobe hacienda is set in a grove of trees on a hill overlooking the town. With the building situated around a courtyard, each of the eight

rooms has a separate entrance and private bath. There's a large veranda for those cool summer evenings (**$** to **$$**).

OUTSIDE TAOS

The Inn at Angel Fire
3530 Highway 434
Angel Fire, NM 87710
(505) 377-2504 or 800-666-1949

This inn has 28 rooms, very reasonable rates, a restaurant, and game room.

Two Pipe
Box 52, Talpa Route
Ranchos de Taos, NM 87557
(505) 758-4774

Another historic hacienda—this one 300 years old—Two Pipe B&B is located in Talpa, a village just south of Taos on the famous High Road. There are lovely gardens and a whirlpool outside, and quiet, comfortable rooms with kiva fireplaces inside. Full breakfast is served. This is a no-smoking establishment, and the hosts have set a 2-day minimum stay. The Antler Gallery is on the premises (**$$**).

Salsa del Salto
Box 453
El Prado, NM 87529
(505) 776-2422

Located on the route to Taos Ski Valley, this southwestern inn has a scenic setting facing

Taos Mountain. There's a tennis court, heated pool, and whirlpool. Each of the six rooms has a king-sized bed, down comforter, and private bath. A full breakfast is served (**$$ to $$$**).

Quail Ridge Inn Resort

P.O. Box 707
Taos, NM 87571
(505) 776-2211 or 800-624-4448

This outstanding resort hotel is a few miles north of Taos, and not far from Taos Ski Valley. The resort has a wide range of rates (from about $70 to more than $300 per night), depending on your needs and budget. There are 110 rooms and suites, with fireplaces in all units and kitchens in the suites. There's a swimming pool (open year-round), whirlpools, and saunas. Recreational activities include tennis, squash, and racquetball. Massage is offered. Packages are available for golfing, skiing, fly-fishing, and mountain biking. The resort has a dining room and lounge (**$$ to $$$+**).

Columbine Inn

P.O. Box 736
Taos Ski Valley, NM 87525
(505) 776-1437

One of several fine places to stay close to Taos Ski Valley, this inn has 20 units and is open year-round. Rooms have queen-sized beds and private baths. There's an indoor whirlpool, and a com-

plimentary continental breakfast is served. Accommodations include streamside suites with kitchens (**$ to $$**).

Hotel Edelweiss

106 Sutton Place/P.O. Box 83
Taos Ski Valley, NM 87525
(505) 776-2301

Close to the ski lifts (ski in, ski out), the Edelweiss is right in the Ski Valley and is open year-round. Rooms with bay windows overlook the slopes and the main restaurant has fine views. Food is particularly well prepared and served here. An eating place on a deck offers lighter meals. The hotel has a whirlpool and sauna, and massage is available. The hotel offers reduced rates during non-skiing months (**$$ to $$$**).

Hacienda de Valdez

Box 5651
Taos, NM 87571
(505) 776-2218

Located in the Sangre de Cristo foothills north of Taos, this Valdez Valley inn has a wonderful southwestern design with two-bedroom, three-bath, condo-style suites. Each unit has a full kitchen and each suite has a balcony with a fine view. There are two whirlpools and outdoor gas grills for guests' use. The inn is located in a natural setting next to the Carson National Forest. This is a place to stay if you want deluxe accommodations and are willing to pay the price, ranging from $100 to $300 ($$$ to $$$ +).

The Abominable Snowmansion

P.O. Box 3271
Taos, NM 87571
(505) 776-8298

This economy place is not for everyone, but if you want a cheap place to stay and don't mind a lot of other people in the same room, it could be for you. This is a dormitory-style operation (bunk 'n breakfast), with a lodge room for socializing. This commercialized hostel with 95 beds is 15 minutes from Taos and 15 minutes from Taos Ski Valley ($).

RED RIVER

Lazy Miner Lodge

P.O. Box 836
Red River, NM 87558
(505) 754-6444 or 800-766-4637

Located on the main street, this affordable hotel has one to three-bedroom suites with kitchens and fireplaces. There's a whirlpool ($ to $$).

Telemark Bed & Breakfast

P.O. Box 907
Red River, NM 87558
(505) 754-2534

There are eight townhouses in this complex, with reasonable rates for the space you get. The suites have fireplaces. There's also a whirlpool and a playground ($ to $$).

Lifts West Condo/Hotel

P.O. Box 330
Red River, NM 87558
(505) 754-2778 or 800-221-1859

With 83 units, this is Red River's largest hotel, and a good place for skiers to stay. It has a full-service ski shop with rentals, lockers, restaurant, swimming pool, and two whirlpools. Kids stay free ($$ to $$$).

TAOS-AREA CAMPING

Cimarron Canyon State Park

(505) 377-6271

Located 3 miles east of Eagle Nest and less than an hour's drive from Taos, the park is part of the state wildlife area. Overnight visitors must have a valid fishing or hunting license to have a night's free stay. The fishing in the Cimarron River is good and you have a good chance of spotting wildlife.

Coyote Creek State Park

(505) 387-2328

Located a bit farther away from Taos, south of Angel Fire on State Route 434, this park offers campsites, as well as fishing for rainbow and cutthroat trout. The creek has beaver ponds, and hiking trails lead from the campground.

Forest Service Campsites

For advance information, call: Carson National Forest, Taos Supervisor's Office (505) 758-6200

Many of the campgrounds in the Carson National Forest are mentioned in the Enchanted Circle and Valle Vidal sections of this chapter, including campgrounds located between Questa and Red River and in the Valle Vidal unit—to the north, near the Colorado border. Hike-in campsites are available in the Wheeler Peak Wilderness and the Latir Peak Wilderness. There is a campground in Taos Ski Valley, across the valley from the ski lifts. Ranger stations are located in Peñasco on State Route 75, 17 miles east of the New Mexico 68 junction, and at the east end of Questa on State Route 38.

Taos RV Park

P.O. Box 729
Taos, NM 87557
(505) 758-2524

Located at Harrison and Sullins, with full hookups.

Taos Valley RV Park

P.O. Box 200
Ranchos de Taos, NM 87557
(505) 758-4469

Located south of the main part of Taos, this campground and RV park with full and partial hookups is operated by Bob and Edith Neumann.

The Roadrunner RV Park

P.O. Box 810
Red River, NM 87558
(505) 754-2286

Located close to the town center and the ski area, the park has full and partial hookups, water, and tables. Operated by Harold and Suzanne Young.

Red River RV Park

Box 777
Red River, NM 87558
(505) 754-6187

This large camping park on the river has full hookups, cable TV, showers, laundry, and propane. Hosts are Lester and Jan Lewis.

Cimarron Camping

There are several private campgrounds in Cimarron including: **Chili's RV Park** (505-376-2218); **Pine Ridge** (Ute Park—505-376-2960); **Kit Carson Motel** (505-376-2288).

PART 3

The Living Desert

There is an eerie power to the desert. You feel it in the cool of early morning as the sun begins to cast its spell—weakly at first, but then with increasing energy. While we supposedly intelligent humans are beginning our day, the really smart denizens of the desert are just finishing theirs, disappearing before the searing heat overtakes the landscape. So we go through our day looking at the desolation, feeling the heat, and missing the essential quality: The desert is a living place where many animals and plants live in harmony with what we consider a harsh land.

Less than 10 years ago I traveled through my first American desert. My only previous desert experience was with a subarctic oddity, a tiny group of sand dunes in the Yukon Territory. The books I had read on the Southwest desert were no preparation for the profound attraction I felt on the day I crossed the high Mojave and the wide washes of the Amargosa before descending into Death Valley. It was a blistering summer afternoon. The car windows were open, and the heat intensified as I plunged down Furnace Creek Wash, below sea level, toward the salt pan. My body and mind were baked, adding to the stupefaction. At that moment, the mysteries of the desert became an obsession.

A visit to Joshua Tree National Monument (now National Park) taught me the difference between high and low desert. I traveled east, into Arizona and New Mexico, to climb into sky islands where an ascent of a few hundred feet presents a whole new ecosystem—far different from that on the desert floor. A few hundred more feet and yet another biological zone appears.

Below the Sonoran sandscape underground rivers flow, sometimes emerging to provide a haven for cottonwoods, willows, and wildlife. Late summer monsoons pound the sand and gravel, filling the washes, supplying the aquifers deep below the surface. Ocotillo flowers pop out and new plants appear. There are mating dances in the air and on the ground. Babies are born. The desert lives. It's powerful and it's magic.

Death Valley and the Amargosa

The legendary landscape haunts visitors long after they leave what, for me, is the most awe-inspiring tourist destination in all of the American West—even grander than the Grand Canyon!

First, there is the heat in this second hottest place on earth, where summer daytime temperatures average 115 degrees. In the winter, it can be one of the wettest places on earth as torrential rains wash the sides of the mountains into the valley, moving earth (and cars) at a prodigious rate. It is also the scene of many individual geologic wonders: brightly colored volcanic ash displays; baked mud that shimmers in the morning light; stark contrasts in elevation including the lowest place in the hemisphere (Badwater) from which you can view the nearby snow-capped peak of Mount Whitney, the highest mountain in the lower 48 states. Huge sand dunes shift across the center part of the valley, while salt pan covers the southern valley floor.

Recently designated a national park, Death Valley was the site of borax mining in the nineteenth century, and is a repository for the bones of many travelers, horses, and burros who attempted to cross its inhospitable expanse. The park is also home to a ranch resort and dune-side motel complex; a deluxe hotel, open during the cooler months; and a bizarre tourist attraction—a desert ranch house called Scotty's Castle.

Most of all, it is the geology of Death Valley that makes the trip worthwhile. High mountain ranges ring the valley, with the nearby Sierra Nevada keeping most of the rainy Pacific weather systems at bay. The majority of visitors come to Death Valley during the cooler winter months. But the real Death Valley summer must be savored, with its biting, dry heat baking the valley floor—sending the surprisingly varied animal species into hiding, only to appear again at night.

To the east—above Death Valley and separated from it by the Black Mountains—is the Amargosa Desert, where the dusty dry channels of the Amargosa River flow across the parched lands, to run with water only during sporadic winter storms. But even now, a rainy winter in the desert causes torrents of water to rush along the washes, nurturing an amazing variety of natural life. This mysterious part of America should be experienced at least once in a lifetime.

Saguaroland—the Tucson Region

Most people think of Tucson as a place to play golf or to relax by the pool at a four-star resort. For me, this charming city on the Sonoran Desert is a starting point for branching out to any number of desert and mountain nature destinations.

Among the most impressive are the two sites of Saguaro National Park, situated at the western and eastern edges of the city. Here the tallest cacti grow, providing shelter and food for many bird species. Animal life is also apparent in the two parks, including pig-like javelina, coyote, and desert tortoise.

Mount Lemmon, northeast of the city, rises 9,000 feet from the desert floor, offering forest recreation such as hiking and fishing. Sabino Canyon, located near the mountain base, is a favorite area for family recreation activity such as hiking, wading in the creek, bird-watching, and nature photography. A wheeled tram provides transportation through the canyon for those who eschew hiking. Pichaco Peak State Park, north of Tucson, features displays of wildflowers blanketing the mountain slope with their muted colors each springtime.

An especially rewarding drive takes visitors north of Tucson toward Florence along the Pinal Pioneer Parkway. Along this road, studded with displays of native trees, shrubs, and cacti, is a memorial to the famed cowboy movie star, Tom Mix, who died on this spot—a strange juxtaposition of the timeless beauty of the desert and the temporary nature of human life. Behind the monument, a stile takes you over a fence into the open desert, where a 2-minute walk will place you into one of the most impressive desert environments in the state. Many species of barrel cactus, skittering lizards, and other wildlife are everywhere, all accompanied by a strange peace that only the desert brings.

Several historic guest ranches of the area are recommended as places to venture by horse, foot, or four-wheel-drive vehicle into the Sonoran Desert. A full-day round-trip from Tucson to the Buenos Aires Wildlife Preserve will reveal 114,000 acres of lakes and grassland—next to the Mexican border—where much wildlife can be seen from nature trails and roads. Add to these excursions the grace and refinement of the city's downtown colonial district, and you have a special region of discovery.

Wickenburg and the Hassayampa River

High in the Bradshaw range, rising out of the desert northwest of Phoenix, water trickles down the mountains and becomes the Hassayampa River. This is one of the strangest and most miraculous of all of Arizona's desert streams.

For more than 60 miles, the river runs beneath a deep channel of gravel—far from human sight. But just south of the Old West town of Wickenburg, the water comes to the surface, nurturing bird and animal life within a cottonwood/willow and mesquite shrub environment. The short appearance of the Hassayampa, with only five miles of open stream, provides a startling contrast to the surrounding desert landscape. In 1986, the Nature Conservancy's Arizona chapter purchased what had been a guest ranch, and created the Hassayampa River Preserve.

Mississippi kites live in the tall cottonwoods, as do rare varieties of hawk, including the Harris', black, and zone-tailed species. In all, 220 species of birds may be seen in the preserve. Spring-fed Palm Lake—more a pond than a lake—has attracted families of water birds including the snowy egret, great blue heron, pied-billed grebe, and the white-faced ibis, plus many migratory species. The lake is also a rearing place for several varieties of endangered desert fish.

The river winds through this narrow valley, creating sand bars where one may walk, repose, and observe the flashing of the tiny transparent desert fish that thrive in this environment.

Nearby Wickenburg, a former mining town, provides accommodations, including several traditional guest ranches from which the visitor may enjoy desert life and recreation. The notable Desert Caballeros Western Museum contains a nineteenth century streetscape, mineral and gem exhibits, collections of western art, and native artifacts from the Anasazi, Pueblo, Hopi, and Navajo history of this area. The museum is a good place to start a visit to this unusual and rewarding community.

A visit of several days in the Wickenburg area offers a superb opportunity for exploring the marvels of nature in the Hassayampa River Preserve, as well as capturing the disappearing ambience of the American West of the late 1800s and early 1900s.

Death Valley and the Amargosa

A t the second hottest place on earth—many Death Valley proponents say it's actually the hottest—the summer heat is at first overwhelming, but then diminishes to a visitor encountering the valley's amazing geological and biological displays. To those who may be intimidated by summer weather reports showing Death Valley temperatures above 110 degrees, I urge you to go! The heat is affecting, but it is only a small part of the traveler's Death Valley experience.

The place has a bad reputation in the United States and Canada. I often face laughter and derision when I mention a recent visit to Death Valley. Who would want to spend time in a location that has landmarks with names such as Badwater, the Devil's Golf Course, the Funeral Mountains, Furnace Creek, Devil's Corn Field, and Dante's View? On the other hand, while many North Americans shun Death Valley, visitors from Europe flock to this newly enlarged national park because they have studied the place. When one begins to understand the natural and human history of Death Valley, it has a mystery and aura that is completely captivating.

Before the mid-1800s, there was no "Dante's View," nor was there a "Devil's Corn Field." These names were coined by hustlers and con men to attract visitors and investors to this burgeoning mining area. As little mining towns were built on the higher slopes of the Funeral, Black, and Panamint mountains, hustlers were busy attracting rubes to invest in their low-grade and no-grade mines. Although several successful mining ventures were launched, much of the hype was bogus. And the fact that a lot of eastern and San Francisco investors lost money is one of the enduring charms of Death Valley, adding a human dimension to the natural mystique.

Sitting just west of the Nevada boundary, in the basin and range district of the Mojave Desert, Death Valley is all but surrounded by mountain ranges, with a few roads connecting the valley to the outside world through narrow passes. On the east side of the valley is the Amargosa Range, comprised of three separate units. The Grapevine Mountains are at the north, with the Funeral Mountains defining the central section. The Black Mountains lie in a north/south direction between Furnace Creek Wash and the southern end of the valley at Jubilee Pass. The Owlshead Mountains lie in a circular position at the extreme south end of the valley.

The western side of the valley is defined by the Panamint Range, with Telescope Peak, at an 11,049-foot elevation, its highest spot. Beyond the Panamints, to the west, is the long, dry Panamint Valley. To the east of the Amargosa Range is the Amargosa Desert, striated by the wide washes of the Amargosa River, which intermittently flows south from Beatty, Nevada, through Death Valley Junction, curving to the west and then north to enter Death Valley below Jubilee Pass.

The valley is more than 100 miles long. The southern portion is the Amargosa River sink, dry most of the time, with a shallow, intermittent lake created by winter rains in some years. The lake disappears soon after the rains cease in the spring. The central part of the valley is hard salt pan. Here is the lowest point in the hemisphere, 282 feet below sea level, and the location of a spring-fed oasis at the mouth of the Furnace Creek Wash on the eastern side of the valley. Today, we find the national park headquarters and overnight accommodations in this area, including Furnace Creek Ranch and Furnace Creek Inn. Zabriskie Point is a major geological feature here. The northern third of Death Valley is bordered by the Panamint and Grapevine mountains, containing a large area of sand dunes near Stovepipe Wells Village.

Farther north is more salt pan, and a dormant volcanic area that includes Ubehebe Crater. Grapevine Canyon is one of the three eastern exit routes from the valley, and the location of

Scotty's Castle. At the extreme north end of the valley—reached by road from Nevada—is the old Palmetto mining area including the hamlet of Lida.

The daily temperature is a popular subject for visitors. The hottest-ever temperature recorded in Death Valley was 134 degrees F. (56.7 degrees C.), on July 10, 1913. This is second only to a higher temperature taken in Africa. However, this reading was made at Furnace Creek, at a point higher than Badwater. Longtime Death Valley residents say that daily temperatures at Badwater are consistently higher than at Furnace Creek. Could Death Valley be the hottest place on earth? We think so!

The First Inhabitants

Before the arrival of white men and women to this desolate place, Native Americans lived in Death Valley for two or three centuries. Wandering over the valley and the nearby Amargosa Desert were three tribes: the Shoshone, the Southern Paiute, and the Kawaiisu. The primary occupants of the region were the Shoshone, whose territory included the Panamints, the northern part of the Amargosa, and most of Death Valley. The Southern Paiute occupied the central and southeastern parts of Death Valley and the southern portion of the Amargosa River. The Panamint range and the most southerly end of the valley was the territory of the Kawaiisu. Another tribe, the Northern Paiute, occupied Owens Valley to the west.

These people lived on mesquite beans and pine nuts, the latter gathered from the pinyon pines that grow above 7,000 feet on the Panamints and other nearby mountain ranges. Wild grapes and other plants also provided food, as did rabbits and the occasional bighorn sheep. The tribes traded supplies, using shell beads for money. Since the warm climate meant that permanent homes were not required, Native Americans built dome-shaped mountain shelters of mesquite and willow branches, and covered them with bark and boughs. Sweat lodges—domes reinforced with mud—functioned as therapeutic and social centers for the Death Valley Shoshone and Paiute. Saratoga Springs, the oasis at the south end of Death Valley, and Tecopa Hot Springs to the east, provided watering and camping spots for the Southern Paiute. At a large settlement at Tecopa Hot Springs in the

Amargosa Desert, Native Americans irrigated the land and grew vegetable crops including squash, melons, corn, and grapes. Relationships between the tribes were friendly, each having its own turf.

The coming of white prospectors caused alarm to the Paiute and the Panamint Shoshone. During the Coso mining rush, the tribes joined forces to oppose the interlopers, killing four prospectors at a camp near Wildrose Canyon on the west side of the valley. The well-armed prospectors killed nine Native Americans, including the Shoshone chief. The skirmishes continued until a peace was arranged about 1867. Most Native Americans kept the peace, with many women from the Oasis Valley marrying white ranchers, but a few warriors raided camps to steal horses, mainly from ranches near Los Angeles. With all the mining action on the mountain slopes, the Native Americans lost their traditional food sources and dispersed, although a few remain in the area today, some intermarried with whites.

Arrival of the Whites

Death Valley provided a shortcut to the California gold fields for Mormons and others who traveled westward to seek riches in the Sierra Nevada. The southern end of the valley proved a hazardous route—difficult because of its dry salt pan, little water, and scorching heat.

Before the California gold rush, two groups of migrant whites passed through the area, disrupting the lives of the Native Americans. In the 1830s, horse traders from New Mexico drove their herds to the growing Los Angeles area through the Amargosa Desert and across the southern Death Valley sink. Their route was called the Spanish Trail. They were followed by caravans of traders. Then came roving bands of raiders—called *Los Chaguanosos*—who looted the ranches of the Los Angeles area, and took horses back east to the Mississippi Valley.

From Santa Fe and Abiquiu, the traders traveled through Monument Valley, across southern Utah, into Nevada around the south end of the Spring Mountains—where Las Vegas now sits—and to the Amargosa River. They followed the Amargosa into Death Valley and followed the route dubbed Jornada del Muerto (the journey of death). They traveled beside Rio Salitrosa, now called Salt Creek, into the Mojave Desert and across the mountains at Cajon Pass to the San Gabriel Valley. The Jornada del Muerto became littered with the bones of expired horses, driven beyond endurance through the long stretches of waterless waste. However, the horse trade continued, as did the horse-thieving trade, carried on by a motley collection of New Mexican, Canadian, and American trappers and mountain men, who were joined in their illicit pursuits by a number of Native Americans. The injured California ranchers organized their own counter-raiding parties, chasing the Chaguanosos.

The battles lasted for several years. Kit Carson, the famous scout, was caught up in this turmoil as a member of an exploring party organized by John C. Fremont. After Paiute raiders stole Fremont's horses, Carson and a companion, John Godley, were soon in hot pursuit. They managed to recover fifteen horses, returning to Fremont's camp with two scalps. The southern California horse trade ended in 1849, as word spread of the gold finds in northern California. Paiute raiders continued to attack traveling parties in the Amargosa until the 1870s.

The tales of the short and secret route to California appealed to an early group of gold rush prospectors. Some passed into the valley with disastrous results. Oxen and horses died, prospectors got lost on the Jornada del Muerto and expired, others stumbled across ledges of gold and silver while en route to the Sierra Nevada and left them behind for what they thought would be larger riches.

Death Valley got its name after the dramatic events of the fall of 1849, when a small army of immigrants from Utah brought their wagons, horses, and supplies down the Spanish Trail, on their way to the gold fields of California's western Sierra foothills. Nearly a thousand people, including children, accompanied by two hundred wagons and more than two thousand horses, mules, and oxen, struggled along a Death Valley trail that no one had wanted to take in the first place. They originally intended to take the northern Nevada route but took the more southerly route because they departed late from Salt Lake. They divided into two groups; the first major party was led by Jefferson Hunt, a former Mexican War captain of the Mormon Battalion, the second led by a Captain Hooker.

By the time the pack trains reached the Amargosa entrance to Death Valley, many animals had died and a majority of the travelers had turned back. Hunt and his diminished party reached the area of Salt Spring, where one of his companions, a man named Pratt, noticed a deposit of quartz in the rock wall and notified Hunt that there might be gold. In the ensuing search, several chunks of gold were found in a 4-inch quartz vein. But Hunt ordered the whole party to continue the trip toward California, and the promising vein was left behind.

The two parts of the wagon train, including Hooker's group, met at Resting Spring, closer to the Nevada border. The first wagons had reached the spring in November 1849. For more than a year after that, struggling groups of migrants passed through the southern end of the valley, most of them disoriented, short of food and water, and despondent. The most desperate group of gold seekers, the Bennett and Arcan families, were rescued and guided out of the valley in February 1850.

The story of the Bennetts and Arcans is a tale of desperation, ignorance of the land and climate, and bad advice. The families were stragglers, following behind several organized groups of easterners traveling along the Spanish Trail toward California. These included the Jayhawkers (from Kansas City) and the Bugsmashers (a dozen men from Georgia and Mississippi including three African Americans). The two straggling families had been joined by other single travelers, including Bennett's friend, William Lewis Manly.

All were under a terrible misapprehension that, by moving north through the arid valley, they'd find an easier, shorter route to the Mariposa gold in California. They'd been told to look for the Walker Cutoff, a route that ran beside a great east/west mountain range. The mountain range was a myth, and the cutoff was to the south, not the north. Finding the Amargosa River, the Jayhawkers turned west at Death Valley Junction, and descended into the valley down Furnace Creek Wash, where Highway 190 now leads into Death Valley. They tried to cross the salt flats but were unsuccessful, so instead they traveled north, up the east side of the valley to McLean Spring. Seeing the high Panamint range directly in their way, they stayed for awhile, killing some of the weaker cattle for food, drying the meat into jerky.

The Bennetts and others had stopped near the Spring Mountains in Nevada. Manley had gone ahead, looking for the Spanish Trail. Climbing a peak near the south of the Spring Mountains, he could clearly see the Spanish Trail, but failed to identify it. Manley returned to the Bennett camp, and his group followed the Jayhawkers into Death Valley where they made another mistake: turning south at the mouth of Furnace Creek. They camped at Badwater, a foul spring, near the lowest point in the hemisphere. The Bennett and Arcan families stayed there a month, in a state of near starvation, with no potable spring water for several miles.

The Jayhawkers were able to leave the salt pan by entering the Panamint Valley—to the west—then heading south to a pass in the Slate Range, traveling around the southern end of the Sierra Nevada. Meanwhile the two families reached the mouth of Furnace Creek on December 27, 1849, and rested for a week at Travertine Springs. Good water, at last!

There were about thirty people and seven wagons in the party that now headed down into the depths of the valley. Manley, the Bennetts, and John Rogers were among the group, which had four wagons with four teamsters to drive them. Starting on January 6, they crossed to the base of the Panamint Mountains. They passed a spring now called Bennett's Well, and then a sulfur spring. Then near Bennett's Well they spotted what they thought was a useable pass through the mountains, but the wagons could not get out of the canyon. Manley and Rogers (who were young and fit) were chosen to go to southern California for help. While Manley and Rogers set out on foot, the rest moved back to Bennett's Well. Bennett was confident that Manley and Rogers would return; most of the others were not. One of the other families (Henry Wade, his wife, and children) left via a route through what is now called Wingate Pass. Except for the Bennetts and Arcans, the others decided to take the same route. It proved to be a good one, getting them to the Mojave River near what is now Barstow in less than a week (though at least one traveler died on the salt pan).

Meanwhile, the Bennetts and Arcans still waited at Bennett's Well, losing hope. They expected Manley and Rogers to return within two weeks. After three more weeks passed, they decided to move on before they, too, died. As they prepared to leave after their 26-day wait, they heard a rifle shot in the distance and soon the two men appeared, but with only one mule and no horses. The three horses they had obtained at the ranches had died on the return trip. But the mule carried food, and everyone ate that night.

After the reunion, Rogers departed with his mule, leaving the remaining animals with Bennett and Manley. By the second morning, they had climbed to the top of Six Spring Canyon, camping in the high reaches of the Panamints. When they reached the summit on February 15, the three men paused to look down into the desolate scene they had just left. One of them cried "Good-bye Death Valley!"

The cry, and the name, have endured. William Manley wrote his classic (though self-serving) true-life adventure book, telling most—but not all—of the horrendous story of the Jayhawkers, Wades, Bennetts, and Arcans. Others, including several Jawhawkers, wrote their own versions of the saga.

SCOUNDRELS AND SCALLIWAGS

The gold seekers were not the first white people to lose themselves in Death Valley. Nor would they be the last; for a crazy, rowdy, greedy period of mining was about to begin. Here, in just about the hottest place on earth, using the backdrop of the Death Valley mystique, confidence men conceived just about the hottest mining promotions ever foisted on an unsuspecting public. It was an amazing period of myth-fueled theater, which completely overshadowed the few real successes of the few honest mining companies. It was the selling of Death Valley for fun and profit.

In January 1850, prospectors were working quartz veins, looking for gold, even before Bennett said good-bye to Death Valley. By 1854, the Comstock Lode at Virginia City had captivated the nation, sending more prospectors into the West, including Death Valley. Gold was again found at Salt Spring, and a rudimentary mining operation was begun in 1852. It failed, and then was restarted in 1861. The first of the valley's mining promoters had an "honest" name—St. Charles Biederman. He found wide-eyed investors in the frenzied San Francisco stock market. A quarter of a million dollars was quickly raised, a small stamp mill purchased and transported to the site. It quickly became choked with salt (from the salty spring). By June 1864, it was all over. The stamp mill would not work, only a small amount of high grade ore had been found, and gold prices had dropped. The mine was abandoned once again.

It was much the same story for at least a dozen other mines in the area over the next two decades. Huge gold and silver finds were floated in the eastern press, with over-eager investors lining up to buy into the latest Death Valley discovery. Railroads (not one, but two) were built across the Amargosa Desert to haul ore from the mines in the eastern mountains. Mining towns were quickly built, and almost as quickly dismantled. The mining district at Rhyolite, now a ghost town near Beatty, was a successful exception to the rule.

One of the most fanciful bubbles to grow, and then burst, was a promotion by Lt. Robert Bailey of Oroville, California. Bailey held claims in several of the Death Valley mining areas, but it was a purported find on the eastern side of the valley—in the Amargosa Range—which was most highly touted. Bailey went to San Francisco in January, 1861, holding a newly unearthed rock that he claimed to have appraised at more than $16,000 a ton, a shockingly high amount. He assured investors and the media that his supply was unlimited. A few wiser investors insisted that Bailey (who wouldn't reveal the precise location of his lode) go back to the find and bring more rock to San Francisco.

He returned in April with several bags of rock and his new partner, Dr. Benjamin Dewey of Stockton. The new rock assayed at a little over $4,000 a ton. Regardless of the disparity, the company was created with an investment of $180,000. Bailey got half of the nine hundred shares and sold them to more investors at $500 apiece. Even more shares were sold by Bailey (1,600 at $500 per share). The promoter became instantly wealthy.

The investors now demanded to see a ton of the ore. Bailey organized a crew, purchased picks and shovels, and proposed to sail by ship to Los Angeles. By sailing date, Bailey had disappeared. The company disbanded in November, with not a hint of the entrepreneur's whereabouts. Two male bodies were soon found in the desert of the San Joaquin Valley, one of them thought to be dressed in Bailey's clothes. Years went by and the mining promotion was forgotten.

In a San Diego bar, some 30 years later, the bartender who told vivid stories of Death Valley and his journey to Tahiti on a French brigantine was identified as Bob—the former

Lieutenant—Bailey. In the intervening years, he had been an Indian scout, a miner in Idaho and Montana, and a deputy sheriff. He remained in San Diego, having worked the bar for more than 20 years. He never did pay for his sins, at least not in this life, and died a free man.

The first profitable mines in Death Valley and the Amargosa were developed in the late 1860s. Small but rich pockets of ore were found and worked successfully. These were tiny operations, employing only a few men each. Mines were opened in the Palmetto district, at the northern head of the valley. Lida was Death Valley's first authentic mining community. Bullion worth $162,000 was mined before the pockets were exhausted.

In the Panamint Range, flanking the west side of Death Valley, silver was discovered, resulting in several lodes being staked, including the "Wyoming," the "Hemlock," and one called "Wonder of the World." A town site was built at the head of Surprise Canyon in 1873. The real Panamint rush began in 1874, when the news went out that two Nevada senators had purchased the Panamint mines for at least a quarter of a million dollars. It was a gigantic and largely false promotion, perpetrated by one Eliphalet P. Rains. Rains arranged the sale of the mines to U.S. Senator John P. Jones, who had made his fortune in the Comstock Lode. Senator William Stewart and a lawyer, T. W. Park, also bought into the mines.

The sale of the mining operations was a sensation and a rush began. The whole promotion was based on a gigantic fraud. There was some gold in the Panamint mining area; however, just about all of it was exposed, to great effect, with little remaining underground. Soon, more than $150,000 worth of ore was shipped abroad, creating more publicity and more interest. What investors didn't know was that most of the available ore had been shipped out and little was left.

Meanwhile Jones and company proceeded to promote the building of a railway, the Los Angeles and Independence Railroad, from Santa Monica to the head of Surprise Canyon. More stock was sold to fund the railroad, and $300,000 was raised in two weeks. Most of the new funds were spent on projects other than the railroad. A reservoir were built in the mountains and water piped to the mines. A grandiose stamp mill, costing more than $200,000, was built. Panamint had become a boomtown of two thousand residents with houses, stores, a newspaper, French restaurant, and saloons. But aside from a few houses on Main Street, most of Panamint's residents lived in squatters' tents, or out in the open. As in all the gold rushes, most people arrived at Panamint to find that all the six hundred claims had been staked. It was a murderous half-year, as five men were dispatched, a rate of almost one per month. By then, the mineral deposits were decimated and another mining town bit the dust.

These are a few typical stories of the mining era in Death Valley. The only lasting mining industry was the borax operation, which started on the salt pan at the Harmony Borax Works, and is now called U.S. Borax. The unrefined borax was hauled out of the valley by 20-mule teams, which became famous in Borax company promotions, and later on the television series "Death Valley Days." There is still some gold in the mountains. After decades of closure, a mining operation near Rhyolite has reopened.

Death Valley Geology

Nowhere else in the Southwest is there such a collection of varied geological wonders as in Death Valley. There is no deep chasm, no immense badlands, no steep cliffs with waterfalls flowing to the valley floor (there is not a single waterfall in the whole valley). Yet, in its immensity and its amazing range of geological features, from the high Panamint Mountains and the mud flats of Zabriskie Point to the below-sea-level salt pan, sand dunes, gravel fans, volcanic craters, and spring-fed oases, Death Valley should rank near the top of anyone's list of geological wonders.

Eons of time, over which the Amargosa River and salt springs have worked to shape the valley floor, have brought an accumulation of salt minerals, which now cover an area of more than 200 square miles. The valley floor is tilted to the east, a movement that continues to this day. This is caused by the thrusting of the Panamint Range, which is faulted on the west and tilts to the east, and the Black Mountains, which are also faulted on the west and tilt east. These earth movements are recent, considering the fullness of geological time. Unlike most valleys, Death Valley was not created by erosion. While ancient seas deposited marine animals, now fossils, on the sea floor, these fossils are found high on the mountain slopes—a sure sign that thrusting has taken place. The Panamint Range is considered to be only 5 million years old, rising one foot every 500 years.

The salt pan is the result of deposits from a large lake that almost filled the valley during the Holocene Age. Since then, the valley has tilted 20 feet to the east. Surveys taken in the valley show a lowering of the eastern side of the valley by 3 to 4 inches between 1907 and 1943. Some of the tilting action of the valley is thought to have occurred during the last great earthquake in the area, about 2,000 years ago, with most of the action occurring along a fault that runs the length of the Black Mountains.

Standing on the salt pan provides a deceptive view of the valley's construction. Since the beginning, the valley has received deposits from the surrounding mountains through erosion. The huge alluvial fans are the most prominent evidence of this movement of rock and sand from the mountains. Under the crust of salt is fill 8,000 feet deep. However, as fast as the fill accumulates, the tilting and shifting actions of the mountains keep the valley floor at below sea level—an amazing geological accomplishment. It began during the late Tertiary period and continues today.

Volcanic action has played a part in the building of the valley as well. Volcanic rocks are found on the east side of the Panamint Range. Ubehebe Crater and the small craters near it provide more evidence of further recent volcanic action. Faults throughout the valley, and through the surrounding mountains, have intrigued geologists throughout the century. All of the surrounding mountain ranges are young. The south end of the Panamint range is made up of Precambrian rock. The northern part of this range and the Funeral Mountains are largely made of Paleozoic limestone. The north end of the Black Mountains is mostly volcanic rock—turned into dry mud flats at Zabriskie Point, the amazingly colorful badlands that cover only a small area, but are more impressive than any other badlands in the nation.

Sand dunes lie between the two major salt pans in the area north of Salt Creek. A small group of dunes is located on the west side of the valley, under Telescope Peak. Gravel fans descend from the mountains on both sides of the valley, with the largest and deepest fans lying on the west side. Some are more than 6 miles long and rise to a height of 1,500 feet. The fan that accommodates the road to the Owens Valley east of Stovepipe Wells provides an amazing downward drive toward the valley floor. The fans provide the windblown sand that made the dunes.

Water is a precious commodity in Death Valley. About 2,000 years ago, the valley was flooded by a lake, to a depth of about 30 feet. A much earlier lake, in the Pleistocene Age, had a depth of up to 500 feet. This lake has been named Lake Manley, after the pioneer traveler who passed through the valley during the gold rush period. The most recent lake was formed in the spring of 1995, when rainwater washed down the Amargosa and down the sides of the mountains. A larger lake was formed in 1969 when 80 square miles of the southern salt pan was flooded after 3 days of rain.

Springs occur on both sides of the valley, but are fed from very different systems. Water that falls into the Amargosa Desert and the Pahrump Valley is routed through the rock structures and emerges at the hot springs near Furnace Creek Ranch. Another source of water in Death Valley is 50 miles away in the Spring Mountains near Las Vegas. The water from this range flows into the Pahrump Valley, discharging in some of the Death Valley springs. Other springs, on the west side of the valley, are fed by water that accumulates in the Panamint Range.

The largest springs are the Travertine, the Texas, and the Nevares, all found in the Furnace Creek fault zone between the Black and Funeral mountains. The springs here have large deposits of travertine (layered calcium carbonate). There are also clumps of travertine deposited by springs that are now dry. A group of springs north of the park visitor center serve to maintain water in Salt Creek.

Another kind of spring, primarily saline, is found in the southern part of the valley. The water that emerged at Bennett's Well, Tule Springs, Short's Well, and Salt Spring, among others, is stored in the gravel fans and under the salt pan. Both Salt Spring and Badwater are charged by this groundwater.

Desert varnish is a fascinating phenomenon. Older gravel and rock surfaces are stained black or dark brown by a coating of manganese oxide and iron. This varnishing occurs in many desert locations, including Death Valley.

Water seeps slowly over the rock, creating the shiny finish. One can identify the age of various rocks by looking at the varnish. Older rock is well stained, while recently formed rock is not, except when flooded with seep water. It is thought that most of the desert varnish on Death Valley rocks is the result of being washed during the Pleistocene lake period about 5,000 years ago.

Life in Death Valley

There is abundant life in what we consider desolate waste. The life is subtle, tolerant of the arid and saline conditions, but it is there. More than nine hundred kinds of plants are found within the boundaries of the national park, ranging from salt-bush and cacti on the valley floor to juniper, pinyon pine, and mountain mahogany, with bristlecone pine at the top of the Panamint Mountains. Spring wildflowers wave delicately on the gravel fans, roadsides, and in mountain valleys. Animals run, skitter. and scrape as they cross the salt pan and the sandy dunes. Bighorn sheep graze on the mountainsides.

Because of the tremendous variation in elevation between the valley floor and the top of the mountain ranges, there is a great diversity in ecosystems. The highest biotic zone in the park is the Canadian, characterized by limber and bristlecone pine. This zone is restricted to the topmost parts of the Panamint Range, north and south of Telescope Peak. Lower, is the pinyon-juniper woodland zone (Upper Sonoran), while still lower stands of creosote bush mix with burroweed near the bottoms of the alluvial fans, with desert holly surviving a little higher on the fans (Lower Sonoran). The spring-fed oases should be considered an anomaly. Furnace Creek Ranch is a freakish version of the Lower Sonoran Zone, one that is largely man-made—not very natural, although pleasant to visit with its palo verde, acacia, and towering date palm trees. A more natural palm oasis surrounds the springs above Scotty's Castle in

Grapevine Canyon, although that, too, has been enhanced with copious plantings.

The pinyon pine grows down to 5,500 feet, while the bristlecone or foxtail pine is seen only at 11,000 feet. At the other end of the ecological scale, no plant grows on the salt pan. In the narrow areas at the sides of the salt pan, creosote bush is the primary vegetation. There is a diversity of life in the briny wetlands of Salt Creek. The desert pupfish, an endangered species, lives in the creek. This is the sole survivor of the fish that inhabited the valley when the water was fresher and more abundant. March is the best time to see this tiny, silvery fish, which lives in water with more salinity than sea water. Only a small percent survive the hot summer months when the creek becomes super-hot and almost dries up. Salt-loving plants are rare, but several live in this harsh environment. Pickleweed and salt grass are found in the salt marsh. They need water, however, and are not found outside this ecosystem. Arrowweed, another salt-tolerating plant, is found in the Devil's Cornfield, near the sand dunes and Stovepipe Wells Village.

Beetles and fly larvae have adapted to the salty water. Insects are prime food for the pupfish. Higher on the food chain, coyotes and larger birds, especially ravens, dine on pupfish. Among the other birds you'll see around the marsh are killdeer, spotted sandpiper, and common snipe. The great blue heron is sometimes a visitor, as is the wood duck. Mallards and eared grebes are infrequently seen throughout the spring months. The turkey vulture is the most numerous raptor in Death Valley. Mississippi kites are seen on a casual basis, as are broad-winged and Swainson's hawks. Coyotes and sidewinders, the kings of the valley floor, feed on small rodents.

Higher in the mountains is another collection of birds and animals. The hardiest survivor is the burro. Death Valley burros were brought here and abandoned by prospectors. Living handily off the mountain vegetation, the burros have had a population explosion, resulting in a live-capture program conducted by the Park Service. The largest native animal is the bighorn sheep, which roam at various levels on the mountain slopes, depending on the time of year. Other animals to be found above the valley floor include deer, bobcat, kit fox, and mountain lion.

Down on the dunes is an amazing aggregation of small game, including rabbits, various rodents, and lizards. The animals and birds were hunted by Native Americans for hundreds of years. Rodents are numerous, and they include the desert wood rat (pack rat), kangaroo rat, antelope ground squirrel, round-tailed ground squirrel, white-footed mouse, and two types of rabbits—jack and cottontail. Many of the same reptiles that live in the deserts of Nevada and Arizona live here too—desert iguana, collard and zebra-tailed lizard, horned and striped lizard, and chuckwalla. A few pests should be avoided, such as the scorpion, which is particularly common on the valley floor, hiding under rocks and on damp ground.

How to Get There

You can enter Death Valley from the north, south, east, and west sides, although it makes sense to plan your visit, including your approach, so you can experience maximum scenery, and don't have to retrace your routes. From the south, California Route 127 leads north from the town of Baker and Interstate 15 southwest of Las Vegas. The road runs across the Mojave Desert, past several dry lake beds and into the Amargosa near Tecopa. Just north of Shoshone, State Route 178 leads west, across Salisberry and Jubilee passes, into the southern end of Death Valley. The road leads north along the eastern side of the valley, past Badwater, to the mouth of the Furnace Creek Wash and national park headquarters.

From the northeast, Nevada State Route 267 runs from State Route 95 north of Beatty, leading down through Grapevine Canyon past Scotty's Castle, then turning south and passing the dunes to a junction with Highway 190.

There is one paved route from the west, accessed by driving through the Owens Valley (U.S. 395). The western end of State Route 190, the main road through the national park, joins Highway 395 south of the dry Owens Lake at Olancha. You may access this highway from Lone Pine, north of Owens Lake, by taking State Route 136. This route leads over the White Mountains, into the Panamint Valley (where you'll find a cafe and accommodations at Panamint Springs), then across the Panamints, descending into Death Valley on a wide alluvial fan. The road reaches the valley floor at Stovepipe Wells Village.

There are two eastern entrances. The main route (State Highway 190) leads west from Death Valley Junction and State Route 127, 28 miles north of Shoshone. Passing across the Amargosa and past Pyramid Peak (6,700-foot elevation), the road drops down Furnace Creek Wash, passes the road to Dante's View, and arrives at sea level near the Furnace Creek Inn. This is the junction with State Route 190; national park headquarters and the Furnace Creek Ranch are a mile north of the junction. From the town of Beatty and Nevada Route 95 in the east, take State Route 374 southwest, through Daylight Pass, for a total of 19 miles. You'll find the junction with the north/south route through the valley here.

An alternative one-way route leads west through Titus Canyon, a worthwhile trip if you're approaching Death Valley from Beatty. Drive southwest from Beatty on State Route 374 and turn right onto Titus Canyon Road beyond the Rhyolite ghost town. This scenic road leads through the ruins of Leadfield, another old ghost town and mining area, and quickly drops into Death Valley through the narrow canyon, meeting State Route 267 on the valley floor. Furnace Creek is to the south.

Enjoying Death Valley National Park

PLACES TO STAY

One of the most important parts of planning your Death Valley vacation is making sure you have a place to stay in the valley. Fortunately, there are several choices, ranging from campgrounds operated by the Park Service; a motel with restaurant and lounge, gas station, and store at Stovepipe Wells Village; the Furnace Creek Ranch, a year-round resort complex next to the park visitor center that includes cabin-style units and upperscale motel units on the Death Valley golf course, plus a store, restaurant, coffee shop, and gas station; and the Furnace Creek Inn, a deluxe hotel operated October through May, at the mouth of Furnace Creek Wash.

If you would prefer to stay outside the park while approaching the park from the west, you'll find motels in Lone Pine and Independence (in the Owens Valley), and at Panamint Springs in the Panamint Valley, just east of Death Valley. Beatty or

Death Valley Junction are good places to stay before a morning drive into the valley from the east. Contact addresses and phone numbers are given in the Where to Stay section, on page 309.

TOURING THE PARK

When Death Valley National Monument became Death Valley National Park in October 1994, the park's boundaries were expanded to create a total park area of 3.3 million acres. This is now the largest park outside Alaska, larger than Yellowstone. It will take a few years for routes to be opened to most of the new areas, which include a giant sand mountain, several new desert valleys, mountains, springs, and a Joshua tree forest. The national park now boasts not one but several waterfalls in its new sections. The most spectacular is Darwin Falls, on the west side of the Panamint Valley.

The first thing to do, after finding your accommodations, is to check out the park headquarters and visitor center. An orientation program is presented every half hour throughout the day. A wealth of interpretive material is available, including a large recreation map, individual trail guides, many books on the history and ecology of Death Valley, and the usual national park souvenirs such as slide sets, T-shirts, and mugs.

Death Valley is a huge place. To get the full benefit of your time, a little advance planning is necessary. If you have only a day to spend in the park, two half-day tours are recommended, one to the southern part of the valley and an afternoon drive to the north.

An Early Morning Drive   A drive to Zabriskie Point, 20-Mule-Team Canyon, and Dante's View can be done before breakfast if you are so inclined. Check with the park visitor center to see the sunrise time and plan to be at Zabriskie Point (on Highway 190) just before then. This wonderfully colored badland is best observed at sunup, when the iridescent yellow and gray mudflats are brilliantly lit and shaded by the low-lying sun.

Then, proceed up the Furnace Creek Wash and take the short one-way tour through 20-Mule-Team Canyon, a detour that takes you back to the highway. Continue west on Highway 190 and turn south on the road to Dante's View. This viewpoint atop the Black Mountains provides a thrilling panorama of Death Valley, the Panamints to the west, and the Sierra Nevada even farther to the west. You'll be back at your Furnace Creek campsite or lodgings in a little over 2 hours.

Badwater and Artist's Drive   This 44-mile round-trip takes you past the Devil's Golf Course on the way south to Badwater, the stinky springs below sea level, just a short distance from the lowest point on the continent. An interpretive booklet for this tour is available at the visitor center or from a box at the Furnace Creek highway junction. On the return trip, turn off the highway at the signpost for Artist's Drive. This fascinating side-trip leads across an alluvial fan, 500 feet above the valley floor, into a deep mountain wash, and to the viewpoint for Artists Palette.

Here, what is thought to be volcanic ash lies in colorful deposits—black, brown, yellow, green, and violet. Scientists have yet to find out what caused these colorful layers to form here. The route winds back to the highway for the return to Furnace Creek. If you have time (an extra half-hour to an hour), stop for a hike through Golden Canyon. Without Golden Canyon, this is a 2-hour tour. In the spring months, you could extend it by driving south of Badwater, all the way to the passes, to take in the wildflower displays. A full day would be required.

Borax Works, Salt Creek, and Sand Dunes   A 42-mile round-trip from Furnace Creek, this tour can take as long as you wish to spend on the dunes. Just north of Furnace Creek, a short loop road leads to the original borax mining operation in the valley, the Harmony Borax Works. The road leads around the old workings and a short self-guided trail runs through what is left of the adobe mill and old borax mining equipment, including a 20-mule team wagon. Back on the highway, drive north to the turnoff to Salt Creek. One mile off the highway you'll find an easy walking trail along spring-fed Salt Creek, the home of the desert pupfish.

A gravel side road leads to the eastern side of the Sand Dunes. To complete this tour, drive past the intersection of Highways 190 and 267, in the direction of Scotty's Castle. Turn left onto the sand dunes road. The historic stovepipe well is on the north side of the road, and the dunes parking area is beyond the well. You can also take the other end of this road from Highway 190, starting west of Stovepipe Wells Village near the Devil's Cornfield.

North-End Tour to Scotty's Castle and Ubehebe Crater

Scotty's Castle, situated in Grapevine Canyon, is 53 miles north of the park visitor center. Ubehebe Crater is a 5-minute drive from the castle. The return trip from Furnace Creek will take about 4 hours, if you are able to get a timely tour of Scotty's Castle, or choose to walk around the outside of the main buildings and look at the palm oasis.

As you drive into the northern portion of the valley, the highway climbs, passing the Grapevine Entrance Station. Drive up Grapevine Canyon for another 3 miles to Scotty's Castle. Albert Johnston, an eastern financier, built this Spanish rococo complex in the early 1900s as a vacation home. The main building, part of Death Valley Ranch, was named for Johnston's friend Walter Scott, known as Death Valley Scotty. Scott was a prospector and genial scoundrel who lived and worked in Death Valley for many years. Albert Johnston and his wife Bessie first visited the area after being approached in Chicago by Scott, who wanted Johnston to help finance a secret gold mine that Scott had discovered.

For several years, the two men roamed the valley, searching for gold. They never did come across Scott's secret find. However, Johnston fell in love with Death Valley and decided to establish a vacation home and ranch in the area. Scott suggested Grapevine Canyon, where there was a flow of water from several springs. The location, at 3,000 feet, was ideal.

Construction began in 1922, and the ranch was built over many years, with Scott playing a large part. Johnston spent more than $2 million on the property, but it was never finished, in part because the Depression intervened. The estate was named Death Valley Ranch, but because of Scott's constant presence and his overwhelming personality, it became known as Scotty's Castle. In his excellent history, Richard E. Lingenfelter described Death Valley Scotty as ". . . a ham actor, a conscienceless con man, an almost pathological liar, and a charismatic bullslinger." Scott and his stories entertained not only Albert and Bessie Johnston but a host of guests including Will Rogers, Betty Grable, Norman Rockwell, and Clark Gable, among many others.

On a guided tour of the castle, you'll learn Walter Scott's story and see the amazing buildings, complete with carillon tower, solar heater, and much more. Scott is buried on the property. At the end of a short hike to Windy Point, you can find the graves of Walter Scott and his dog Windy. Other short walking trails take you to the springs and Tie Canyon. It's important to register for a tour as soon as you arrive at the site. There may be a wait of about an hour for the next tour, and fees are charged ($6 for adults, $3 for seniors and children 6 or over). There is a snack bar, as well as a gift shop and gas station at the castle. The site is usually open at 8:30 A.M. and tours begin at 9 A.M.

Returning south from the castle, turn right onto the road that leads to Ubehebe Crater, 5 miles from the junction. This explosion pit is 5 miles wide, 750 feet deep, and less than a thousand years old. The large crater is flanked by several small craters that were formed more recently.

Death Valley Hikes

There are several easy day hikes and a few backcountry hikes that are mostly strenuous and suitable for only the most fit and experienced. The most difficult mountain hike leads from the Mahogany Flat Campground, climbing 3,000 feet to Telescope Peak, the highest spot in the park. A more moderate backcountry route leads through Jayhawker Canyon, starting on Highway 190 (2.3 miles past Emigrant Junction, at the 3,000-foot elevation sign). This trail was used by gold seekers in 1850, some of whom signed their names on a large boulder about 2 miles from the trailhead. The trail runs 5 miles to the base of Pinto Peak.

Sand Dunes Hike   This 4-mile round-trip hike leads across the central sand dunes from the parking area, 2.2 miles east of Stovepipe Wells. You'll see animal tracks on your way to the 80-foot-high dunes. It's best to do this in the early morning or late afternoon. The area is also open for moonlight hiking.

Keane Wonder Mine Trail   This 2-mile round-trip starts from the parking area at the mouth of Titus Canyon. Drive 3 miles from Scotty's Castle Road on a gravel road. This very steep trail climbs from the ruins of a mill to the mine, 2,000 feet above the road. From the mine you'll see fine views of Death Valley.

Keane Wonder Springs Trail Another 2-mile round-trip hike, this trail departs from the Keane Wonder Mill parking area, 2 miles off the Beatty Cutoff Road. From the trailhead, follow the pipeline north along the base of the mountain to the sulfur springs and travertine mounds. An old stamp mill and cabin are located beyond the springs.

Mosaic Canyon Trail The trailhead for this 2-mile return walk is located 2 miles from Stovepipe Wells. Take Mosaic Canyon Road from State Route 190. This is an easy, and very popular, hike up the narrow canyon, some of it over slick rock. The Mosaics are rock fragments that are cemented together in the walls of the canyon. You may see bighorn sheep as you walk.

Golden Canyon Trail Another 2-mile route, its trailhead is at a parking lot at the end of a short side road that leads from Highway 178 (Badwater Road) south of Furnace Creek. An easy, self-guided trail with trail guides available at the park visitor center, the walk leads through the narrow canyon. Red Cathedral is located half a mile up the canyon, beyond the final trail marker.

BACKCOUNTRY HIKES

Jayhawker Canyon Trail This moderate backcountry hike on State Highway 190, 2.3 miles past Emigrant Junction, has an elevation gain of 2,600 feet, starting at the 3,000-foot level. The route offers a 10-mile return hike. The trail starts with a mild grade to the base of Pinto Mountain. A topographical map (#851 Emigrant Canyon) is available at the park visitor center for this part of the famous Jayhawker route of 1850. Two miles into the trail, you can see where Jayhawkers signed their names on a large boulder.

Wildrose Peak Trail This trail, which begins at the north end of the Charcoal Kilns parking area on Upper Wildrose Canyon Road, provides a 4.2-mile, one-way hike to the mountain peak at 9,064 feet. The elevation gain is 2,200 feet. There are great views as you approach the peak. The last mile is considered strenuous.

Telescope Peak Trail Only for the most hardy hikers, this trail offers a 7-mile, one-way climb to the highest point in the park. The trailhead is at the Mahogany Flat Campground on upper Wildrose Canyon Road. Drive to the Charcoal Kilns and continue on the rough, steep road. This strenuous trail has an elevation gain of 3,000 feet; the high altitude is known to take its toll. You'll see bristlecone pine trees above 10,000 feet. There's a fine view of Mt. Whitney from the top. Badwater, the Black Mountains, and the Amargosa Desert can all be seen to the east. The Park Service advises that winter climbing is possible but hazardous, with crampons and ice axes required. The peak is usually free of snow by June. You can pick up a special leaflet on the Wildrose and Telescope Peak hikes at the park visitor center.

Nearby Attractions

TECOPA AND TECOPA HOT SPRINGS

Located southeast of Death Valley and 50 miles north of Baker, these are two of the most bizarre communities in the nation. Tecopa is a hamlet located a mile off Highway 127, with a store, saloon, and a few mobile homes. To the north, on a loop road, is Tecopa Hot Springs. This trailer village is devoid of life during the summer months, then awakens when a flood of RVs and trailers arrive for the winter.

There's a large county park across from the public hot spring pools, and several private RV parks offer a little more than the basic desert accommodations of the county RV park. The private parks have their own hot spring pools. Tecopa was a favorite encampment and resting place for the Shoshone Indians before the late 1800s. As zany as the present-day winter encampment may be, there is fine soaking to be had in the geothermal pools at any time of year. You'll have a good chance of being a lone soaker after May and throughout the summer. Men's and women's bath houses are located across the road from the county RV park.

AMARGOSA OPERA HOUSE

By following the same route toward Death Valley (Highway 127), you'll arrive in the atmospheric hamlet of Death Valley Junction. This used to be a much larger community with railroad stations and mining companies. What used to be a busy mining town is now reduced to the white-painted Amargosa Motel—just about the only structure still standing.

Attached to the motel is the Amargosa Opera House, where dancer Marta Becket performs her one-woman show, as she has done for decades, on most nights during the winter season and on Saturday evenings during summer. Marta Becket has become a renowned institution. To find this cultural outpost in the middle of the Amargosa Desert is a stupefying experience.

OWENS VALLEY

This valley—more than 100 miles long—lies to the west of Death and Panamint valleys, and east of the Sierra Nevada. It is one of the most outstanding outdoor attractions in California, yet it is virtually unknown to most Americans. It has a checkered history, which is reflected in several museums. The main streets of the valley's small towns retain an Old West atmosphere. The geological profile of the Owens Valley is quite amazing. It lies between the highest peaks of the southern Sierra Nevada and the Inyo/White Range. The valley floor is sage desert land, somewhat changed from its natural state with pockets of irrigated fields. U.S. Highway 395 runs the length of the valley, entering north of Mojave and rising out of the valley into higher Sierra country north of Bishop, the valley's major town.

In earlier years, it was home to nomadic tribes of Native Americans, mainly the Northern Shoshone, but also Paiute, who hunted and gathered pinyon nuts and fruit. More recent history features one of the most depressing stories of western settlement, involving the first (and probably the worst) major water grab in the state. Los Angeles—in 1904—was growing at an extreme pace, and needed more water to slake the thirsts of the millions of people migrating to what was (and still is) a desert that meets the salty sea. Since the Los Angeles basin required a secure, long-term supply of water, by 1907 the City of Los Angeles purchased water rights to the Owens River and quickly diverted much of the Sierra snowmelt into the quickly built Los Angeles Aqueduct. By 1917, most of the small streams flowing from the mountains to the Owens River were also bought up by the Los Angeles water interests. As the aqueduct transported the water to the ever-thirsty city, the lush valley and farms began to disappear (their water rights had been sold to L.A.) and the green valley largely reverted to desert.

The greatest tragedy was the desiccation of Owens Lake. As the aqueduct siphoned the Owens River water over the mountains, this large, salty lake (50 feet deep, 15 miles long, 9 miles wide) lost its source. Where steamboats once plied, and abundant brine shrimp provided food for thousands of shore birds, there is nothing but a huge, dry lake bed.

It is a desolate salt pan where, in a breeze, the sand and sodium blow in great clouds. The same situation—again due to the ever-thirsty L.A.—has affected Mono Lake north of the Owens Valley. However, since this is not 1907, Mono Lake has met a different fate.

Environmentalists and government agencies have joined to protect this shrinking lake, and feeder streams are now flowing into Mono Lake again. Looking at this mountain lake, with nearby cinder cones and pine forests, one can only imagine how the Owens Valley (and Los Angeles) might look today had the L.A. leaders of the century's first decade decided to restrict city development instead of import Owens River water.

From the moment you enter the Owens Valley (from the north, south, or from the east and Death Valley), you are struck with an ever-changing panorama, featuring the highest peaks of the Sierra Nevada. Here, the Sierra forms a gigantic rock wall, almost perpendicular compared with the slopes of the eastern side. The Whitney group of peaks are over 14,000 feet high, forming the crown of the Sierra and providing a magnificent series of views from almost any point around the town of Lone Pine. The Lone Pine area, at mid-valley, has several geological points of interest. A paved road leads east from town, through the Alabama Hills, now a recreational area that provided the scene for many early Hollywood westerns with stars such as Tom Mix, Hopalong Cassidy, Gene Autry, Roy Rogers, and Gary Cooper, and for series such as *The Lone Ranger*. Movie Road leads through an array of jumbled rock formations, on a loop trip past the old movie sites. In 1969, 30,000 acres of this arid but spectacular landscape, with the High Sierra as a backdrop, were set aside as the Alabama Hills Recreation Area. You'll find campgrounds, picnic areas, and many places for exciting photography here.

However, Mt. Whitney is the star attraction in the Lone Pine area. The main road, leading west from the center of town, is Whitney Portal Road. This short road leads up the side of the mountain, past three campgrounds, to Whitney Portal, a park with a lovely pond fed by a roaring mountain stream.

You'll find the trailhead for the Mt. Whitney Summit Trail at the Portal. The trail usually takes intermediate hikers 3 days to reach the summit and return, with overnight stays at Trail Crest Camp. Extremely fit hikers are able to make the round-trip from the Portal in one long day. The summit trail crosses several ridges with stupendous views. It also crosses the John Muir Trail at Trail Crest, and arrives at the summit (14,495 feet) where there is a small stone hut built by the Smithsonian Institution. Here you can view the rugged rock of the High Sierra and glacial cirques that hold snow year-round to the north and west. The summit is relatively flat, with huge boulders and rock slabs scattered across the 1.5 acres of mountaintop. There is a campground at Whitney Portal, plus a pack station and a small store that sells camping supplies. Various shorter mountain trails lead from the portal park.

Several small towns in the Owens Valley include Big Pine and Independence (the Inyo County seat). The Museum of Eastern California, in Independence, has indoor displays including artifacts of early Native American life in the valley and memorabilia from the days when Independence was an army camp in the 1860s. Another Sierra adventure lies waiting at the end of Taboose Creek Road, which leads west from the highway. Two campgrounds in the high desert are located on Goodale Creek and Taboose Creek. At the end of the road, a trail climbs to Taboose Pass (11,366 feet) and leads through the basin of the South Fork of the Kings River. The view of the Sierra (Mt. Ruskin and Striped Mountain) and the valley's volcanic field is worth the hike. Red Mountain (5,188 feet) lies to the west of this area. The red cone is 600 feet high. For a close-up view of the cone and the nearby Poverty Hills, take Fish Springs Road. This route circles the hills, with Tinemaha Creek Campground providing a place for an overnight stay in a desert setting with the looming Sierra peaks.

The town of Big Pine provides a gateway to several areas of interest, including a route through the extreme north end of

Death Valley (Palmetto mining area), and also provides access to the Ancient Bristlecone Pine Forest in the White Mountains. State Highway 168 climbs Cedar Flat Plateau at 7,000 feet, where you'll find a campground. Past the summit, the road wanders through Payson Canyon, with great views of Deep Springs Valley, before it enters Nevada. The bristlecone pines in the Inyo National Forest are not only the oldest of the bristlecone trees in America, but are the oldest living things on earth. There are national forest campsites on the plateau. Visiting the bristlecone groves takes some walking, and even summer weather may be crisp. However, the effort and inconvenience is minor compared to the thrill you will get from being in the presence of these long-enduring trees.

By taking Highway 168 into Nevada to its junction with U.S. 95, you can access the north end of Death Valley. Drive south on U.S. 95, then take State Route 374 through Grapevine Canyon to Scotty's Castle and on to Furnace Creek.

The Owens Valley comes to an end a few miles north of Bishop. To the north is the resort town of Mammoth Lakes, Mono Lake, and the Tioga Pass Road leading into the high country of Yosemite National Park. U.S. 395 continues northward, to Carson City and Reno.

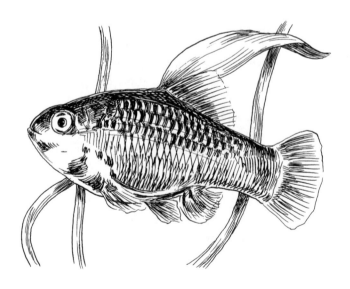

DEATH VALLEY WILDLIFE

During summer days, Death Valley seems almost devoid of creatures. Only humans are silly enough to wander around in those temperatures. But in the evening, birds and animals venture out to look for food and water. During the late fall, winter, and spring, bird and animal watching is much easier.

The best place to see bird life is from the boardwalk that runs around the Salt Creek marsh. Located north of the park visitor center, this little riparian habitat harbors only a few kinds of low-growing plants, but you can spot a diversity of wildlife if you are patient. The palm oases at Furnace Creek Ranch and Scotty's Castle attract different kinds of birds in summer, including migrants on their way to cooler homes.

Wildflowers such as desert-gold and evening primrose are found at higher elevations: on the alluvial fans and in mountain pockets. Roadsides are also good places to look for wildflowers.

The valley floor is home to beavertail and hedgehog cactus, as well as little "bellyflowers,"

which you may not even notice unless you get close to the ground—on your belly! The wildflowers begin to bloom in February, in areas on and near the valley floor. The show continues through March and April, when the mountain passes are filled with profuse, colorful displays, particularly in the southern part of the valley.

BIRDS

Broad-winged Hawk
Buteo platypterus
One of several hawks that fly over Death Valley, the broad-winged is a small, husky bird, about the size of a crow. This hawk is best identified by the noticeable dark bands in a curved pattern on both sides of its tail, separated by white bands of the same size. It also has dark brown wing linings. This is quite a rare bird, breeding in the Canadian prairie (mostly in Alberta). According to its regular migration patterns, it is not supposed to be seen here, but it is.

Common Poor-will
Phalaeenoptilus nuttallii
This is the smallest member of the nightjar or goatsucker

family, growing to a length of about 9.5 inches. Compared with a nighthawk, it has a shorter tail, which is rounded and has black bars and white end tips. The black tail bars are longer than those on the whippoorwill. It has a grayish brown body with a light collar under its black throat. You'll hear its plaintive song at night.

Its range is from southern Canada to Mexico, where it lives in the desert, chaparral woodlands, and in other upland ecosystems. It sometimes hibernates in the desert.

Spotted Sandpiper
Actitis macularia
This small shore bird is often seen in the West, beside lakes and streams. It winters in Death Valley and can be seen beside Salt Creek, several miles north of the park visitor center. While it has round spots on its breast in summer, it loses them in winter. It is an olive-brown color above with a thin white line over the eye. It has a white, wedge-shaped mark on the shoulder. In summer its range is from Alaska through Canada; in winter from the Southwest U.S. to Argentina. Its voice is a sharp *peet* or *peet-wheet*, or a combination of both.

Yellow-headed Blackbird
Xanthocephalus xanthocephalus
Another dweller in the Salt Creek area, this marsh bird also winters here, flying in from southern Canada and the northern U.S. It prefers freshwater marshes but manages to survive well with this water, which is as salty as the ocean. There is quite a difference in coloration between the male and female. The male has the brightly colored yellow head and chest, otherwise is black with a white patch on the wing that is best seen when it flies. The female has a yellow throat and breast with white flecks at the edge of the yellow patch. This bird loves to sing, and its song is a distinctive low, rasping sound: a repeated *kruk* or *kack*.

Horned Grebe
Podiceps auritus
The grebes are a family of duck-like birds that dive into the water for their food. They have a very sluggish flying style, and when they dive, they usually dive from the surface. Sometimes they just sink into the water. Their primary food is small fish.

The horned grebe is identified by its ear tufts, which are dark in the winter (when you'll see it in Death Valley) and golden in summer. It has a thin, straight bill. It lives in both fresh and salt-water regions, preferring salt water environments in winter.

American Coot
Fulica americana
It walks, swims, and talks like a duck. This member of the rail family (also referred to as coot) is seen during winter at the Salt Creek marsh. It is a blackish-gray color, with two white patches (or a single, divided patch) on the tail. It has large feet with puffy lobes on its toes. It seems to have difficulty when it takes off from the water, skittering along the surface and dragging its feet. Ranging from southern Canada to Argentina, as well as Eurasia, the American coot spends most of its time on the water, unlike its rail cousins. They are often seen on the water in flocks. Its voice is varied, and loud. It repeats a croak, similar to *kruk*, or *kup*, and also gives out a repeated *kek*. And that isn't all—this coot also indulges in a series of cackling sounds.

OTHER ANIMALS

Desert Pupfish
Cyprinodon macularis
Five species of pupfish live in Death Valley's salt marshes. One of these, the cottonball marsh pupfish (*cyprinodon milleri*) lives in Cottonball Marsh near the Harmony Borax Works, in water three to five times as salty as seawater. Other varieties of the tiny, silvery fish live in Salt Creek and its marsh. Still other pupfish inhabit northwest Mexico and the Anza Borrego Desert in Arizona. The desert pupfish lives in the waters created by desert springs and marshes. Of the thirteen species in the United States, several are endangered. The pupfish has a stout, chunky shape, and a silvery body (sometimes an olive color), with six to nine dark bars on the sides. Males, when breeding, are an iridescent blue. The mouth is upturned. It grows to a length of about 2 inches.

Desert Kangaroo Rat
Dipodomys deserti
Several kangaroo rats live in Death Valley and the nearby mountain slopes, including the Panamint Kangaroo rat (*d. panamintinus*). The more numerous desert kangaroo rat is also found in Nevada and southwestern Arizona. It lives in sand dunes and in other sandy areas under creosote bush. Beige above and white below, it has white marks above and below the eyes. The long tail has a crest and a white tip. Each foot

has four toes. This timid creature can be best seen at night.

Sidewinder
Crotalus cerastes
This toxic rattlesnake is defined by the way it moves—traveling over sandy surfaces by "sidewinding," in which it uses static electricity to maintain its place when crossing soft areas such as the Death Valley sand dunes. You'll see its distinctive sidewinding pattern on the dunes and other sandy areas of the valley, which is a favored habitat for this snake. It thrives in sandy areas from below sea level to an elevation of 5,000 feet. Its range is from this area to southern Utah and into Mexico. The sidewinder found in Death Valley is one of three subspecies; others are the Sonoran and Colorado desert sidewinders. It is a light brown color with white and dark brown, and has rough scales with a triangular projection above each eye. It grows to a length of about 32 inches.

Chuckwalla
Sauromalus obesus
A large lizard with a prominent stomach area, the male chuckwalla is black on the head, front legs, and the front part of the body, with red, yellow, or gray on the back part of the body. Female and immature chuckwalla often have yellow and gray bands. Three subspecies are found in southern California, southern Nevada, western Arizona, and into Utah. They all emerge from their nighttime nests (under rocks) in the early morning, moving around when temperatures are over 100 degrees F. They eat foliage and fruit.

Desert Iguana
Dipsosaurus dorsalis
Although not as pot-bellied as the chuckwalla, this large lizard still has a round body and a long tail. It has a crest of scales that extends from the neck almost to the end of the back. Its head is brown. The body has more red, showing in a net-like pattern with gray and white spots on the neck and body. The tail is whitish or gray with round rows of darker spots. It is found across the deserts of southern California, the southern tip of Nevada, and western Arizona, where it lives in sand and rocky areas, usually with creosote bush. It, too, is diurnal, enjoying the heat of Death Valley even on the hottest days, retreating under bushes only during the hottest afternoon hours.

Zebra-tailed Lizard

Callisaurus draconoides

This large gray lizard has pairs of darker spots down the back, with bands across the tail of the same color. The male lizard has two black bars on each side that become blue spots or blotches on the belly. The female does not have the belly spots, and the bars are fainter than on the male. This lizard does not rely on creosote bush but lives in more sparse, arid areas, sometimes among small rocks. Its range includes Nevada and southwestern Utah near St. George, through much of Arizona and into Mexico. There are twelve subspecies of the zebra-tailed lizard, with three living in the Southwest (Mojave Desert, Nevada, and Arizona). Eggs hatch in summer and fall.

Texas Antelope Squirrel

Ammospermophilus interpres

Resembling a chipmunk, this little desert squirrel grows to a length of about 9 inches. It has white stripes on both sides of the back. A blackish-brown color, the squirrel's tail is white underneath. It has very short ears. This squirrel is found not on the valley floor but higher up the sides of the surrounding mountains, with its den at the base of boulders. It feeds on seeds and fruit.

Round-tailed Ground Squirrel

Spermophilus tereticaudus

This larger cinnamon-gray-colored squirrel grows to a length of 10.5 inches. It has a long, slender tail that has a lighter underside. Its range extends from this region, through southern Nevada, into Arizona. It lives near the valley floor in the creosote bush scrub environment. Visitors see this squirrel in the cooler parts of the day.

Desert Tarantula

Aphonopelma chalodes

You may see this desert spider in Death Valley, crawling over the sand dunes or beside the highways, mostly after sunset or before dawn. That's the male looking for a friendly female. Its range includes the desert areas of Arizona, California, and New Mexico. The male grows to 2.5 inches, the female slightly larger. Both have heavy, hairy bodies, an almost black abdomen, and a grayish-brown cephalothorax.

PLANTS

Creosote Bush

Larrea tridentata

The haven and food supply for many desert animals, the creosote bush is a vital part of the deserts of southern California,

Arizona, and Texas. It is the most widespread plant in the region. Its companion, in Death Valley and elsewhere, is the burrobush (*hymenoclea salsola*). Creosote bush is an evergreen shrub that usually grows to a height of about 4 feet, but sometimes up to 12 feet (Death Valley does not have enough water for this kind of growth). It grows on well-drained slopes, and you'll see it on the alluvial fans, including the accessible Furnace Wash fan. The flowers are yellow, about 1 inch wide with five sepals. The fruit is white and globe-shaped. After a good rain, the bush exudes a strong odor.

Desert Holly
Atriplex hymenelytra
This shrub, common in Death Valley, is a rounded, compact silvery shrub, covered with leaves that resemble those of the holly plant. The flowers are hardly visible. It produces oval bracts about half an inch long with wings and fruit attached. It prefers gravelly areas and washes below 3,000 feet. Particularly suited for growing on the alluvial fans above the Death Valley floor, it grows to its height of about 3 feet. Its range extends into southwestern Utah, and into northwestern Arizona, in a line south of Death Valley.

Arrowweed
Pluchea sericea
Featured in the Devil's Cornfield just south of the sand dunes in Death Valley, arrowweed is a salt-loving shrub, somewhat like the willow, with vertical branches. While the bush grows to a height of 40 inches in other places, it is shorter, about 30 inches, in this area. It is called arrowweed because Native Americans used to fashion arrows from the tough, straight branches. The plant sends down deep roots to tap the low-lying groundwater after the winter rains recede into the sand. The effect of wind blowing through the Devil's Cornfield, washing earth from around the arrowweed, has left large distinctive clumps of sand imprisoned by the roots. Its purple flowers are arranged in clusters at the end of the branches.

Pickleweed
Salicornia rubra
Pickleweed is one of the most salt-tolerant plants in the Southwest deserts. Needing plenty of water, this succulent grows only on salt pans with a high water table and in salt marshes, including a sizable stand in the Salt Creek area. You won't see pickleweed growing on the Death Valley salt pan, except in a few places where there is sufficient seep-

age at the edges. At Salt Creek, it grows beside salt grass (*destichlis*), another plant that can tolerate very salty situations (up to 6 percent salinity).

Burrobush
Hymenoclea salsosa
Found in desert washes, and close to creosote bush, this medium-sized shrub often brings hay fever to those who come too close. There is another subspecies found in southeastern Arizona and New Mexico that does not cause the same discomfort. The plant has slender, sparse, white branches, growing to a height of about 3 feet. The leaves are very thin, almost like threads, alternative, and about 3 inches long. The fruit, accompanied by silvery colored wings, is very small. The bush is found above the valley floor up to an elevation of 1,800 feet. Look for it as you drive up Furnace Creek Wash.

Dodder
Cuscuta denticulata
This unusual and fascinating parasitic plant can be seen strangling other plants on the Death Valley roadsides. You'll recognize it by its bright yellow-orange color. Both leafless and rootless, it looks like a thin, stringy, spaghetti-like substance. These stems become entwined around the stems and branches of the host plants, like a vine. Dodder is widely found in the United States. In agricultural areas it is a terrible pest, ruining many crops. In the desert in grows on burrobush, arrowweed, and goldenrod. In Death Valley, it also grows on creosote bush. This strange plant produces flowers that are white to pale yellow. The flowers grow at the ends and along the yellowish strands.

Date Palm
Phoenix dactylifera
If Death Valley were its own country, the date palm would be its national tree. The palm trees planted at Furnace Creek Ranch by the U.S. Borax Company are not only a striking contract to the sparse vegetation in the rest of the valley, but produce a good crop of tasty dates each summer. You can buy the dates at the ranch. There are several varieties of date palm, including a dwarf variety (*P. humilis*) native to Laos. The date palms of Death Valley, and the most common date palm in the Indio/Palm Springs area, is *dactylifera*. It is not a North American native but was imported from the Middle East. It has a slender trunk that grows to 80 feet. These trees can take any kind of heat, and are hardy to 20 degrees F.

California Fan Palm
Washingtonia filifera
This palm, a native of the California desert, can be seen at Scotty's Castle. It is often used to line city streets in California and Arizona. Growing to 60 feet, it occurs naturally near springs or moist spots. It is the classic tree of California's palm oases. Mature trees are identified by the long leaf stalks, which stand apart, and by the long beards composed of dried leaf stalks (that is, if the stalks and beards haven't been cut down by beautifiers). The thatch tapers inward, toward the trunk. This palm survives winter temperatures down to 18 degrees F. The Mexican fan palm (*W. robusta*) is a more compact and slender tree.

Beavertail Cactus
Opuntia basilaris
This small cactus featuring "paddles" (or nopals), grows to a height of 1 foot, with the clump of paddle-like stems growing out to about 6 feet. It has marvelous flowers, about 3 inches wide, with many bright pink or reddish-lavender petals. The flat stems have small spines (up to 0.25 inches long) and are a matte, light green color. The brownish fruit is egg-shaped, about 1.25 inches long, with many seeds inside.

The cactus, which flowers in March, is found along the roadsides at an elevation slightly above the valley floor (above sea level). Its range is from southeastern California to the southwest corner of Utah, and south from western Arizona into the Sonoran desert. The profusion of beautiful flowers make this a prime landscaping specimen.

Four-wing Saltbush
Atriplex canescens
Nine varieties of phreatophytes grow at the edges of the salt pans in Death Valley. These are plants whose roots reach perennial groundwater or the capillary fringe around the water table. The four-wing saltbush, a round, woody shrub with branches that become scaly with age, is found in this zone. The evergreen leaves, about 2 inches long and less than a half-inch wide, are alternately positioned. The fruit is its most distinctive feature, with four diaphanous wings around a circular seed. The plant grows to a height of 3 feet. It has small yellow flowers.

WILDFLOWERS

Desert Sand Verbena
Abronia villosa
A creeping plant with flower stalks that grow to about 10 inches, this sand-loving verbena

flowers from March, and—depending on the heat and accumulated rainfall—continues to flower after many other wildflowers have become dormant. The stems lie on the ground, growing to a length of 6 feet. Its runners and stalks are sticky, with small hairs. It bears bright pink, trumpet-shaped flowers, and also bears fruit having three or five wings. The leaves grow opposite, to about 1.5 inches in length, and have scalloped edges. Its range stretches into western Arizona.

Desertgold
Geraea canescens
This sunflower family member is also called desert-sunshine, desert sunflower, and hairy-headed sunflower. Blooming very early—from January to May—it has one of the most sweet-smelling flowers, located at the end of stalks that grow from 6 inches to 2 feet tall. The leaves and bracts enclosing the flower heads have many small hairs. The desertgold is an important source of food for rodents, particularly mice. Bees and hummingbird moths perform pollination duties. It has a range to Utah and southeastern Colorado to southern Arizona and the Sonoran desert in Mexico. It can also be seen in several other national parks, including Saguaro National Park

and Organ Pipe National Monument, both in Arizona.

Desert Paintbrush
Castilleja chromosa
The red and orange flowers, and the brightly colored bracts make sighting of this plant easy during the spring period. It grows in open, dry soil, often accompanied by sagebrush, to a height of 4 to 16 inches. The leaves are almost 2 inches long, with the lower leaves quite narrow and single and the upper leaves displayed as 3 or 5 narrow lobes. The brightly colored flower bracts are also divided. The plant's range is from the Great Basin desert (southern Idaho) to Northern Arizona, and from northwest New Mexico to Colorado and Wyoming.

Desert Fivespot
Malvastrum rotundifolium
This is one of the most distinctive wildflowers growing in Death Valley. The globe-like flowers are a purplish-pink color, with a dark red center. Around the center of the flower, on each of the five petals, are distinct, round spots. Thus the name. The plant flowers from March to May.

The plant grows to a height of 4 to 24 inches; in Death Valley its height is closer to 6 or 8 inches. The fan-shaped leaves are from 1 to 2 inches wide, quite round and toothed. The fivespot may be seen along the roadside in Death Valley, as well as in several desert washes. This is one of those "bellyflowers," best seen by crawling over the ground on your stomach.

Mojave Aster
Machaeranthera tortifolia
Growing on dry rocky slopes and in washes, this fragile plant with a delicate pastel flower grows to a height of about 2 feet, with several gray stems growing out of a woody base. Although there are leaves along the stems, the stem ends are reserved for the 2-inch-wide flower heads that are a very pale lavender or violet color. The leaves, covered with gray hairs, are about 1 inch long with teeth on the edges and a little spine at the leaf tip. Its range is from the Death Valley region to southwestern Utah and western Arizona. A relative, the Big Bend aster

(*M. wrightii*), is seen in western Texas and Mexico.

Goldfields
Lasthenia californica
One of the smallest members of the sunflower family, goldfields have a daisy-like flower with a large yellow center and yellow petals. Because the flowers are very tiny (it's another bellyflower), you may miss a plant that's standing alone. However, most goldfields are seen by the thousands or millions, presenting a carpet of finely spun gold. The plant is seen from southern Oregon to Arizona, and across California. It requires considerable rain to activate the seeds, which lie dormant for several years until the proper climate conditions awaken them. It grows quickly and blooms early, the seeds maturing and dropping to the ground before the really hot weather arrives. The plant grows at elevations under 3,500 feet.

BAKER, CALIFORNIA

Bun Boy Motel

I-15 and State Route 127
P.O. Box 130
Baker, CA 92309
(619) 733-4363

There's not much to choose from in this small desert town. In fact, the Bun Boy is just about it, but it's a good launching point for a trip to Death Valley. This is a standard motel beside the I-15, with showers, TV, and a 24-hour restaurant with all-night room service ($).

BEATTY, NEVADA

Exchange Club Motel

P.O. Box 97
Beatty, NV 89003
(702) 553-2333

Easily found on U.S. Highway 95, this basic motel has 44 units (one with whirlpool bath), a coin laundry, and 24-hour coffee shop. There's also a small casino here ($ to $$).

Burro Inn

P.O. Box 7
Beatty, NV 89003
(702) 553-2225

Just south of the main part of town—at Third Street on U.S. 95—the Burro Inn has 62 rooms, laundry, a 24-hour cafe, lounge, and casino ($).

Beatty Camping

The town has several private RV parks, one at the **Burro Inn** (see above). There are 42 sites here, with hookups, laundry, and a casino to attract or distract you. For reservations, call (702) 553-2225 or 800-843-2078. **Bailey's Hot Springs**, 6 miles north of Beatty, has 14 sites with hookups as well as swimming—(702) 553-2395. The largest RV park in the area is the **Rio Rancho RV Park**, with 58 sites (including hookups), laundry, and playground. For reservations, call (702) 553-2238 or 800-448-4423.

DEATH VALLEY JUNCTION, CALIFORNIA

Amargosa Motel

Death Valley Junction, CA 92328
(619) 852-4441

This stark white motel is just about the only remaining relic in what used to be a larger town—when the borax mines were active in the area. The famed Amargosa Opera House is part of the motel, and staying in a motel room gets you a ticket to one of Marta Becket's performances, which run from mid-October through early May ($).

Ash Meadows National Wildlife Refuge is a desert oasis and wetland in Nevada, protecting 26 plant or animal species that are seen nowhere else in the world. The refuge, located 7 miles from Death Valley Junction, contains 12,736 acres of desert uplands and wetlands.

DEATH VALLEY NATIONAL PARK

Furnace Creek Ranch Resort
P.O. Box 1
Death Valley, CA 92328
(619) 786-2345 or 800-528-6367

This year-round ranch resort with deluxe motel and connected cabin-style units is located at the palm oasis next to the park headquarters on State Route 190. There is a golf course, tennis courts, riding, archery range, large pool, saunas, and whirlpool. The complex includes the fascinating Borax Museum, and you can buy dates fresh off the palms. The ranch has several restaurants including a cafeteria and coffee shop. Deposit required ($$ to $$$).

Furnace Creek Inn
P.O. Box 1
Death Valley, CA 92328
(619) 786-2361

This Spanish mission-style resort hotel is perched on a hillside overlooking the depths of Death Valley. Palms shading the garden terrace help it retain some of the ambience of an earlier era. There are 67 rooms, a heated pool, saunas, whirlpool, and lighted tennis courts. Not open during the torrid summer months, the inn is just the place for winter socializing with visitors from around the world. There are two dining rooms. The Sunday brunch is a Death Valley tradition ($$$+).

Stovepipe Wells Village
Death Valley, CA 92328
(619) 786-2387

A quasi-rustic resort complex near the sand dunes, 24 miles from the ranch on State Route 190. There are 82 units with full baths and shower units, a hot spring pool, store, and service station. The restaurant and bar are open from 7 A.M. to 2 P.M. and from 5:30 P.M. to 9 P.M. ($$).

SHOSHONE, CALIFORNIA

Shoshone Inn and RV Park
P.O. Box 67
Shoshone, CA 92384
(619) 852-4335 or 852-4224

This standard motel, the only one in this tiny village, has

24 rooms. There is also a warm pool, fed by a natural spring ($).

The motel management also operates an RV and trailer park. A cafe, bar, and general store are nearby. The Shoshone Museum was first built in Greenwater as a hospital, then became the town's first general store and gas station.

TECOPA HOT SPRINGS, CALIFORNIA

You wouldn't think anyone would haul a large trailer to a remote desert location, more than a 90-minute drive from the nearest large town, and stay for the winter in a landscape devoid of normal vegetation. This is one of the oddest places to stay in the nation, but every winter hundreds do stay here. The hot springs and a county campground (at the southern edge of the Amargosa Desert) attract these sunbirds with their trailers. The hamlet of Tecopa, 2 miles down the loop road, has a small store and saloon.

Inyo County Hot Springs Campground

For information, write or call:

Tecopa Hot Springs Park
P.O. Box 158
Tecopa, CA 92389
(619) 852-4262

The campground, across the road from the two public bathhouses that are fed from the springs, covers 40 acres. Some of the 362 sites have electrical hookups. The maximum stay is nine months. The park facilities include showers and a community center that offers a wide range of social activities such as exercise and dance classes, lectures, game nights, and movies. Part of the winter ambience is the busy social schedule (most of the "residents" are seniors), including potluck dinners and arts and crafts classes. The park has horseshoe pits, a picnic site with ramadas and barbecue pits, and an outdoor dance area. Bathing in the hot pools is free. There's a store and tavern in Tecopa. The community is 5 miles south of Shoshone, 3 miles off U.S. Highway 127.

Las Vegas is 100 miles away. The southern entrance to Death Valley is to the north, as is Death Valley Junction.

Saguaro National Park

Deserts mean different things to different people. Some scientists think of a desert as a place that has low rainfall and high evaporation, with soil consisting of various particle sizes to permit enough water to soak into the sand to allow plants to grow. Others believe a true desert is a dry, warm, breeze-drenched landscape that is host to myriad unique plants, mammals, birds, and amphibians.

Those who begin to fall for the desert in an emotional way soon realize that the deserts of North America and the world are marvelously varied in both their physical characteristics and in the plants and wildlife that inhabit them. These mysterious, silent landscapes must have been created for their spiritual value. They are places we can contemplate our existence outside our normal living environment; places we can walk in quiet solitude and discover the true person.

Having grown up on the northern Precambrian Shield in the midst of lakes, under spruce and pine forests, I experience a psychic shock every time I explore a Southwest desert, which is often. Nowhere else can a person walk into a micro-environment, stand and observe the small circle of life, and hear one's own heartbeat. Occasionally, one can hear the faint sounds of the desert—breezes whistling through the shrubs, a cactus fruit dropping to the ground, and perhaps the skittering of a tiny lizard or the soft thumping of a furtive rabbit. Tiny sounds seem amplified in the overwhelming silence of the desert landscape.

I have seen "accidental" deserts, in Canada of all places. There's a pocket desert in the southern Yukon Territory, a small area of dunes where strong winds, a freakish lack of rain and snow, and results of glacial scrapings have created a deposit of sand so dry that the few trees growing there are severely stunted. There's another, slightly hotter desert in southern British Columbia—a finger of dryness poking northward from the Great Basin. But it is the hot, arid Sonoran desert that really captures my imagination.

Lying south of the Great Basin and Mojave deserts, most of the Sonoran Desert is in Mexico. The northern portion is found in southeastern California and Arizona, contained in what is known as the Basin and Range Province, a vast low-lying area of 106,000 square miles, punctuated by a few small mountain ranges—sky islands. The Mexican Highland region stretches from the southeastern corner of California across the middle of Arizona, south of the Mogollon Rim, and into the southwestern corner of New Mexico. The Arizona Uplands subregion covers the area around Tucson.

Sonoran Climate

One thinks of the low desert as being unalterably dry. Yet the Sonoran Desert surrounding Tucson has abundant plant life— saguaro and other cacti, many varieties of shrubs, palo verde trees, and wildflowers. Because of the seasonal changes in weather patterns, winter storms move from the southwest across the Gulf of California, washing the desert with almost daily late-summer rainfall. Unlike the Chihuahuan Desert to the west, the Sonoran desert areas receive some winter rains, although they differ from the summer storms in their longevity and lower intensity. The summer rains are heavier and shorter, propelled by convective thunderstorms. Unlike Death Valley, which receives no rainfall at all in some years, the Tucson region can always count on its share of life-giving rain, beginning in late July or early August.

Summers are scorchingly hot in the north Sonoran Desert. Altitude and latitude both have a role in determining summer and winter temperatures in Tucson. The summer heat is achingly dry. Winters are very different, when the evening thunderstorms bring high humidity along with temperatures that can be well over 100 degrees Fahrenheit. These are the times to dive into an air-conditioned building, although you won't want to miss the desert smells following a thunderstorm.

Summer temperatures in Tucson are surprisingly comfortable, permitting long walks in the surrounding desert (as long as sufficient water is carried to counteract the fast evaporation rate). Evaporation is what makes the hot desert experience more comfortable than a hike in a more northern, more humid environment. Yet, as moisture evaporating from the human skin makes the desert fairly comfortable, the heat can be hard on desert plants. And this is what leads to the survival of only a few distinctive species that have either the ability to switch into a dormant state or the water-storage capacity to beat the dry heat. The saguaro is a fine example of the latter. Fog and dew also play a part in sustaining desert plants over the long hot summer.

Plant and Animal Life

The Arizona Uplands are also known as the Palo Verde Cacti Desert. It is characterized by the two largest forms of cacti, saguaro and organ pipe. There are many smaller cacti in the uplands, and this small part of the Sonoran Desert has the most diverse collection of cacti in the world. Cholla, prickly pear with its flat paddles, and barrel cacti are all seen in abundance and sometimes all together in a magnificent display. The cacti are often seen in the company of shrubs, ranging from the ubiquitous creosote bush, to bur sage, brittlebush, and ocotillo.

The dominant tree is the foothill (blue) palo verde, which grows along the sides of the desert washes that ripple across the Sonoran landscape. The ironwood and acacia are also widespread. Less numerous but noticeable plants include jojoba, desert buckwheat, and limber bush. Palo verde, the state plant of Arizona, is often seen with other desert wash inhabitants such as desert brook, burrobush, and desert willow. You'll see the wash trees and plants along the roadsides of the Tucson region, where the ditches gather enough water to foster willow and palo verde growth.

Saguaro is king of the Sonoran Desert. Growing mostly on hillsides and bajadas—alluvial fans anywhere else—the tall cacti dominate the landscape and provide homes for animals and birds, including the elf owl. While there are stands of saguaro as far north as the Phoenix area, they are at their most splendorous in the southern part of the state, particularly in the Tucson area. The federal government has protected two of the most significant saguaro forests in Saguaro National Park. The two sites flank the city of Tucson on its east and west sides. It is here that we explore the full range of plant and animal life seen on the Arizona Uplands.

Most desert visitors set out with a fear of spiders and scorpions. To be sure, these creatures are here in quantity—after a rainstorm, tarantulas appear by the thousands. However, these fearsome-looking spiders are not nearly as dangerous as they look; and when they do bite, on very infrequent occasions, their sting has less effect than a honeybee's. Although scorpions leave people alone unless harassed, caution is still advised should you meet one. I have never heard that any acquaintance of mine actually suffered a scorpion sting.

The spiders are joined on the ground by beetles, termites, flies, and wasps, most showing brilliant colors. On the other hand, the resident grasshopper is so subtly colored as to be almost invisible. This is the Green Valley grasshopper, a large specimen whose green coloration blends perfectly with the leaves of the palo verde and willow trees.

The different species of lizards and other amphibians are surprisingly few. Only six species of toads are commonly seen, along with a dozen varieties of lizard, including the tubby chuckwalla, iguana, and Gila monster. The desert tortoise is the only one of its family living in the region. Snakes are more profuse, with twenty-one desert species in the Tucson area. The sidewinder of Death Valley is present here, along with five other rattlesnakes, plus the boa constrictor and fourteen other non-poisonous species.

While the Sonoran desert has more than 250 identified bird species, fewer than twenty-five are known to breed in the region. The raptor clan is confined to two hawks (American kestrel and red-tailed hawk) and the turkey vulture. The common raven is everywhere, and acts as if it owns the desert. The elf and burrowing owls are the only native owls in the whole upland. Gnatcatchers and flycatchers are numerous, as are four species of thrasher, and four doves. The greater roadrunner and Gambel's quail are also on the list of natives.

The desert is a temporary home for many migratory birds, which stop in riparian areas during their journey along the interior flyway. You have to travel south from Tucson to the Santa Cruz watershed to see most of the temporary residents in a cottonwood/willow habitat. When on the desert floor, the black-throated sparrow, roadrunner, and cactus wren may be the only birds you'll see on or near the ground. Fortunately, the nearby mountains and park areas are home to songbirds and woodpeckers.

Coyote and bighorn sheep are the largest of the mammal population. Most desert animals are very small and drought-tolerant, particularly the many varieties of rabbits, mice, and rats that live on the desert floor—at the base of saguaro and other plants, or in nests under rocks. Four species of squirrel are found here (round-tailed ground, rock, white-tailed antelope, and Harris' antelope). Many of these small animals are more likely to be seen at night, also a time when the kit fox, collared peccary, and badger come out to look for something to eat.

When starting a Sonoran vacation, the best place to visit first is the superb Arizona–Sonoran Desert Museum, located in Tucson Mountain Park west of the city. This zoological park exhibits not only native animals and birds of the region, but also has native plants in habitat displays (see page 324).

Saguaro National Park

Some of Arizona's finest stands of the saguaro cactus are found in the two sections of the Saguaro National Park that flank the east and the west of the city. The larger (and older) saguaro forest is located east of town at the end of Old Spanish Trail in the Rincon Mountains. The western site, just north of Tucson Mountain Park and the Arizona–Sonora Desert Museum, features a younger stand of saguaro, most of it in a bajada (sloping alluvial fan) environment. The preserve areas were known as Saguaro National Monument until October 1994, when it was upgraded to full national park status, thanks to federal legislation that included the California Desert Protection Act.

The park areas are at the east and west sides of the Santa Cruz River Valley, and each is set on the western side of a mountain range. The eastern site sits on the Rincon Mountains; the western site on the Tucson Mountains. Differences in the base elevation and the height of the two mountain ranges affect the age and size of the saguaro and results in the presence of somewhat different plants and animals at each site. The western (Tucson Mountain) site sits at an elevation of 2,200 feet, while the eastern (Rincon Mountain) portion is at 2,700 feet. This difference of several hundred feet means that wildlife like the Steller's jay and white-tailed deer are seen only in the Rincon portion of the park.

Additional factors influence the growth of saguaro and other desert plants in the two sites. During the long period (late 1800s to 1958), when cattle grazing was permitted in the Rincon Mountain section, much of the lower saguaro forest near the visitor center was trampled to extinction or damaged by other grazing practices. What is visible is a stand of aging cacti, unless one looks closely. This portion of the park is actually in a state of recovery. Since cattle left the park, thousands of young saguaro have germinated and the saguaro forest will, one day, look much as it did a hundred years ago.

Saguaro East, which has been less disturbed, is a saguaro forest at full throttle. Rising on the slopes of an alluvial fan, the tall saguaro stand with other, smaller cacti and desert bushes, in a typical open desert environment that includes a wide range of desert animals. Visiting the two portions of the national park offers unique insight into the fragile nature of deserts, and illustrates what we must do to ensure that such superb examples of desert ecosystems are protected from our instinctive desire to use land for human benefit only. The protection of the areas as a national park is an appropriate response to mistakes of an earlier age.

SAGUARO WEST

This portion of the national monument is located north of Tucson Mountain Park on Kinney Road, in the vicinity of the Old Tucson Studios (theme park) and the Arizona–Sonora Desert Museum. The easiest way to get to Saguaro West from downtown Tucson is to drive west from town on Speedway Boulevard. The road becomes Gates Pass Boulevard, then crosses the Tucson Mountains.

Turn right onto Kinney Road, and you'll find the park a 2-minute drive from the intersection. From the south, the route into Tucson Mountain Park is via Ajo Way (Highway 86) and Kinney Road.

Native Americans lived in the valley below the park for at least 8,000 years. Petroglyphs carved into the rock at the Signal Hill Picnic Area are reminders of these early inhabitants. Later, the Hohokam people grew vegetable crops—corn and beans—and irrigated the desert valley. The Hohokam are considered the ancestors of the present-day Tohono O'odham.

Saguaro West is much more a desert biotic zone than is its eastern counterpart. The base is low, and the areas that rise to the mountains are gravel bajadas. The mountain ridges are dry, rocky barrens, with no vegetation. A small grassland transition zone is found at the southeastern corner of the park, in an area not traversed by roads. This transition zone—from 3,500 feet to 4,500 feet—does not contain any saguaro, but is sparsely covered with low shrubs and yucca. The lower areas are a typical desert scrub environment, full of great numbers of saguaro and cacti. In the lower elevations, the ironwood, with its grayish-blue leaves, is a common tree. It does not occur farther west. The palo verde is also present. In the winter and spring, brittlebush shrubs come into bloom with masses of yellow flowers. From February to May, many flowering shrubs and wildflowers provide a variety of colors, although less in this section of the park than in many other locations. Plants that do bloom here include desert marigold and desert chicory.

Animal life differs somewhat according to the elevation. The desert rodents live at the bottom, among the cacti and under the saguaro. Coyote and javelina are seen in the lower zone, along with mice, gophers, snakes, and desert rats. Others, including the gray fox and great horned owl, live in all three zones. A year-round resident at lower levels is the noisy desert thrasher. This native bird, about the size of a robin, lives amongst the mesquite and cholla, feeding on insects and fruit. Gambel's quail is widely seen, as are roadrunners dashing along the desert washes, picking up insects and spiders, seeds, fruit, and even small lizards. The gilded flicker and Gila woodpecker are often seen close to the saguaro they live in. These carpenter birds drill nests into the stems of the cactus with their sharp, hard bills. After the woodpeckers leave to peck a new home, the elf owl moves into the cavities, called shoes or boots.

Mourning doves are year-round residents. Inca doves are also seen here regularly. The rock wren and house finch have their nests in the protected spaces within thickets of mesquite and cholla cactus.

Desert animals are often seen in the vicinity of the visitor center. Other park wildlife includes the abundant kangaroo rat, gopher and coachwhip snakes, the diamondback, javelina (the collared peccary), and varieties of birds including quail, Gila woodpeckers (which live in the saguaro), and several species of thrasher. There are two garden areas featuring native desert plants, with interpretive trails close to the visitor center.

Longer trails lead into the foothills, where there are several old mine sites, and higher up the mountainsides. Camping is not permitted in this section of the park. Located near the park gate, the Red Hills Information Center is open daily, offering guided walks during winter months, as well as books and brochures on the park attractions. With a scenic drive through the saguaro forest and several hiking trails available, a day passes quickly.

Bajada Loop Drive The 6-mile Bajada Loop Drive passes through thick forests of saguaro, interspersed with other cacti and desert bushes. This graded unpaved road begins half a mile from the information center and leads in a counterclockwise direction (although portions of the road have two-way traffic). The Valley View Trail provides a 0.75 mile (one-way) walk to a viewpoint where the Avra Valley stretches before you.

The loop road continues until it meets Golden Gate Road near Apache Peak. Turn left, and you'll soon see a sign for the Signal Hill Picnic Area. This area was used by the prehistoric Hohokam people—probably the ancestors of the Tohono O'odham Indians. Their petroglyphs are found on rocks near the picnic area. The loop drive continues via Kinney Road, returning to the starting point, with the visitor center another 2 miles on. Near the beginning of the route is the Sus picnic area.

SAGUARO WEST TRAILS

Cactus Garden Trail This short interpretive trail is situated beside the visitor center, following a level (wheelchair-accessible) walkway. The garden features a collection of native plants. Taking a short stroll through the cactus garden will help you identify plants before you set out to fully explore the park.

Discovery Nature Trail   A circular loop located a half-mile past the visitor center, this trail also follows a level path for a half-mile at the downward edge of the Tucson Mountain bajadas.

Valley View Overlook Trail   To reach the trailhead for this scenic trail, drive along the one-way route of the Bajada Loop Drive. The trail is to the left of the road, off a parking lot. It offers a 1.5-mile round-trip with fine views of the desert, saguaros, and mountain ridges. The valleys of this area are thought to have been created not by the thrusting of the mountains but by the sinking of the land between the ranges. You'll get a good feel for this theory by looking down at the Avra Valley, which lies below the trail. As the mountains eroded, creating the huge bajadas, the fill covered the valley. You'll be able to see Baboquivari, the mountain to the south that is sacred to the Tohono O'odham. Also to the south are the Quinlan Mountains, identified by the domes of Kitt Peak National Observatory. To the north are the Silverbell Mountains and Picacho Peak.

Hugh Norris Trail   Backcountry hiking across desert ridges is the prime feature of this longer trail, which departs from the early stretch of the Bajada Loop Drive. To the east of the road, the trail leads across the ridges of the Tucson Mountains, with access to Amole Peak and Watson Peak (4,587 feet). At the halfway point, the Norris Trail intersects.

Sendero Esperanza Trail   This connects the Ez-kim-in-zin picnic site (to the north) with King Canyon Trail (to the southwest). The Hugh Norris Trail continues in a southeasterly direction, meeting two other trails. The Sweetwater Trail leads east, along a wash, toward Tucson. The King Canyon Trail heads southwest along another wash, intersecting Kinney Road at the park boundary, near the Arizona–Sonora Desert Museum. Trail leaflets are available from the rangers in the Red Hills Information Center.

Saguaro East

The topography of the Rincon Mountains division of Saguaro National Park holds a very different mix of biotic zones from that of the western site. While Saguaro West is primarily desert, with some grassland, the eastern section has a desert base at the lowest elevations near the park entrance. A band of transitional grassland follows at a slightly higher level, changing into an upland oak woodland characterized by stands of oaks placed well apart with grasses and thickets of bushes—a typical oak chaparral zone. Another transition zone continues the oak woodland, adding stands of pinyon pine. This "pygmy" woodland features small trees of both types decorated with standing rock formations.

At higher elevations is a large forest of ponderosa pine—without oaks—covering most of the mountain ridges. A Douglas fir forest sits on top of the highest mountains, forming a circle around Rincon Peak and Mica Mountain, both located in this large park section. The defining geological feature is Tanque Verde Ridge, which runs across the park from southwest to northeast.

The variation in elevation, and the cooler temperatures and additional moisture that nurture plant communities, brings many animals and birds not found in the western site. Species that are more common in northern regions are found here: Steller's and scrub jays, deer, skunks, ringtails, and raccoons. Coatimundi and javelina are seen in the Rincon Mountains, usually in large groups. Most of Saguaro West is not accessible by road. Backcountry hiking is required to climb into the mountain areas.

Ranger-led programs are offered during winter months. There is a visitor center that includes a shop with books and park guides for sale, plus a slide show about the saguaro, the Sonoran Desert, and its wildlife.

Cactus Forest Drive   This 8-mile, one-way loop road winds through the extensive, aging saguaro forest, at the park's lowest level. The loop begins near the park visitor center and leads in a clockwise direction. Side roads lead off the loop route to picnic areas at Mica View (near the start) and Javelina (near the end of the loop). For those who wish to have a walk through the saguaro, a trail leads from the north side of the loop (past the Mica View road) to the visitor center. You'll see trailheads beside the road.

SAGUARO EAST DAY HIKES

Desert Ecology Trail   This short interpretive trail is located off Cactus Forest Drive. The trail is a paved quarter-mile path that is wheelchair-accessible. Signs along the way illustrate how water is used by the animals and plants of the desert. Situated beside a wide wash, the trail provides several opportunities for venturing into the wash during the dry spring and fall months, and into adjacent desert areas to observe the rich plant life of this lowland area. Visitors in the rainy months should beware of the power of water as it can suddenly fill, and sometimes race down, the washes.

Freeman Homestead Nature Trail   There is a two-way section of the Cactus Forest Loop Road (leading to the Javelina Picnic Area), from which one starts along this one-mile interpretive loop. The trail descends, gradually, from the typical desert land to a sandy wash and climbs back to the trailhead.

BACKCOUNTRY TRAILS

This section of the park is perfect for longer hikes, with more than 75 miles of trails leading through the desert and mountain landscape. Several longer hiking trails climb into the mountains, where the landscape changes from desert scrub and grassland to oak and pine woodlands and—at the top—to a mixed evergreen forest. Backcountry camping is permitted, but only at designated campsites, and permits must be obtained at the visitor center in advance of an overnight trip.

Cactus Forest Trail   The shortest of the backcountry trails, an easy half-day hike, this trail leads in two directions from the visitor center area. The most popular part of the trail lies between the visitor center and the northern part of the Cactus Forest Loop Road. Should one member of your party be willing to drive to that point, there's no need to walk back to the visitor center. The more southern section of this trail leads to the park boundary at Old Spanish Trail—another opportunity to have a car sent to save you time and energy (something you might wish to conserve on a hot summer day).

Tanque Verde Ridge Trail   This long backcountry route is extendible by continuing on the Cow Head Saddle Trail and the North Slope Trail. As the trail names suggest, this combined hike will take you from the vicinity of the Cactus Forest Loop Road, all the way across the park, crossing the Rincon Mountains on the Tanque Verde Ridge. Horses are not permitted on this trail. A backcountry campsite is located at Juniper Basin, about 6 miles along the ridge.

The combined three trails continue in a northeast direction to Tanque Verde Peak (2,148 feet) and farther up the mountain range past the peak of Mica Mountain at 8,666 feet. There is a network of intersecting trails atop the mountain range, and it is possible to spend a week or more in this varied landscape of mountain peaks and creek valleys. Manning Camp, with a ranger station and campground, is located about a mile south of where Cow Head Saddle Trail meets the North Slope Trail. The campground is a departure point for other trails including the Heartbreak Ridge Trail, which leads south, and the East Slope Trail, which forms a loop with access to Spud Rock Spring and the Spud Rock backcountry campground.

Douglas Spring Trail   Leading to the higher reaches of the Rincon Range, this trail is reached by hiking the Tanque Verde Trail past the Juniper Basin Campground to Cow Head Saddle. The Douglas Spring Trail leads north and south from the saddle. Running north, it moves up a drainage system to Douglas Spring and then turns west, running near the northern edge of the park. South of Cow Head Saddle, it leads beside Chiminea Canyon, passing the Madrona ranger station. It connects with the Rincon Creek Trail, which leads east to a campground at Happy Valley Saddle and the intersection with the Heartbreak Ridge Trail.

Rincon Creek Trail   This trail starts at the Madrona ranger station, in the south-central portion of the park, heading east to Happy Valley Saddle (campground) turning south.

Rincon Peak Trail   Starting just east of Happy Valley Saddle, this trail climbs to Rincon Peak, ending at an elevation of 8,482 feet.

Because many of these trails (and several others) intersect one another, it is possible to plan an extensive backcountry adventure. Horseback riding is permitted on all trails except the Tanque Verde Ridge Trail, Rincon Peak Trail and Miller Creek Trail (which leads from the Happy Valley Saddle area, past the eastern park boundary). Camping is permitted only at designated sites and permits must be obtained at the park visitor center in advance of overnight trips.

The most comfortable time to visit the park, and expend a lot of energy, is from October through April. Daytime temperatures are usually in the 60s and 70s. Nighttime temperatures may fall to 30 degrees F. at lower levels, and into the 20s at the higher mountain areas. There are two rainy seasons in the Sonoran Desert. Thunderous monsoon storms scour the region from late July through September. Gentler rains fall from January to March.

Nearby Attractions

Tucson Mountain Park

Much of the Tucson Mountain range is included in this county park, which features stands of saguaro and other desert plants. There are picnic areas, hiking and riding trails, and a campground. The park is 8 miles west of the downtown district via Speedway Boulevard. There is no entrance fee. The park is reached by taking Speedway west from Tucson, north of the downtown district. From the south end of the city, take State Route 86 west from Interstate 19 and turn north on Kinney Road.

Inside the park is one of the finest wildlife museums in the country, the Arizona–Sonora Desert Museum. More than two hundred species of desert animals and birds are housed in realistic settings, and the museum includes pathways that connect habitat-based botanical gardens filled with desert plants. There's a fine picnic area sheltered with ramadas, in addition to two restaurants, a snack bar, and gift shop. For information, call (602) 883-2702.

Old Tucson, a Wild West theme park used by many studios for filming movies, TV series, and commercials, burned to the ground in a spectacular nighttime fire in April 1995. The false-fronted streets of Old Tucson had long been a favorite family attraction. Check to see if the attraction has reopened. It is located near the museum in Tucson Mountain Park.

Sentinel Peak

The finest panoramic views of the city and surrounding mountains are seen from several vista points on top of the peak called "A" Mountain for the whitewashed "A" provided by students at the University of Arizona. In earlier days, settlers posted a sentinel on the peak to watch for approaching Native Americans. To see the views (spectacular day or night), drive 2 miles west of the city on Congress Street and take Sentinel Peak Road. The road loops around the mountain.

SABINO CANYON

This superb area of forest-clad mountains sits northeast of the city, offering several recreation areas that include campgrounds. Narrow Sabino Canyon has a marvelous display of desert vegetation beside a creek that cascades down the hills of the Catalina Mountains in the Coronado National Forest. You can easily spend a day in the canyon, particularly if you are a hiker or walker. To get there, take Tanque Verde Road from the city and turn onto Sabino Canyon Road. Visitors park next to the visitor center. From here, you walk, cycle, or ride a horse or tram into the canyon.

Sabino Dam, built in 1937 as a New Deal project, is a short walk from the visitor center. The dam holds back Sabino Creek, and in dry months it is not a spectacular sight. Wintry weather increases the flow of the creek and water often cascades over the dam, turning to white water below. To visit the dam, take the path to Bear Canyon Road from the canyon parking lot, then take the Lower Sabino path at a fork.

I prefer exploring the canyon in the late afternoon and into the dark hours. This is when the javelina herds run around—best seen in the dam area—and when other wildlife shake off their hot-weather stupor. Of all the times of year to visit the canyon, the wet months provide the most exciting experiences, when the creek is flowing briskly and the cool temperatures permit the birds and other wildlife to appear in the daytime hours. Being in the canyon when a storm occurs is a wonderful Sonoran Desert experience.

A shuttle tram operates on a half-hourly schedule. The main road within the canyon park is closed to vehicular traffic, except for the tram, for which a fee is charged. It runs from the visitor center at the park entrance, up the canyon beside the creek, for a round-trip of 7.6 miles. There are picnic areas and swimming places along the paved roadway. A variety of trails offer recreation for hikers of all levels.

Paved Road   The easiest hike in the canyon is along the road-way that is used by the tram. Since this is the most popular walking place in the park, daytime crowds may be too much for a dedicated hiker. It does have the advantage of passing several picnic and rest areas.

Phoneline Trail   This maintained trail provides a 9-mile round-trip from the visitor center, past the Sabino Dam, and through the canyon to the north end of the paved road. The trail leads along a ledge which perches about 400 feet above the floor of the canyon. It's an easy walk, but offers some thrilling moments when the ledge narrows against the high rock walls, with the canyon lying far below. You have a good chance of seeing white-tailed deer along this trail. There is always the option of catching the next tram back to the park entrance.

Saddleback Trail   A shorter walk, with a steep climb, Saddleback Trail is found a short distance up Phoneline Trail, from whence it veers slightly to the east, climbing to the top of a saddle (4,400 feet) that separates Sabino and Bear canyons. There are excellent views of Tucson from a dizzying height. The city is about 1,500 feet below the trail.

Hutch's Pool Trail   This trail starts where the paved road and the Phoneline Trail end. It continues up the canyon to an elevation of 4,000 feet, where you'll find an old-fashioned swimming hole. The round-trip from the end of the tram ride is 7.2 miles. The trail passes through two biotic zones as it gains elevation.

The entrance to the canyon, the parking lot, and the visitor center are at the corner of Sunrise Drive and Sabino Canyon Road, in the northeastern corner of Tucson. For information on trails in this and other national forest lands, call the Santa Catalina Ranger District at (520) 749-8700.

MT. LEMMON RECREATION AREA

There's an exciting driving tour available in this same area, leading to and through the eastern part of the Mt. Lemmon Recreation Area. A paved road climbs the Catalina Mountains to the 9,000-foot level, through a range of ecological regions— from cactus scrubland to mixed conifer forest. Turnouts near the top offer fine views of the basin and city. There are picnic areas, campgrounds, and hiking trails along the route, and skiing is available during winter months. To get there, drive east from the city on Broadway Boulevard and take Catalina Highway, which soon becomes General Hitchcock Highway.

As the road climbs along the eastern side of the Catalina Mountains in the Coronado National Forest, it provides access to campgrounds in Rose Canyon. You'll find a picnic area at the end of the campground road, as well as a park amphitheater offering nature interpretation programs. The road continues to climb, with a back road leading off to the east to Bear Wallow campsites, a picnic area, and the Mount Bigelow Lookout Tower.

The road climbs toward the peak of Mt. Lemmon, offering more camping and additional picnic areas. At any of these points are fine vistas. The route ends at Lemmon Park, an area surrounded by mountain springs. Hiking trails and four-wheel-drive roads lead from the park into the adjacent wilderness area. A sizable community, known as Summerhaven, is also found atop the mountain. Mt. Lemmon is a year-round destination. When backpackers cease hiking in the late fall, skiers arrive. This is the location of a popular downhill ski area.

PUSCH RIDGE WILDERNESS

As the General Hitchcock Highway curves and switches back across the slopes of Mt. Lemmon, it passes the boundaries of the Pusch Ridge Wilderness: 56,933 acres of protected forest lying at elevations between 3,000 feet and 9,000 feet. This is an area of canyons and ridges, with biotic zones ranging from Upper Sonoran to Alpine. Sabino Canyon runs the entire length of the wilderness area, in a general north/south direction.

While ponderosa pine blankets most of the slopes, the upper area is covered with a Douglas fir and aspen forest. The difference in vegetation is striking, and it all depends on the rainfall. While about 11 inches of rain falls yearly at the lowest level, the upper zones receives more than 30 inches in most years. The abundant runoff is what makes the viewing of the falls at Sabino Dam so interesting during stormy months.

You may access trails from various points outside the wilderness area boundaries, including the General Hitchcock Highway that leads to the top of Mt. Lemmon. Two trails climb into the wilderness from the Sabina Canyon park area, including a long backcountry trail (#23), which begins at the end of the paved Sabino Canyon road and climbs up the canyon, almost to Mt. Lemmon's peak. Another (trail #29) begins at the lower part of Bear Canyon, at the end of unpaved Forest Road 100A. This trail climbs from the 2,800-foot level to about 4,600 feet, where it joins Trail #339 and continues the climb to Sycamore Reservoir following East Fork Sabino Canyon. It meets the trail that starts at the bottom of the Sabino Canyon.

CATALINA STATE PARK

Several wilderness trails are accessed from Catalina State Park on the west side of Mt. Lemmon. A major trail from the park descends through Romero Canyon. Another trail uses Cargodera Canyon, leading east in an area just north of the wilderness area boundary (but still in the national forest) before reentering the wilderness preserve. The state park is reached by taking U.S. Highway 89 north from Tucson. The park entrance is north of the community of Oro Valley.

In addition to providing access to the Pusch Wilderness, this large park offers picnicking, hiking, camping, horseback riding, and wildlife viewing. Riders may bring their horses into the park in trailers to a staging area. The park encompasses more than 5,500 acres of prime Catalina Mountains desert and forest land.

PICACHO PEAK STATE PARK

The peak rises abruptly to a height of 1,500 feet above the desert floor. This is the best place in the Tucson area to see wildflowers in the spring. After winter rains have fallen, the slopes of the park are covered with blankets of colorful flowers. At any time of year the park features picnicking, camping, and nature trails, including one that leads to the peak's summit. There are 34 tent and trailer sites in the campground. The park is located north of Tucson via Interstate 10.

TOHONO CHUL PARK

This wonderful botanical park was the gift of Richard and Jean Wilson, who donated the property to be used as a nonprofit public park. When the property was first developed, it lay in the open desert north of the downtown Tucson area. It was the estate and winter residence of a prominent eastern family. Organized as an educational establishment, the park exists to give the public an opportunity to experience the wealth of native desert plants, and to study the minimum use of water for landscaping—as a way of developing arid regions. It has been open since 1985.

It is a living natural history museum, with trails that wind through a natural desert environment. The historic Exhibit House, an original adobe building, has displays in a gallery-like atmosphere. The galleries include collections of southwestern painting, sculpture, and crafts. A landscaping library can be accessed for research and reference purposes. The Park Greenhouse has a variety of native and other arid plants for sale. The Ethnobotanical Garden focuses on the ways in which Southwest Native Americans used water for irrigation and adapted the plants for their purposes. A weather station is located next to this garden.

Although it is now in a large urban area, the park attracts desert animals. The desert tortoise lives here, and other animals—such as rabbits, foxes, and coyotes—live in or visit the park. Docents lead bird-watching tours through gardens planted to attract hummingbirds and other species. Picnic areas are covered by ramadas for shady box-lunching. A tea room and cafe are located in a lovely Spanish Colonial courtyard, where breakfast, lunch, and afternoon tea are served. There is a suggested entry donation of $2. The park grounds are open daily from 7 A.M. to sunset. Exhibit house is open from 9:30 A.M. to 5 P.M. Monday through Saturday, and from 11 A.M. to 5 P.M. on Sundays. The Tea Room is open daily from 8 A.M. to 5 P.M. For park information, call (602) 742-6455.

TUCSON BOTANICAL GARDENS

Located at 2150 North Alvernon Way, the botanical park features a Tucson-area garden, tropical greenhouse, and displays of iris, herbs, and wildflowers, as well as North American vegetables. There's an admission fee, and the gardens are open daily from 8:30 A.M. to 4 P.M. (520-326-9255).

ORGAN PIPE CACTUS NATIONAL MONUMENT

All of the wonders of the Sonoran Desert are on display in this reserve comprised of mountains and flatlands at the Mexican border southwest of Tucson. The park is renowned for the variety of desert plants that thrive here, including the eponymous cactus that is common in Mexico but found north of the border only here. The prime flowering time for the large upright cacti is May and June.

To reach the park from Tucson, drive west on Arizona Route 86. This highway leads 119 miles to the village of Why, with most of the drive spent in the Tohono O'odham Indian reservation. Turn south at Why onto Arizona Route 85. The park lies a few miles south of the village. For park information, write or call:

Superintendent,
Organ Pipe Cactus National Monument
Rt. 1, Box 100
Ajo, AZ 85321
(602) 387-6849

In addition to the organ pipe cactus, the monument has stands of saguaro, prickly pear, cholla, hedgehog, and barrel cacti (twenty six species of cacti), as well as ocotillo and several varieties of trees including palo verde and ironwood. Organ Pipe is unusual in that it contains two Sonoran Desert zones: Lower Colorado (hot and dry) and Arizona Upland (where most of the large cacti are found). Each area contains plants and harbors animals of its regions. In addition, the park has a few plant species that have migrated from Mexico and are not found elsewhere in U.S. desert regions. This unusual confluence of desert ecosystems makes the monument a special place indeed, and several days are required to fully explore the area.

The visitor center and other park services are located near the southern edge of the park, within sight of Mexico. Several shorter trails are in this area, with trailheads at the visitor center and at the campground. There are picnic areas on several of the park side roads, two of which offer extensive loop drives. The campground, located a few minutes' drive south of the visitor center, is open year-round. It has water, restrooms, grills, and a dump station. The park amphitheater is a short walk from the campsites. The short trails within this vicinity offer good desert walks with views of the nearby Ajo and Sonoyta mountain ranges.

The two maintained loop roads provide your best opportunity to fully explore the variety of plant and animal life in the park, as well as to catch some fine desert and foothills scenery.

Ajo Mountain Drive Skirting the foothills of the 4,000-foot high Ajo Mountains, this loop winds around the eastern side of the monument. This is where the best stands of organ pipe cactus grow, along with other plant varieties. After turning onto the side road, the drive leads around a one-way loop. There are three picnic areas along the drive. The first, in the hills, provides a view of Tillotson Peak (3,374-foot elevation). The second is located at Angel Canyon, the farthest point along the loop road. Next is the trailhead for the Estes Canyon–Bull Pasture Trail, with the third picnic area located across the road from the trailhead. The Ajo range is to the east, with the Diablo Mountains directly to the west of the picnic area. The road then leads across the Sonoyta Valley, returning to Highway 85.

Puerto Blanco Drive   This loop leads around the Puerto Blanco Mountains, providing a wide range of scenery along the 53-mile route. Plan for at least a half-day's drive, which should include a stop at a desert oasis (Quitobaquito Springs). This is a one-way gravel route beginning at the visitor center. After passing along the northern foothills of the mountain range, the road reaches the site of the former Golden Bell Mine. There's a picnic area at Bonito Well and the oasis here is a few feet from the international border. Puerto Blanco Drive continues east from the oasis, running beside the border to Highway 85.

Several easy and moderate hiking trails wind through Organ Pipe National Monument:

Palo Verde Trail   This easy walk leads between the campground and visitor center, a 1.3-mile (one-way) walk.

Visitor Center Trail   This 1-mile round-trip trail is wheelchair-accessible and offers visitors a self-guided introduction to the desert scene.

Perimeter Trail   This is a level mini-trail that circles the campground, forming a 1-mile loop.

Desert View Trail   Another loop trail leading from the campground, this trail leads west to views of the Sonoyta Valley and the Cubabi Mountains across the Mexican border.

Victoria Mine Trail   Offering a 4-mile round-trip walk, this trail runs to the Victoria Mine, one of several gold and silver mines that operated within the monument area in the early 1900s. The trailhead is located on the Campground Perimeter Trail.

Estes Canyon–Bull Pasture Trail   This is the longest trail in the park, a round-trip of 4.1 miles. The trailhead is off Ajo Mountain Drive. The route ascends to a high plateau, where ranchers once kept cattle during winter months.

Tom Mix — Desert Guardian

Without becoming maudlin, I recommend a visit to the picnic area in which stands a touching statue. Located on the road that is called the Pinal Pioneer Parkway, this interesting piece of flat desert roadway, U.S. Highway 89, leads north from Oracle Junction (about 20 miles north of downtown Tucson) and ends south of the town of Florence. Along the parkway, trees and shrubs of the desert are identified. The area is scored by several washes.

The memorial statue pays tribute to the great western movie star, Tom Mix, who died at this spot on October 12, 1940, the victim of a car accident. Mix shot many of his movies in this same desert region. What is most interesting about this little picnic site is the desert that surrounds it. At the back of the roadside pull-off, a stile crosses the highway fence. Beyond the fence is pure unspoiled desert, the type you just have to enter to investigate the plants and wildlife. Vegetation includes numerous varieties of fruiting cactus, mesquite thickets, and ironwood trees. Palo verdes line the nearby wash. Wrens hover over the cacti; tiny rodents and amphibians scuttle across the sand. This is just the place to sample a desert micro-environment.

I lost myself here for an hour on my first drive along the parkway, and returned for another visit. I heartily recommend a stroll on this abundantly full, living desert landscape. It provides a sense of irony, considering the nearby reminder of a fatal car accident, and the desert—growing generation after generation in a great jumble of exuberant life. While vehicles zoom along the parkway—full of people in a great hurry to be somewhere, anywhere—the desert lives quietly, growing at an imperceptible rate, but with a permanency that neither Tom Mix, the guardian on his bronze horse, nor any of the rest of us, could envision for ourselves.

SONORAN DESERT WILDLIFE

In the Tucson area, particularly on the Rincon Mountains, changes in elevation offer chances to see plants, animals, and birds in five biotic zones: Lower Sonoran—desert scrub; Upper Sonoran—grassland transition; Upper Sonoran—oak/pine woodland; Transition—Ponderosa pine/Gambel oak; and the beginning of the Canadian zone—Douglas fir/aspen. Wildlife varies with each change in zone, as does the amount of precipitation. With each 1,000-foot rise in this part of Arizona, temperatures drop about 4 degrees Fahrenheit, and rainfall increases 4 to 5 inches per year. You have to visit Saguaro East to see this wide range in biotic zones and wildlife, and you have to be prepared to hike to get the full effect. However, a drive to the top of Mount Lemmon will help, as the highway passes through several zones, from the desert scrub on the east side of Tucson to the pine forest near the summit. The listing of wildlife that follows represents the diversity found on this drive.

In this southern climate, where the sun brings heat in any season, the early mornings and late afternoons provide the best opportunities to see the wealth of life found in the region. Walking the desert washes and climbing above the desert floor provide unforgettable meetings with wildlife at any time of year.

BIRDS

Elf Owl

Micrathene whitneyi
This is the smallest of the American owls, not larger than a sparrow, although somewhat more rounded. It is a mottled brown color, with buffy underparts, white eyebrows, and no ears. Its very short tail extends only to its wingtips. The elf owl uses the holes drilled by woodpeckers in saguaro, trees, and poles to hide during the daytime hours, coming out at night to feed on insects. Its range extends from southern British Columbia, throughout the western U.S., to Mexico and Guatemala, where it lives not only in saguaro desert but also in wooded canyons.

Cactus Wren

Campylorhynchus brunneicapillus

Living amongst cactus in the desert and in thickets of mesquite or yucca on arid hillsides, this large wren inhabits only the U.S. Southwest and northern Mexico. It has a brown head and white underparts, and is identified by the white eye stripe and the white spots on its outer tail feathers. The tail has prominent crossbars. You will probably see this bird on the ground late in the morning, hunting under cacti and shrubs for its food. Look for cactus wren nests, which are built in the shelter and protected areas of cacti and shrubs. Their call is unmusical: a repeated *kuh kuh kuh* or *chug chug*.

Canyon Wren

Catherpes mexicanus

With white throat and breast, the canyon wren is a rusty color, with the upper back and wings flecked with white. The belly has a reddish-brown tinge. You'll find this bird in desert canyons, on cliffs, rocky slopes, and sometimes in man-made structures including stone buildings and rock walls. It ranges from southern British Columbia's Okanagan desert area through Montana and south to southern Mexico. Unlike the cactus wren, the canyon wren has a pleasing, musical voice, with notes descending down the scale: *tew tew tew tew tew*, or *tee tee tee tee*.

Northern Cardinal

Cardinalis cardinalis

This beautiful crested bird is the only American cardinal found in the Southwest. Male and female are decidedly different in coloration. The male is completely red, darker red on top, with a lighter red crest, throat, breast, and belly. The female is brownish-buff with olive underparts, and red on wings and tail. While widely found in the eastern U.S., its natural western habitat is restricted to southern Arizona, Baja California, and northern Mexico. It lives in mesquite thickets beside streams, and in riparian woodland areas. It has also adapted to urban gardens. You'll see it coming to bird feeders in Tohono Chul Park in Tucson. Its song is a clear, slurred *cheer cheer cheer* or *woit woit woit*. The call is a short, soft *tick* or *tsip*.

Pyrrhuloxia

Cardinalis sinuatus

A Mexican bird, the pyrrhuloxia is shaped like a cardinal. The male has a crimson-red crest, a gray body with a red to rose-colored stripe down the underside, and dark red flashes on the wings and tail. The female is more buff-colored and has fewer red markings—only on the wings, crest, and the eye stripes. The bill of both male and female is yellow in summer and darker in winter. The pyrrhuloxia is definitely a desert dweller, living in a mesquite environment rather than in riparian habitats. In the U.S., it is found only in south-central Arizona, in southeastern New Mexico, and western Texas, where it feeds on insects and seeds. You will probably see this bird in pairs. Its voice is like a cardinal's: a descending *tseu, tseu tseu tseu*. Its call, uttered when startled, is a clear *quit quit.*

House Finch
Carpodacus mexicanus
Originally found only in the west, from Mexico to southern British Columbia, this sparrow-sized bird was introduced to the eastern U.S. and is now common there as well. The male has red or orange on the crown, breast, and rump. The female is a plain, striped brown, with an unstriped head and a streaked underside. The house finch lives in oak woodlands and chaparral, as well as in deserts. It also finds a home in orchards and urban areas, where you'll often hear its song—a long series of warbles ending in *zeee*— as it sits on wires or high trees.

Black-throated Sparrow
Amphispiza bilineata
Known as the desert sparrow in the Southwest, this little bird breeds in a narrow range on both sides of the U.S./Mexican border. It is a transient in more northern states including Nevada, Utah, and southern Wyoming. It is gray above with white face stripes and a distinctive black throat and chest. Look for white markings—eyebrows, mustache, and below the eye. The sexes look similar. Young desert sparrows do not have the black throat.

This bird is well adapted to the harshest desert conditions, living in sagebrush country and cactus areas, particularly in cholla gardens. In the summer it feeds on seeds, staying close to a water supply. During the rainy seasons, the birds join in large flocks and feed mainly on grasshoppers and insects, which contain all the water the sparrows need. It has a varied song, usually a combination of musical notes and phrases, ending with a trill.

Inca Dove
Columbina inca
This is one of the smallest birds in the dove/pigeon family. It has a scaled-looking back, with rufous wings and other primaries, distinctive white sides, and a long, narrow tail with a

square end. It is similar to the ground dove, except that it is more pale, has a narrow rather than fan-shaped tail, and its white tail markings are more pronounced. It lives the southern desert areas of the Southwest, in southern Texas, and south to Costa Rica. It has been a longtime resident of the desert valleys around Tucson, including the lower elevation of Saguaro National Park-West. It has also found a home in suburban gardens, farmers' fields, and ranches. Its voice is a repeated *coo-hoo*, the first note higher than the second.

Black-tailed Gnatcatcher
Polioptila melanura
This little bird with the upright tail is similar in size and color to the blue-gray gnatcatcher found in southern Utah. Gray above and whitish below, it has a band of shaded light gray below its neck and wings. The long black tail has white on the outer parts. This southern California resident also ranges east to Texas and south into Mexico. Its scolding call is usually *chee chee* or *chee chee chee*.

Gilded Flicker
Colaptes auratus
This is one of several woodpecker-type birds under the banner of northern flicker. The desert or "gilded" variety lives only in the deserts of southern California, including Baja, and in southern Arizona. The more widespread western variation is the red-shafted flicker. The gilded flicker, which grows to 14 inches, has yellow wings and a black-edged tail. The male has a red mustache. Both male and female have a white rump and a whitish, barred back. The flicker's voice is a loud repeated *wick, flick-a*, and an abrasive *klee-yeer*.

OTHER ANIMALS

Green Valley Grasshopper
Schistocerca shoshone
One of the most common grasshoppers in the desert Southwest, this hopper is green with a yellow stripe at the middle of the head and on the upper part of its thorax. The hind tibia are a rosy pink. As small as 1.5 inches, it grows to a length of about 2.75 inches. Its range is across the U.S. Southwest from Colorado to Texas and into Mexico. It lives in tall grass and in other open areas, including desert lands with trees and shrubs, and in woods with a sandy floor. One of the largest grasshoppers in America, its frequent appearance in huge numbers has caused great damage to grasses and other plants.

Tiger Beetle
Cicindela pusilla
You'll see this colorful beetle running across the open desert, and flying very fast. Ranging in size from less than half an inch to almost an inch, the tiger beetle has a shiny shell that's a metallic blue, green, or gray. The elytra (forewings) are wider behind the middle part. Their antennae grow from above the jaw base. The various sub-species of tiger beetle are found throughout North America. They live in sunny areas, on sand dunes, on sandy flat areas between shrubs and trees, and on alkali flats such as those in Death Valley. This subspecies, and several more, are found in the deserts of Arizona, Utah, and New Mexico.

Gila Monster
Heloderma suspectum
One of only two venomous lizards (the Mexican bearded lizard is the other), the Gila monster is a large, black-headed lizard with small scales covering its back. The yellow body is covered with uneven brown crossbands and blotches, which can also be yellow, pink, or or-ange. The subspecies found in the Tucson area is more mottled than another (*H. s. cinctum*) found in Utah, southern Nevada, and the Yuma district of Arizona. While it is somewhat active dur-ing daylight hours in the colder months, it is primarily noctur-nal. A Gila monster attack is not normally fatal to humans, be-cause the venom is not injected through fangs, but is secreted as it chews on its prey.

Coyote
Canis latrans
You can best distinguish the coyote from a dog by looking at the tail and nose. The coy-ote's nose is more pointed and the tail is much bushier. Otherwise, it looks very much like a medium-sized dog. This predator is a grizzled gray or reddish-gray with light brown underparts. Its legs are often a rusty brown or a yellowish brown with a dark line on the lower foreleg. Besides fulfilling its role in the desert—dispos-ing of the remains of dead ani-mals—it also eats berries, grass, and melons. You'll find the coy-ote in the desert floor and in the mountain zones except in Canada. It is thought to be the most widespread mammal in the Southwest.

Desert Tortoise
Gopherus agazzizi
This terrestrial creature is adapted for dry desert living, going underground to keep cool, rather than into water like most amphibians. It has a small, brownish-red head. The iris of

its eye is a greenish-yellow. It has a brown, oval-shaped carapace and the legs are flat, with webless toes (made for digging). Growing to a length of about 14 inches, the desert tortoise lives in southeastern California, southern Nevada, and in this small part of Arizona. It is not usually found east of the Rincon Mountains. It lives on sand or gravel surfaces populated by creosote bush and cacti, and also on the floors of canyons, in palm oases and washes. It feeds on grass and other plant material. During the day, it escapes the heat by going into burrows, which are usually dug in the walls of washes and have tunnels as much as 20 to 30 feet deep.

Kit Fox
Vulpes macrotis
This small fox has very large ears and a bushy tail tipped with black. Its back is gray and buff, changing to a whitish buff under the chin and tail. The upper legs have short, dark bars. Kit foxes usually build their dens in soft bajadas, protected against flooding by mounds. Each burrow has several entrances with sharply angled tunnels, which in turn connect to the main tunnel that leads to the main den. Sometimes they use old burrows left by ground squirrels and kangaroo rats. The kit fox is a

social animal. Mother and father raise their children together, although the male normally hunts for food for the whole family. The kangaroo rat is the prime source of food, but this species will kill and eat many kinds of rodents. Its tracks are about 1.5 inches long. Because hairs under its feet allow it to glide over the sandy soil, tracks rarely show the foot pads. You'll see the heel and four toes with claws. The mainly nocturnal kit fox has a wide range, from the southern Canadian prairies through Idaho and Utah, to New Mexico and Texas. In Arizona, the kit fox is found in the Lower Sonoran zone.

Coachwhip (snake)
Masticophis flagellum
This Sonoran desert native can grow to great lengths. As small as 36 inches at maturity, under the right conditions it can grow to a stupendous length of 102 inches. It usually has long, rust-colored bands separated by paired pink bands, although the bands can also be uniformly rust or black. Other subspecies are found in other parts of the Southwest, such as *M.f. cingulum*, which is found in the Tucson area. This one is also seen in Baja California and the San Diego area. It lives in open, rocky hillsides and in grass-

lands, as well as desert scrub and chaparral, to an elevation of about 7,000 feet. This very fast snake climbs trees when chased and uses its tail to strike at its enemy. During the day, it looks for rodents and lizards.

PLANTS

Saguaro Cactus
Carnegia gigantea
Standing over the Sonoran Desert like tall sentinels, the saguaro grows to 50 feet tall, and can weigh 12 tons. Arizona's state flower, it has a life span of 170 years, or more. Standing on some of the driest earth in Arizona, including bajadas that quickly lose their moisture, the saguaro's secret is in its great water storage capacity. Taking in water after rains, the cactus stores an enormous amount of moisture—up to 95 percent of its weight. It supports this weight with its strong outer ribs, which are enclosed in a wax-like outer skin or cuticle. It begins to grow arms and to reproduce when it reaches 25 years of age. It grows buds at the topmost part of its stem, from May to June. The waxy-white 3-inch flowers unfold at night, remaining open until the next afternoon. Birds are attracted by insects that land on the flowers. The long-nosed bat is its symbiotic partner, pollinating the saguaro. The fruit

matures in July, looking like small cucumbers, then bursts open, revealing deep-red pulp and shiny black seeds. The fruit is eaten by rodents and birds. The saguaro provides a home for birds—woodpeckers and flickers, who drill their nests, and elf owls—as well as insects and reptiles. A young plant has only a slight chance of surviving unless it is sheltered by a "nurse" tree, usually a mesquite or palo verde. The trees protect the saguaro seedling from the heat of the summer sun and the force of winter winds.

Organ-pipe Cactus
Tenocereus thurberi
This is one of two upright cactus species that grow in Mexico but only within Organ Pipe Cactus National Park southeast of Tucson in the U.S. Both look alike, except that the Senita Cactus (*Lophocereus schotti*) has pink flowers, while the blossoms of the organ pipe (*Tenocereus thurberi*) have a lavender tint. Both cacti grow with clumps of tall stems, up to 15 feet high. The name Senita (or "whisker cactus") refers to the hairs or spines which are found at the upper ends of the stems. Both varieties bloom at night, with the flowers at the tips and sides of the stems, and close earlier in the day than the saguaros.

Barrel Cactus

Ferocactus acanthodes

With a single stem, this barrel-shaped cactus flowers in April and May. It generally grows along washes, on bajadas, and along canyon walls. It is a native of southern California and south-central California, growing to a height of 10 feet. Most in the Tucson area are much shorter. They grow in washes, on bajadas and other gravel slopes, and along canyon walls. Clusters of yellow or reddish spines—up to 3 or 4 inches long—grow from the stem. On other species of barrel cactus, some spines are hooked at the end. Following rainstorms, yellow, orange, or pink flowers grow in a crown near the top of the stem. Egg-shaped fruits follow the flowers, maturing in the late summer and attracting many rodents, as well as deer.

Jumping Cholla

Opuntia fulgida

This very spiny cactus is like all other cholla, a plant with jointed branches. This is the largest of the species. The plant gets its name because the branches detach easily when touched, sticking into clothes or skin. It pays to be careful around the jumping cholla. It grows as a shrub and as a tree with a short trunk, maturing to a height of 15 feet.

The leaves are narrow and cylindrical, about 1 inch long, and a light green color. They are placed in joints or segments about 8 inches long, with many egg-shaped tubercles, each of which bear two to twelve large, brown spines. The flowers, which have five to eight white or pink petals with lavender streaks, grow near the ends of joints and on the fruit in late spring and summer. The fruit, a spineless, pear-shaped berry with many seeds, is connected into long chains. Fruit can remain for years, bearing flowers every year.

Teddybear Cholla

Opuntia bigelovii

This tiny tree-like cactus has short branches covered with yellowish spines. The name comes from its resemblance to a fuzzy toy bear, but it is not something to hug. The spiny joints easily detach, striking deep into flesh. Beware. The teddybear grows on arid, rocky slopes and flowers in March and April, bearing green or yellow blossoms, sometimes with lavender streaks. The fruit is egg-shaped, about 0.75 inches long with distinctive knobs.

Ocotillo

Fouquieria splendens

The ocotillo grows from the ground with several woody

(often dead-looking) stems. The plant is leafless for most of the year but suddenly breaks out in leaf immediately following a rainstorm. As soon as the soil dries, the leaves wither and fall off. This growing cycle is repeated several times through fall and winter. Red tubular flowers grow at the branch tips, in clusters up to 10 inches long. Blooms are seen from March into June. Eleven species of ocotillo are found in the Southwest, and most species are found in Mexico. The Boojum tree of Baja California is a relative.

Blue Palo Verde

Cercidium floridum

Arizona's state tree, this small tree has an amazing annual cycle, unlike that of most trees. Like the ocotillo, these trees are leafless for most of the year; then, following winter rains, they sprout small compound leaves with tiny leaflets that wither and disappear as soon as the soil dries. They bloom in April and May, following the late rains, bearing thousands of tiny yellow flowers that attract myriad flies, beetles, and honey bees, which in turn attract spiders and predatory bugs. The flowers change into flat seed pods containing one to eight seeds. The pods then drop off, providing food for rabbits and rodents. The tree is

found along washes and on the lower slopes of the desert. The other palo verde tree in Arizona (foothill) is the nurse tree for young saguaro.

Desert Ironwood

Olneya tesota

This short, spiny tree is well named, for it is so dense that it sinks in water. This evergreen tree has a short trunk, spreading branches, and a broad crown. The ironwood looks like a wisteria in late May and early June, when it bursts into bloom with thick clusters of lavender-to-violet flowers. Following the flowers, seed pods appear. These cylindrical pods contain shiny, brown, bean-like seeds that are prized as food by squirrels, javelina, mice, rats, and even people, who sometimes roast and eat them as a good-tasting snack. This is another plant that grows leaves only after rainstorms, shedding them as soon as the earth dries. A type of mistletoe often grows on the ironwood, producing berries that attract birds.

Spanish Dagger

Yucca sarizonica

One of three broad-leafed yuccas, this plant is also called Spanish Bayonet. This is the subspecies that grows in Arizona; the other two are *Y. schidigera* (California) and

Y. torreyi (Texas). All reach a size of 10 to 15 feet. You can see the Spanish dagger in clusters and even "forests" in Arizona. They produce tall flower stems, which bear clusters of creamy, white, bell-shaped flowers. The yucca has long been a useful plant. Roots were used by Native Americans for making soap.

WILDFLOWERS

Phacelia
Phacelia crenulata
This annual plant, also called wild heliotrope and scorpionweed, is widespread across southern Arizona, New Mexico, and California. A member of the waterleaf family, it blooms from February to June, bearing violet to purple flowers. The name scorpionweed comes from the curled flower heads that resemble a scorpion's tail.

Filaree
Erodium texanum
Also called heronbill and alfilaria, this member of the geranium family, introduced to the region by Spanish settlers, is a common winter annual in the Tucson area. Its leaves are geranium-shaped, and the pink-to-violet flowers that bloom in February and March are succeeded by fruit, which are long and slender like a heron's bill.

Bladderpod
Lesquerella gordonii
This mustard species decorates great swaths of the desert with bright yellow when it blooms each February to May. It is one of the earliest of the Sonoran wildflowers, growing at under 4,000 feet, and an important forage for cattle. Plants grow to a height of 8 inches.

TUCSON

The city of Tucson has many excellent hotels and motels, most of which belong to chains of one kind or another. Here we provide listings of several fascinating guest ranches, desert inns, and bed-and-breakfast homes that offer something different for people interested in exploring the natural environment of the Tucson area.

Tanque Verde Ranch

14301 East Speedway
Tucson, AZ 85748
(520) 296-6275

This country inn at the very end of Speedway Boulevard east of the city has an Old West ambience and a focus on riding. The ranch has a hundred horses for riding over the desert hills. The rooms and suites are luxurious—many with fireplaces; all with private patios. Breakfast, lunch and dinner are served. The Dog House is the ranch barroom. You bring your own bottle and the management provides a locker for it. There are indoor and outdoor pools, tennis, riding, a health spa, and a ranch program for children. Mobil has given the Tanque Verde Ranch its 4-star rating ($$$).

White Stallion Ranch

9251 W. Twin Peaks Road
Tucson, AZ 85743
(520) 297-0252

This ranch at the base of the Tucson Mountains features horseback riding, but you can just sit around, do a bit of swimming, enjoy a hayride, or simply relax. The ranch, which has rooms in the main lodge as well as cottages, operates on the American Plan—lodging and all meals included in the daily rate. Cookouts are a regular feature. Other ranch activities include dances and performances by entertainers. Ranch facilities include a swimming pool, whirlpool, tennis courts, and a lounge. Meals are served in the dining room, unless there's an outdoor event.

Lazy K Bar Guest Ranch

8401 N. Scenic Drive
Tucson, AZ 85743
(520) 744-3050 or 800-321-7018

Located on the desert in the Tucson Mountains area, 17 miles northwest of the city by Interstate 10 and Ina Road, the Lazy K Bar is in the middle of a saguaro forest. As with the other area guest ranches, this one focuses on riding, but other activities such as tennis and swimming are available, as are desert nature trails and a whirlpool. The ranch, which operates on the American plan (all meals included), is closed during July and August.

Leowe's Ventana Canyon Resort

7000 N. Resort Drive
Tucson, AZ 85715
(520) 299-2020

With 398 units, this golf and tennis resort at the foot of the Catalina Mountains has everything: two pools, whirlpool, saunas, bicycles, steam room, tennis (10 courts), two dining rooms, restaurant, and lounge. If you need to walk off all the food, there are nature trails in the nearby Catalina State Park. There are several other fancy resorts in the Tucson area, but Leowe's has always had top ratings (**$$ to $$$+**).

Westward Look Resort

245 Ina Road
Tucson, AZ 85704
(520) 297-1151 or 800-722-2500

If you're looking for the Tucson resort life, but at affordable prices, this may be what you want. Westward Look, north of town on State Route 77, was one of the earliest resorts in Tucson. It has undergone renovations in recent years and offers rooms, dining, and recreational facilities at a reasonable cost. Facilities include 244 units, 3 swimming pools, whirlpools, tennis courts, dining room, and coffee shop (**$$**).

Lodge on the Desert

306 N. Alvernon Way
Tucson, AZ 85733
(520) 325-3366

A hacienda-style inn in northern Tucson, this is a relaxing place to stay while you explore the nearby desert. Behind the adobe walls of the compound is a distinctive operation that used to be out in the desert but is now in the urban area. An old ranch house—a grouping of Spanish buildings (casas), many with fireplaces and patios—is the main lodge for this B&B inn. A swimming pool is located in the central garden, with casita-style rooms around the central plaza. There is a restaurant, and all-inclusive treatment via the American plan is available. The Tucson Botanical Garden and several notable restaurants are nearby (**$ to $$**).

Tucson Camping

There are several deluxe RV parks near Tucson, including the **Cactus Country RV Resort**, (520) 574-3000, 16 miles southeast of town via I-10 and Houghton Road (Exit 275). The resort has 260 sites with full hookups, a dump station, laundry, propane, pool, and whirlpool. Many of the area campgrounds are located on federal and state lands, which include several campsites in the **Coronado National Forest**. See the earlier pages in this section for the location of Forest Service campgrounds and campsites in **Catalina State Park**. **Tucson Mountain Park**, a civic park located west of the city, offers camping as well.

AJO

Guest House Inn
3 Guest House Road
Ajo, AZ 85321
(520) 387-6133

This highly recommended B&B inn is one of several places to stay in this little town north of Organ Pipe Cactus National Monument. The four guest rooms are in the middle of this charming house, which was built in 1925 to house guests of the Phelps Dodge mining company. There are combination or shower baths, a patio with picnic table, and shops and restaurants nearby. The Walker family provides fine hospitality, serving breakfast and afternoon tea ($).

Mine Manager's House
1 Greenway Drive
Ajo, AZ 85321
(520) 387-6505

Another home from the Ajo copper-mining days, this B&B inn has five units, all with unique decor and names (the Maid's Room, the Cornelia Suite, etc.). Hosts Faith and Martin Jeffries serve a full breakfast and offer afternoon refreshments. You may also reserve a table for dinner ($ to $$).

Marine Motel
P.O. Box 446
Ajo, AZ 85321
(520) 387-7626

This standard motel 1 mile north of the town center on U.S. Highway 85 has 20 units, some with showers. Refrigerators are available ($).

Ajo Camping

The Shadow Ridge RV Resort
431 N. 2nd Avenue
Ajo, AZ 85321
(520) 387-5055

Located a half-mile north of town. All 46 sites have RV hookups. Laundry and recreation room are available.

Wickenburg and the Hassayampa River

Whatever faint glimmer of memory remains of the Old West of movie myth is brought back by a visit to this region in west-central Arizona. This is not the lawless Wild West of Tombstone, nor is it the staid and genteel Spanish-colonial ambience of Tucson. This the West of Mexican caballeros riding across the upland range, chasing herds of cattle on ranches that stretch to the horizon; and later the West of the cowboys who came after the miners, herding dogies on drives to the nearest railway town of Maricopa. And yet, there's a little bit of Tombstone in Wickenburg, and a bit of Spanish colonial heritage, too. It's just that the land is so immense, so made for riding, that a visitor's lasting impressions are of ranching. Today, that theme is carried out in a half-dozen guest ranches, which people visit to experience what remains of the real West.

The story of Wickenburg—at least the recent part—begins with the Spanish conquistadors who came to the area, bringing with them horses (caballos) and a new athletic way of riding, which they taught to the local Apache. These caballeros, gentlemen on horseback, were the first white people to see the immense desert vistas north of the Mexican border and south of the Mogollon Rim. They were followed by Mexicans, and then by prospectors who found ore in the hills surrounding Wickenburg, creating a series of gold rushes. Little towns were built on the mountain slopes—most of them abandoned within a year or two—and the life of the caballeros was never the same.

Large-scale ranching became the successor to mining in the area. A logical extension of the cattle industry in the early years of the twentieth century was the dude ranch, and Wickenburg has long been known as the world's capital of dude ranching (now more civilly called "guest ranching"). That tradition continues today, with a dozen uplands guest ranches offering visitors a chance to see the Old West as we imagine it might have been. Of course, modern variations such as golf, tennis, mountain hiking, and nature study are included in some guest ranch programs. So it's really the New Old West, an atmosphere that retains the romance of the pioneer era but makes it a little more comfortable than either the Spanish caballeros or the ranch cowboys experienced.

The Arizona Uplands is high desert—the landscape of the Joshua tree, saguaro, cholla, and ironwood—situated south of the Date Creek Range, west of the Hieroglyphic Mountains and east of the Buckskin and Harcuvar ranges. This is the most northerly section of the Upper Sonoran desert.

Through this region flows the Hassayampa River. For the most part, it's a typical desert river, more of a deep wash than a flowing stream, moving underground for much of its 100-mile journey from the Bradshaw Mountains to join the Gila near Phoenix. The source of the Hassayampa is across the summit from Prescott, a series of little mountain creeks that drain the snowmelt in the spring. The river picks up water from springs along the way. Its course is mainly unseen, as it flows deep under the visible stream of river rock. Here and there it comes to the surface (or is it the other way around?) and when the Hassayampa surfaces, magical things happen in this hot dry desert otherwise meant for cacti and sagebrush. Cottonwoods and willows grow next to bosques of mesquite. Both habitats (cottonwood/willow and mesquite bosque) attract a raft of birds and animals, which live in a symbiotic relationship with the plants.

When you cross the river in summer, over a bridge in Wickenburg, you will see its waterless course of large-sized river stone winding through the community. A mile south of town, the river appears for a few miles, nurturing an amazing range of plants, animals, and birds. Beside the stream is a former guest ranch—one of the first in the area, called the Garden of Allah when it opened in 1913.

This oasis of a different kind is now one of the prime nature preserves owned and operated by the Nature Conservancy, which protects the river and its riparian habitat. Less than 5 percent of the riverside desert habitats that existed in Arizona before settlement now remain. Great desert rivers—like the Gila—are now funneled into aqueducts to supply drinking, industrial, and lawn water for the state's growing urban areas. As the riparian areas have disappeared, so have the birds that lived in or visited the cottonwood/willow groves. Animals of the desert dropped in numbers, having no life-giving water on which to survive. The protection of a little bit of open river near Wickenburg is not only a demonstration project in stream protection, but a vanguard of the type of wildlife protection that governments and private agencies alike need to carry out.

For nature lovers, the Hassayampa River Preserve is an important place to visit on a trip to or near Phoenix. Spend a day or two at the preserve with a not-quite-natural-but-close-enough ranch vacation, and you have the best of both worlds: great wildlife viewing—on the open desert and in a very special riparian habitat—and the comfort of a ranch home.

Out Wickenburg Way

> . . . *you won't believe your eyes.*
> *It's like angels painting rainbows in our Arizona skies.*
> *Come relax and hear the breezes hummin'*
> *western lullabies, out Wickenburg Way.*
>
> —LYRICS BY MORT GREENE

The old western song still captures the relaxed desert lifestyle available to visitors to this small ranching community. Yet at times the humming breezes and artistic angels would have been a bit hard to take, particularly on Vulture Mountain.

The Wickenburg area has had ups and downs since before the town was founded in the mid-1800s. The Arizona Uplands had been the purview of the nomadic Apache, the caballeros, and their rancher successors; all, except for grazing cattle, pretty much left the land alone. Then, a German immigrant, Henry Wickenburg, became interested in potential mineral deposits on

Vulture Mountain. He began exploring a ledge, and exposed a rich vein of gold. He promptly named his claim the Vulture.

Vulture Mountain is small as mountains go, but has a distinctive upright, rounded peak, like a bald head on a tall thick neck. Several stories are told about how Wickenburg came to name his mine the Vulture, but the most believable has it that Henry discovered the gold while turkey vultures were flying over the peak. Since vultures fly every day in this area, there's a good chance they were flying that day. One apocryphal story has it that Wickenburg killed a vulture on the ground and saw the gold when he picked up the bird.

Henry Wickenburg could have become rich, but he had neither the mining experience nor any financial sense. He didn't actually mine the ore himself, but let others pay him for the ore they took out of the mine, which left the customers the job of milling their own ore. In 1886 Wickenburg was mostly bought out by Benjamin Phillips, who got together an organization to actually mine the mountain's ore. He took out some $2.5 million in gold by the end of 1872. Phillips could have made larger profits, but up to half the gold was high-graded by his own miners. It is said that 18 of these larcenous employees were hanged at the mine site.

Meanwhile, a little town with a population of three hundred had sprung up at the mine site. By 1875, without rail transportation for the ore, the mine was bankrupt. James Seymour, a New Yorker, reopened the mine in 1879, and installed an 80-stamp mill to partially refine the ore. Water for the stamp mill was diverted by pipe and flume from the Hassayampa River. But like every other mining operation, this one closed, in the 1890s. The Vulture post office didn't last that long either; it shut its doors in 1897.

Henry Wickenburg benefited only by having a town named after him, not likely a great pleasure. He was not paid a fair amount for his share of the Vulture Mine and had given away much of the land he had owned for the town site. He died in poverty, taking his own life with a six-shooter in 1905.

Mining did take place for a while—on and off—until the 1940s, when the war brought a closure of all nonessential mines. In recent years, the current ownership has mined the tailings for the remaining gold.

The end of mining was a blow to Wickenburg, but the town was also developing as a ranching center, supplying the needs of the area ranchers. Other gold finds had been made north of Wickenburg, at Congress Junction, and the cow town continued to grow. By the spring of 1895, a spur railway came from Prescott to the mines at Congress and Wickenburg. Hotels and saloons were constructed on Railroad Street, and a Wells Fargo freight office was opened.

Aside from the substantial buildings on Railroad Street, most of the structures—the ice company, pool hall, barber and bath shops, and livery stable—were very basic wooden buildings, constructed without artistic design or any thought of permanence. Several pioneer families built more long-lasting homes out of cement blocks or wood and stucco. The bank and school were more sturdy, built of red brick. While Congress and other nearby mining towns developed and soon closed, Wickenburg managed to hold on, becoming—in the 1930s—the "dude ranch capital of the West."

The relaxed town still serves the needs of the area ranchers, but also draws tourists who come to see what remains of the Old West. The classic railway station is now the town's visitor information center and Chamber of Commerce office. The Chamber offers a walking tour map, which will lead you to all of the historic buildings in the town.

The Desert Caballeros Western Museum features an extensive series of displays on the early settlement of the area, along with an outstanding small collection of western American sculpture and painting. Art exhibitions change throughout the year. Located at 21 North Frontier, between the highway and Railroad Street, it is open Monday through Saturday from 10 A.M. to 4 P.M., and on Sunday from 1 P.M. to 4 P.M.

Hassayampa River Preserve

As the Hassayampa River flows from the Bradshaw Mountains through the open desert to empty into the Gila, it runs primarily underground, beneath a deep wash of sand and gravel. It surfaces in only a few places. A short stretch of open water is located north of Wickenburg; another 5-mile long section just south of the town creates one of the outstanding riparian habitats in the desert Southwest. In 1986, the Nature Conservancy purchased the property known through most of the twentieth century as the Brill Ranch, Garden of Allah, then the Lazy RC Ranch. The Conservancy bought the land in order to protect what is considered one of the last and finest Sonoran Desert streamside habitats. It is open to the public for recreation and nature study.

The property, which includes a main adobe building built in the 1860s as a ranch house, is listed on Arizona's State Register of Historic Places. Frederick Bill, a Prussian immigrant, arrived in the area in 1871 and occupied the property, which he called Brill Ranch. There he operated a stagecoach station, raised cattle, was a fruit farmer with several orchards, and also created the first carp farm in the state. After Brill sold the property in 1913, the Brill Ranch became a dude ranch, the "Garden of Allah," so named because of the extensive groves of palm trees near the ranch house and near Palm Lake, an oversized pond on the property. Later owners called it the Lazy RC Ranch.

Most of the 5 miles of riparian habitat are accessed by the main lane into the preserve, 2 miles south of Wickenburg off U.S. Highway 60/89. Just off the parking lot is the main ranch building, now the Conservancy preserve office and nature center where you can get information on the two short trails and on opportunities for wildlife viewing. There is a picnic area beneath the Garden of Allah palms.

The riparian habitats are amazingly complex. At the edges, away from the river, is the Upper Sonoran desert scrub community, which is characteristic of the hilly desert lands throughout the Wickenburg area. Mesquite bosque or forest is the transition zone between the desert and the riverside habitat. Beside the river Fremont cottonwoods and Goodding willows create a forest in the middle of the Sonoran Desert. The river itself is a habitat—for the longfin dace, lowland leopard frogs, and Sonoran mud turtles, as well as many kinds of bugs and insects. Cattails, almost absent from the riverside in recent years, are now making a comeback in the preserve. Watercress grows along the water's edge.

Storms in 1993 and 1994 brought rampaging floods through the preserve that scoured the riverbanks, removed trees, and reshaped the floodplain. Although they wiped out part of the floodplain trail, the floods have brought some beneficial changes as well. On newly created areas of the floodplain, tiny cottonwoods and willows are growing—a sign of the regenerating power of nature.

One of the most beneficial results of opening the reserve to the public is that the local community has become thoroughly involved in the operation of the reserve. Volunteers devote more than 6,000 hours a year to maintaining trails, giving demonstrations, staffing the bookstore, and taking part in the annual "tammywhacking expeditions." This activity is performed to eradicate the obnoxious imported plant species, the tamarisk, which grows so fast and extensively that it crowds out native plant species. The volunteers also raise funds in the community (including holding garage sales) for the benefit of the preserve's educational programs.

PRESERVE TRAILS

Staff naturalists lead guided walks through the preserve on a seasonal schedule. The walks, which usually last 90 minutes, are booked in advance. Two trail systems lead through the preserve in the area adjacent to the visitor center, taking visitors to the floodplain, to riverside locations, and also around the small pond that nurtures an impressive aggregation of wildlife.

River Trail   Two loop trails in the form of a figure eight make up the River Trail, covering both the existing river channel and a former channel that lies at a higher elevation than the present one. Numbered markers along the trail match trail interpretation in a trail guide that is available at the visitor center. The two loops are accessed from the main walkway that runs about 50 yards from the visitor center toward the river. The main interpretive loop (leading north) is a mile long.

Passing the palm grove, the trail heads to the floodplain, where you'll see the extensive cottonwood/willow woodland crossing older river channels. In addition to the willow trees (*Salix gooddingii*), the seep willow (*Baccharis glutinosa*) grows on the riverbank. This shrub digs its roots into the floodplain, helping to control erosion. It is often removed, however, during strong flooding. The seep willow serves as a nurse plant for cottonwood and willow seedlings. As the trail crosses the floodplain, you'll be able to walk on sandy bars in the river. The north trail returns to the main junction after passing along the higher terrace, a former river channel. Across the river to the south-west, you can see a large wash coming to the stream.

Palm Lake Trail Palm Lake is a 4-acre pond with a marsh, making a wonderful bird habitat. At the pond, you can see several water birds not usually seen in desert areas; these include the great blue heron, white-faced ibis, snowy egret, and pied-billed grebe. These birds live and breed in the preserve. In addition to the resident waterfowl, an ever-changing collection of migrating birds visit the pond.

The pond is being used by federal and state fish and wildlife services to preserve and grow several species of endangered desert fishes, including the Colorado river squawfish, razorback sucker, bonytail chub, Gila topminnow, and the desert pupfish. The fish are bred in an attempt to increase the numbers of these species, all of which are close to extinction.

The Palm Lake Trail leads south from the main visitor center walkway, forming a half-mile loop. Passing by the palms, it leads along the southern edge of the pond and around the hooked end where the main marsh begins. You'll want to have your bird book or preserve checklist along on this walk.

DESERT RANCHES

As the world capital of dude ranching, the Wickenburg area offers a range of guest ranch experiences. You may stay in a bunkhouse at a small cattle ranch and take part in the daily ranching operations—eating with the cowboys, herding cattle, and repairing fences. On the other end of the scale, you can stay at a deluxe ranch resort—eat gourmet meals in a dining room, enjoy cocktails in a lounge with a view, bask by the swimming pool, golf on a championship course, play tennis, tour the desert in a rented Jeep, and maybe ride horseback to a chuckwagon dinner in the desert. All are available. What is new to guest ranching is the emphasis on nature appreciation and study that has been introduced to the Wickenburg ranch scene. Many ranches, such as the Kay El Bar, Flying E, Rancho de los Caballeros, and Rancho Casitas offer different things for different people, depending on interests. See details on each of these places in the Where to Stay section on page 367.

Vulture and All Those Mines

Many nature lovers are disgusted when they come across old mining ruins and ghost towns. The despoiling of the natural environment is a touchy subject for many, including myself. Any mine opened today must have a well-planned environmental protection program and a restoration process. That was not the case a century or more ago.

It's beneficial that the earth has a way of healing itself. Volcanoes have erupted, bringing devastation around the globe; floods and ice ages have changed vast sections of continents. Humans, too, have wreaked havoc on the earth and, especially in less sensitive times, have neglected to restore damaged sites to anything like their original states. This is the major sin of the mining industry—not necessarily of the original mining process, but later neglect in the service of economics. However, neglect of a few old communities, built and later abandoned in the mid-to-late 1800s and the first decade of the 1900s, has left us a legacy. Together with the low humidity of the Sonoran Desert, neglect has left these communities much as they existed more than 100 years ago.

Vulture, neglected by its ownership and by most of the public for a century, is one of the best preserved mining towns. This fascinating place is open to the public, causing excitement amongst dedicated ghost town fans. It's easy to find and is accessible by roads that accommodate normal cars. The town is not a state park, nor is there an interpretation program with tours. It is a town in a state of slow decay, open for exploring. What I find most interesting is how nature slowly but surely undertakes its recovery program.

The original operation was called the Gold Leaf, later renamed the Nellie Meda Mine. It was originally developed by Westly Rush, a miner who began mining in 1917. He and his daughters, Nellie and Almeda, dug the shaft themselves, all by hand. The mine was later purchased by Phoenix newspaper owner Ned Creighton, who named the mine in honor of Rush's two daughters. The Robsons obtained the property in 1980.

To get to Vulture Mine from Wickenburg, start on Wickenburg Way, and drive west from town for 13 miles. Turn onto Vulture Mine Road and drive past the Rancho de los Caballeros for 13 miles. The mine town is open to the public from mid-September through mid-May from 9 A.M. to 5 P.M. Thursday through Monday, and from mid-May through mid-July on weekends only from 8 A.M. to 4 P.M. It is closed from mid-July to mid-September. You can pick up a walking tour brochure at the mine office when you pay the admission fee and sign a liability waiver (required). For information, write or call:

Vulture Mine
P.O. Box 1869
Wickenburg, AZ 85358
(520) 377-0803

More than a dozen old buildings, many in a surprisingly well-preserved condition, are spread over several acres. A marked trail leads around the property which, in addition to the buildings, displays a jumble of old mining equipment, including the headframe and hoist. There are two school buildings, built in 1877 and 1936. The stone assay office, built in 1884, offers a glimpse into the conditions under which the inhabitants of this town worked. Henry Wickenburg's first house, later used as the town jail, is still here. You can see the hanging tree from which greedy high-graders swung. There's a stone bunkhouse, the mess hall, and a crumbling apartment building. Saguaro cactus and shrubs are proceeding to take over the area, offering their own stoic commentary on this one-time busy community.

I have mixed feelings on the further preservation of this amazing little historical spot. It is a powerful artifact of life in the late 1800s, a town in which living, breathing people worked and played, kids trudged to school, bad people committed crimes, and good people went to church. Yet, perhaps nature should be allowed to have its way and, in another half-millennium, the saguaro will grow and reproduce, and other cacti, grasses, and shrubs will move in on the town and continue nature's healing work. Wind and water will increasingly wear away at the buildings, eventually putting it all back onto and then into the ground. In the meantime, the mining operation welcomes visitors to see the site as it was left when the mining stopped and people deserted the boomtown. As there is no restoration work planned, nature is likely to have its way.

There are other old mining towns in the area, including the near-ghost town of Congress, north of Wickenburg via

Highway 89. However, there is a fascinating one-street town in the Harcuvar Mountains, a half-hour's drive southeast of Wickenburg. Now called Robson's Mining World, this former mine site in the remote mountain range has been developed into a re-creation of a little mining town of the 1800s.

On the foundations of the old boardinghouse, Charles and Jeri Robson have built a two-story hotel with 24 rooms. The main street is a museum of mining lore, with false-fronted buildings and a boardwalk on one side, and displays of mining equipment on the other. There is one restaurant and a few shops. Outside is the best collection of antique mining equipment in the state.

Jeep Tours

One way of seeing the desert is in an off-road vehicle. Desert & Alpine Jeeps of Wickenburg conduct guided four-wheel-drive tours of the desert on a daily basis. The basic cross-country tour lasts about 2 hours. Special destination tours are offered: to the Vulture Mine ghost town, the Hassayampa River Box Canyon, and a cattle company line camp. Moonlight tours are given 3 days per month. For information and reservations, call Desert and Alpine Jeeps, (520) 684-0438 or 800-596-5337 (JEEP).

HASSAYAMPA WILDLIFE

The birds listed here are those found in or near the riparian habitats of the Hassayampa River, in the Nature Conservancy's preserve south of Wickenburg, or in the open, flowing section north of the town. Animals and plants include the prominent residents of the Hassayampa River Preserve and the desert surrounding it.

BIRDS

Zone-tailed Hawk
Buteo albonotatus
A black-colored hawk with slender wings, this bird has a two-toned underwing, much like the turkey vulture. It is identified by the white tail bands: one large and one small band at the tip of the tail. Young zone-tailed hawks have a narrower whitish band, as well as small light spots on the body. This large bird, with a wingspread of about 4 feet, flies with its feet tucked over the base of the tail. It breeds in this part of Arizona, as well as the central and southeast parts of the state. Ranging from Arizona to northeast New

Mexico and into West Texas, to the northern countries of South America, it lives in woodlands along desert rivers, in mountains and canyons. A family has been nesting in the Hassayampa River Preserve during the past couple of years, although no young have been seen recently.

Red-shouldered Hawk
Buteo lineatus
The shoulder is the giveaway for this small hawk with a wingspread of about 2 feet. It has dark brown bands on its tail, separated by narrower whitish bands. The underpart of the bird is a rufous red color. This hawk lives in riverside woodlands, such as the cottonwood/willow environments along the Hassayampa River, as well as in bottomland woods. It has a wide range, from southeastern Canada to California and Mexico. Its voice is a loud scream, in two dropping syllables: *kee yer*.

Mississippi Kite
Ictinia mississipiensis
Another raptor that winters in Arizona and other southern states, this bird is similar to a falcon. Gray in color with a light

head, it is darker above and a lighter blue-gray below. There is a pale patch on the rear of the wing, which you can only see when the bird is resting. The slim tail of the adult is a dark blue. The young kite has mottled brown underparts and head, darker brown mottled back and wings, and white spots on the tail. Its range is throughout the U.S. to its winter home in Central and South America. It prefers to live in streamside wooded habitats, and in groves where it can be sheltered. You will rarely hear the Mississippi kite, except for an infrequent *phee phew* when it is resting.

Great Blue Heron
Ardea herodias
More gray than blue, this heron is an infrequent desert dweller, although it can be seen in the Hassayampa River Preserve and along the San Pedro River in southeastern Arizona. It nests in the mesquite thickets beside the preserve's Palm Lake. A large bird, the great blue heron stands 3 to 4 feet tall, and grows to about 50 inches long. It has long legs, a long, sharp, yellow bill, and lower neck feathers that fan out to create a fuzzy "bib." The head is largely white, with distinctive black plumes during breeding. Its food is fish, frogs, and other small water life,

as well as mice and insects. The Great Blue is found from Canada to Mexico. It usually winters in South America, living in swamps, shoreline marshes, and other intertidal areas. Its voice is a grating croak: *frahnk frahnk*.

Gila Woodpecker
Melanerpes uropygialis
One of several "zebra-backed" woodpeckers (others include the ladder-backed, also found in the desert; red-bellied; and Nuttall's), the Gila has a round, red cap atop its head, while the rest of its head and underparts are a light grayish brown. The female lacks the red cap. You can see a white wing patch when the bird is in flight. The Gila Woodpecker is seen across the desert Southwest, and has a range that includes northern and central Mexico. It lives in riverside habitats, in saguaro forests where it pecks a nest hole in the cactus, and in desert washes. Its voice is a *churr*.

Ash-throated Flycatcher
Myiarchus cinerascens
This medium-sized bird with a slender bill is about 8 inches long. It has two white wing bars, a slender whitish throat and pale yellow underparts. The primary feathers and wing feathers are cinnamon or rust-

colored. Distinguished from other flycatchers in the desert by its rusty tail, its range includes southern Washington and Idaho to the north, and California and Mexico to the south. It lives in a wide range of habitats, from open mixed woods, oak and pinyon-pine woodlands, to riverside groves and pine-oak canyons. Its main voice is a whistle: a long *queeeeeeeer*. It also has *pip* and *pwip* notes.

Mourning Dove
Zenaida macroura
A permanent resident of the Hassayampa River Preserve, this is the common dove of the southern states, although it migrates to cooler areas, even into central Canada. The name comes from its plaintive cooing sound. It is a light brownish-gray above, with pale reddish-buff below. The sharply pointed tail has white spots on the edges. The wing feathers are a dark brownish black. It has a prominent black spot behind the eye, in front of the shoulder patch. Its range is throughout North America from southeast Alaska to Panama, always in moderate climes. It is a game bird but reproduces quickly, up to four times each year. The distinctive, sad voice is a descending *wooh, wooh, wooh*.

Verdin
Auriparus flaviceps
This tiny bird, related to the titmouse and bushtit, is gray with yellow head and throat. It has a rufous patch at the bend of the wing (adult only) and whitish underparts. The tail is shorter than the bushtit's. Its habitat is primarily the low desert; the elevation of this area is just about its highest range. Found in southeastern California, ranging to south Texas and into Mexico, verdin live in areas where there is an adequate amount of low shrubs and scrub for security. This includes desert slopes with mesquite and oak, and open fields with tall grass. Verdins feed on insects, berries, and seeds. It is not found in large flocks. The song is a three-part *clep-urr-zee* or *see,see*. Its call is a bossy *see-lip*.

Abert's Towhee
Pipilo aberti
This desert bird is sparrow-like, a pale brown color with a black patch around the bill. The belly is buff-colored, and the bottom of the tail is a darker, tawny shade. It has a small range, restricted to the desert areas of Arizona, and barely into southern Utah, Baja California, and Mexico. It lives in washes and desert thickets, along desert

streams, and in mesquite groves that are near the cottonwood/willow habitat (Hassayampa Preserve). This very shy bird hides most of the time, foraging on the ground under mesquite or shrubs for the insects and seeds that comprise its diet. It is closely related to the brown towhee.

OTHER ANIMALS

Lowland Leopard Frog
Rana berlandieri
Also called the Rio Grande leopard frog, this pale green amphibian has dark spots between the brown ridges where its back meets its sides. Its light jaw stripe is difficult to see. Usually nocturnal, this frog survives the desert heat by making burrows under rocks. It is better off along the Hassayampa River with adequate vegetation for cover. It is found more widely in the extreme southern edge of New Mexico, in at least half of Texas, and into Mexico. In Arizona, it lives only in this part of the state, from around Sedona to the Mexican border. It breeds year-round. The voice is a low, rapid trill, unlike the voice of a bullfrog.

Sonoran Mud Turtle
Kinosternon sonoriense
During the hotter months, you'll see this small turtle in small patches of water, where it is protected from the summer sun. It lives in ponds and creeks, in desert foothills, or in water holes in the oak-pinyon woodland. It prefers higher elevations, up to about 6,700 feet, in ponderosa pine and Douglas fir forests. This mud turtle nests in May, laying up to nine eggs. The smooth oval-shaped carapace (hard outer shell) sometimes has several keels (plates). Its range extends from the southwest corner of New Mexico, in the Gila National Forest, throughout southern Arizona and south into Mexico. It feeds on snails.

Tree Lizard
Urosaurus ornatus
This diurnal lizard is found in all parts of Arizona, as well as southern and eastern Utah, in western New Mexico, and part of Texas. It has also been seen in the most southern part of Wyoming. The tree lizard has the ability to leap into a tree when startled or pursued. Two subspecies of tree lizard are found in this region, the northern (*U. o. wrighti*) and Colorado River (*U. o. symmetricus*). The northern has large back scales in three or four rows, and its belly patches are connected. The Colorado River species has bands of larger back scales separated by an area larger than the

band. It has a loose fold across the back of the throat. The tree lizard lives in rocky areas, in trees, near dry washes, and by streams. You may see it in pairs or larger groups.

Desert Spiny Lizard
Sceloporus magister
This large lizard has rough scales of a brownish and yellow coloring with crossbands and a black triangular patch with a light rear edge. The male has a blue throat and blue belly patches. The females and young have more definite crossbands than the male. This lizard generally lives at low elevations. The eggs are laid in May, and young appear eight to eleven weeks later. Its range extends from southern Nevada to Baja California, into Arizona, Mexico, and west Texas. It is one of five subspecies of spiny lizard that live in the Southwest deserts. You may also see this lizard in a tree, where it's looking for food.

Hog-nosed Skunk
Conepatus mesoleucus
The Wickenburg area is the most northerly part of this unusual skunk's range. A desert dweller, the hog-nose is found in both the Sonoran and Chihuahuan deserts, and across much of central and southern Texas. In this area, it joins the much wider-spread striped skunk (*Mephitis mephitis*). It has a white head, back and tail, with black underside. Its most distinctive feature is its long, broad snout—without fur on top. The broad nose pad is adapted for scooping up insects, reptiles, and small rodents. The large foreclaws make its footprints larger than that of the striped skunk. Its habitat includes desert scrub, brushy areas, and foothills. This skunk normally rests by day and is active at night. Dens are found in rocky crevices.

Western Patchnose Snake
Salvadora hexalpsis
This slender snake grows to a length of 22 to 45 inches. Its scales are triangular-shaped, and are curved over the snout, giving it the "patch" over the nose. It has a broad yellow or tan stripe, bordered by dark stripes. Its range extends from southern California, throughout western and central Arizona, into Nevada, southwest Utah, and northern Mexico. Here, it lives in desert sagebrush country. In other locations it inhabits oak chaparral and arid lands where you'll also find creosote bush, up to an elevation of 7,000 feet. In this part of Arizona, it can be found on most mountains, as well as in the high desert. Females lay

four to ten eggs in the summer and babies emerge in the fall.

Arizona Pocket Mouse
Perognathus amplus
Six species of pocket mice reside in the Southwest. The Arizona mouse is found in central and southern Arizona and into the northern edge of Mexico, directly south of Nogales and Tucson. This little rodent grows to about 6.5 inches long and is a tawny brown color (with black hairs mixed with the brown hairs) with a pink tinge above. The underside is whitish. The tail is much longer than the body (about a two to one ratio). It lives in scrubby desert areas of fine, sandy soil populated with shrubs. Like the other pocket mice, its primary food is seeds. When food is in short supply, Arizona pocket mice enter a state of hibernation, shutting down many body functions.

Botta's Pocket Gopher
Thomomys bottae
Found widely across the Southwest deserts, this rodent builds burrows and long underground tunnels. A solitary creature, living one to a burrow, it ranges from southeast Oregon to California, and southwest Colorado to Arizona, New Mexico, and west Texas. It is dark brown but can have gray tinges above, with a purple wash on the sides. The tail is hairless, tan or gray. In Arizona, this gopher has white spots under the chin, unlike those found in other regions. The rounded ears have a black patch. In the Wickenburg area, it lives in the open desert and in mountain meadows, preferring softer, wetter soils, although it survives in sandy areas as well.

PLANTS

Foothill Palo Verde
Cercidium microphyllum
Larger than the blue palo verde, this tree is also called the "yellow" palo verde, because of its yellowish-green bark. This spiny tree, which is bare of leaves for most of the year, grows to a height of about 25 feet. When the leaves do appear for a short time, following rains, they appear in alternate, compound order, with three to seven very small leaflets. The short, stiff twigs end in spines 2 inches long. Pale, yellow flowers, with white outer petals, cover the tree in spring. Flowers are followed by fruit in the form of long pods with seeds inside. The foothill palo verde grows on foothills and mountain slopes, as well as on the open desert. They are usually seen where saguaro are found, at elevations up to 4,000 feet.

Gooddings Willow
Salix gooddingii

This large, sheltering willow tree was once widely seen in riparian areas across the Arizona desert. However, with the loss of many streams and urban development, it is restricted to only a few places, including the Hassayampa River Preserve. Here it stands in combination with the Fremont cottonwood. When mature, the bark is dark, rough, and fissured. It is much larger than the ordinary desert willow (*Chilopsis linearis*) and makes an excellent home for birds, including Bell's vireo and the yellow warbler.

Seep Willow
Baccharis glutinosa

Growing in dense clumps along the side of streams, the seep willow provides protection from erosion by digging its roots into river banks. It is very supple and, when floods occur, it bends with the water flow, surviving when larger trees and shrubs are torn away. It serves as a nurse plant, protecting seedlings of cottonwood and willow trees against flowing water during high water periods. You'll see the seep willow along the banks at the Hassayampa preserve, recognizable by its bright green color.

Prickly-pear Cactus
Opuntia phaeacantha

One of the most numerous cacti in the Sonoran and Chihuahuan deserts, the prickly pear has several dozen varieties, including the Engelmann (*O. engelmanii*), which grows to a height of 6 feet, and grizzly-bear cactus (*O. erinacea*), which is found in the Grand Canyon area of northern Arizona. The cactus blooms in the spring with brilliantly colored flowers. The egg-shaped fruit follows. All Opuntia have jointed stems, the flattened pads studded with barbed bristles. Each pad can root a new plant. The pads store water after a rainstorm. In dry years they discard some of their stems to stay alive. These cacti are closely related to the cholla, which have cylindrical stems instead of flat pads. You'll find one kind or another of prickly pear from the low Chihuahuan desert in New Mexico to ponderosa pine uplands as far north as Canada.

Screwbean Mesquite
Prosopis pubescens

This small tree or shrub has long branches and fascinating screw-like seed pods. These are the fruit of this mesquite, about 2 inches long, light brown or yellow, and coiled like a screw. The tree's bark is smooth and light brown. When mature, the bark separates into long hanging strips. The flowers are a whitish yellow, formed in clusters during the spring and early summer. The spiral pods, which grow several to a stalk, hold many seeds. They fall intact to the ground in the fall, where they are eaten by the desert wildlife and provide food to cattle. The screwbean mesquite grows in thickets close to streams, including the Hassayampa. It is found from Texas to southeastern Utah and west to southern California.

Velvet Mesquite
Prosopis velutina
A spiny tree, the velvet mesquite is seen in large numbers in the Hassayampa preserve, in mesquite bosques (woodlands). It has a short, forked trunk, with hairy dull green leaves. Like the screwbean mesquite, the velvet has brown bark that shreds into long strips. The fragrant flowers are light yellow in two–three-inch clusters. This tree, found in central and southern Arizona, was a favorite tree of early settlers who used the trunks for fence posts. It is also used as fuel, as in mesquite-flavored steaks. The flower of this mesquite also is used by bees to make the popular honey.

Fremont Cottonwood
Populus fremonti
The major tree of all southwestern riparian habitats, the Fremont cottonwood provides shelter for the hundreds of varieties of birds that live in or visit the desert rivers and streams. It is found at elevations as high as 6,000 feet. You'll always find it with its "feet" in water, as it requires abundant water to grow. The leaf is heart-shaped or triangular and, like the willow with which it lives, changes color in the fall before shedding its leaves. The combination of cottonwood, willow, and nearby mesquite at the Hassayampa preserve provides the most perfect type of riparian home for birds and small animals.

Desert Catclaw Acacia
Acacia gregii
This is another tree that grows along desert streams and in valleys, although it is found on rocky slopes. It is quite spiny, usually seen as a large shrub, but sometimes as a tree. It can grow to a height of 20 feet. Its compound, alternate leaves have three to seven pairs of dusky green leaflets. Bark is gray, becoming furrowed when mature, and twigs are covered with fine hairs. The catclaw bears light yellow flowers in clusters from early spring to

summer. The pods that follow are flat and curved, remaining on the tree until winter. Also called devilsclaw, the catclaw has a bad reputation because of its dangerous spines. Jackets and pants can easily get torn when hikers walk into this tree.

Brittlebush
Encelia farinosa
This is one of the noticeable wildflower plants in the southwestern desert, producing clusters of bright yellow flowers that cover the plant. The yellow petals surround a brown center (yellow in more northern areas). It grows in washes and other sandy parts of the desert, with a range from southeast California, including Death Valley and the Anza-Borrego Desert, to Utah and northwestern Mexico. This bush grows to a height of 5 feet, although you'll usually find it at about 3 feet. It is a fragrant plant, with resin produced by the stems. Native Americans chewed the resin. It also yields a small, seed-like fruit.

Bur Sage
Ambrosia deltoidea
A low shrub, a little over 1 foot tall, the bur sage has dark brown branches. Its sticky leaves are triangular (sometimes oval) and are toothed. The underside of the leaves are fuzzy. The fruit is spiny, giving the plant its name. Male and female flowers grow separately, with the female (which has lateral spikes) below the male flowers. Bur Sage is found in a restricted zone in southwestern Arizona, and in a small adjacent part of Mexico. It grows in gravel, particularly on alluvial fans (bajadas), or flatter soil that has washed down from mountains. It's part of the same genus as the ragweeds, of which the canyon ragweed (*A. ambrosiodes*) is found in southern Arizona, also in washes and on dry, well-drained soil.

American Mistletoe
Phoradendron tomentosum
The American mistletoe is found in the higher uplands of the Southwest and far beyond. This parasitic shrub lives on a host plant, getting all of its nutrients from the host. At the Hassayampa preserve, mistletoe is found on the cottonwood trees. You'll also see the desert mistletoe in the preserve, sitting on mesquites, acacia, and on palo verde trees. It also uses the ironwood as a host. Mistletoe berries provide food for birds that stay during the winter months. The desert mistletoe also provides a nesting site for a bird, the phainopepla, a black member of the waxwing family.

Tamarisk

Tamarix chinensis

The presence of this shrub or small tree is one of the greatest landscaping mistakes ever made in America. Also called saltcedar, it was imported to this hemisphere in the early 1900s to control erosion and to be used as a decorative plant. Instead of helping the environment, it has become a prime pest. It has deep roots and needs lots of water. It survives so well that it has crowded out native plants—to the extent that eradication programs are now taking place, including in the Hassayampa preserve. Tamarisk, which grows in large thickets, does provide shelter for birds, but its obnoxious character far outweighs its benefits. A native of Asia (thus the botanical name), it has a reddish bark and green twigs. It flowers abundantly in the spring, with pink petals in clusters.

Joshua Tree

Yucca brevifolia

Many people think that the Joshua tree is grotesque, a plant without any aesthetic appeal, which looks dead most of the time. That is far from accurate. The largest of the yucca family, it grows mainly in the Mojave Desert but is also seen in a fine Joshua tree forest in the hills north of Wickenburg. It requires an elevation of over 4,000 feet in most areas, although it does grow almost at sea level in Baja California. It has yucca-like leaves that cluster around the top of the gray trunk. Older, dead leaves hang down in a beard, much like the California fan palm. The blades of the leaves are 3 to 5 inches long, and are split into several parts, with threads hanging from the edges.

It flowers after the rainy season, and a Joshua tree forest in flower is a beautiful sight. The nearly half-inch-long blossoms consist of a corolla with three lobes, and have a mild fragrance. The flowers are clustered together in groups that can be as much as a foot long. The fruit is an egg-shaped berry, about 1.5 inches long, a kind of pod that dries in the summer sun. The young berry is sweet and provides food for birds and animals. Inside the berry is one brown seed. The Joshua tree grows where the soil retains some moisture, and beside alkaline streams. It grows out in the open and in mountain canyons, from southeastern California to central Arizona, and around Yuma. It was named by Mormon travelers who saw this tree with raised arms as a likeness of the biblical prophet.

GUEST RANCHES

Flying E Ranch
P.O. Box EEE
Wickenburg, AZ 85358
(520) 684-2690

Located 4 miles west of Wickenburg, with Vulture Peak rising in the near-distance, the Flying E is a small guest ranch operation focusing on riding and friendly service. A working ranch (staff members call their visitors "guest hands"), the business of taking care of cattle goes on as other activities are staged—riding horses on the open desert; playing tennis, table tennis, shuffleboard, horseshoes; swimming; soaking in a heated whirlpool; golfing at two nearby courses; rockhounding Vulture Mountain. Rides with wranglers are available twice daily and riding instruction is available.

Sixteen rooms and suite with private baths, TVs, and refrigerators can accommodate 32 people, giving the ranch a cozy feeling. Guests are invited to bring their own bottles to the saloon (no bar). This ranch operates from November to May, on the American Plan (excluding riding). Food is served "family style" in the ranch dining room and cookouts are frequently held. Plenty of land for riding—20,000 acres—lies outside the ranch door. Rates for two range from about $185 to $200 per day for the regular rooms, to $250 for the most deluxe accommodations. Children are welcome at a modest additional rate. Vi Wellik is the owner (**$$$**).

Kay El Bar Guest Ranch
P.O. Box 2480
Wickenburg, AZ 85358
(520) 684-7593

Situated north of Wickenburg, via Rincon Road, and on the Hassayampa River, this is a small, comfortable guest ranch, on which you could base a vacation. Owned and operated by sisters Jane Nash and Jan Martin and their husbands Jay and Charlie, the ranch is a national historic site.

The main activity is horse riding on trails that reach into the hills above the Hassayampa River. Wildlife is seen regularly, including javelina, jackrabbits, deer and coyote. Roadrunners are almost tame. Other birds gather by the river. The ranch is not far from the Joshua tree forest—in the hills north of Wickenburg—or the Bradshaw Mountains.

This family-style vacation place has rooms (all with private baths) in the main lodge and a two-bedroom, two-bath cottage. Rates are American Plan, three meals included, with a 4-day minimum stay required from February 15 to May 1 and a 2-day minimum stay from mid-October until February 15. The ranch is closed during the summer months. Daily rates begin at about $225 for two people, and a week's stay for two runs about $1,510. Taxes and a 15 percent gratuity are extra. Riding is the main event (**$$$**).

Rancho Casitas
Prescott Highway (89)
P.O. Box A-3
Wickenburg, AZ 85358
(520) 684-2628

This is the smallest of the area guest ranches, with only seven units. It's located 3 miles north of town and is owned by Louise Craig. Operating with the European Plan, each casita has a full kitchen and fireplace. Horse riding is available and there is a swimming pool. Maid service is provided on a weekly basis (**$$** to **$$$**).

Rancho de los Caballeros
1551 South Vulture Mine Road
Wickenburg, AZ 85390
(520) 684-5485

This longtime deluxe ranch resort, founded in the 1940s, still sets the standard for Arizona guest ranches. While horse riding remains a major attraction, "Los Cabs" also has a championship 18-hole golf course that guests are invited to play for pay. Rated one of the West's top courses, it plays 7,025 yards, par 72, from the championship tees. Four acrylic tennis courts are located near the horse corrals, from which wranglers lead two desert rides each day. Trap and skeet-shooting are available on a private range.

The original swimming pool, a marvel for its day, is still a focal point, with the main lodge curving around the pool deck. Inside the main building is an excellent dining room, a large living room, and a bar with full service. A variety of 73 rooms and suites are in casita buildings, all within a 3-minute walk of the main lodge, which houses the dining room, a large living room with fireplace, and saloon. The ranch operates on the American plan and has special golf packages. Rates for two (daily) run from about $150 with an adjoining living room costing about $75 per day. These rates are for the slower October to January season. In February, the rates rise until April (**$$$**).

Wickenburg Inn
Tennis & Guest Ranch

P.O. Box P
Wickenburg, AZ 85358
(520) 684-7811 or 800-942-5362

This fine guest ranch and tennis center is located 8 miles north of Wickenburg, via State Route 89. A lane runs through the hills between the highway and the main lodge building, which is set in a beautiful desert hollow. Casita-style buildings are positioned on a hillside with wonderful views. The ranch owns a 4,700-acre area, which is operated as a nature preserve. This is prime Sonoran desert, rolling with great views in every direction. The grounds are lushly landscaped. Accommodations are deluxe but relaxing. There's a dining room and a saloon. Tennis is a main concentration here, but riding is also a major activity, available to adults and children. The ranch arts and crafts center is a fine place for kids, as is the desert museum, both on the property. Rates in lodge rooms run from about $185 (double) per day for the low season (May 1–November 25) and from $275 per couple per day during the busy months. The American plan includes all meals, horseback riding, and tennis privileges. Rooms in casitas are more expensive (**$$$**).

MOTELS AND B&BS

Best Western Rancho Grande

293 E. Wickenburg Way,
Highway 60
Wickenburg, AZ 85358
(520) 684-5445

This large downtown motel located on the main highway is the most sophisticated place to stay in Wickenburg, excepting the guest ranches outside the town. It has large standard rooms (**$$**).

AmericInn Motel

East Highway 60
Wickenburg, AZ 85358
(520) 684-5461

This recently opened economy motel provides good accommodations for the price. It also offers the benefit of the Willows Restaurant and cocktail lounge, plus a pool and whirlpool (**$ to $$**).

Westerner Motel

580 W. Wickenburg Way
Wickenburg, AZ 85358
(520) 684-2493

A standard motel in downtown Wickenburg, with a swimming pool, morning coffee, and refrigerators in rooms (**$**).

Robson's Mining World

P.O. Box M2
Wickenburg, AZ 85358
(520) 684-5838 or 684-3160

This unusual hotel is located on a former mine site where

Charles and Jeri Robson have established a one-street mining theme town and a large display of antique mining equipment. The hotel is recently built, on the foundations of the original mine boarding house. Meals are served at the Gold Leaf Saloon. This unusual and fascinating place to spend an evening or two is open from October 1st to the end of May (**$$**).

Vista del Oro
6700 Hacienda, P.O. Box 3191
Wickenburg, AZ 85358
(520) 684-3827 or 684-3991

A bed-and-breakfast home, this Mission-style building with 7,000 square feet was built in the early 1940s. Large rooms and a suite have private baths. There's a swimming pool with breakfast served on the lanai. Non-smoking. Hiking, riding, and desert tours can be arranged.

CAMPING

Hospitality RV Park
P.O. Box 2525
Wickenburg, AZ 85358
(520) 684-2519

This RV park is located 2 miles east of the main Wickenburg stoplight, on the highway to Phoenix, U.S. 89, at milepost 112. It offers pull-through spaces, full hookups, laundry, and game room.

PART 4

The Ultimate Outdoors

As the passenger pigeon disappeared from North America, wilderness proponent and longtime federal bureaucrat Aldo Leopold mourned its loss in his book *Sand County Almanac:*

> There will always be pigeons in books and in museums,
> but these are effigies and images, dead to all hardships
> and to all delights. Book-pigeons cannot dive out of a cloud
> to make the deer run for cover, or clap their wings in thun-
> derous applause of mast-laden woods. Book-pigeons cannot
> breakfast on new-mown wheat in Minnesota, and dine on
> blueberries in Canada. They know no urge of seasons;
> they feel no kiss of sun; no lash of wind and weather.
> They live forever by not living at all.

Aldo Leopold felt that, like the passenger pigeon, the wild lands of America's wilderness were in danger of becoming extinct. He believed in preserving "a harmony between humans and the natural land," and proposed what he called a "land ethic" based on government conservation of wilderness areas. As a result of Leopold's urging and his political contacts, the district forester in New Mexico's Gila River district named the forest region surrounding the headwaters of the Gila River a designated wilderness area. This act was the precursor of a national system of such protected areas, created through the National Wilderness Protection Act of 1964. Leopold became a founder of the influential Wilderness Society.

Wilderness is not stopping the car beside the highway to venture into a grove of trees. Wilderness is not walking a nature trail in a state or national park, with a few hundred other people in close pursuit, although a walk in a park can be enjoyable as its own kind of recreation. Wilderness is not camping with full hookups and the glare from the lights of the surrounding community obscuring the stars.

No, wilderness is the quiet of the forest or another natural environment, experienced alone, or maybe with no one else except your closest loved one(s). Wilderness is sitting beside a clear, quiet, burbling stream that flows unimpeded by human engineering. Wilderness is the quiet of the midnight hour—black except for the moonlight. An owl hoots; there are brushing noises in the bush. An animal's young one cries in the distance, or perhaps close enough to banish your serenity for awhile.

The first chapters of this book explored sublime natural places, but none as pristine and untouched as the Gila Wilderness. Real wilderness provides an extra dimension—the solitude which, at the least, enables a person to leave the civilized world long enough to regenerate the psychic batteries, and at its emotional best, provides a life-changing experience. Wilderness is living as close to other living things and the land as possible, without the distractions of motels, stores, cars, and especially hordes of other travelers. Wilderness is finding a new dimension in your life.

Wilderness can be forest, prairie, or desert. It can be a field of tundra at the Arctic Circle, or a clearing in a rain forest—in the American Northwest or at the equator. Pristine natural landscape, and opportunities for solitude and serenity are, to me, the defining elements of wilderness. While the Southwest has superb natural places in abundance, the type of wilderness considered here is in very short supply. For instance, the Wheeler Peak Wilderness near Taos offers some of the attributes of a wilderness experience, but not all. The land is too rugged to offer good backcountry camping for most people, and more surrounding area is required to provide the ultimate wilderness experience, with mountain creeks and enough space for that essential ingredient called solitude.

Our ultimate wilderness has just about everything: unfettered rivers, a combination of desert river-bottom and pine-clad mountain ecosystems, hot springs, hiking and riding trails in an unspoiled landscape, and the highly symbolic reminders of an earlier people, who once lived in and enjoyed the solitude and serenity of the Gila Wilderness.

What Is Wilderness?

What do we really want from the wilderness? What do we want it to be? Why should a dam not be built in an isolated canyon visited by only a few hundred people a year? These challenges have been at the focus of the environmental movement since the days of John Muir.

Some recent philosophers of what is becoming the post-environmentalist age debunk the idea of wilderness for wilderness' sake. They state that a wilderness area is really just another park, an artificial environment just like all the others, except with fewer creature comforts. They say that the concentration on preserving "wilderness" as an area free of any future natural or man-made alterations contradicts nature, of which we are a part. The preservation of a pristine environment such as the Gila Wilderness came long after Native Americans were forced to leave their traditional living and hunting region. Is the wilderness a natural place without its longtime native inhabitants, who lived on the land and used the land in harmony with the rest of nature?

These and other related arguments are already on the political front burner. Western ranchers have largely won a hard-fought battle over grazing rights. Some say, why not substitute cattle for buffalo on the rangelands of the American West? Plagues, volcanoes, and other natural disasters have wiped out many animal species. Is the decimation of the American buffalo any more catastrophic than the natural disappearance of the dinosaur?

Were humans, Native Americans, part of the ecological mix of the southwestern forests, or were they an aberration to be removed? This question haunts me when I visit the Gila Cliff Dwellings, a place of human history, of a long-ago tribe whose successors were not permitted to live their traditional life in this bountiful forest.

The other side of the coin is apparent across the Arizona border. If Canyon de Chelly were designated a national park, the Navajo farmers who practice agriculture on the bottomlands of two fantastically scenic canyons would have to leave. But Canyon de Chelly is a national monument, permitting some "commercial" activity. The canyon is no less marvelous a place to visit because of the farming that has taken place for thousands of years in this river valley. I wonder what the Gila Wilderness would be like if the descendants of the Gila Cliff Dwellers now lived here and used the forest for their own benefit. We would be the intruders.

Instead, we, who come largely from urban areas for rest, relaxation, recreation, and renewal have a forest that is protected from outside influences, including many natural ones such as wildfire. I'm unable to resolve these questions, so suggest that we enjoy this "park" for what it is: one of the many opportunities we have created in this modern age for reflection and personal development. The Gila Wilderness is not a true primeval place—free of modern-day American influence—but it serves well enough; at least until someone else comes along who is able to solve the philosophical questions surrounding the issue of what is wilderness.

As we visit the Gila Wilderness, it quickly becomes apparent that this landscape is not true wilderness, untouched by outside influences. It is a living museum of earlier human inhabitants, and of their struggles to make America what it is. This area, centered at the confluence of the three forks of the Gila River, has long been a confluence of Native American and American pioneer life. Geronimo was born and raised in this area. He and other Apaches battled with the U.S. Cavalry in what is now the wilderness. Prospectors came to explore for minerals, and mines were opened in the nearby forests.

So there is history here, as well as wilderness. Far-sighted Washington bureaucrats first designated this area the Gila River Forest Reserve in 1899, before New Mexico was a state. They began the process of protecting forest lands, which led to Aldo Leopold's accomplishments of 1924. By protecting the headwaters of the three forks of the Gila River, and keeping it as a wilderness (or "park" if you like), we have a place available for personal reflection in a quiet atmosphere. The Gila Cliff Dwellings give us a sense of continuity, of our part in the overall natural scheme of things.

We are simply part of the natural world, which we interact with in different ways. We need natural places to remind us from whence we came, to help us contemplate why we use the land as we do, and to allow us to ponder where we and the land are going. These are the psychic benefits of the wilderness experience.

Gila Wilderness

E stablished in 1924 as the first forest wilderness preserve in the United States, the Gila Wilderness offers the ultimate outdoor experience in the Southwest. This vast tract of 569,792 acres set in the much larger Gila National Forest (2.7 million acres) is a refuge for outdoor lovers with its deep canyons featuring desert agave vegetation, hot springs, 400 miles of fishing streams and—on the upper slopes—thick forests of spruce and fir. Together with the adjacent Aldo Leopold Wilderness, the protected area covers more than 1,000 square miles.

Located in southwestern New Mexico, you can reach the wilderness area by taking State Highway 90 from Lordsburg (on Interstate 10), driving through the historic mining towns of Silver City and Piños Altos, and continuing north into the national forest. Next to the protected wilderness is the Gila Cliff Dwellings National Monument, a series of homes set in high caves above the middle fork of the Gila River. The monument, with its visitor center, is the information and take-off point for hiking and riding in the Gila Wilderness.

The Mogollon tribe lived here for only 10 years, nearly 700 years ago. Their structures were built with stone, mud, and timbers, which still remain on view. The Mogollon used the cliff dwellings as a base for farming, hunting, and fishing.

Three hot springs located near the cliff dwellings can be accessed by short hikes. The Scorpion campground, near the base of the dwellings, is the main entry point to the Gila Wilderness.

This is a place where time stands still and feelings of peace and natural grandeur overcome the visitor.

Other more "civilized" recreation areas lie within the national forest at Lake Roberts, Bear Canyon Lake, and the Mimbres Valley. Here, the legacy of the Mimbres, a branch of the Mogollon, is seen: abandoned villages, farming lands, and hot springs where the Mimbres gathered.

Remnants of the early Spanish age of exploration, and of Tchi-he-nde Apache habitation, are also on display. It is a region of few gas stations, motels, and modern distractions—an incomparable, wild place.

There are few places where one can watch a herd of longhorn antelope or javelina quietly go about their daily routine— feeding, frisking, making sounds, spending quiet moments resting—without the artificial environment of a national park, in which a few hundred other people may be gazing at the same display. Finding a hot spring disgorging water near the riverside, with natural pools created over thousands of years is another experience only a very few special places offer. In the Gila Wilderness, such experiences are possible.

Yet it is only dedicated nature lovers, expending their own energy, hiking to get there, who discover the essence of a wilderness area. Parking in a parking lot and walking around for a few minutes won't do it. Even camping in an organized campground does not provide the ultimate natural experience. You have to work to fully appreciate the natural wonders of the Gila Wilderness. Set apart, miles from the urban scene and commercial functions of society, this truly special place, once the refuge of Geronimo and his Chiricahua Apache warriors, is now preserved for all to enjoy.

Geology

To thoroughly enjoy the wilderness experience, a look at the topography is essential. The Mogollon Mountains provide the main accent to the landscape. This is the high point of the drainage area for the Gila River system, which drains the slopes of the Mogollon Rim. From the headwaters, the creeks flow into the three forks of the Gila, two of which (the West Fork and Middle Fork) meet at the visitor center and join the East Fork a few miles south of the small community of Gila Hot Springs. From here, the Gila turns west and then south on its journey south of the Mogollon Range into Arizona.

The mountains and canyons of this region have been formed by a combination of forces, including volcanic action, faulting, and erosion. Sixty-five million years ago, a great series of volcanic eruptions shook the area. Later, more than 20 million years ago, another period of volcanism occurred. This activity created large mesas that began to erode, creating today's canyons. A later earthquake period brought faulting. It is thought that the Mogollon Range was created by this thrusting action. The earlier volcanic eruptions are thought to have brought the precious minerals, the gold and silver for which Silver City is famous, close to the surface. All of these geological changes have turned what was an inland sea 70 million years ago into the heavily scored landscape of today.

The Mogollon, Pueblo, and Apache

The Mogollon people occupied the Gila River headwaters more than 800 years ago. These early ground-dwellers built pit houses, grew beans and corn, gathered food and hunted game. Later in the period, the Mogollon crafted distinctive black-on-white pottery.

By the 1200s, the Mogollon no longer lived here; they had disappeared or moved to other regions, and the area was occupied by pueblo dwellers. These people lived in the open, as did the Mogollon, but also built protected homes in the cliff of a side canyon. The cliff dwellings found here date back to the 1200s. The Pueblo occupied five of the seven caves that are located far above stream level and farmed on the mesa above the cliffs. Some forty rooms were constructed in the cave, housing about seventy people. The timbers supporting the ceilings have been dated at A.D. 1280.

A 1-mile loop trail begins next to a small visitor center at the cliff dwellings parking lot. The trail is level for awhile, providing a good view of the dwellings high above. A series of stairs takes visitors to the dwellings, 180 feet above trail level. "Triple Cave" is the most impressive of the caves, having three large openings. Using stone, the occupants built rooms on two levels, supporting the upper level with wooden beams. Since they brought their corn down to the cave to grind, they built a food storage area, and also a ceremonial room.

But, like the Mogollon and the Anasazi, the Pueblo people abandoned the secure and comfortable cliff homes, in about A.D. 1300. Much later, Apache used the region for hunting and lived in villages, up to the time of the Gadsden Purchase and the arrival of American homesteaders. A small army camp was established in the late 1800s where the village of Gila Hot Springs now sits, to guard the settlers from the dreaded Apache.

The troubles between foreigners and the Apache had their roots during the Spanish period, from about 1600. The inevitable result of Spanish settlement in the nearby Santa Cruz Valley and the Rio Grande Valley to the east was an ongoing conflict for power over the land. Apache were captured and put into slavery and, beginning in 1835, those with Apache scalps were awarded a bounty. The Gadsden Purchase only made things worse.

In 1856, gold was discovered at Piños Altos, north of Silver City, bringing more prospectors and miners to the region. A major incident occurred at Piños Altos in February 1861, involving Cochise, his followers, and a small U.S. Army unit. Three members of Cochise's family were killed by soldiers in the ensuing conflict, and the wars began in earnest. Several incidents ensued in the mountainous Gila River country. The last Apache to live in the area that is now the Gila Wilderness departed by 1900.

How to Get There

Located in the southwest corner of New Mexico, the Gila National Forest covers 3.3 million acres of tree-covered mountains: the Mogollons, Tularosas, Diablos, and the Black Range. From a base elevation of 4,500 feet in the high desert, the peaks rise to almost 11,000 feet, covering biotic zones from desert to alpine. The Continental Divide snakes across the national forest for 170 miles. Within the larger national forest are three major protected areas. In addition to the Gila Wilderness, the forest encircles the Aldo Leopold Wilderness (202,016 acres) and the Blue Range Wilderness, which crosses the mountains into Arizona.

Much of the national forest is designed for multiple use, including logging, mining, and other human endeavors. The Gila Wilderness comprises over half a million acres covering more than 1,000 square miles. It is located north of the New Mexico towns of Deming and Lordsburg, both on Interstate 10, and even closer to Silver City, which is 44 miles northeast of Lordsburg via State Route 90. It's another 42 miles to the visitor center and the Gila Cliff Dwellings via State Route 15.

You can take an alternate 88-mile scenic route to the wilderness by leaving Interstate 10 at Deming (to the east of Lordsburg) driving northwest for 23 miles on U.S. Highway 180, then heading northeast on State Route 61 through the Mimbres River Valley. This route will lead you to the Lake Roberts Recreation Area before it meets Highway 15, which you'll drive for the final 19 miles to the Gila Wilderness parking lots, visitor center, and campground. Combining the two routes as a loop trip makes for a fine in-and-out drive.

Enjoying the Gila Wilderness

This is an area of dense alpine forest, the Canadian biotic zone with Douglas fir and Engelmann spruce at the higher reaches. Aspen provide shelter for the young fir and spruce seedlings. This is elk country, where the decaying trees nurture an abundant undergrowth. Heavy snows provide a constant supply of water for wildlife and trees. The herbs and shrub berries, a source of food for the Apache, today continue to serve the animals of the region. You'll find wildflowers and ferns in the more open stands of aspen. However, because of firefighting policies that suppressed wildfires over the past century, there are fewer aspens than there might have been through natural adaptation.

At lower levels is the uplands or transition zone, where most of the animals and birds are found, and ponderosa pine predominates. Here the tall pines are in different stages of growth. The portions of the forest that were logged (or burned by wildfires) are densely packed. The older trees, unaffected by earlier logging, are widely spaced, permitting a healthy undergrowth to thrive. Visitors may walk through these stands, off the trails, to see what a natural forest is really like. Along the lower slopes, and those that face south, is the pinyon-juniper woodland. The short pines and junipers are joined here by Emory and Gambel's oaks, an important source of animal food, as are the pine nuts. Throughout this more arid zone live the plants of the high desert: yucca (primarily Spanish dagger) agave, prickly pear, and manzanita. The creeks that flow from the Gila River's three forks tumble through the Uplands zone. The grasses in this zone provide forage for elk, deer (mule and white-tailed), and antelope. Foxes and prairie dogs are numerous, as are hawks and eagles.

The bottomlands are in the high desert—the Upper Sonoran zone—much higher than the neighboring desert areas of southern New Mexico and the San Pedro Valley across the Arizona boundary. Here, streams flow year-round, creating riparian habitats beside the rocky bottoms of the creeks and the river forks. These are trout streams, with fast-moving sections and quieter pools that house insects on which the fish feed. Along with the trout, including the endangered Gila trout, are dace, chubs, suckers, bass, and catfish. The streamside habitats are populated by an amazing variety of trees and shrubs: alder, cottonwood, willow, walnut, maple, ash, and box elder. Vines (Virginia creeper), wild onions, and plants bearing fruit—grapes, strawberries, raspberries—spread over the riverbanks.

On more arid slopes are all the succulents and other plant life of the desert: sagebrush, creosote bush, yucca, and scrub brush. You'll see the effects of periodic flooding, massive movements of soil and vegetation brought about by rampaging rivers after heavy rainstorms. The proximity of the rich, dense riparian habitats to the high, arid desert brings constant wonder. In addition, ponderosa pine is also found at the lower levels, keeping to the south (north-facing) slopes, while the pinyon-juniper woodland covers the north slopes.

The weather and climate are important to a visitor to the Gila Wilderness. This is not the low desert zone of Lordsburg and Las Cruces. It is typical of the higher desert uplands, bringing 20 inches of precipitation on the higher mountains, and 10 to 12 inches at the canyon bottoms. Summer daytime temperatures at river level are normally in the 90s, with summer nights in the 60s. Winter nights are generally below freezing, into the 20s, while daytime winter temperatures rise to the mid-60s. Higher elevations bring cooler temperatures at any time of year.

The mild temperatures cause an early melting of snow at the lower and mid-level elevations, making it possible to begin mountain trail hikes in late March and early April. After heavy snowfall, the topmost trails have been closed until late June or early July. Late March and early April provide the best windows for viewing the full range of wildflowers that grow at river level. Many people visit the wilderness area in May and June when temperatures are crisp but easy to take, plants are flowering in the lower and middle levels, and trails are largely deserted. Fall is another period for full enjoyment of the area, without the summer traffic. Then, the deciduous trees—including maple, walnut, and aspen—are changing color. Hunters come to hunt for elk and deer during the short bow and rifle hunting season. Winter on the canyon floor is mild, offering walks to the steaming hot springs and relaxed soaking in complete solitude.

NATIONAL FOREST FACILITIES

The visitor center for the Gila Wilderness and the Gila Cliff Dwellings National Monument is located at the end of State Route 15, beside the confluence of the east and west forks of the Gila River. It is open year-round, except for December 25 and January 1. The visitor station is staffed by rangers who are knowledgeable about wilderness trails and the cliff dwellings. A selection of books on the natural history of the area is available. The cliff dwellings are located 1 mile beyond the visitor center. Two adjacent park campgrounds are accessed by the same road. These are the only developed campgrounds in the monument, equipped with picnic tables, a water supply, and toilets.

DAY HIKES

The following short hikes begin in the area of the Gila Cliff Dwellings National Monument visitor center. They are relatively easy routes that lead along the river forks or into nearby canyons. The trails cross the rivers, requiring good footwear and the use of caution. Because the water level of the forks can change within a short time, using common sense is necessary before you walk into the streams.

West Fork Trail   The first 5-mile portion of the much longer West Fork Trail is probably the most popular hike from the National Monument. With the trailhead at the cliff dwellings parking lot (#151), the trail crosses the river often, making summer and fall the best seasons for the hike. Along the way you'll see the Grudging Cabin on the south bank. Some walkers only go as far as the rock cave, another cliff dwelling, at mile 3.1. White Rocks Canyon, a side canyon, is at mile 3.75. Ring Canyon is at 8.5 miles. Hell's Hole Canyon, a very scenic ending point for many, is 12.75 miles from the trailhead.

Middle Fork Trail   This is another short hike along a portion of a longer trail (see below). The trailhead (#157) is near the end of the visitor center parking lot. Go to the end of the parking area and turn right. Like the one on the West Fork, this trail stays at river level. Two miles along the trail are hot springs, a popular Apache recreation spot in the days of Geronimo and Cochise. It's a fine place to soak in the early morning and evening hours. The hike continues along and across the river, passing several side canyons. This is one of the most scenic walks in the wilderness area, with a mixed forest on the canyon bottom and high rock cliffs ascending from the riverside.

Stock Bypass Loop Trail   From the trailhead at TJ Corral, take Trail #729. The corral is 1 mile from the visitor center on the road to the cliff dwellings. Follow Trail #729 and bear left at the junction, onto the bypass trail. Walk down the bypass trail for 2.75 miles until you reach the West Fork Trail (#151). Take the West Fork Trail to the east, ending at the cliff dwellings parking lot. The loop is 4.25 miles long.

EE Canyon Loop   This longer hike covers 0.8 miles with an ascent of 970 feet. The trailhead (#160) is at Woody's Corral, 1 mile along the road to the cliff dwellings. The trail climbs on the first 3.25 miles, to a junction at the top of the ridge that separates the West Fork and Little Creek canyons. Take Trail #162 to the right (west) and follow the ridge for .75 miles until you arrive at the junction with EE Canyon Trail (#151). Take EE Canyon Trail north, descending for 2 miles through EE Canyon, arriving at the West Fork Trail. Turn right and walk downriver for 1 mile to the cliff dwellings parking lot. Woody's Corral is 1 mile from the trailhead.

Little Bear Canyon Loop   This 8-mile hike begins at TJ Corral, via Trail #729. Walk for 2 miles to the top of the ridge between the West Fork and the East Fork. This route crosses the junction with Trail #164, but we keep on a straight course for another 2 miles through Little Bear Canyon, arriving at the Middle Fork. Retrace the route to return to TJ Corral.

BACKCOUNTRY HIKES

With more than 300 miles of hiking and riding trails in the Gila Wilderness and more trails leading through the surrounding national forest, a hiker has a grand buffet of hiking routes from which to choose. A comprehensive listing of these trails would take a book of its own. Serious backpackers interested in backcountry hiking should pick up a copy of John Murray's excellent book *The Gila Wilderness, A Hiking Guide*.

The following trails are among the most well-traveled and well-marked backcountry routes in the wilderness preserve, some of which lead to other trailheads and to further exploration. All five trails are accessed from roads in or near the Gila Cliff Dwellings National Monument.

Meadows Trail (Cliff Dwellings to the Meadows)   *Access:* The West Fork trailhead is located at the Gila Cliff Dwellings parking lot. Drive from the national monument visitor center, past the Scorpion campgrounds, and park at the lot next to the small cliff dwellings information center.

The Hike: This is a popular 2- or 3-day hike, with a length of 9 miles. This short backcountry hike may be used by too many people during July and August to be a fulfilling experience. Therefore, I suggest a spring or fall visit to see the beautiful Meadows.

The Trail: Take Trail #151, the West Fork Trail from the trailhead. This popular trail follows the river before it reaches the junction with Trail #28. This is the Zig Zag Trail, which leads toward the Meadows. Originally carved out by cattle, this trail climbs to the top of the canyon. After the ascent (about 3 hours), it meets Trail #164, the Woodland Park–Lilley Park Trail. Stay on Trail #28, climbing to the top of a ridge and then descending to cross Trail #156, the Prior Cabin Trail. Stay on Trail #28 to reach the rim of West Fork Canyon.

The river is 1,000 feet below the rim. The trail descends into the Meadows, a wonderfully open, grassy area, perfect for an overnight stay, either in the grassy meadow area or amidst the pine trees. This trail can be done as a day hike, but you'll wind up having no time at all to spend in the Meadows. Camping overnight is the solution. Many people who hike to the Meadows are so enchanted that they stay for two nights.

West Fork (National Monument to Willow Creek)   *Access:* If you're riding, the place to saddle up is TJ Corral, which provides access to the West Fork side trail along the river that leads to the main trailhead at the Gila Cliff Dwellings parking lot. Those without horses should head straight for the cliff dwellings parking lot.

The Hike: Almost 35 miles long, this trail (#151) is best taken in the summer months when the river is low and the frequent river crossings are relatively easy. For experienced backcountry people, this is a 3-day hike. Many do it in four.

The Trail: The first part of the hike is along the West Fork Trail described above. There will be other people on the first 5 miles or so, the popular day-hike route. White Creek Canyon is at 15.5 miles. After passing the mouth of White Creek, the trail leads along the West Fork for half a mile, then leaves the West Fork and ascends 940 feet to Cub Mesa. The route traverses Cub Mesa and crosses Packsaddle Canyon into Jackass Park before dropping down into West Fork Canyon at the mouth of Cub Creek. It leads for 1.25 miles up the West Fork before reaching the beginning of the fork, where Turkeyfeather Creek and Cub Creek meet to form the Gila. The route (still Trail #151) leads up Turkeyfeather Creek to higher country at Turkeyfeather Pass, then descends to Iron Creek. The trail climbs to Iron Creek Lake, crosses Iron Creek Mesa, then descends to Willow Creek, the Willow Creek Campground, and Forest Road 507, which meets Bursum Road (Route 159).

Middle Fork Trail (Visitor Center to Gilita Campground)
Access: This trail (#157) is the longest single trail in the Gila Wilderness system. The trailhead is located at the end of the parking lot for the national monument visitor center. Drive to the end and walk to the right edge of the lot.

The Hike: It is 36 miles from the trailhead at the visitor center parking lot to the campground at Snow Lake. Walk another 5.1 miles if you want your hike to end at Gilita campground, which has quick access to Bursum Road. Forest Road 142 leads from Snow Lake to Bursum Road. The benefit of ending your hike at Snow Lake is a possibility of a night beside the lake before pickup. At least 6 days should be reserved for this trip, starting with a soak in the hot springs at the 2-mile point.

The Trail: This moderately difficult trail should be taken in the summer and early fall, when the river is low enough to permit crossing. The trail follows the Middle Fork for almost all of the route, passing through deep canyons, across lava flows, past cliff dwellings, and through wonderful streamside woodlands. There are many river crossings—about a hundred—over sand or cobble. As with the West Fork Trail, this route intersects with numerous other wilderness trails, including the Meadows Trail. A side trip to the Meadows could add an extra day.

A warning about quicksand: There are patches of quicksand along the Middle Fork, and hikers should be cautious before setting out to cross the river at one of the many crossings. It helps to stay out of wet areas and cross where you see a definite dry crossing.

Gila River Trail (Grapevine Campground to Turkey Creek)

Access: This trail (#724) does not begin at the national monument but is across the road from Grapevine campground, at the Upper Gila River Bridge, south of the village of Gila Hot Springs. This is another long streamside walk on the main river below the confluences with tributaries.

The Hike: Since this part of the Gila is also a prime rafting stream, you may see rafters on the river. The hike is 32.5 miles long—from the bridge to a back road near Turkey Creek.

The Trail: Starting in the Gila Wilderness, the trail follows the river out of the wilderness boundary, and then proceeds through the national forest for another 25 miles. There are hot springs along the way, including an early possible soak less than 2 miles from the bridge trailhead. Another hot spring pool is at Turkey Creek. The trail passes several cliff dwellings. There is good fishing for a variety of fish, including trout and catfish.

Granny Mountain Loop (Woody's Corral to/from Gila River)

Access: The trailhead is at Woody's Corral, on the road to the Gila Cliff Dwellings in the national monument. Woody's Corral is halfway down this road, between the area of the visitor center and the cliff dwellings trailhead.

The Hike: A 35-mile route (trails 160, 159, 155, 161), this is just one of the many possible loop hikes you can take through the Gila Wilderness by using several trails for a circle trip. Only the limits of your imagination will limit the choices.

The Trails: Granny Mountain Trail (#160) runs down the West Fork, in a southerly direction, until it meets the Gila River. However, we will leave this trail before reaching the river.

At Miller Spring, where there is good drinking water, take the Miller Spring Trail (#159) to the junction with the Turkey Creek Trail (#155), then take Turkey Creek Trail to Little Creek Spring. You'll find the Little Creek Trail (#161), which leads back to the Granny Mountain Trail and Woody's Corral.

This long trip with ups and downs along the side of several mountains requires a minimum of 3 days.

House Log Canyon and Meadows Hot Springs   *Access:* Via the Middle Fork Trail (#157). Drive into the national monument visitor center parking lot, go to the end, and find the trailhead to the right of the lot.

The Hike: This 9.5-mile hike along the Middle Fork can be arduous for novice hikers, with more than forty river crossings. It does result in finding a very satisfying primitive hot spring pool (unmarked on any map) where water flows out of the ground at a temperature of 92 degrees F., then directly into a small, natural pool. Hike a mile farther up the Middle Fork and you'll find another hot spring pool (Meadows), where Indian Creek Canyon meets the Middle Fork.

The Trail: The Middle Fork Trail is best hiked during low water periods, in the summer and fall months. It is not a strenuous hike, as the route follows the canyon bottom for the entire route. Because there are so many crossings in the 10.5-mile walk to the two hot springs, this adventure should not be considered earlier in the year. The Gila Wilderness Visitor's Travel Guide and Map is a good guide to the canyon locations along the Middle Fork.

Camping

Two campgrounds in Gila Cliff Dwellings National Monument provide little more in services than the basic forest recreation campsites. The side-by-side campgrounds (Scorpion 1 and Scorpion 2) are located on the road that leads to the cliff dwellings trail. There is a private campground with RV spaces in the nearby village of Gila Hot Springs. Additional Forest

Service campgrounds are located outside the wilderness boundary, on State Route 15 (Forks and Grapevine), and farther from the monument on State Route 35. These campsites are in the Lake Roberts Recreation Area (15 minutes' drive from the intersection of Route 35 and State Route 15).

BACKCOUNTRY ADVISORY

Backpacking permits and the filing of trip itineraries are not required in the Gila Wilderness. Topographical maps and other information are available at the visitor information center in the Gila Cliff Dwellings National Monument. For advance information and ordering of maps, call (505) 536-9461. One map that provides an excellent overview of the wilderness is the "Visitors Travel Guide and Map of the Gila Wilderness." This is not the usual colored forest map but is a special semi-waterproof map, three feet square (200 feet contour), selling for $5.00. It has all the maintained trails marked with numbers and also has prominent topographical features including mountain peaks, springs, rivers, creeks, and perimeter roads for trail access. USGS topos (40 feet contour) are available at $2.50 per map.

You have to cross rivers on the major trails that lead along the Gila River and its forks. There is not a single footbridge on the trail system (after all, this is wilderness). The four riverside trails require several crossings per mile. Crossings are often hazardous from mid-March through late April. There are places along the East Fork that are privately owned, and hikers must receive written permission to cross these properties, all shown on the wilderness map.

Campers should put their tents on high ground, above the forks or river. Water sources, including the three forks and the river, are generally reliable. There are springs with potable water along several of the most popular trails. Check with the rangers before you set out to confirm water sources on your route. It is advisable not to immerse your head in hot spring water, or splash water on your head or chest. There is a tiny organism in some of the spring pools which, when inhaled through the nose, may cause serious medical problems.

Finding a camping spot is easy, as camping is permitted anywhere in the backcountry wilderness, except within 300 feet of a spring, 100 feet of a stream, or within 300 yards of a tank or other man-made water supply. Firewood may be gathered for campfires, but only that wood which is both dead and down. Do not remove dead branches from living trees. Fire rings are not permitted within the wilderness, and campers are asked to scatter any rings they might find. Pets are allowed, although not particularly welcomed because of the presence of wildlife.

Nearby Attractions

LAKE ROBERTS RECREATION AREA

Twenty-five miles to the southeast is a peaceful, 71-acre reservoir with national forest campgrounds that are superior to most basic campgrounds. There are two campgrounds, several picnic areas, and a grocery store in the tiny village of Lake Roberts. About a half-hour drive to the Gila Wilderness visitor center, these campgrounds provide a pleasant place to stay while you take day-hikes in the wilderness and visit the cliff dwellings. The lake is perfect for canoeing.

WHITEWATER CANYON CATWALK

The Gila National Forest extends to the Arizona border, west of the Mogollon Range. This western forest area is an historic area: first, the home of Apache communities, and later the scene of several large gold strikes in the 1800s. There were many outlaws in these forests during the gold period, gravitating from nearby Tombstone and other rowdy mining towns. This is the location of the Catwalk National Recreation Trail, located in Whitewater Canyon near the town of Graham. This area of the national forest is accessed via U.S. Highway 180, leading north from Silver City. It can also be reached—from the northeast—via Bursum Road (State Route 159). The site is 5 miles west of Glenwood and U.S. 180.

The gold produced in the Whitewater Canyon area could not be milled near the mines because of the narrow canyon. Water for the town and the mill had to be provided by a 4-inch pipeline running 3 miles up the canyon. Construction was completed in 1893. The present-day catwalk follows the route of the pipeline. The mill closed in 1913 and the pipeline and catwalk lay dormant until the Depression, when the Civilian Conservation

Corps rebuilt the catwalk as a recreational attraction. What was the work camp for the CCC workers is now the Glenwood Community Park. The wooden catwalk finished in 1936 was replaced by a metal catwalk in 1961.

The nature trail and suspended metal pathway provide an exhilarating walk through 3 miles of the canyon and the ponderosa pine forest. Many people visit the canyon each year, picnicking at the Whitewater Picnic Grounds. This attraction provides a good reason to visit the Glenwood district, including San Francisco Gorge southwest of Glenwood.

SILVER CITY AND PIÑOS ALTOS

The old mining town of Silver City is a picturesque little community, located next to the Gila National Forest and only 40 miles south of the Gila Cliff Dwellings. Situated at an elevation of 5,850 feet, 44 miles northeast of Lordsburg, the college town is focused more on tourism than mining these days, although the discovery of large copper deposits south of Silver City has given new life to the town.

Silver City has an historic business district. A walking tour map, obtained from the town information center, leads to a collection of Victorian houses and other buildings from the late nineteenth and early twentieth centuries. The information center is located at 1103 N. Hudson St., (call 505-538-3785). There are two museums that provide information on the early mining days in this area as well as display art and artifacts. The Silver City Museum (312 W. Broadway St., downtown), formerly an 1881 silver magnate's mansion, holds exhibits on the history of the mining town of Tyrone. An annex houses other regional exhibits. The Western New Mexico University Museum is at 12th and Virginia streets. While this museum has displays of photographs from the mining camp period, its major focus is on African folk art, and Native American pottery and jewelry.

Seven miles north of Silver City, the pioneer mining town of Piños Altos survived early Apache attacks to produce over $8 million of gold, silver, copper, lead, and zinc before the mines played out in the early 1900s. Some of the original buildings remain, including a fine old saloon and dining house. The original fort has been recreated, on a slightly smaller scale.

WILDERNESS WILDLIFE

With a high desert environment on the canyon floors, the mountains bring a series of rich biotic communities, including that of the Rocky Mountains (Canadian, fir/spruce), the pinyon-pine woodland, and the Transition Zone, characterized by ponderosa pine that grows on north-facing slopes in the river canyons. Desert plants, including yucca, agave, cacti, and sagebrush, are found on the south-facing canyon slopes. The semidesert environment is startling to observe, only a few yards away from and above the riparian environment of the riverside.

Higher in the mountain meadows, the wildflowers bloom. The selection of wildflowers in the Gila Wilderness is much the same as that seen in the high Bryce Canyon area. The mule deer is the most numerous mammal in the Gila Wilderness. The original elk herd was decimated by hunting before the wilderness area was protected, but Merriam's elk were introduced and are now seen in small numbers. The best time to see elk is in winter, when they migrate to lower levels to obtain food. Other native mammals include black bear, mountain lion, bobcat, mink, skunk, porcupine, javelina and coatimundi. The bird spectrum, while not quite as rich as in the nearby San Pedro Valley, offers wonderful bird-watching. From the forest woodpeckers to water and song birds, there's a plentiful supply.

BIRDS

Acorn Woodpecker

Melanerpes formicivorus
Red, black, and yellow are prominent colors on and around the head of this woodpecker. The crown is red, with the area between the crown and the bill a bright yellow. This yellow extends to the throat. The front of the crown is yellow, as a connecting band. The bird's back is black. It has white wing patches and a white rump. You'll find the acorn woodpecker in all four woodland zones in the Gila Wilderness, from pinyon-pine to spruce-fir. Its loud and persistent calls include a *ja-cob, ja-cob, ja-cob, ja-cob*—with the accent on the *ja*—and *wack-up, wack-up, wack-up, wack-up*. It also makes a hitting sound with

its bill, similar to a drumroll. This is a territorial marking sound.

Hairy Woodpecker
Picoides villosus
This common woodpecker is found here, and across most of North America, wherever there are trees in which to drill holes. It is easy to spot, by noting its large bill, white back, and the small red "skullcap," a red patch at the back of the crown. The black wings have white spots and there are white patches (sideburns) on the head. The underpart is whitish. You'll find this bird in groves by the rivers, and in the pine and spruce-fir forests.

Cinnamon Teal
Anas cyanoptera
This small duck is found in ponds and marshes throughout the West, from southwest Canada to Mexico and South America. Both male and female can be identified by the grayish-blue (longitudinal) strip on the fore edge of the wing. The male has a general cinnamon color throughout, with a deep cinnamon-brown on the head and below, and dappled wings. The female's bill is longer than the male's. Both grow to a length of about 17 inches. The cinnamon

teal is a summer resident of the Gila Wilderness.

Lesser Scaup
Aythya affinis
This bay duck is a winter resident of southwestern New Mexico. The scaups (lesser and greater) have wide white stripes on the trailing edge of the wings. The stripe on the lesser scaup is shorter than on the greater. The male and female are quite different in coloration. The male has a black head and chest, and also a black tail. Its back is a mottled gray-white. The female is brown, with a sharp white band (like a mask) around its bill. The bill—on both male and female—is blue. With a range extending from Alaska and western Canada to South America, the scaup lives in rivers, lakes, marshy ponds, and estuary environments. Its voice is a very loud *scaup*. Male and female make purring notes and the male calls with a low whistle. The lesser scaup lives in open marsh area in the Gila Wilderness.

Blue Grouse
Dendragapus obscurus
For a grouse, this bird is large, with a bluish-gray color and a yellow to orange comb over the eyes. The male has mottled, dark brown wings. There is a

wide, light blue band at the end of the tail on blue grouse that live in the northern Rockies, and only a slight tinge of gray-blue in other regions. The female is a lighter, mottled brown on its back, head, neck, and tail. In the spring, the male performs a mating ritual that deserves a bird "Oscar." It perches on logs and stumps, giving a series of five to seven loud hooting or booming notes, by inflating and deflating the large yellow or purple pouches on each side of the neck. This grouse lives at the edge of mountain forests, including the subalpine spruce-fir forest at the topmost level of the Gila Wilderness.

Purple Martin
Progne subis
A summer dweller in the highest reaches of the wilderness area, this large swallow spends the summer from southern Canada to northern Mexico, and winters in South America. The purple martin is similar to the tree swallow, except much larger. The male and female are vastly different in color. The male has such a dark-blue color, that it seems almost black above and below. The female has a light, mottled belly, with less mottling toward the tail. Gliding in a circular pattern, its song is a repeated, deep *tchoo-wuw*.

Western Kingbird
Tyrannus verticalis
One of 21 tyrant flycatchers living in the western U.S., the western kingbird is the most frequently seen kingbird in the Southwest. The tyrant family also includes becards, flycatchers, phoebes, and peewees. The western kingbird breeds here, and is a summer resident, living at all elevations except the spruce-fir zone. It has a gray head and a yellowish belly. The narrow black tail has a tracing of white at the edges. Wintering in Mexico and Costa Rica, it lives in open areas, meadows, fields, and near forest clearings. Its call is a quick *whit, whit*, or *whit-kee-wit*.

Cordillaran Flycatcher
Empidonax occidentalis
This is one of two "western" flycatchers. The other is the pacific-slope flycatcher. The cordillaran is a summer resident, and breeds in the Gila Wilderness. This species is originally Canadian, with a dull gray-green back and head, blackish wings, and yellowish throat and belly. It has two curved bars at the upper part of the wing. The eye ring is oval. This bird spends its summers in the Gila Wilderness because of the high elevations, otherwise it would be found in Canada or the northeastern United States.

It winters from Mexico to Panama. The differences between the two "western" flycatchers is mainly in their voice. While the pacific-slope flycatcher's song is an uplifted *tseep*, the cordillaran's song is a squeaky *pit-wheet*, with each note issued separately.

Yellow-rumped Warbler
Otus flammeolus
Formerly called Audubon's warbler, this bird is found at lower elevations in the Gila Wilderness than many of the resident birds, ranging from the pinyon-pine woodlands to the spruce-fir forest. It is easily identified by the bright yellow rump just above the tail. The male has a yellow crown, as well as yellow throat and side patches. It has white chin and wing bars. This wood warbler spend its summers from Alaska to Guatemala and winters as far south as Panama. It prefers conifer forests in summer, although it is found in the pinyon-juniper zone in southwestern New Mexico. Its song is in two parts, either up or down in pitch: *seet-seet-seet-seet*, *trrrrrrr*. Its note is a distinct *chek*.

Red-faced Warbler
Cardellina rubrifrons
The only wood warbler with a red face to be found in the U.S., its distinctive head and chest make it easy to spot. The forehead and chin are bright red and there is a black patch on the head. The back is gray, with a white patch on the rump. Preferring a warmer environment, it lives mainly in mountainous regions of the southwestern U.S. and Mexico, including the pinyon-juniper and pine areas in the Gila Wilderness. It is sometimes seen as a casual visitor at desert oases, far from its preferred habitat. The song is a bright, rapid *tsee-tsee-tsee-tsee-titi-wee*, or *weet-weet-weet-weet-tsee-tsee*. Its primary food is insects.

Brown-headed Cowbird
Molothrus ater
A smallish blackbird, the male has a reddish-brown head. The female is gray with a lighter, grayish-brown breast and belly. Immature male cowbirds molt in the late summer, giving them a mottled look. Male and female have a short bill. You'll see them on the ground with their tails lifted. They are found in all zones within the Gila wilderness, from the riparian habitat of the canyon bottoms to the spruce-fir forest. Its range is from southern Canada to Mexico. It often lives in river groves, but also inhabits the edges of forests, farms, fields, and roadsides. Its song is a bur-

bling *glug-glug-gleeee* (as if sung through water). The call is a whistle: *weeee-tete*.

Dark-eyed Junco
Junco hyemalis
Looking like a sparrow, the "gray-headed" junco is one of four regional subspecies of this bird, living in the southern Rockies and nearby ranges and the Great Basin. It has a gray head and sides, a rufous back, and white outer tail feathers that can be seen when it is flying. The dark-eyed junco is a summer resident and breeds in the deciduous riparian areas of the Gila Wilderness. It is also seen in Arizona's San Pedro Valley and conifer forests. Wintering in northern Mexico, Texas, Louisiana, and other gulf states, it lives in mixed woodlands, along roadsides and brushy areas. Its song is a light, pleasant *chip-chip-chip*. Its note is a series of *click* notes or *tick* notes.

OTHER ANIMALS

Tiger Salamander
Ambystoma tigrinum
This large, chunky land-dwelling salamander (the world's largest) lives in a wide range of biotic zones, from low desert to mountain areas up to 11,000 feet. While it lives on land, it breeds in pools, quiet river areas, and lakes—early in the spring. The larvae transform into baby amphibians in mid-summer. Aside from its approximate tiger-like appearance, it has a varied coloration including light spots on a dark background or dark spots on a light background. Tubercles are located on the soles of its feet. Its range is from southern Canada to Mexico and Florida. In the Gila Wilderness, it lives in the pine and spruce-fir forests and meadows, preferring damp soil. It is best seen at dusk, after a spring rain. It feeds on worms, insects, mice, and smaller amphibians.

Greater Earless Lizard
Cophosaurus texanus
Living at the wilderness area's mid-level ranges (oak woodland and pine forest), this large (7-inch) lizard blends into its habitat, taking on gray to brown coloration. It has broad brown bands on the underside of its long flat tail. The male has two bars on its side. The female has no side bars. Ranging from central Arizona to southern Texas and northern Mexico, it lives in cliffs, sandy rivers, and creek beds—generally, in rocky areas including washes. It's active in the daytime hours.

Short-horned Lizard
Phrynosoma douglassi (ornatissimum)
This unusual, wide and flat-bodied lizard is the same shape as its relative, the Texas short-horned lizard (*P. d. cornutum*). Both have heads topped by short spines, but cornutum is smaller. Behind the spines is a depression in the skull. It has two rows of spots in a darker shade of brown than the rest of the back, which is yellow to light brown. Its belly has smooth scales. This is the desert subspecies, which lives in oak and pinyon woodlands and sometimes in lower-level conifer woodlands such as the ponderosa pine groves in the Gila River canyons. Ants make up its main food supply.

Great Plains Skink
Eumeces obsoletus
This reptile with an exceptionally long tail likes to live beside a permanent water supply. Running down its back and tail is a set of horizontal scales. Under this set of scales, on its side, are rows of scales that are oblique to the row of back scales. This large skink has a yellowish-brown color, getting more yellow toward its tail. The young are black with white spots on the lips, and have a blue tail. Its range is from southern Nebraska and the Great Plains states to Mexico and into Texas. In this part of the desert Southwest, it lives in open rocky areas fairly close to its water supply. Mating occurs in April and May, eggs hatch in July and August. It feeds on small lizards, insects, and spiders. Beware of handling: it bites!

Southwestern Toad
Bufo microscaphus
This olive to pink toad is a plump specimen, which may or may not have dark spots. There is often a whitish patch on the back and head. The underside is lighter, from the throat to belly. The "Arizona" subspecies, found in the Gila Wilderness, is *A. m. microscaphus*, the desert dweller found also in southwest Utah, Arizona, southern Nevada, and into Mexico. This toad has a very musical trilling call, which runs for about ten seconds and then stops abruptly. It can be seen during evening and early morning hours, hopping around and looking for food, which includes spiders and insects.

Bullfrog
Rana catesbeiana
The largest frog in America, the bullfrog lives in open marshes and riparian areas where there are deciduous trees, primarily

the cottonwood/willow habitat. It doesn't like flowing rivers, but prefers ponds, backwaters, and lakes. The top part of the bullfrog is a yellowish-green color. The underside is much lighter: creamy to almost white, with gray mottling. An unusual feature is the frog's large round external eardrum, visible behind the eye. The enormous thighs are also standouts. Like other amphibians, it is nocturnal, resting during the day. It can be found along the edges of the rivers and ponds. The voice is the well-known croak: *chug-o-rum* or *jug-o-rum*.

Western Rattlesnake
Crotalus vividus
Usually found in the Great Basin, and a small portion of the Mojave Desert, the western rattlesnake has somehow taken residence in the Mogollon and Chiricahua ranges. It is harder to identify than other, more distinctively colored rattlesnakes. Its back has a brownish, blotched appearance, with a light stripe behind the eye. It has noticeable black and (wider) white rings around the tail. This rattler lives at elevations up to about 8,000 feet. Here it lives on canyon floors, in the high desert zone, and in the woodlands surrounding the rivers, except for the spruce-fir

forest. It lives in scrub desert lands, near cactus, mesquite, and creosote bush. But here, it also lives on rocky hills and in woodlands, especially the pinyon-juniper zone. It roams mainly at night, and is most often seen near streams. With extremely strong venom, this is the most dangerous rattlesnake in America.

Southwestern Myotis
Myotis auriculus
One of eighteen bats found in the Gila Wilderness, the Southwestern myotis is a small bat (about 3.5 inches long) with dull brown fur. It has a long tragus (lobe) extending from the ear. Unlike many bats, it lives in desert areas, as well as oak chaparral, pinyon-juniper woodlands, and pine forests. It nests in rocky outcrops and caves. It is sometimes found in buildings. This bat is found only in southeast Arizona, and southwest New Mexico, and into central-northern Mexico.

Silver-haired Bat
Lasionycteris noctivagans
This very widespread, medium-sized bat is almost entirely black, but has fine silver hairs on its back. It has short, rounded ears. This bat usually comes out of its cave at dusk

and flies much more slowly than many other bats, looking for insects, particularly moths. It ranges throughout southern Canada, most of the U.S., and farther south, except southern California, Texas, and the gulf coast states including Florida. It migrates south for the winter, spending the summers in this region. Each night it roves over a wide area, traveling as much as 100 miles from its home roost.

Spotted Bat
Euderma maculatum
This very rare North American bat is also called the "Death's Head" bat. It does not have a wide range, living only in southeastern California, the tip of Nevada, throughout Arizona, into the Durango area of Colorado, and into this corner of New Mexico. It has a distinctive pattern of fur—black above with three large white spots. Its lower parts are white. With a body length of only 4.5 inches, the spotted bat has an extremely wide wingspan. It has very large ears (as long as its body). It makes a loud, high-pitched call when flying. It lives in caves and on rocky cliffs and canyons. It can be seen flying out of crevices in the Gila river canyons. The most common bat in the Southwest, the Brazilian free-tailed bat, is not found in this area.

Rock Squirrel
Spermophilus variegatus
One of ten squirrels found in the Gila Wilderness, this is the largest of the ground squirrels found in Arizona and New Mexico. It is the only squirrel found in all five biotic zones in the wilderness area. Since it rests during the midday period, be on the lookout for this squirrel during the early morning and early evening hours. It has a gray-brown front and a plain brown back, with white or a buff color below. The rock squirrel is also seen in a much darker, even-colored variation. Its range is from southern Nevada, Utah, Colorado, and into Oklahoma to West Texas on the east. It lives in open rocky areas, particularly in the lower oak-juniper habitat.

Gray Fox
Urocyon cinereoargenteus
As its name suggests, this fox is largely gray, but with a reddish tint on the back of the head and underneath. Its throat is white. The upper part and tip of the tail have long black hairs. It has large ears and its feet are a rusty-red color. This fox has the ability to jump into low-lying trees, doing so to eat and to escape enemies. It lives at the mid-level areas of the Gila Wilderness, in the three zones that have juniper and pon-

derosa pine. It prefers to live in thickets and other brushy areas with large rocks. Its range includes most of the United States except for the Great Basin and Rocky Mountain regions. Its foreprint shows four clawed toes, with a "winged" heel pad.

PLANTS

Arizona Madrone
Arbutus arizonica
This tree is a member of the heather family, along with other unlikely members including azalea, cranberry, rhododendron, and bearberry. This particular arbutus grows only in a small area of southeastern Arizona and southwestern New Mexico. An evergreen tree, it grows to 45 feet tall. Its trunk is from 18 to 24 inches in diameter. The leathery green leaves grow on thin twigs, which are red. Its bark is its most distinctive feature, gray and scaly, peeling from the trunk in thin sheets, much like all arbutus trees. It bears clusters of white to light pink flowers from April to September, and its berries are a bright orange-red.

Apache Pine
Pinus engelmannii
Another tree found in the Gila Wilderness, the Apache Pine has a narrow range, growing only in the immediate region and into Mexico, mainly along the Continental Divide that runs through the Mogollon Range. It is similar to the ponderosa pine, growing to an age of up to 500 years. It has long, light green needles, usually about 10 inches long. The bark is dark brown, growing yellow with age. The dark red cones, oval-shaped, are about 6 or 7 inches long, grow in pairs, or in groups of three to five. Birds eat the dark brown seeds. Native Americans used the soft inner bark of this tree for food, and obtained the resin for waterproofing purposes.

Pinyon Pine
Pinus edulis
Growing throughout the Southwest, the pinyon (or piñon) is the state tree of New Mexico. Small for a pine, it grows to 35 feet (but that height is unusual). It has a distinctive crooked trunk with a reddish-brown bark. Usually part of a plant community with Utah or one-seed juniper, in the Gila Wilderness, it is accompanied by the one-seed, alligator, and Rocky Mountain junipers. This very useful tree produces plump cones that contain the pine nuts used by humans, animals, and birds for food. Wood rats gather and store the pine nuts for their winter supply. This is a slow-growing,

long-lasting tree, living up to 150 years.

Lanceleaf Cottonwood
Populus acuminata
Unlike the more common desert riparian tree, the Fremont cottonwood, the lanceleaf grows at elevations from 4,500 to 8,500 feet, making it perfect for this high Mogollon environment. It is thought to be a crossbreed of the narrowleaf and plains cottonwoods. Growing to a height of about 50 feet, it is seen along creeks and rivers, in the Southwest and north to Canada. Its leaves grow at the end of yellowish-brown twigs. Like other members of the willow family, the buds and catkins of this cottonwood are eaten by animals, including deer and elk. Native Americans also ate the tender buds, and made drums from cottonwood logs.

Gray Oak
Quercus grisea
This oak grows in the oak-juniper zones, here and in other parts of the Southwest. It is accompanied, in the Gila Wilderness, by the Gambel oak. It is also called the shin oak, or *encina blanca* (white oak). Its grayish-blue leaves are small and oval, sometimes toothed. It

is easily identified by the blue tinge to its leaves. Growing to elevations of about 7,800 feet, the gray oak's range is from southern Arizona into southern New Mexico and West Texas, as well as into Mexico. It grows mainly on slopes and mountain ridges. The acorns are eaten by birds and animals. Mule deer forage on the leaves.

Pennycress
Thlaspi montanum
Pennycress is only one of more than 150 wildflowers found in the Gila Wilderness. This member of the mustard family is also called wild candytuft. You'll see the pennycress flowers early in the spring, before most other mountain plants are in bloom. Leaves form an unusual rosette on the ground. The stem leaves are opposite, rising along the stalks that branch from ground level. The leaves are dark green and smooth. The white flowers have four petals and six stamens. The flowers grow in clusters, making it a beautiful springtime sight. Triangular seed pods follow the flowers. Springtime in the wilderness is a wildflower lover's delight, with lupines, goosefeet, and many other species in the hillside and meadow displays.

GILA CLIFF DWELLINGS NATIONAL MONUMENT

Two campgrounds, **Scorpion 1 and 2**, are located near the national monument visitor center. These are the only maintained campgrounds with drinking water and toilets within the Gila Wilderness boundaries. The campsites are secured on a first-come, first-served basis. To get there, take State Route 15 north past the community of Gila Hot Springs and drive past the bridge over the river. Turn left just before reaching the national monument visitor center. Drive 1.5 miles toward the Gila Cliff Dwellings trailhead. The campgrounds and a picnic area are on the right. Trailers are restricted to a length of 17 feet. For information on camping, including backcountry camping in the Gila Wilderness, call the Wilderness Ranger District: (505) 536-2250.

Two additional Forest Service Campgrounds are located just south of the small village of Gila Hot Springs, on State Route 15. The **Forks** and **Grapevine** campgrounds are of the basic, primitive type. There is a small store in Gila Hot Springs that stocks campers' supplies. Grapevine campground is said to have the world's largest grapevine.

GILA HOT SPRINGS

Doc Campbell's Post
Highway 15, Route 11
P.O. Box 80
Silver City, NM 88061
(505) 536-9551

This is a longtime institution in this tiny community located on State Route 15, just south of the Gila Cliff Dwellings National Monument. Also called the Gila Hotsprings Vacation Center, the operation has RV and trailer spaces and a hot spring pool with thermal water piped from the nearby spring.

PIÑOS ALTOS

Continental Divide R.V. Park is 7 miles north of Silver City in this old mining town. There are 14 sites. For information, call (505) 388-3005.

Camping near Piños Altos
The U.S. Forest Service operates the **McMillan** and **Cherry Creek** campgrounds, located just inside the Gila National Forest, 12 miles north of Silver

City and 5 miles north of Piños Altos. There are 14 basic sites.

SILVER CITY

Bear Mountain Guest Ranch
P.O. Box 1163
Silver City, NM 88062
(505) 538-2538

One of the finest attributes of this guest ranch is the energy and enthusiasm of its owner, Myra McCormick. She has instituted a Lodge & Learn program, providing classes in birding, for example. Excursions to nearby attractions such as the Gila Cliff Dwellings are also popular with guests. All rooms (15, including some suites) have private baths, and the ranch is open all year ($$).

Copper Manor Motel
710 Silver Heights Boulevard
Silver City, NM 88062
(505) 538-5392

This modern motel has 68 units with color TV and phones in each room, in addition to an indoor pool, whirlpool, a cafe, and lounge ($).

Holiday Motor Hotel
3420 Highway 120E
Silver City, NM 88061
(505) 538-3711

A pool and coin laundry are two of the features of this Best Western operation. It also has a restaurant that serves beer and wine. There are 79 units available at a reasonable rate ($).

The Carter House B&B Inn and Hostel
101 N. Cooper Street
Silver City, NM 88061
(505) 388-5485

This unusual place is a combination of a small bed and breakfast inn and an AYH (American Youth Hostel).

Silver City Camping
KOA Kampground
Highway 180 East
Silver City, NM 88601

This typical KOA Kampground with 75 sites is the most complete campground and RV facility in the area.

Silver City RV Park is located at Bennett and 13th streets, with 13 sites. (505) 538-2239.

LAKE ROBERTS

Lake Roberts Recreation Area is located beside a 72-acre lake in the Gila National Forest, less than a 40-minute drive from the national monument visitor center. There are two campgrounds in the recreation area. Mesa Campground has 24 sites near the lake. Trailer or RV length is restricted to 22 feet. Lake Roberts Upper-end Campground is at lake level. This campground has 10 sites and the same trailer stipulation —22-foot maximum—applies.

WILDLIFE CHECKLIST

Birds of the Southwest

This checklist of birds is a selected guide to the species that are permanent, seasonal, or transient residents of the Southwest.

Residency Key: P—permanent, T—transient (most pass through in spring and fall), W—winter resident, S—summer resident, I—irregular (varies from year to year or not enough is known). *—Asterisks indicate birds that have been identified but are rarely seen.

Loons and Grebes

☐ Arctic Loon	T
☐ Pacific Loon*	T
☐ Common Loon	T
☐ Pied-billed Grebe	T
☐ Horned Grebe	T
☐ Eared Grebe	W
☐ Clark's Grebe*	T
☐ Least Grebe*	T
☐ Western Grebe	P

Cormorants and Pelicans

☐ Double-crested Cormorant	T
☐ Olivaceous Cormorant*	S
☐ American White Pelican	T
☐ Brown Pelican	T
☐ Magnificent Frigatebird*	T

Herons and Allies

☐ American Bittern	T
☐ Least Bittern	T
☐ Great Blue Heron	P
☐ Great Egret	T
☐ Snowy Egret	T
☐ Little Blue Heron*	T
☐ Tri-colored Heron	T
☐ Reddish Egret*	T
☐ Cattle Egret	T
☐ Green-backed Heron	P
☐ Black-crested Night Heron	P
☐ Louisiana Heron*	T
☐ White-faced Ibis	T
☐ Wood Stork*	T

Swans, Geese, and Ducks

☐ Fulvous Whistling Duck*	S
☐ Black-bellied Whistling Duck	S
☐ Tundra Swan	T
☐ Greater White-fronted Goose*	W
☐ Snow Goose	W
☐ Ross' Goose	W
☐ Brant*	W
☐ Canada Goose	W
☐ Wood Duck	W
☐ Green-winged Teal	W
☐ Mallard	P
☐ Northern Pintail	W
☐ Garganey*	I
☐ Blue-winged Teal	W
☐ Cinnamon Teal	W
☐ American Widgeon	W

☐ Gadwall	W
☐ Canvasback	W
☐ Redhead	W
☐ Ring-necked Duck	W
☐ Greater Scaup	T
☐ Lesser Scaup	W
☐ Oldsquaw*	T
☐ Black Scoter*	T
☐ Surf Scoter	T
☐ White-winged Scoter*	T
☐ Common Goldeneye	W
☐ Barrow's Goldeneye*	W
☐ Bufflehead	W
☐ Hooded Merganser	T
☐ Common Merganser	T
☐ Red-breasted Merganser	T
☐ Ruddy Duck	W
☐ Northern Shoveler	W

Raptors

☐ Black Vulture	S
☐ Turkey Vulture	S
☐ Osprey	T
☐ Black-shouldered Kite	T
☐ Mississippi Kite	T
☐ Bald Eagle	T
☐ Northern Harrier	W
☐ Sharp-shinned Hawk	W
☐ Sparrow Hawk	P
☐ White-tailed Hawk	T
☐ Cooper's Hawk	P
☐ Northern Goshawk	T
☐ Common Black Hawk	T
☐ Harris' Hawk	P
☐ Gray Hawk	S
☐ Red-shouldered Hawk*	I
☐ Broad-winged Hawk	T
☐ Swainson's Hawk	S
☐ Zone-tailed Hawk	T
☐ Red-tailed Hawk	P
☐ Ferruginous Hawk	P
☐ Rough-legged Hawk	W
☐ Marsh Hawk	W
☐ Golden Eagle	P

☐ Crested Caracara	I
☐ American Kestrel	P
☐ Merlin	W
☐ Peregrine Falcon	T
☐ Prairie Falcon	W

Turkey, Quail, and Grouse

☐ Sage Grouse	P
☐ Turkey	P
☐ Scaled Quail	P
☐ Gambel's Quail	P
☐ Harlequin Quail	P
☐ Montezuma Quail	T

Cranes and Allies

☐ Black Rail*	T
☐ Clapper Rail*	T
☐ Virginia Rail	W
☐ Sora	W
☐ Purple Gallinule	T
☐ Common Moorhen	W
☐ American Coot	P
☐ Sandhill Crane	T
☐ Whooping Crane*	T

Shorebirds

☐ Black-bellied Plover	T
☐ American Golden Plover*	T
☐ Snowy Plover	T
☐ Semipalmated Plover	T
☐ Mountain Plover	W
☐ Black-necked Stilt	S
☐ Greater Yellowlegs	T
☐ Lesser Yellowlegs	T
☐ Solitary Sandpiper	T
☐ Red Knot*	T
☐ Willet	T
☐ Spotted Sandpiper	T
☐ Upland Sandpiper*	T
☐ Killdeer	P
☐ Whimbrel	T
☐ Ruddy Turnstone	T
☐ Long-billed Curlew	T
☐ Semipalmated Sandpiper	T

☐ Western Sandpiper	T
☐ Least Sandpiper	T
☐ Dunlin	T
☐ White-rumped Sandpiper*	T
☐ Baird's Sandpiper	T
☐ Pectoral Sandpiper	T
☐ Stilt Sandpiper	T
☐ Sanderling	T
☐ Short-billed Dowitcher	T
☐ Long-billed Dowitcher	T
☐ Hudsonian Godwit*	T
☐ Marbled Godwit	T
☐ American Avocet	S
☐ Red Phalarope	T
☐ Red-necked Phalarope	T
☐ Wilson's Phalarope	T
☐ Common Snipe	W

Gulls and Terns

☐ Laughing Gull*	T
☐ Franklin's Gull	T
☐ Bonaparte's Gull	T
☐ Heermann's Gull*	T
☐ Ring-billed Gull	W
☐ California Gull*	T
☐ Herring Gull	T
☐ Sabine's Gull*	T
☐ Western Gull*	T
☐ Gull-billed Tern	T
☐ Caspian Tern*	T
☐ Common Tern	T
☐ Arctic Tern*	T
☐ Forster's Tern	T
☐ Least Tern	T
☐ Black Tern	T

Pigeons and Doves

☐ Rock Dove	P
☐ Band-tailed Pigeon	T
☐ Black-tailed Pigeon	S
☐ White-winged Dove	S
☐ Mourning Dove	P
☐ Inca Dove	P
☐ Common Ground-Dove	P

☐ Ruddy Ground-Dove	T

Cuckoos, Roadrunners, and Anis

☐ Yellow-billed Cuckoo	S
☐ Greater Roadrunner	P
☐ Groove-billed Ani	T

Owls

☐ Common Barn Owl	P
☐ Flammulated Owl	T
☐ Western Screech-Owl	P
☐ Whiskered Screech-Owl	P
☐ Great Horned Owl	P
☐ Northern Pygmy Owl	P
☐ Feruginous Pygmy Owl	P
☐ Elf Owl	S
☐ Burrowing Owl	T
☐ Spotted Owl	P
☐ Long-eared Owl	P
☐ Short-eared Owl	W
☐ Northern Saw-whet Owl	T

Goatsuckers

☐ Lesser Nighthawk	S
☐ Common Nighthawk	S
☐ Common Poorwill	S
☐ Buff-colored Nightjar	S
☐ Whippoorwill	S

Swifts

☐ Black Swift*	T
☐ Chimney Swift	T
☐ Vaux's Swift	T
☐ White-throated Swift	T

Hummingbirds

☐ Broad-billed Hummingbird	T
☐ White-eared Hummingbird	S
☐ Beryline Hummingbird	S
☐ Violet-crowned Hummingbird	S
☐ Blue-throated Hummingbird	S
☐ Magnificent Hummingbird	S

☐ Lucifer Hummingbird	S
☐ Black-chinned Hummingbird	S
☐ Anna's Hummingbird	P
☐ Costa's Hummingbird	T
☐ Calliope Hummingbird	T
☐ Broad-tailed Hummingbird	T
☐ Rufous Hummingbird	T
☐ Allen's Hummingbird	T
☐ Rivoli's Hummingbird	S
☐ Plain-capped Starthroat	T

Trogons and Kingfishers

☐ Eared Trogon	W
☐ Elegant Trogon	T
☐ Belted Kingfisher	W
☐ Green Kingfisher	P

Woodpeckers

☐ Lewis' Woodpecker	W
☐ Red-headed Woodpecker*	T
☐ Acorn Woodpecker	T
☐ Gila Woodpecker	P
☐ Yellow-bellied Sapsucker	W
☐ Red-naped Sapsucker	T
☐ Red-breasted Sapsucker	T
☐ Williamson's Sapsucker	W
☐ Ladder-backed Woodpecker	P
☐ Downy Woodpecker	P
☐ Hairy Woodpecker	T
☐ Strickland's Woodpecker	P
☐ Arizona Woodpecker	P
☐ Yellow-Shafted Flicker	P
☐ Red-shafted Flicker	P
☐ Gilded Flicker	P

Kingbirds and Flycatchers

☐ Northern Beardless Tyrannulet	S
☐ Olive-sided Flycatcher	T
☐ Greater Pewee (Coues' Flycatcher)	T
☐ Western Wood-Pewee	S
☐ Willow Flycatcher	T
☐ Hammond's Flycatcher	T
☐ Least Flycatcher	T

☐ Dusky Flycatcher	W
☐ Gray Flycatcher	W
☐ Pacific-slope Flycatcher	T
☐ Buff-breasted Flycatcher*	T
☐ Black Phoebe	P
☐ Eastern Phoebe	T
☐ Say's Phoebe	P
☐ Vermillion Flycatcher	S
☐ Dusky-capped Flycatcher	S
☐ Ash-throated Flycatcher	S
☐ Brown-crested Flycatcher (Wied's Crested)	S
☐ Sulphur-bellied Flycatcher	T
☐ Tropical Kingbird	S
☐ Cassin's Kingbird	S
☐ Thick-billed Kingbird	T
☐ Western Kingbird	S
☐ Eastern Kingbird	T
☐ Scissor-tailed Flycatcher	T

Becards and Larks

☐ Rose-throated Becard	T
☐ Horned Lark	P

Swallows

☐ Purple Martin	T
☐ Tree Swallow	T
☐ Violet-green Swallow	T
☐ Northern Rough-winged Swallow	S
☐ Bank Swallow	T
☐ Cliff Swallow	S
☐ Barn Swallow	S

Jays and Crows

☐ Steller's Jay	W
☐ Blue Jay	T
☐ Scrub Jay	W
☐ Gray-breasted Jay	T
☐ Pinyon Jay	W
☐ Clark's Nutcracker	W
☐ American Crow	T
☐ Chihuahuan Raven (White-necked)	P
☐ Common Raven	P

Chickadees, Titmice, Verdin, and Bushtits

- ☐ Mexican Chickadee — P
- ☐ Mountain Chickadee — P
- ☐ Bridled Titmouse — P
- ☐ Plain Titmouse — P
- ☐ Verdin — P
- ☐ Common Bushtit — P

Nuthatches

- ☐ Red-breasted Nuthatch — P
- ☐ White-breasted Nuthatch — P
- ☐ Pygmy Nuthatch — P

Creepers

- ☐ Brown Creeper — P

Wrens

- ☐ Cactus Wren — P
- ☐ Rock Wren — P
- ☐ Canyon Wren — P
- ☐ Bewick's Wren — P
- ☐ House Wren — P
- ☐ Winter Wren — W
- ☐ Marsh Wren — W

Dippers

- ☐ American Dipper — W

Thrushes, Solitaires, and Bluebirds

- ☐ Eastern Bluebird — W
- ☐ Western Bluebird — W
- ☐ Mountain Bluebird — W
- ☐ Townsend's Solitaire — P
- ☐ Gray-cheeked Thrush* — T
- ☐ Swainson's Thrush — W
- ☐ Hermit Thrush — W
- ☐ Rufous-backed Robin — T
- ☐ American Robin — W
- ☐ Aztec Thrush* — T
- ☐ Varied Thrush* — T
- ☐ Wood Thrush* — T

Mockingbirds and Thrashers

- ☐ Gray Catbird — T
- ☐ Northern Mockingbird — P
- ☐ Sage Thrasher — W
- ☐ Brown Thrasher — T
- ☐ Bendire's Thrasher — P
- ☐ Curve-billed Thrasher — P
- ☐ Crissal Thrasher — P
- ☐ Le Conte's Thrasher — P

Gnatcatchers and Kinglets

- ☐ Golden-crowned Kinglet — W
- ☐ Ruby-crowned Kinglet — W
- ☐ Blue-gray Gnatcatcher — T
- ☐ Black-tailed Gnatcatcher — T

Pipits

- ☐ American Pipit (Water Pipit) — W
- ☐ Sprague's Pipit — W

Waxwings

- ☐ Bohemian Waxwing* — T
- ☐ Cedar Waxwing — W

Silky Flycatchers

- ☐ Phainopepla* — P

Shrikes

- ☐ Loggerhead Shrike — P
- ☐ Northern Shrike — T

Starlings

- ☐ European Starling — P

Vireos

- ☐ White-eyed Vireo* — T
- ☐ Bell's Vireo — S
- ☐ Black-capped Vireo* — T
- ☐ Gray Vireo — T
- ☐ Solitary Vireo — T
- ☐ Yellow-throated Vireo* — T

☐ Hutton's Vireo	T
☐ Warbling Vireo	T
☐ Philadelphia Vireo	T
☐ Yellow-green Vireo*	T

Woodwarblers

☐ Golden-winged Warbler*	T
☐ Blue-winged Warbler*	T
☐ Tennessee Warbler	T
☐ Orange-crowned Warbler	T
☐ Nashville Warbler	T
☐ Virginia's Warbler	T
☐ Lucy's Warbler	S
☐ Northern Parula	T
☐ Yellow Warbler	S
☐ Chestnut-sided Warbler	T
☐ Magnolia Warbler	T
☐ Cape May Warbler	T
☐ Black-throated Blue Warbler	T
☐ Yellow-rumped Warbler (Audubon's)	W
☐ Black-throated Gray Warbler	T
☐ Townsend's Warbler	T
☐ Hermit Warbler	T
☐ Blackburnian Warbler*	T
☐ Yellow-throated Warbler*	T
☐ Grace's Warbler	T
☐ Prairie Warbler*	T
☐ Palm Warbler	T
☐ Bay-breasted Warbler*	T
☐ Blackpoll Warbler*	T
☐ Cerulean Warbler*	T
☐ Black-and-white Warbler	T
☐ American Redstart	T
☐ Prothonotary Warbler*	T
☐ Worm-eating Warbler*	T
☐ Ovenbird	T
☐ Pine Warbler*	T
☐ Northern Waterthrush	T
☐ Louisiana Waterthrush	T
☐ Kentucky Warbler	T
☐ Mourning Warbler*	T
☐ Fan-tailed Warbler*	T
☐ MacGillvray's Warbler	T

☐ Common Yellowthroat	S
☐ Hooded Warbler*	T
☐ Wilson's Warbler (Pileolated)	T
☐ Canada Warbler*	T
☐ Red-faced Warbler	T
☐ Painted Redstart	T
☐ Slate-throated Redstart	T
☐ Yellow-breasted Chat	S
☐ Olive Warbler	S

Tanagers

☐ Hepatic Tanager	T
☐ Summer Tanager	S
☐ Scarlet Tanager	T
☐ Western Tanager	T
☐ Streak-backed Tanager*	T

Blackbirds and Orioles

☐ Bobolink	T
☐ Red-winged Blackbird	S
☐ Eastern Meadowlark	P
☐ Western Meadowlark	W
☐ Yellow-headed Blackbird	W
☐ Rusty Blackbird	T
☐ Brewer's Blackbird	W
☐ Great-tailed Grackle	P
☐ Common Grackle*	T
☐ Bronzed Cowbird	S
☐ Brown-headed Cowbird	P
☐ Orchard Oriole	T
☐ Hooded Oriole	S
☐ Streak-backed Oriole*	T
☐ Scott's Oriole	S
☐ Bullock's Oriole (Northern Oriole)	S

Grosbeaks, Buntings, Towhees, and Sparrows

☐ Northern Cardinal	P
☐ Pyrrhuloxia	P
☐ Rose-breasted Grosbeak	T
☐ Black-headed Grosbeak	T
☐ Blue Grosbeak	S
☐ Lazuli Bunting	T

☐ Indigo Bunting	S
☐ Varied Bunting	S
☐ Painted Bunting	T
☐ Dickcissel	T
☐ Green-tailed Towhee	W
☐ Rufous-sided Towhee	W
☐ Canyon Towhee	P
☐ Abert's Towhee	P
☐ California Towhee	P
☐ Botteri's Sparrow	S
☐ Cassin's Sparrow	S
☐ Rufous-winged Sparrow	T
☐ Rufous-crowned Sparrow	P
☐ Chipping Sparrow	W
☐ Clay-colored Sparrow	T
☐ Brewer's Sparrow	W
☐ Black-chinned Sparrow	T
☐ Vesper Sparrow	W
☐ Lark Sparrow	T
☐ Black-throated Sparrow	P
☐ Sage Sparrow	P
☐ Savannah Sparrow	W
☐ Baird's Sparrow	W
☐ Grasshopper Sparrow	W
☐ Fox Sparrow	W
☐ Song Sparrow	P
☐ Lincoln's Sparrow	W
☐ Swamp Sparrow	W
☐ White-throated Sparrow	W
☐ Golden-crowned Sparrow	W
☐ White-crowned Sparrow	W
☐ Harris' Sparrow	W
☐ Dark-eyed ("Oregon") Junco	W
☐ Yellow-eyed Junco	T
☐ McCown's Longspur	T
☐ Chestnut-collared Longspur	W

Finches

☐ Pine Grosbeak	T
☐ Purple Finch	W
☐ Cassin's Finch	W
☐ House Finch	P
☐ Red Crossbill	T
☐ Pine Siskin	P
☐ Lesser Goldfinch	P
☐ Lawrence's Goldfinch	W
☐ American Goldfinch	W
☐ Evening Grosbeak	T

Weaver Finches

☐ House Sparrow	P

Other Animals of the Southwest

This is a selective listing of fish, amphibians, reptiles, and mammals that are found in our natural places of the Southwest.

The current status of the listed species is shown following the name: E—endangered, T—threatened, S—sensitive.

Bats are identified with their residency in the southwest, particularly in the Gila Wilderness: P—permanent resident, S—summer resident, W—winter resident, T—temporary.

Fish

☐ Largemouth Bass	
☐ Smallmouth Bass	
☐ Bluegill	
☐ Black Bullhead	
☐ Yellow Bullhead	
☐ Carp	
☐ Channel Catfish	
☐ Flathead Catfish	
☐ Chihuahua Chub	E
☐ Gila Chub	
☐ Roundtail Chub	S
☐ White Crappie	
☐ Longfin Dace	
☐ Speckled Dace	
☐ Spikedace	T

☐ Fathead Minnow
☐ Loach Minnow   T
☐ Mosquitofish
☐ Desert Pupfish
☐ Beautiful Shiner   E
☐ Red Shiner
☐ Desert Sucker
☐ Gila Mountain Sucker
☐ Rio Grande Sucker   S
☐ Sonora Sucker
☐ Green Sunfish
☐ Longear Sunfish
☐ Gila Topminnow   E
☐ Brown Trout
☐ Gila Trout
☐ Rainbow Trout
☐ Rio Grande Cutthroat Trout

Amphibians
☐ Bullfrog
☐ Chiricahua Leopard Frog
☐ Lowland Leopard Frog
☐ Western Chorus Frog
☐ Canyon Treefrog
☐ Mountain Treefrog
☐ Tiger Salamander
☐ New Mexico Spadefoot Toad
☐ Red-spotted Toad
☐ Southwestern Toad
☐ Woodhouse's Toad

Reptiles
☐ Western Banded Gecko
☐ Gila Monster
☐ Desert Iguana
☐ Chuckwalla Lizard
☐ Clark's Spiny Lizard
☐ Collared Lizard
☐ Crevice Spiny Lizard
☐ Desert Spiny Lizard
☐ Eastern Fence Lizard
☐ Greater Earless Lizard
☐ Lesser Earless Lizard
☐ Madrean Alligator Lizard

☐ Plateau Lizard
☐ Round-tailed Lizard
☐ Short-horned Lizard
☐ Texas Horned Lizard
☐ Tree Lizard
☐ Great Plains Skink
☐ Many-lined Skink
☐ Plains Blackhead Snake
☐ Southwestern Blackhead Snake
☐ Texas Blind Snake
☐ Western Blind Snake
☐ Ring-necked Coachwhip Snake
☐ Arizona Coral Snake
☐ Black-necked Garter Snake
☐ Checkered Garter Snake
☐ Narrowhead Garter Snake
☐ Western Terrestrial Garter Snake
☐ Gopher Snake (bull)
☐ Common Kingsnake
☐ Sonora Mountain Kingsnake
☐ Big Bend Patchnose Snake
☐ Desert Patchnose Snake
☐ Mountain Patchnose Snake
☐ Blacktailed Rattlesnake
☐ Rock Rattlesnake
☐ Sidewinder Rattlesnake
☐ Western Diamond-backed
   Rattlesnake
☐ Western Rattlesnake
☐ Striped Whipsnake
☐ Chihuahuan Spotted Whiptail
☐ Desert-grassland Whiptail
☐ Gila Spotted Whiptail
☐ Western Whiptail
☐ Ornate Box Turtle
☐ Sonoran Mud Turtle
☐ Spiny Softshell Turtle
☐ Desert Tortoise

Mammals
☐ Prong-horned Antelope
☐ Badger
☐ Allen's (Mexican)
   Big-eared Bat   S

☐ Big Brown Bat	P	
☐ Hoary Bat	T	
☐ Hognose Bat	S	
☐ Longnose Bat	S	
☐ Lump-nosed Bat	P	
☐ Mexican Freetailed Bat	T	
☐ Pallid Bat	S	
☐ Silver-haired Bat	S	
☐ Spotted Bat	S	
☐ Western Mastiff Bat	P	
☐ Western Red Bat	S	
☐ Western Yellow Bat	P	
☐ Bison		
☐ California Myotis	S	
☐ Cave Myotis	S	
☐ Fringe-tailed Myotis	P	
☐ Little Brown Myotis	S	
☐ Long-eared Myotis	S	
☐ Long-legged Myotis	S	
☐ Southwestern Myotis		
☐ Southwestern Myotis	S	
☐ Western Small-footed Myotis	P	
☐ Yuma Myotis	S	
☐ Western Pipistrelle	S	
☐ Black Bear		
☐ Beaver		
☐ Bobcat		
☐ Cliff Chipmunk		
☐ Coatimundi		
☐ Coyote		
☐ Mule Deer		
☐ White-tailed Deer		
☐ Elk		
☐ Gray Fox		
☐ Kit Fox		
☐ Botta's Pocket Gopher		
☐ Valley Pocket Gopher		
☐ Yellow-bellied Marmot		
☐ Mountain Lion		
☐ Brush Mouse		
☐ Cactus Mouse		
☐ Deer Mouse		
☐ Northern Grasshopper Mouse		
☐ Southern Grasshopper Mouse		

☐ Grateful Mouse
☐ Harvest Mouse
☐ House Mouse
☐ Pinyon Mouse
☐ Arizona Pocket Mouse
☐ Desert Pocket Mouse
☐ Silky Pocket Mouse
☐ Rock Mouse
☐ White-footed Mouse
☐ Muskrat
☐ River Otter
☐ Collared Peccary (javelina)
☐ Pika
☐ Porcupine
☐ Gunnison's Prairie Dog
☐ Raccoon
☐ Desert Cottontail
☐ Eastern Cottontail
☐ Antelope Jackrabbit
☐ Black-tailed Jackrabbit
☐ Desert Kangaroo Rat
☐ Merriam's Kangaroo Rat
☐ Ord's Kangaroo Rat
☐ Hispid Cotton Rat
☐ Yellow-bodied Cotton Rat
☐ Ringtail (Cat)
☐ Mexican Woodrat
☐ Stephen's Woodrat
☐ White-throated Woodrat
☐ Rocky Mountain Bighorn Sheep
☐ Desert Shrew
☐ Merriam's Shrew
☐ Vagrant Shrew
☐ Hog-nosed Skunk
☐ Spotted Skunk
☐ Striped Skunk
☐ Abert's Squirrel
☐ Texas Antelope Squirrel
☐ White-tailed Antelope Squirrel
☐ Arizona Gray Squirrel
☐ Golden-mantled Ground Squirrel
☐ Spotted Ground Squirrel
☐ Thirteen-lined Ground Squirrel
☐ Kaibab Squirrel

- ☐ Red Squirrel
- ☐ Rock Squirrel
- ☐ Long-tailed Vole
- ☐ Meadow Vole
- ☐ Mexican Vole
- ☐ Long-tailed Weasel

Plants of the Southwest

Following are some of the more prevalent cacti, trees, vines, shrubs, grasses, and wildflowers found across the Southwest, listed by their common names.

Cacti

- ☐ Barrel Cactus
- ☐ Desert Christmas Cactus
- ☐ Fishhook Cactus
- ☐ Hen and Chicken Cactus
- ☐ Claret Cup Hedgehog
- ☐ Fendler Hedgehog
- ☐ Simpson's Hedgehog
- ☐ Beavertail Prickly Pear
- ☐ Plains Prickly Pear
- ☐ Purple Fruited Prickly Pear
- ☐ Pygmy Prickly Pear
- ☐ Smooth Mountain Prickly Pear
- ☐ Sprawling Prickly Pear
- ☐ Cane Cholla
- ☐ Chain Fruit Cholla
- ☐ Jumping Cholla
- ☐ Organ Pipe Cactus
- ☐ Rainbow Cactus
- ☐ Saguaro
- ☐ Senita Cactus
- ☐ Teddybear Cactus

Trees and Shrubs

- ☐ Arizona Alder
- ☐ Single-leaf Ash
- ☐ Velvet Ash
- ☐ Quaking Aspen
- ☐ Bitterbrush
- ☐ Inland Boxelder
- ☐ Birchleaf Buckhorn
- ☐ Southwestern Chokecherry
- ☐ Cliffrose (Buckbrush)
- ☐ Fremont Cottonwood
- ☐ Lanceleaf Cottonwood
- ☐ Narrowleaf Cottonwood
- ☐ Creosote Bush
- ☐ Arizona Cypress
- ☐ Red-osier Dogwood
- ☐ Box Elder
- ☐ Blue Elderberry
- ☐ Cliff Fendlerbush
- ☐ Douglas Fir
- ☐ White Fir
- ☐ Netleaf Hackberry
- ☐ Narrowleaf Hoptree
- ☐ Alligator Juniper
- ☐ One-seed Juniper
- ☐ Rocky Mountain Juniper
- ☐ Utah Juniper
- ☐ Arizona Madrone (Arbutus)
- ☐ Greenleaf Manzanita
- ☐ Pointleaf Manzanita
- ☐ Alder-leaf Mountain-mahogany
- ☐ Curl-leaf Mountain-mahogany
- ☐ Rocky Mountain Maple
- ☐ Screwbean Mesquite
- ☐ Velvet Mesquite
- ☐ Arizona White Oak
- ☐ Emory Oak
- ☐ Gambel Oak
- ☐ Gray Oak
- ☐ Scrub Oak
- ☐ Silverleaf Oak
- ☐ Ocotillo
- ☐ New Mexican Olive
- ☐ California Fan Palm
- ☐ Date Palm
- ☐ Blue Palo Verde
- ☐ Foothill Palo Verde

- ☐ Apache Pine
- ☐ Bristlecone Pine
- ☐ Chihuahua Pine
- ☐ Limber Pine
- ☐ Mexican White Pine
- ☐ Ponderosa Pine
- ☐ Southwestern White Pine
- ☐ Two-needle Pinyon Pine
- ☐ Dwarf Rabbitbrush
- ☐ Golden Rabbitbrush (Chamisa)
- ☐ Rubber Rabbitbrush
- ☐ Arizona Rosewood
- ☐ Bur Sage
- ☐ Bladder Sage
- ☐ Death Valley Sage
- ☐ Rocky Mountain Sage
- ☐ Big Sagebrush
- ☐ Utah Serviceberry
- ☐ Blue Spruce
- ☐ Engelmann Spruce
- ☐ Arizona Sycamore
- ☐ Tamarisk (Salt Cedar)
- ☐ Arizona Walnut
- ☐ Arroyo Willow
- ☐ Goodding's Willow
- ☐ Sandbar Willow
- ☐ Seep Willow

Herbs, Grasses Vines, and Wildflowers

- ☐ Desert Anemone
- ☐ Arrowweed
- ☐ Apache-plume
- ☐ Common Aster
- ☐ Grand Aster
- ☐ Mojave Aster
- ☐ Spine Aster
- ☐ Western Aster
- ☐ Bahia
- ☐ Balloon Flower
- ☐ Beargrass
- ☐ Bedstraw
- ☐ Beebalm
- ☐ Beeblossom

- ☐ Rocky Mountain Beeplant
- ☐ Parry Bellflower
- ☐ Bitterweed
- ☐ Black Medic
- ☐ Bladderpod
- ☐ Blanketflower (Firewheel)
- ☐ Arizona Blue-eyes
- ☐ Aspen Bluebell
- ☐ Bluedicks
- ☐ Bracken
- ☐ Brickellbush
- ☐ Brittlebush
- ☐ Buckbush
- ☐ Birchleaf Buckthorn
- ☐ Buffalo Gourd (Coyote Melon)
- ☐ Bullgrass
- ☐ Burrobush
- ☐ New Mexico Butterweed
- ☐ Threadleaf Butterweed
- ☐ Desert Calico
- ☐ Carlessweed
- ☐ Catclaw
- ☐ Cattail
- ☐ Century Plant (Agave)
- ☐ Night-blooming Cereus
- ☐ Chia
- ☐ Desert Chicory
- ☐ Chinchweed
- ☐ Chuparosa
- ☐ Scarlet Cinquefoil
- ☐ Shrubby Cinquefoil
- ☐ Clammyweed
- ☐ Rocky Mountain Clematis
- ☐ Cloakfern
- ☐ Colorado Columbine
- ☐ Golden Columbine
- ☐ Cutleaf Coneflower
- ☐ Cosmos
- ☐ Cranesbill (Storksbill)
- ☐ Scarlet Creeper
- ☐ Golden Currant
- ☐ Desertgold
- ☐ Blackfoot Daisy
- ☐ Tahoka Daisy

- ☐ Woolly Daisy
- ☐ Feather Dalea
- ☐ Desert Dandelion
- ☐ Sacred Datura (Western Thornapple)
- ☐ Birdbill Dayflower
- ☐ Mojave Desert Star
- ☐ Devil's Claw
- ☐ Winged Dock
- ☐ Dodder
- ☐ Dogbane
- ☐ Fagonia
- ☐ Fairy Duster
- ☐ False-indigo
- ☐ Feathergrass
- ☐ Filaree
- ☐ Fireweed
- ☐ Desert Five Spot
- ☐ Blue Flax
- ☐ Fleabane (Wild Daisy)
- ☐ Desert Four O'Clock
- ☐ Trailing Four O'Clock
- ☐ Meadow Gentian
- ☐ Parry Gentian
- ☐ Purple Geranium
- ☐ Ghost Flower
- ☐ Scarlet Gilia
- ☐ Coulter's Globemallow
- ☐ Desert Globemallow
- ☐ Fremont Globemallow
- ☐ Mountain Glory
- ☐ Meadow Goatsbeard
- ☐ Goathead
- ☐ Goldeneye
- ☐ Goldenrod
- ☐ Goldensmoke
- ☐ Goldfields
- ☐ Fremont Goosefoot
- ☐ Canyon Grape
- ☐ Black Greasewood
- ☐ Purple Groundcherry
- ☐ Broom Groundsel
- ☐ Ragwort Groundsel
- ☐ Threadleaf Groundsel
- ☐ Sweet-scented Heliotrope
- ☐ Heronbill
- ☐ Desert Holly
- ☐ White Flower Honeysuckle
- ☐ Horehound
- ☐ Horsetail
- ☐ Giant Hyssop
- ☐ Common Ice Plant
- ☐ Indian Blanket
- ☐ Desert Ironweed
- ☐ Poison Ivy
- ☐ Bristly Langloisia
- ☐ Spotted Langloisia
- ☐ Nuttall's Larkspur
- ☐ Desert Mariposa Lily
- ☐ Rain Lily
- ☐ Sego Lily
- ☐ Starlily
- ☐ Melon Loco
- ☐ New Mexican Locust
- ☐ Coulter's Lupine
- ☐ Silvery Lupine
- ☐ Macomb's Trumpet
- ☐ Desert Marigold
- ☐ Marsh Marigold
- ☐ Fendler's Meadow Rue
- ☐ Curly Mesquitegrass
- ☐ Milkvetch (Loco Weed)
- ☐ Freckled Milkvetch
- ☐ Poison Milkweed
- ☐ White Milkweed
- ☐ Wild Mint
- ☐ American Mistletoe
- ☐ Dwarf Mistletoe
- ☐ Juniper Mistletoe
- ☐ Scarlet Monkeyflower
- ☐ Monkshood
- ☐ Mormon Tea
- ☐ Star Morning Glory
- ☐ Mullein
- ☐ Onion
- ☐ Desert Paintbrush
- ☐ Southwest Indian Paintbrush
- ☐ Pennycress

- [ ] Common Pennycress
- [ ] False Pennyroyal
- [ ] Beardlip Penstemon
- [ ] Markagunt Penstemon
- [ ] Purple Penstemon
- [ ] Rydberg Penstemon
- [ ] Peppergrass
- [ ] Phacelia
- [ ] Scalloped Phacelia
- [ ] Varileaf Phacelia
- [ ] Longleaf Phlox
- [ ] Pickleweed
- [ ] Esteve's Pincushion
- [ ] Pink Windmills
- [ ] Spectacle Pod
- [ ] Great Desert Poppy
- [ ] Prickly Poppy
- [ ] Broadleaf Plantain
- [ ] Poison Hemlock
- [ ] Portulaca
- [ ] Desert Primrose
- [ ] Birdcage Evening Primrose
- [ ] Bronze Evening Primrose
- [ ] Lavender Evening Primrose
- [ ] New Mexico Evening Primrose
- [ ] Tansy-leaved Evening Primrose
- [ ] Parry Primrose
- [ ] Purple Mat
- [ ] Rabbitbrush
- [ ] Rattlesnake Weed
- [ ] Indian Ricegrass
- [ ] Desert Rock Nettle
- [ ] Desert Rosemallow
- [ ] Rush
- [ ] Yellow Salsify
- [ ] Four-wing Saltbush
- [ ] Sedum
- [ ] Mexican Silene
- [ ] Wright Silktassel
- [ ] Skyrocket

- [ ] Snakeweed
- [ ] Yellow-Twining Snapdragon
- [ ] Little Snapdragon Vine
- [ ] Net-cup Snapdragon Vine
- [ ] False Solomon's Seal
- [ ] Southwest Solomon's Seal
- [ ] Wood Sorrel
- [ ] Spurge
- [ ] Ridgeseed Spurge
- [ ] Starflower
- [ ] Bullet Stickleaf
- [ ] Stickleaf Mentzelia
- [ ] Stinging Nettle
- [ ] Sunflower
- [ ] Southwestern Stoneseed
- [ ] White Sweetclover
- [ ] Yellow Sweetclover
- [ ] Limestone Thistle
- [ ] New Mexico Thistle
- [ ] Desert Tobacco
- [ ] Tobacco Weed
- [ ] Angel (Pale) Trumpets
- [ ] Desert Trumpet
- [ ] Desert Sand Verbena
- [ ] Dakota Vervain
- [ ] Canada Violet
- [ ] Watercress
- [ ] Douglas Water Hemlock
- [ ] Western Wallflower
- [ ] Wooly White
- [ ] Louisiana Wormwood
- [ ] Western Yarrow
- [ ] Baccata Yucca
- [ ] Joshua Tree (Yucca)
- [ ] Narrowleaf Yucca
- [ ] Spanish Dagger (Yucca)

Mushrooms
- [ ] Buried-stalk Puffball
- [ ] Desert Stalked Puffball

INDEX